CHRYS PANAYIOTOU

DATE DUE

WITHDRAWN

THE 8080, 8085, AND Z80

Hardware, Software, Programming, Interfacing, and Troubleshooting

David LaLond

Learning Resources
Brevard Community College
Palm Bay, Florida

 PRENTICE HALL, Englewood Cliffs, New Jersey 07632

Library of Congress Cataloging-in-Publication Data

LaLond, David, (*date*)
   The 8080, 8085, and Z80.

   Includes index.
   1. Intel 8080 (Microprocessor) 2. Intel 8085
(Microprocessor) 3. Zilog Z-80 (Microprocessor) I. Title.
QA76.8.I28L35 1988   004.165   87-32796
ISBN 0-13-247008-X

Editorial/production supervision and
   interior design: **Kathryn Pavelec**
Cover design: **Lundgren Graphics, Ltd.**
Cover photo courtesy of: **Slide Graphics of New England, Inc.**
Manufacturing buyer: **Peter Havens**

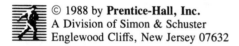
Printed in the United States of America

10 9 8 7 6 5 4 3 2 1

ISBN 0-13-247008-X 025

PRENTICE-HALL INTERNATIONAL (UK) LIMITED, *London*
PRENTICE-HALL OF AUSTRALIA PTY. LIMITED, *Sydney*
PRENTICE-HALL CANADA INC., *Toronto*
PRENTICE-HALL HISPANOAMERICANA, S.A., *Mexico*
PRENTICE-HALL OF INDIA PRIVATE LIMITED, *New Delhi*
PRENTICE-HALL OF JAPAN, INC., *Tokyo*
SIMON & SCHUSTER ASIA PTE. LTD., *Singapore*
EDITORA PRENTICE-HALL DO BRASIL, LTDA., *Rio de Janeiro*

To Donna—
knowing you has been a blessing—
and to my family and yours.

To Jim King, mentor, colleague, and friend;
to Jim Tammen, colleague and friend;
to Bob Wooton, colleague and friend;
your dedication and professionalism have made
working with you a rewarding experience.

Special thanks to Mike Fagan,
who took the time to review this text three times.

CONTENTS

PREFACE   *xi*

1 INTRODUCTION   *1*

1-1   The Computer Chip   *2*
1-2   8080 Introduction   *2*
1-3   Overview of the I/O Bus   *6*
1-4   Memory Terminology   *7*
1-5   Program Entry   *10*
1-6   Program Execution   *11*
1-7   Single-Tasking Processors   *11*

1-8   Introduction to Computer
        Architecture   *12*
1-9   8085 Introduction   *14*
1-10 Z80 Introduction   *16*
1-11 Closing Thoughts   *18*
        Summary   *18*
        Questions   *19*

2 BASIC INSTRUCTIONS   *20*

        Introduction   *21*
2-1   Mnemonics and Op Codes   *21*
2-2   Assemblers   *21*
2-3   High-Level Languages   *22*
2-4   Machine-Level Coding   *22*
2-5   Instruction Formats   *23*
2-6   Move Instructions   *23*
2-7   The Memory Operand   *24*

2-8   Register-Pair Operations   *25*
2-9   The Memory Pointer   *26*
2-10 The Move Immediate
         Instructions   *26*
2-11 IN and OUT   *26*
2-12 Some Program Examples   *27*
2-13 Branch Instructions   *28*
2-14 Flag Control   *30*

2-15 Counting Instructions   *31*
2-16 Programming Longer Loops
      (Nesting)   *33*
2-17 Programming Longer Loops
      (Extended Loop Counters)   *36*
2-18 Logical Instructions   *38*
2-19 Masking   *43*
2-20 Compare Instructions   *46*
2-21 Rotate Instructions   *47*
2-22 Understanding Flag
      Response   *48*

2-23 Arithmetic Instructions   *52*
2-24 Terminating Program
      Execution   *54*
2-25 Closing Thoughts   *54*
      Summary   *55*
      Questions   *55*
      Lab Assignments   *56*
      Lab Questions   *57*

3 PROJECT DEVELOPMENT   *58*

      Introduction   *59*
3-1   Computer Science
      Techniques   *59*
3-2   Project Development   *61*
3-3   Software Development   *64*
3-4   8080/8085/Z80 Subroutine
      Support   *75*

3-5   An Order-Filling Routine   *79*
3-6   Software Debugging   *85*
3-7   Closing Thoughts   *95*
      Summary   *95*
      Questions   *96*
      Lab Assignments   *97*
      Lab Questions   *98*

4 TIMING   *99*

      Introduction   *100*
4-1   Master Clocks   *100*
4-2   Power-Up Timing   *104*
4-3   Cold/Warm Resets   *106*
4-4   State Definitions   *106*
4-5   Machine Cycles   *110*
4-6   Instruction Cycles   *114*
4-7   Software Timing   *121*

4-8   Hardware Timing
      Support   *130*
4-9   8253 Project Discussions   *141*
4-10 Closing Thoughts   *143*
      Summary   *144*
      Questions   *144*
      Assignments   *145*
      Lab Questions   *145*

5 DIGITAL INTERFACING   *147*

      Introduction   *148*
5-1   Bus Standards   *148*
5-2   Isolated I/O   *151*
5-3   Bus Wiring   *152*
5-4   Device-Select Pulses   *152*
5-5   Memory-Mapped I/O   *165*
5-6   Using Select Pulses as Control
      Pulses   *171*
5-7   The 8212   *173*

5-8   The 8255   *177*
5-9   Date Code Stamp Project   *183*
5-10 Data Communications   *190*
5-11 Closing Thoughts   *201*
      Summary   *202*
      Questions   *202*
      Lab Assignments   *203*
      Lab Questions   *204*

6 DIAGNOSTICS 205

Introduction 206
6-1 Memory Pointers 206
6-2 Data Tables 207
6-3 The 7432 Diagnostic
Project 209
6-4 The 74155 Diagnostic
Project 220

6-5 Closing Thoughts 230
Summary 230
Questions 230
Lab Assignments 232
Lab Questions 232

7 ADVANCED INSTRUCTIONS 234

Introduction 235
7-1 STA, LDA 235
7-2 More Arithmetic
Instructions 236
7-3 Stack Operations 243
7-4 Multiple Memory
Pointers 250

7-5 Address Tables 253
7-6 Addressing Modes 257
7-7 Closing Thoughts 259
Summary 260
Questions 260
Assignments 261
Lab Questions 262

8 MEMORY 263

Introduction 264
8-1 Memory Machine Cycles 264
8-2 Read-Only Memory 266
8-3 Read/Write Memory 273
8-4 Direct Memory Access 280
8-5 Dynamic RAM 289

8-6 Closing Thoughts 291
Summary 291
Questions 292
Lab Assignments 293
Lab Questions 293

9 ANALOG INTERFACING 294

Introduction 295
9-1 Digital-to-Analog Conversion
Principles 295
9-2 Analog-to-Digital Conversion
Principles 306
9-3 Sample and Hold 314

9-4 Control Loops 315
9-5 Closing Thoughts 317
Summary 317
Questions 318
Lab Assignments 319
Lab Questions 319

10   SYSTEM OPERATION   320

Introduction   *321*
10-1   Loading Considerations   *321*
10-2   Circuit Speed   *331*
10-3   Standardized Bus
        Systems   *334*
10-4   Keyboard and Display
        Ports   *340*

10-5   System Monitors   *347*
10-6   Closing Thoughts   *368*
        Summary   *368*
        Questions   *369*
        Lab Assignments   *370*

11   INTERRUPTS   371

Introduction   *372*
11-1   8080A Interrupt
        Architecture   *373*
11-2   Implementing a Single-Line
        System   *375*
11-3   Restarts as Vectors   *381*
11-4   Priority Chains   *382*
11-5   Priority-Interrupt
        Controllers   *383*
11-6   8085 Interrupt
        Architecture   *400*

11-7   Z80 Interrupt
        Architecture   *403*
11-8   Security Door Project   *406*
11-9   Closing Thoughts   *420*
        Summary   *421*
        Questions   *422*
        Lab Assignments   *423*
        Lab Questions   *423*

12   HARDWARE TROUBLESHOOTING   425

Introduction   *426*
12-1   What NOT to Do   *426*
12-2   Standard Equipment   *427*
12-3   Troubleshooting
        Techniques   *429*
12-4   Advanced Test
        Equipment   *452*

12-5   Closing Thoughts   *455*
        Summary   *456*
        Questions   *457*
        Assignments   *458*

Appendix A   TWO'S COMPLEMENT NUMBERS   459

Appendix B   TIME-DELAY SUBROUTINES   462

Appendix C   8080 INSTRUCTION SET   465

Appendix D   Z80 SPECIFICATION SHEETS   *469*

Appendix E   8085 SPECIFICATION SHEETS   *477*

Appendix F   8085A SPECIFICATION SHEETS   *480*

Appendix G   NUMBER CONVERSION TABLES   *485*

GLOSSARY   *487*

ANSWERS   *492*

INDEX   *501*

PREFACE

Introduction

Microcomputer electronics is one of the fastest-changing areas within the electronic field. Recent advances have allowed memory chips to increase dramatically in storage capacity; new designs for faster, more powerful computer chips; and a rapidly-growing set of support chips that perform complex functions, freeing the central processing unit for computational work.

It would be very difficult for a two- or four-year curriculum to cover in depth every processor or computer chip currently on the market. Survey courses that take a quick look at many different products are best left for accomplished professionals and advanced students. This text is meant as an introduction to the area of microcomputer electronics; as such it forgoes the survey approach.

The microprocessor chips chosen for study in this text are the 8080, 8085, and Z80. These numbers will be used to represent all the versions of such chips currently available. The chips are widely used, use 8-bit architectures, and are found on a large number of reasonably-priced computer trainers.

There is little doubt that computers based on 16-line data buses are finding their way into many new designs. As a rule, the 16-bit chips are faster and more powerful, contain richer instruction sets, and can access larger amounts of memory without the aid of external support chips, such as memory manager units. Yet these very features, which make them so appealing to design engineers, can be a detriment to the student just being introduced to the subject of computer electronics.

This text takes the position that a first course in microcomputer electronics should concentrate on the simpler, easier-to-understand 8-line data bus processors. A second course could then delve into the intricacies of 16-bit processors or survey the computer chips currently on the market.

Usability

The text has been written so that both hardware and software examples have good portability. Trainers based on 8080, 8085, and Z80 processors were used to test examples and projects discussed throughout the text. To obtain this portability, hardware and software features specific to certain trainers are not discussed. Concepts that can be applied to a wide number of trainers based on these CPUs are included. There should be enough information, presented through these general concepts, to make it possible to understand the features found on any 8080-, 8085-, and Z80-based trainer.

A notable exception to the attempt to maintain portability is the information presented on the 8259A. This chip is an interrupt controller that does not seem to interface to Z80-based computers. The design philosophy on handling interrupts is significantly different when the 8080/8085 CPUs are compared to the Z80. Details on both interrupt systems can be found in Chapter 11.

Suggested Background

The skills obtained in a DC and AC circuit analysis class are assumed to be part of the background of a student who will be using this text. The ability to measure currents, voltages, and resistance are required for work performed when learning this material. In addition to these two courses, an introduction to digital electronics covering small-scale integration and some medium-scale integration is useful. Breadboarding skills and the use of a logic probe will be helpful. A software course is not a prerequisite to the material found in this text. Finally, the ability to interpret and use manufacturers' data sheets will open avenues for additional work by the students.

Objectives of the Text

This text is meant to present an in-depth examination of three microprocessor chips. As already mentioned, these chips are the 8080, 8085, and Z80. Although there are differences between these chips, the similarities are many. The principles explained will relate to many other processors as well. It is hoped that after completing a course based on the material found in this text, the student will be familiar with the concepts of microcomputer operations. This will include a study of the processor chip, the I/O bus, and the subsections of the computer such as memory and the I/O ports. Programmable support chips also are covered in this text. General-purpose peripheral interfaces, timing controllers, interrupt controllers, and direct memory access controllers are included in the study of support chips.

The interaction between the software and the hardware is stressed. Concepts taken from computer science are used where appropriate. The text takes the position that a computer technician needs to understand both the hardware *and* the software in a system.

Interfacing skills are examined in detail. The ability to expand a system or tailor it for a particular operation is considered important. Examples of how this can be done are found throughout the text.

Implementation

The text starts with an overview of a typical microprocessor and discusses some general characteristics of the three processors to be studied.

The second chapter begins the study of the software that is an integral part of computer operations. This text restricts the code used to the 8080 instruction set. This allows program examples to be used in all three processors, since the 8080 instruction set is a subset of the 8085 and Z80 instruction sets. Since this is the case, the instruction mnemonics used by the 8080 and 8085 will be used in program examples. To facilitate ease of use for all users, we include op codes in every listing. When appropriate, we explain certain instructions not found in all three processors.

The text programs were developed using machine-level coding and hand assembly. The text takes the approach that coding at this level can be used as a tool to teach the student about the architecture of the computer. High-level languages such as COBOL, FORTRAN, and BASIC obscure many of the architectural features of a computer. In conjunction with this idea, we use both hexadecimal notation and octal notation. It is true that many programmers and technicians prefer hexadecimal. Octal, however, leads to certain insights about internal CPU architecture. Condition codes and register numbers, for example, were assigned based on the octal system.

Chapter 3, while introducing important concepts such as software development and software debugging, stresses organization and documentation as tools a good technician will use throughout a career. In particular, we examine structured programming methods, top-down software design, and the project layout sheet.

Chapter 4 returns to the hardware features of the computer. This alternation between software and hardware continues throughout the texts so student's hardware and software skills can develop in tandem. The focus of Chapter 4 is computer timing. We examine the master clocks of each processor. After this, there is a study of machine cycle and instruction cycle operation. This information is used to explain and develop software timing loops. The chapter concludes with an examination of the 8253 programmable interval timer.

Chapter 5 continues an examination of the hardware found in a system. The focus of this chapter concentrates on the skills and information the technician needs for digital interfacing.

The sixth chapter, while short, looks at two software projects that determine if hardware connected to the computer is functioning correctly. The interaction between the software and the hardware being tested is an important part of this chapter.

Chapter 7 returns to examine more instructions. We explain and use the instructions in examples that highlight some important software topics. The chapter includes a second, more detailed look at stack architecture. The closing section of the chapter discusses the addressing modes used by the processor chips studied in the text.

Next we turn to memory, examining ROM, RAM, and memory interfacing. Chapter 8 includes a section on a direct memory access controller.

Chapter 9 investigates analog interfacing, concentrating on digital-to-analog principles and analog-to-digital principles. A typical DAC chip is used in several examples in the chapter. ADC chips are not examined. Many ADC chips are difficult to use in laboratory situations, being very sensitive. We examine alternatives, though, allowing the student to gain experience with ADC techniques.

Chapter 10 examines the computer from an electrical perspective while looking at overall system operation. Up to this point in the text, the focus has been logical operation. We discuss loading problems and timing concerns such as propagation delays. We include bus standards and a look at a system monitor in this chapter.

Chapter 11 deals with interrupts, describing the interrupt architecture of all three processors. Interrupt controller circuitry and a special-purpose interrupt controller chip, the 8259A, are included in this chapter.

The last chapter, Chapter 12, looks at one way to troubleshoot the microcomputer system. While it does not claim to be the end-all in troubleshooting technique, the goal of the chapter is to lay a foundation that the prospective technician can use once on the job. We also examine waveforms taken from a computer in this chapter. The text concludes with short descriptions of some advanced microcomputer test equipment.

DAVID LaLOND

1

INTRODUCTION

At the end of this chapter you should be familiar with:

1. the internal organization of 8080 CPU, 8085 CPU, and Z80 CPU
2. the functional breakdown of a typical processor bus
3. preliminary memory concepts such as RAM, ROM, and memory maps
4. the flags available within the 8080, 8085, and Z80
5. some differences between register-intensive architecture and memory-mapped architecture

The digital computer is both easy and difficult to understand. The difficulty lies in its overall complexity; the easy part lies in its restriction to a basic unit known as a *bit*. Unlike analog electronics, where every possible voltage can occur, within a digital computer the electronics is restricted to two different voltages. In the computers that this text covers, these voltages are ideally 5 and 0 V. (In a TTL-compatible system, 2 to 5 V is used to indicate a logic 1. Any voltage between 0 and .8 can be used to indicate a logic 0.) The *bit* is a representation of this situation. A logic 1 is used to represent the 5 V state, while a logic 0 is used to denote the 0 V state. Thus a single *binary digit* (bit) can be used to answer questions that have yes/no, true/false, and on/off answers. The output of such a circuit is easy to test. It is a logic 1 or a logic 0 or it is bad. A digital computer, however, can do much more than answer yes/no-type questions. This is where the additional complexity becomes necessary.

Bits are grouped together in standard lengths. A *nibble* is a group of 4 bits. With a nibble the computer can distinguish between 16 different possible conditions. A *byte* is a group of 8 bits. This grouping is the one most often used in the computers we will learn about in this text. A byte allows the computer to differentiate between 256 different outcomes.

Words are 16 bits in length. Words are used more often in the computers most people refer to as minicomputers. There are 65,536 possible combinations when using 16 bits. A *long word* is made up of 32 bits. The large mainframes often use long words as the standard length in storing and manipulating data. With a long word more than 4 billion possibilities can be handled.

1-1 THE COMPUTER CHIP

Most of the computer circuitry is found within one IC. This particular IC often comprises 75 percent or more of the decision-making circuitry in the computer. The chip is referred to as a central processing unit (CPU) or a microprocessing unit (MPU). The CPUs this text focuses on are examples of register-intensive CPUs. The 8080, 8085, and Z80 all have a set of general-purpose registers incorporated in their internal electronics. The 6502, 6800, and 6809 are examples of memory-mapped architectures. The differences between these two types of CPUs will become obvious as you proceed through the text.

1-2 8080 INTRODUCTION

General-Purpose Registers

Figure 1-1 is a block diagram of the various sections within the 8080. The register array contains the general-purpose registers. These registers, B through L, are used for internal storage of information that the CPU needs to access quickly. Subtotals and values associated with ongoing computations are often kept in these registers. All of these registers are 8 bits in width. Therefore, the 8080 uses the byte as its basic data width. The

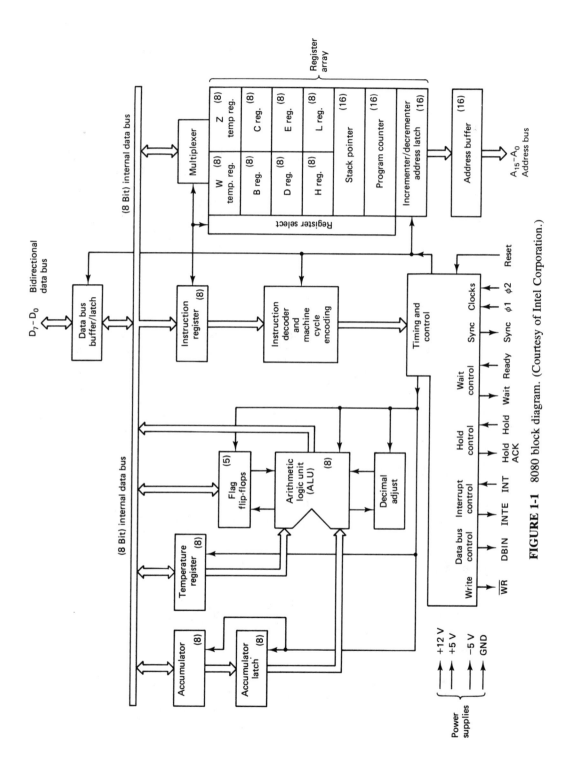

FIGURE 1-1 8080 block diagram. (Courtesy of Intel Corporation.)

3

register select section of the register array, coupled with the multiplexer, allows information from a specific register to pass between the register and other sections of the CPU.

Instruction Register

The instruction register located to the top left of the register array will hold the *operation code* that tells the CPU what function to perform. The operation code will be sent to the instruction register from memory chips external to the CPU. These memory chips will contain the program that the computer will execute. The op code is then decoded by the instruction decoder found just to the left of the register array in the 8080 block diagram. The decoded information will affect the functional section of the CPU, which determines what timing and control signals the CPU needs to produce to carry out the instruction in the instruction register.

Accumulator

The accumulator is a special-purpose register. This register must be used in all arithmetic and logical operations the 8080 will perform. The second operand—that is, the register or memory location that will be used in an arithmetic or logical instruction—is specified by the instruction in the instruction register while the instruction is being performed. This means that the second operand is under the control of the programmer. Later in the text we will learn how to prepare arithmetic and logical operations by moving a value into the accumulator prior to the actual arithmetic or logical operation being performed.

Arithmetic Logic Unit

The arithmetic logic unit is the functional section of the CPU that performs the actual arithmetic and logical operations. This ALU has two inputs. The first input is the *accumulator latch*. The latch is a temporary holding place for information that was in the accumulator. It is transparent to the programmer. This means that the programmer does not have direct control over the accumulator latch with any of the instructions in the 8080 instruction set.

The second input to the ALU is the *temporary register*. Like the accumulator latch, this register is used by the 8080 for internal operations associated with the instruction being performed. It is also transparent to the programmer. Frequently a value from one of the registers in the register array is placed in the temporary register in preparation for performing a logical or arithmetic operation.

The result of an arithmetic instruction is placed back into the accumulator. Most of the logical instructions also place the result of the operation back into the accumulator. The chapter covering the basic instructions will indicate which of the logicals store results in the accumulator and which do not.

Flag Register

The flag register found just above the ALU in the 8080 block diagram is also affected by what happens in the ALU. This register contains the flag bits which allow the 8080 to make decisions. A flag is a status bit used to indicate something about the outcome of an operation. The 8080 has five flags in its flag register that it can use to make decisions. Figure 1-2 is an expanded view of the flag register layout.

The first flag bit, located at D7, is used to determine the sign of an answer. If the *sign bit* is a logic 1, then the result was negative. If the sign bit is a logic 0, then the answer was positive. This follows the convention of two's-complement arithmetic. If you are not already familiar with two's-complement arithmetic, see the appendices for further details.

The next flag in the flag register is the *zero flag*. This bit is used by the computer to test if a result was zero. If the zero flag is a logic 1, then the result of an operation was zero. This is often confusing at first. It might help to think of the flags as true/false indicators rather than 1s and 0s; then a logic 1 represents a true condition. So when the zero flag is true, the result is zero. Of course when the zero flag is false—that is, a logic 0—then the result was not zero.

Bit position D5 is always zero. It has no significance as far as the programmer is concerned.

Bit position D4 is the *auxiliary carry flag*. This flag is used to check for illegal numbers when performing binary-coded decimal arithmetic. There is just one instruction that uses this flag in the 8080 instruction set. That instruction is *decimal adjust the accumulator*.

D3 is another unused bit position in the flag register.

D2 is the *parity flag*. This flag is used to determine if the result of an operation was even or odd parity. If the total number of logic 1s in a result is even, then the parity flag is set to a logic 1. If the opposite is true—that is, the result has odd parity—then the parity flag is reset to a logic 0.

Starting programmers often use the parity flag incorrectly to test if an answer is even or odd. This will not work. Consider the number 2. In binary it would be written as 0000 0010 where the computer operates with bytes. Even though this is an even number, it has odd parity.

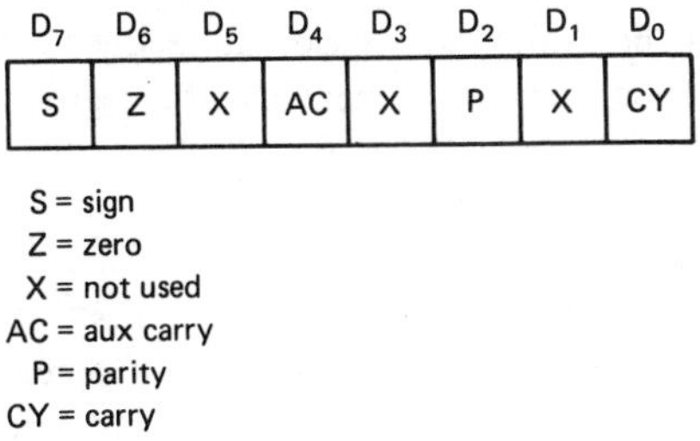

D_7	D_6	D_5	D_4	D_3	D_2	D_1	D_0
S	Z	X	AC	X	P	X	CY

S = sign
Z = zero
X = not used
AC = aux carry
P = parity
CY = carry

FIGURE 1-2 Flag register layout.

D1 in the flag register is always 1. The programmer can ignore this bit.

The last bit position in the flag register is used for the *carry flag*. This flag is set whenever an operation results in an overflow or a borrow. In the case of an overflow, consider the addition of the decimal numbers 210 and 200. The result is 410, but this will not fit into an 8-bit register. Remember, an 8-bit register is capable of handling 256 possible states. Consequently, 410 will not fit back into the accumulator and the carry flag will be set. The carry flag will be reset whenever an operation does not produce overflow or a borrow.

It might seem from the foregoing that arithmetic with numbers larger than 255 base 10 is impossible in a computer that has byte-wide operands. Software routines can be written that use the carry flag to perform arithmetic operations to deal with numbers larger than 255 base 10. The answers from such computations are stored in multiple bytes.

The Buffers

The 8080 has two internal buffers. The first of these is found at the top of the 8080 block diagram of Figure 1-1. The *data bus buffer* is used to isolate the internal data bus from the data bus that will be connected to the computer chip. The *internal data bus* is used to transfer information from one section to another section of the CPU. This buffer is controlled from the timing and control section of the CPU. The timing is important. Information on the external bus will at times need to be transferred into the 8080. If the CPU is working, this can only be done when the internal data bus is not transferring information.

The *address buffer* is used to transmit information from the 8080 to the external address bus. It is controlled indirectly by the timing and control section through the address latch.

The questions that you should have—that is, what is a bus and what is the difference between an address bus and a data bus—are explained in the next section.

1-3 OVERVIEW OF THE I/O BUS

The computer chip must communicate with the circuitry that comprises the rest of the computer. This communication takes place on the processor bus.

A computer bus can be considered as a group of individual transmission lines that share a common purpose. In the computer's case, these lines are transferring digital information. This information will be subdivided into three groups for further discussion.

Data Bus

The data bus is an 8-bit bus in the 8080, 8085, and Z80. This means that the amount of information moved in a single data transfer is a byte. Timing is a very important consideration when the data bus is used. The data bus is bidirectional. At times the information flow is out of the CPU; at other times the information is flowing into the computer chip. If the computer attempted to transfer information into and out of the CPU simultaneously, the information would be garbled and the computer would not be able to operate. The timing of data transfers into and out of the CPU is controlled by the computer chip. This leads to the next section of the bus, the control bus.

Control Bus

The control bus generates or monitors information that regulates what happens on the data bus and address bus. It will let external chips know if the CPU is sending or expecting to receive information. Other control signals indicate if an output is to be directed to a memory chip or an output port, such as a bank of LEDs. Other control signals can be used to determine if bus lines are active or in the tristate condition. The control signals will be discussed in greater detail in later sections of the text dealing with I/O interfacing, timing, and system operation.

Address Bus

The address bus is a 16-bit bus structure. This part of the I/O bus is used by the computer chip to specify which section of the computer is to receive or send the information. The address bus is unidirectional. That is, the CPU outputs the address of the circuit with which it will communicate. The computer circuitry supporting the CPU will have the ability to respond to a specific address while ignoring addresses which for that circuit are incorrect. Since the address bus is 16 bits wide, the computer chip can select 65,536 different locations within the computer. This means that the 8080, 8085, and Z80 can communicate with 64K (this is the standard way of indicating 65,536) of memory. To communicate with larger amounts of memory, the computer chip needs the help of additional circuitry, frequently a memory manager unit (MMU). Of course the memory circuitry need not be fully implemented. Smaller amounts of memory can be used. The amount of memory selected for use will most likely come in blocks of 1K, 4K, or 16K, where these designations represent the nearest power of 2. This would be 1024, 4096, and 16,384 bytes of memory.

1-4 MEMORY TERMINOLOGY

The CPU will use the bus to communicate with the memory chips that help make up the computer system. Each well-documented computer system should include in its documentation a *memory map*. (See Fig. 1-3.) The memory map will indicate which sections of memory are available for program storage, which are read only, which are to be used by the computer's control program, and where the memory chips are wired. That is, the memory map will list the addresses to which the memory chips will respond. In so doing, the memory map will indicate where *holes* exist in the memory architecture. These holes

HEX

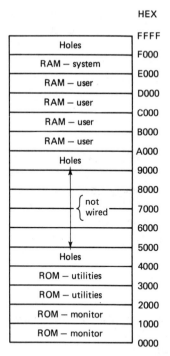

	HEX
Holes	FFFF
	F000
RAM — system	
	E000
RAM — user	
	D000
RAM — user	
	C000
RAM — user	
	B000
RAM — user	
	A000
Holes	
	9000
	8000
{ not wired	7000
	6000
	5000
Holes	4000
ROM — utilities	
	3000
ROM — utilities	
	2000
ROM — monitor	
	1000
ROM — monitor	
	0000

FIGURE 1-3   Memory map.

may be used for future expansion of the memory system or may be reserved for memory mapped I/O. Once again, the preceding paragraph raises questions that need to be answered.

Programs the user writes and enters into the computer's memory are stored in *read/ write memory*. This type of memory is often called *RAM* for *random-access memory*. The use of the term RAM is somewhat confusing to someone just beginning to learn about computers. There is actually nothing random about how these memory chips work. The computer chip is able to specify exactly which memory chip it wishes to activate. Furthermore, if the memory chip has many locations in its internal architecture, the CPU can specify exactly which *memory location* is to be used. A single memory location in the computers that we will study are 8 bits wide. This width matches the width of the general-purpose registers inside the 8080, 8085, and Z80. It also is the width of the data bus. Consequently, a memory location can transfer its 8 bits over the data bus in a single data transfer.

What then does random access mean? Random access indicates the ability of the computer architecture to address any memory location directly without having to sequence through lower-order addresses. *Sequential access* occurs when a memory location is addressed after the computer has addressed lower-order locations, one after another, without skipping any locations to finally reach the destination. Obviously, sequential access is slower than direct access. Surprisingly, there are times when sequential access is used in computers. Certain software structures lend themselves to sequential access. As far as hardware is concerned, there are certain devices that are sequential, such as a tape drive. There is no way to reach a byte stored in the middle of a tape without having traversed prior information.

The memory map of Figure 1-3 indicates the types of uses read/write memory finds within a computer system. The first and most obvious use is program storage; the second function is data storage. The variables and answers that the program manipulates must be available to the program in memory operands that can be changed as data is updated. These sections of the memory map are labeled "user RAM." This particular example has user ram starting at hex address A000 and ending at DFFF. This means a user of this system has 16K memory to work with.

The third use of read/write memory indicated by the memory map of Figure 1-3 involves the storage of information that will be used by the control program operating the computer. This section of the memory map is labeled "system RAM." This section of the memory can be written to by user programs. To do so, however, could cause the control program to crash, perhaps shutting down some hardware functions. It might also turn on circuitry at the wrong time. When this happens, it is frequently necessary to reset the system by rebooting (restarting) the control program.

Figure 1-4 shows an expanded section of system RAM. Notice here that certain locations are associated with hardware functions. E000 is used to remember how fast data bytes are to be sent to a modem. The next location contains the bit rate for cassette storage. The next four cells interact with game paddles. The digitized resistance of the game paddle potentiometer as well as the condition of the game paddle button are stored here. The last location, E006 in the example of Figure 1-4, contains a code that tells the control program whether to perform a cold or warm reset when the reset pin of the CPU is pulsed. Of course, in a complicated system the memory map of system RAM may be very detailed.

The control program, often called a *monitor,* which makes use of the section of system RAM that we have just discussed begins at hex address 0000. The program takes up an 8K block of ROM. *Read-only memory* is used for software programs that must be available to the computer every time power is applied. This type of memory chip must be nonvolatile. Nonvolatile memory retains its information after power is off. Most nonvolatile memory currently available is ROM. A growing number of read/write chips are

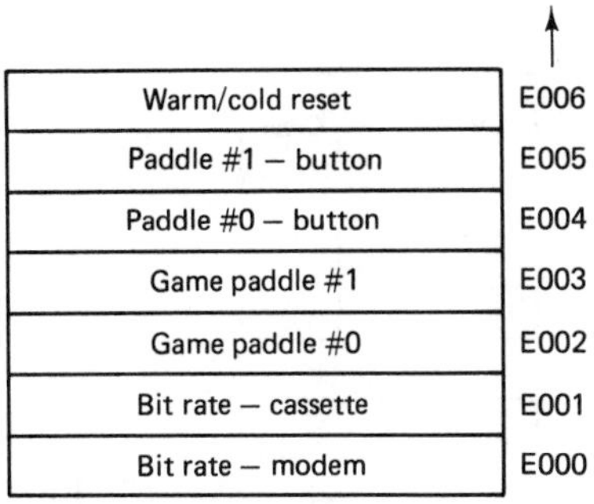

Warm/cold reset	E006
Paddle #1 — button	E005
Paddle #0 — button	E004
Game paddle #1	E003
Game paddle #0	E002
Bit rate — cassette	E001
Bit rate — modem	E000

FIGURE 1-4   Expanded system RAM.

capable of retaining information when power is removed. These chips are usually more expensive than ROM or standard volatile read/write ICs.

The chips beginning at address 2000 contain ROM utilities. These type of programs are functions that may be used frequently by programmers but are not essential to the operation of the system. A cassette interface routine is an example of such a program.

1-5 PROGRAM ENTRY

The microcomputer trainer you are most likely to use as an electronic technician usually contains a hex pad for data entry. Figure 1-5 shows a typical hex-pad keyboard. In an inexpensive trainer it is necessary for the technician to hand assemble his programs. This involves looking up the operation codes that will be used to write a program. The operation codes will be entered through the hex pad, then stored in a memory location by

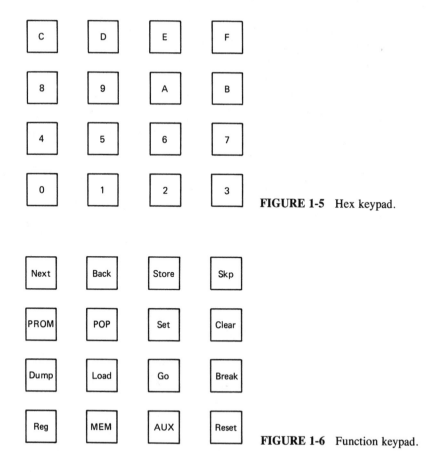

FIGURE 1-5 Hex keypad.

FIGURE 1-6 Function keypad.

pressing the store button on a function keypad. Figure 1-6 shows a typical function keypad.

The computer keeps track of where to place the op codes in memory through the function keypad and the monitor program. Each time an op code is stored, the monitor program should increment an address counter so the op codes can be stored in sequence for later use. This takes us back to the 8080 block diagram of Figure 1-1.

1-6   PROGRAM EXECUTION

The *program counter,* located within the register array, is a special-purpose register. It is 16 bits wide, which enables it to address up to 64K of memory. It is used by the CPU to locate an op code stored in memory. The contents of the program counter are placed on the address bus every time the 8080 wishes to fetch an op code. Without any branch or jump instruction the program counter retrieves the stored op codes sequentially. Consequently, the order in which the instructions were stored has a great deal to do with the order in which the instructions will be performed. When the "go" button on the function pad is pressed, the monitor transfers control of the computer to the user program.

The program counter in the 8080, 8085, and Z80 is reset to 0000 hex whenever the computer chip is reset. This means that when power is first applied the computer chip must be able to find the control program at 0000 hex.

In most available trainers there is some method of performing a program one instruction at a time. This function is usually implemented by pressing the *step button.* Take time to find this feature on the computer trainer you will use; it will be useful when you troubleshoot the software you have written.

Another feature of many trainers that is also useful when it is necessary to troubleshoot software is the ability to set *breakpoints.* A breakpoint is a location within a program where execution of the program can be stopped temporarily.

Once the program execution is interrupted, it is possible to look at the contents of the general-purpose registers and the flags. Frequently the trainer will facilitate examination of the registers through the use of a *register mode,* where the contents of the registers can be displayed on the trainer's output circuitry. These functions will be looked at in more detail later in the text when we discuss software troubleshooting techniques.

1-7   SINGLE-TASKING PROCESSORS

The processors we will study are capable of performing one program at a time. Such processors are frequently referred to as single-tasking processors. This means that a program will run until completed unless the processor is informed that some task not handled by the program controlling the computer needs to be performed. The processor will be informed of such a situation by an external circuit generating an *interrupt.* An interrupt, when accepted, breaks the flow of logic in the program underway. At this time the computer is free to begin execution of another program. This concept will be explained in detail in Chapter 11, Interrupts.

1-8 INTRODUCTION TO COMPUTER ARCHITECTURE

A Simple Block Diagram

Now that we have taken a look at a computer chip, it is time to see how the computer chip would fit into a computer system. Figure 1-7 shows the organization of a simple computer system. The central processing unit communicates with the support circuitry via the three sections of the I/O bus previously discussed.

An unidirectional address bus is depicted at the top of the block diagram. The address lines are connected to the memory subsection and the I/O subsection through address decoders and *port number decoders*. Port number decoders are used to create a device-select pulse that will activate an I/O port. The address decoders for the memory subsection of the computer will create memory-select pulses. The generation of these pulses will be explained in detail in the chapters on digital interfacing and system operation. These decoders are activated at the proper time by control logic generated by the computer chip. The control signal created by the CPU to activate the decoders must be generated just after the address is placed on the address bus.

The memory chips and I/O ports that are turned on by the computer chip communicate with the CPU via the bidirectional data bus shown at the bottom of the dia-

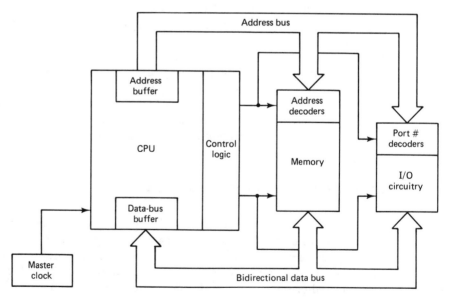

FIGURE 1-7 Computer block diagram.

gram. The support circuitry will not place information of the data bus unless the proper control signal indicates that it is the proper time.

The circuitry in the memory subsection includes the types of memory talked about in the section on memory terminology. That is, it contains user RAM, system RAM, and ROM.

The I/O port circuitry must have, at a minimum, a keypad for program and data entry which allows the user to access functions within the monitor program; it must also include some form of output display that indicates which section of memory is being used and what is stored in that memory operand. In a simple computer system these displays are usually LEDs or seven-segment displays. While the monitor controls the computer, the displays are used as indicated above. When the user program has control of the computer, the displays can be used for the output of results.

The master clock is input to the computer chip. This master clock is usually generated by a crystal oscillator; some divide by circuits that lower the crystal frequency to a value usable by the computer chip. It is common to select a crystal that oscillates much higher than the computer chip can handle. This results in a very stable master clock signal. The master clock signal times the generation of the control signals, which then activate the address bus and data bus at the correct times. It is not too early in our discussion of computer architecture to emphasize that the computers we will be studying are synchronous devices. This means that almost every operation the computer performs is tied to the master clock. Interrupts are a notable exception to the preceding statement.

Register-Intensive Architecture

A computer setup as indicated by the block diagram of Figure 1-7 performs most of its input and output through the accumulator. In fact, no other register can transfer its contents to the I/O bus without going through the accumulator. This accumulator I/O, often called *isolated I/O,* depends on the generation of control signals labeled IN and OUT found on the computer's control bus. If the signals are active low, as is often the case, a bar will be written above the designations. These control signals combine with a port number placed on the address bus to generate a device-select pulse as mentioned previously. The instruction set of computers like this include an IN and an OUT instruction that tell the computer chip to generate the control signals and the timing necessary to input or output information. The 8080, 8085, and Z80 are CPUs that use this type of I/O. These CPUs also have many general-purpose registers within their internal architectures. This is why we will refer to these chips as *register-intensive.*

Memory-Mapped Architecture

A memory-mapped computer system will replace the I/O ports shown in Figure 1-7 with memory-mapped ports. In this type of architecture every I/O device is treated as if it were a memory chip. Consequently, the control signals used for memory operations are also used for memory-mapped I/O.

These control signals are RD and WR, abbreviations that stand for *read* and *write.*

Once again, if the signals are active low, a bar will be placed over the designation. The types of computer chips that use memory-mapped I/O create a memory-select pulse when communicating with a memory-mapped port. Another difference between register-intensive and memory-mapped architectures becomes apparent when looking at the instruction set of these types of CPUs. The 6502 and the 6800 do not have IN and OUT instructions in their instruction set. These CPUs also lack a general-purpose register set, relying on an accumulator (two accumulators in the 6800) and specialized registers that make some programming tasks easier.

Memory-Mapped vs. Isolated I/O

The chapter on digital interfacing will show that when using isolated I/O, 256 output and 256 input ports are available. In most small systems this is much more than adequate. In memory-mapped systems, since each I/O operation is treated as a memory operation, the memory-mapped computer can in theory with a 16-bit address bus have 65,536 memory-mapped ports. The problem with this concept is that the computer must have memory for program and data storage, not to mention a place to keep the control program. Therefore, in a memory-mapped system, memory must be sacrificed for I/O.

The 8080, 8085, and Z80 can all be wired to support memory-mapped I/O with support from external circuitry. Most users of these chips, however, make use of the isolated I/O logic already available. This gives these chips greater flexibility when choosing an I/O system, as the memory-mapped architectures do not have the provision in their instruction sets for the IN and OUT operations.

1-9 8085 INTRODUCTION

A block diagram of the 8085 is shown in Figure 1-8. Many of the features found in the 8080 are also included in the 8085. The register array includes the general-purpose registers B through L. The stack pointer, the program counter, and the address latch are also part of the register array. So far this is the same as the 8080. The instruction register, the instruction decoder, the flag register, the arithmetic logic unit, and the temporary register are still part of the internal architecture of the 8085.

The first difference we will discuss is the presence of the in-chip clock generator. The 8085 can connect directly to a crystal oscillator. This cuts down some of the circuitry found in the CPU subsystem when compared to the 8080. An analysis of clock circuitry will be found in the chapter on timing. The power supply requirements are simplified in the 8085; it needs a single 5-volt power supply. This contrasts to the 8080 power supply requirements, which call for a positive 12 and 5 volts and a negative 5 volts.

The differences discussed so far are conveniences that do not actually affect the architecture of the computer circuitry. The 8085, however, does have some significant enhancements when compared to the 8080. To achieve these enhancements and retain

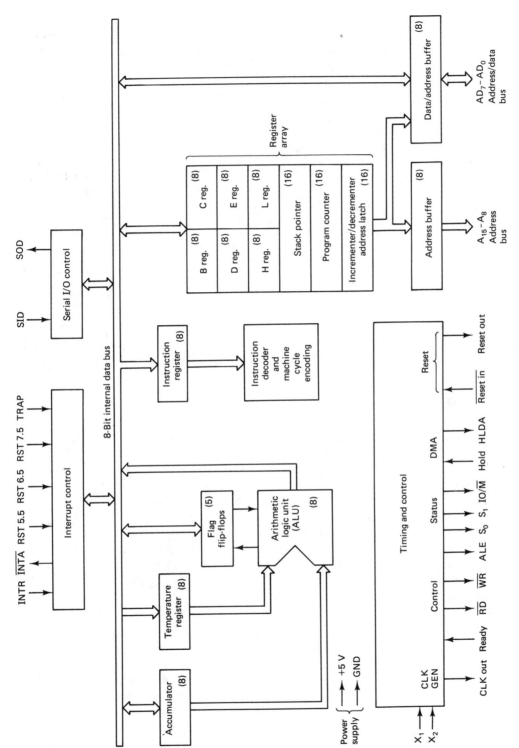

FIGURE 1-8 8085 block diagram. (Courtesy of Intel Corporation.)

the same pin count as the 8080, the low-order address bus and the data bus are multiplexed.

The low-order address bus and the data bus share the same pins; therefore, they share the same buffer. Each will be present at a specific time controlled by the CPU. A special control signal, address latch enable, ALE, is generated by the 8085 when the low-order address byte is present. External circuitry must use this control signal to gate the low-order address byte into latches. The latched low-order byte is then combined with the high-order address to complete the 16-bit address. When the address latch enable signal is not active, the multiplexed pins are available for data transfers.

The first added features gained from multiplexing the low-order address bus with the data bus are the serial input and serial output pins. These pins allow the CPU to communicate directly with serial devices. The 8085 has a control section that monitors the operation of this feature.

Another control section in the 8085 not found in the 8080 is the interrupt control section. This control section allows external devices to temporarily break the flow of a program executing in the CPU. The overview of the 8080 already presented did not mention interrupts. The 8080 has a simple interrupt system consisting of a single interrupt pin and an interrupt flip-flop. The 8085 has a more sophisticated interrupt system consisting of five interrupt inputs, an interrupt output, and an interrupt mask. A detailed look at interrupts and how the different CPUs handle them will be presented in chapter 11, Interrupts.

1-10 Z80 INTRODUCTION

Figure 1-9 is a block diagram of the internal logic of the Z80 processor. This processor has an instruction register, an instruction decoder, an arithmetic logic unit, a register array, buffers, and control logic similar in function to equivalent sections in the 8080 and 8085. The register array of the Z80 differs from the arrays found in the 8080 and the 8085. An expanded view of the Z80 register array is found in Figure 1-10.

The most obvious difference is the greater number of registers. The Z80 has two register sets with 12 general-purpose registers. The main set of registers are still designated with the letters B, C, D, E, H, and L. A register in the alternate set is designated by placing a prime after the register letter. The accumulators and flag registers are grouped in with the register arrays. The greater number of registers gives the Z80 more flexibility; however, just one register set can be active at a time. The Z80 has special instructions that allow a programmer to switch between register sets.

The 16-bit registers include two special-purpose registers not found in the 8080 and 8085. These are the index registers, IX and IY. The index registers are very useful in applications involving the manipulation of data tables. Additionally, these registers expand the number of addressing modes available to the Z80. Addressing modes are explained in the chapter on advanced instructions. Underneath the 16-bit registers are two 8-bit registers. The memory refresh register can be used to support dynamic memory. The interrupt vector register is part of the Z80 interrupt system. It combines with the interrupt flip-flops and the interrupt mode flip-flops to determine how the Z80 will

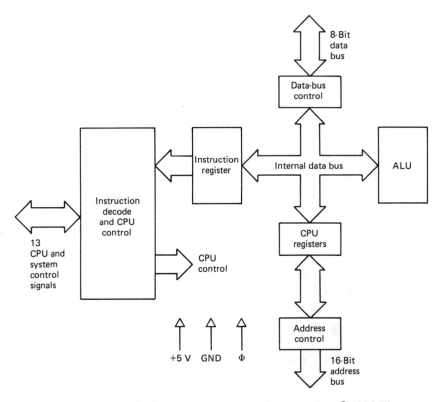

FIGURE 1-9 Z80 block diagram. (Reproduced by permission. © 1986 Zilog, Inc. This material shall not be reproduced without the written consent of Zilog, Inc.)

Main register set		Alternate register set	
Accumulator A	Flags F	Accumulator A'	Flags F'
B	C	B'	C'
D	E	D'	E'
H	L	H'	L'

General-purpose registers

Interrupt vector I	Memory refresh R
Index register IX	
Index register IY	
Stack pointer SP	
Program counter PC	

Special-purpose registers

FIGURE 1-10 Z80 register array. (Reproduced by permission. © 1986 Zilog, Inc. This material shall not be reproduced without the written consent of Zilog, Inc.)

$$D_7 \quad D_6 \quad D_5 \quad D_4 \quad D_3 \quad D_2 \quad D_1 \quad D_0$$

S	Z	X	H	X	P/V	N	C

FIGURE 1-11 Z80 flag register.

handle interrupts. As can be seen from the register diagram, the Z80 handles interrupts differently than the 8080 and the 8085. These differences will be explained later in the chapter on interrupts.

The flag register in the Z80 differs from the flag registers in the 8080/8085 CPUs. The sign flag, the zero flag, and the carry flag are still present. The auxiliary flag has been renamed the half-carry flag. The parity flag now shares a bit position with the overflow flag. Logical operations affect the flag so that it responds by indicating parity. Arithmetic instructions will set this flag if the operation resulted in overflow. When the N flag is set the last arithmetic operation performed was a subtract. The programmer cannot test the condition of the H flag and the N flag. The bit positions in the flag register marked with an X are unused bits.

1-11 CLOSING THOUGHTS

This chapter has presented an overview of three computer chips, the 8080, 8085, and Z80. The 8080 launched our investigation into computer electronics. We presented an extensive explanation of the internal 8080 logical construction. Next we discussed the I/O bus, the method used by the computer chip to communicate with external circuitry. This bus system was subdivided into three sections: the data bus, the address bus, and the control bus.

The ability to perform stored instructions is a characteristic of computers. We introduced the circuitry needed to store programs and data using the concept of the memory map. Program entry and execution were briefly detailed.

We presented the overall organization of a computer. This led to a comparison of register-intensive versus memory-mapped architecture. The different I/O techniques used by each type of architecture were highlighted.

After we laid a foundation, comparisons were made to other CPUs. We made an overview of the 8085 and Z80 based on information obtained from the 8080 introduction. Differences were indicated, where appropriate, with advanced material held for later in the text.

SUMMARY

1. Bits, nibbles, bytes, and words are groups of binary digits on which a computer operates.

2. A central processing chip often comprises more than 75 percent of the electronics found in a computer. The CPU forms the "heart" of a computer system.

3. The 8080, 8085, and Z80 processors are examples of register-intensive architectures.

4. An ALU is the functional section of the CPU that performs the arithmetic and logical operations carried out by the CPU.

5. The instruction register decodes the instructions that will be performed by the CPU.

6. Flag registers are a collection of status flags that allow the CPU to make decisions.

7. The processor bus has three major functional groups: the data bus, the address bus, and the control bus.

8. The logical organization of a typical computer consists of three sections: the CPU, the memory section, and the input/output circuitry.

QUESTIONS

1. What is a *bit?*
2. What is a *nibble?*
3. What is a *byte?*
4. What does MPU represent?
5. What type of CPU architecture is represented by the 6502?
6. What is the function of an instruction register?
7. What is the function of an ALU?
8. List the functions of the carry flag.
9. What is the function of an address buffer?
10. What are the three functional groups that comprise a processor bus?
11. What is meant by *sequential access?*
12. List three uses for read/write memory.
13. What is another name for a *control program?*
14. What is the purpose of the program-counter section of a CPU?
15. What action is carried out when a step button is pressed?
16. What is the purpose of register mode?
17. Of the 8080, 8085, and Z80, which has the largest number of general-purpose registers?
18. What control signals indicate that an isolated I/O operation is underway?
19. In a system built around an 8085, what purpose does the ALE control signal have?
20. What are the power supply requirements of an 8085?
21. How many interrupt pins are found on an 8080?
22. List an application where the Z80 index registers are useful.

2

BASIC INSTRUCTIONS

At the end of this chapter you should be familiar with:
1. the use of the MOV instructions
2. how register pair H is used in conjunction with the M operand
3. register pair operations
4. the use of the IN and OUT instructions
5. flag response to instruction execution
6. the construction of simple looping programs
7. the function of masking operations
8. the use of the logical and arithmetic instructions

INTRODUCTION

This chapter will introduce a subset of the 8080/8085 instruction set. The instructions and the programming examples will provide you with enough information to begin writing simple programs and then enter them into a microcomputer trainer. The introductory programs in this chapter should serve as a guideline in the development of your own software and help you complete the assignment at the end of the chapter.

2-1 MNEMONICS AND OP CODES

The instruction sets of the 8080/8085 and the Z80 are listed using mnemonics. A *mnemonic* is an Englishlike abbreviation of the instruction name. Mnemonics are designed to help us remember the instruction set without having to refer constantly to an instruction set card. The first group of instructions we will talk about are the *move instructions*. The mnemonic for the move instruction is MOV in the 8080/8085 instruction set. The Z80 instruction set has an equivalent instruction, the *load instruction*. The mnemonic for load is LD. Although the mnemonic is different, the entire 8080 instruction set will work in a Z80 CPU. The 8080 instruction set is a subset of the Z80. The reason the 8080 instruction set will work in the Z80 even though the mnemonics may be different has to do with the operation codes the computer chips can interpret. An *operation code* for these computer chips is an 8-bit binary pattern that, once loaded into the instruction register, tells the computer what function to perform. Even though the Zilog instruction set uses different mnemonics for the 8080 instructions, the op codes for these instructions were kept the same. This allows any 8080 program to work in a Z80. The Z80, however, has a larger instruction set. This means that not every Z80 program will work in an 8080 or 8085. The 8085 has two additional instructions not included in the 8080, SIM and RIM. These instructions work specifically with a special-purpose register known as the interrupt mask.

As indicated in the preface, all programs in this text will be restricted to the 8080 instruction set. Therefore, the programs will work in the 8080, 8085, or Z80. Since we are using the 8080 instruction set only, the mnemonics used in the programs will be those found in the 8080 instruction set. To allow you to use or test the programs in your computer trainer, the op codes will be included as part of every program listing.

2-2 ASSEMBLERS

An *assembler* is a special-purpose program written to translate mnemonics into machine code (op codes). An assembly language consists of the mnemonics of the instruction set that is to be translated and the rules (syntax) that govern how the mnemonics are to be entered into the computer. Assembly languages are referred to as low-level languages in computer science. They free the programmer from having to enter machine code, while still allowing the programmer a great deal of control over the machine. An assembly-level programmer is apt to know a great deal about the logical construction of the computer.

2-3 HIGH-LEVEL LANGUAGES

A *high-level language* such as FORTRAN or COBOL is translated into machine code by a program called a *compiler*. The higher-level languages rarely make reference to the logical or electronic construction of the computer. In fact, a COBOL programmer may not even know the computer contains registers. This is not surprising when you consider that a high-level language strives to be as Englishlike as possible. The compiler will take the variables listed in the program and place them into whatever section of the computer is necessary to carry out the instruction given in the code. Thus, a variable may be stored in a register or in a memory location. As you should be able to tell from this discussion, the lower-level languages give the programmer greater control over what is happening in the computer. Each level of computer language has its advantage: the assembled languages with greater computer control and the compiled languages with greater ease of use.

2-4 MACHINE-LEVEL CODING

Many of the microcomputer trainers available to the electronics technician require computer programs to be hand assembled. This means that the technician will write the program using mnemonics, then, once done with the listing, will look up the op codes on a mnemonic-to-op code card. The op codes will then be entered by hand. This can be time-consuming and frustrating. Machine-level programming can offer insights into computer architecture and operation that do not seem to be available in the assembly languages and the compiled languages. The programs in this text were all hand assembled. From this experience, a great deal was learned about the program counter, I/O port architecture, stack operations (discussed in the chapter on project development), memory architecture, and so on. Thus machine-level programming can serve as a tool in learning the electronics of a computer system.

Fortunately, the binary representation of the op code does not have to be entered into the machine. The op codes can almost always be entered into the computer using the octal or hexadecimal representation of the binary code. Each of these numbering systems has an advantage. The octal system is, of course, base 8. This fits in well with the internal architecture of the CPUs we are studying. These computer chips are sometimes referred to as *octally driven*. The general-purpose registers, the instruction register, and the data bus are all 8 bits wide. The basic unit of information in the system is the byte.

Furthermore, the 8080 instruction set follows patterns that are easily remembered when using the octal numbering system. The general-purpose registers, then memory, and finally the accumulator are numbered 0 through 7, the digits allowable in base 8.

The hexadecimal system compresses the binary op code even further. Rather than needing three octal digits to represent the byte, two hex digits are required. This cuts down on keystrokes during program entry, which usually leads to fewer errors. In printing large amounts of data, such as a memory dump, the hex system saves on paper and ink costs. The hex numbering system is also very convenient when using the newer 16-bit machines. Finally, it is the preferred method of data representation.

As an electronic technician, you should be able to use both octal and hexadecimal systems. Each listing in this text will include both numbering systems, which should make it possible to read addresses and op codes in whichever base you find convenient.

2-5 INSTRUCTION FORMATS

The instructions in the 8080/8085 instruction set come in 1-, 2-, and 3-byte lengths. The first byte will always be the op code. The second and third bytes have functions that depend on the op code. These functions will be detailed when specific instructions are explained. The mnemonic representation of the instruction will include the mnemonic and, when appropriate, an operand field. The operand field may include one or two operands. When two operands are present they will be separated by a comma. (See Table 2-1.) Please note that the operand field is separated from the mnemonic by a space. The operands in the example of Table 2-1 are registers. The registers are represented by the generic designation r. The number after the r indicates that more than one register is being used. This instruction will move the contents of r2 into r1. Let us now take a detailed look at the move instructions.

TABLE 2-1   The Move Mnemonic

MOV r1, r2

2-6 MOVE INSTRUCTIONS

The move instructions are part of the *data transfer group*. As part of the data transfer group, the move instructions can be performed by the computer without changing any of the flags in the flag register. In Table 2-1, r2 is the *source register*. This means that the source of the information to be moved is currently stored in r2. The *destination register* is r1. A copy of the information in r2 will be moved into r1 when the move instruction is executed. The previous contents of r1 are gone. The information from r2 simply replaced the old information. The move instruction does not alter the contents of the source register. Whatever was in r2 is still in r2 after the move has been performed. All the move instructions listed in Table 2-2 follow this pattern. The second register listed in the operand field is always the source register. The first register is the destination register.

TABLE 2-2   The Move
Mnemonics

MOV A, s	MOV H, s
MOV B, s	MOV L, s
MOV C, s	MOV M, s
MOV D, s	MOV E, s

s = A, B, C, D, E, H, L, M
Note: MOV M, M = HLT

TABLE 2-3
Register Number
Representations

B = 0	C = 1
D = 2	E = 3
H = 4	L = 5
A = 7	

Note: the memory operand = 6.

Table 2-3 shows the number representation of the registers. Each register can be represented by a letter or a number. The B register is also the 0 register. The A register is also register 7. The number 6 is missing from this table. Six is used to designate operations where one of the operands is a memory location.

The op code for all the move instructions begins with an octal digit of 1. The next octal digit of the op code specifies the destination register. This number is taken from the information shown in Table 2-3. The last octal digit of the move instruction is the source register. This number is also taken from Table 2-3. Consider the instruction MOV A,B. This instruction will move a copy of what is in the B register into the A register or accumulator. The op code written in octal would be 170. The instruction MOV C,D would have an octal op code of 112. The 170 and 112 can be converted into hex, of course. Most mnemonic-to-op code cards have the op codes listed in both hex and octal. If not, they include an octal-to-hex conversion chart.

2-7 THE MEMORY OPERAND

A careful examination of the move instructions listed in Table 2-2 shows that some of the move instructions have an M operand. This operand is not a register. The letter M is used to indicate a data transfer between a register and memory. The instruction MOV M,C will move a copy of the contents of the C register into a memory location. The instruction MOV E,M will move a copy of information stored in a memory location into the E register. The computer chip can talk to a potential of 64K memory. Which location does it use for these data transfers? The answer lies in an explanation of the memory pointer.

2-8 REGISTER-PAIR OPERATIONS

The 8080 allows for register-pair operations. Certain instructions will manipulate registers as if they were 16-bit registers. The pairings are not under the control of the programmer. The internal architecture allows us to use register pairs B, D, H, and the stack pointer. The stack pointer is a special-purpose register explained in the chapter on project documentation. Each of these pairs has a high-order byte and a low-order byte. This is also shown in Table 2-4. Like the individual registers, the register pairs have number designations. The register-pair number is used in an op code to tell the computer chip which register pair to use. Figure 2-1 lists the mnemonic that will load a register pair. The mnemonic LXI represents *load extended immediately.* As can be seen from the diagram, this is a 3-byte instruction. The second and third bytes of the instruction are immediate-data bytes; that is, the data to be loaded into the register pair follows immediately after the op code representing the mnemonic. The second byte in this instruction will be loaded into the low-order register of the pair. The third byte of the instruction will be loaded into the high-order register. The LXI instructions are part of the data transfer group. Like the move instructions, the LXI instructions do not alter the contents of the flag register. So it would be possible to load register pair H without disturbing the contents of the flag register. Register pair H is numbered 10. Fitting this number into the binary format shown in Figure 2-1 yields an op code of 041 in octal or 21 in hex. We are focusing on register pair H because it has a special bearing on the discussion in progress.

TABLE 2-4 Register Pairs

PAIR	HIGH ORDER	LOW ORDER	PAIR NUMBER
B	B	C	00
D	D	E	01
H	H	L	10
SP	SPH	SPL	11

LX1 rp

Byte 2

Byte 3

0	0	R	P	0	0	0	1

FIGURE 2-1
Binary op code layout.

2-9 THE MEMORY POINTER

Register pair H is used by the 8080/8085/Z80 to designate which memory location will be accessed when an instruction using the M operand is performed. To use properly an instruction with the M operand, the computer chip must first be told which memory location to read from or which to send data. This is done by using the LXI instruction to load a 16-bit number that corresponds to the address of the location that will be used. The low-order register of the pair, L, will be used to hold the low-order byte of the address of the location in question. The H register, which is the high-order register of the pair, will contain the high-order address of the location. Together, then, register pair H points to the memory location. This makes register pair H the *memory pointer* for the instructions using the M operand.

2-10 THE MOVE IMMEDIATE INSTRUCTIONS

The first operand of the MVI instruction is specified in the operand field; the second operand is implied. This means that it is an integral part of the instruction. The MVI instructions are 2-byte instructions. The first byte is the op code representing MVI. The second byte is an immediate data byte that follows the op code. This data byte will be placed into the operand specified. This means that the immediate data byte acts as the source of the information, while the operand specified in the instruction is the destination of the information.

There are two forms of the move immediate instruction. The first move immediate instruction lists a register as the single operand. It would be written MVI r. The second form of the MVI instruction is written MVI M. Of course, to use this form the memory pointer must contain the address of the memory location to be used. The MVI instructions are part of the data transfer group. They are listed in Table 2-5.

TABLE 2-5 The Move Immediate Instructions

MVI A	MVI H
MVI B	MVI L
MVI C	MVI M
MVI D	MVI E

2-11 IN AND OUT

The IN and OUT instructions form their own subset of the 8080 instruction set. Neither instruction will affect the contents of the flags. These instructions are used to move information into and out of the computer chip using accumulator I/O. They are both 2 bytes in length. The first byte is of course the byte that specifies the op code. The second byte is a data byte. This data byte has a special purpose in the IN and OUT instructions. It is used to indicate which I/O port is to be selected. The port number is taken from the instruction during the actual transfer of information into or out of the computer and placed on the address bus. In the 8080 the port number appears on address lines A0 through A7 and is duplicated on A8 through A15. The 8085 places the port number on A8 through A15. The Z80 places the port number on the lower half of the address bus. The top half of the address bus of the Z80 does not duplicate the port number during I/O operations.

After the port number has been passed to the I/O bus, the data bus is opened to data transfer. In the case of the OUT instructions the CPU places the contents of the accumulator onto the data bus, where external circuitry can latch the information. If an IN instruction is in progress, external circuitry is signaled to place information onto the data bus. This information will then be placed into the A register.

The port number is just a single byte. This means that the CPU can designate 256 possible port numbers. The port numbers can logically combine with the IN and OUT control signals to form 512 device-select pulses. The generation of device-select pulses will be discussed in the chapter on digital interfacing.

2-12 SOME PROGRAM EXAMPLES

We have now discussed enough instructions to build some simple programs. The first program is found in Example 2-1. This program begins in page 03 of memory, location address 00. Each page of memory consists of 256 cells. The entire memory space has

EXAMPLE 2-1

HEX ADDRESS	HEX OP CODE	MNEMONIC	COMMENTS	OCTAL ADDRESS	OCTAL OP CODE
03 00	21	LX1 H	Point to memory location to	003 000	041
01		00	be used	001	
02		05		002	
03	7E	MOV A,M	Move data into the A register	003	176
04	D3	OUT	Display the data	004	323
		01		005	
06	76	HALT		006	166

256 pages of memory. The first instruction of the program loads register pair H with 05 00. The 05 will be placed in the H register. The 00 will be placed in the L register. In this program, register pair H is being used as a memory pointer. This is apparent when the next instruction of the program is examined. The instruction at location 03 moves the contents of the memory location pointed to by H and L into the accumulator. The contents of the A register is then output to port 01 for display. The HLT mnemonic at 06 terminates the program. Please remember that the only way to output without memory-mapped I/O is through the accumulator. Therefore, it was necessary to move the contents of location 05 00 to the accumulator if a user wished to examine the contents of this location.

Example 2-2 illustrates the use of the IN instruction. The first instruction inputs information from port 05, which, we are informed by the comments, comes from some switches. This information is then moved from the accumulator into the B register. This movement is required so the second input instruction does not erase the information from the first input operation. The second data byte from the switches is then moved into register C for storage. The program is then halted.

EXAMPLE 2-2

HEX ADDRESS	HEX OP CODE	MNEMONIC	COMMENTS	OCTAL ADDRESS	OCTAL OP CODE
04 00	DB	IN	Get data from the switches	004 000	333
01		05		001	
02	47	MOV B, A	Save the byte	002	107
03	DB	IN	Get a second byte	003	333
04		05		004	
05	4F	MOV C, A	Save the second byte	005	117
06	76	HLT		006	166

2-13 BRANCH INSTRUCTIONS

So far the program examples have been straight-line algorithms. This means the flow of the program proceeded from one instruction to the next instruction and then to the next until the halt statement was encountered. At that time the program flow would terminate. The ability of a computer to repeat tasks over and over is one of its major attributes. To repeat a task, a program must have the ability to loop back to a prior instruction. The loop construction will be examined at length in Chapter 3. At this time we will examine how to build simple loops that allow us to repeat a section of code.

The computer performs looping by using a jump instruction. In the instruction set we are using, JUMPs are part of the branch group. This group includes the JUMP, CALL, RETURN, and RESTART instructions. The CALL and RETURN instructions are associated with subroutine usage. These instructions will be found in the section of Chapter 3 that deals with 8080/8085 support of subroutines. The RESTART instructions are used by external circuitry to select interrupt software. This group of instructions is examined in the chapter on interrupts.

As a group, the branch instructions do not change the flags. *The branch instructions react to the flags.* The 8080/8085 and the Z80 make decisions based on the settings of the flags. The breakdown of the flag registers for each of the CPUs can be found in Chapter 1. At this time we would like to look at the flags in a different manner. Condition codes are testable codes that allow the CPU to execute or ignore a conditional JUMP instruction. These codes are controlled by the condition of the flags. Thus, testing for a condition code is the same as testing the condition of a flag.

Table 2-6 lists the eight condition codes recognized by the CPUs. The binary code is listed in the left column. The meaning of the code is given in the center column. The right column contains the mnemonic of the conditional jump instruction, which reacts to the condition code in the left column. Suppose an operation performed by the computer resulted in a zero result. Then, if a JZ instruction was inserted into the program right after the zero result, the condition code would match the mnemonic. Therefore, the JZ instruction would be performed. Whenever the condition code matches the conditional jump instruction chosen, the jump will be performed. If the conditional jump does not match the condition code, the jump instruction is ignored. When a conditional jump is ignored, program flow proceeds to the instruction following the jump instruction.

Example 2-3 shows a section of code that contains a JNZ mnemonic. If the condition code does not match the not-zero condition, the jump is ignored. When this happens the program "drops through" the JNZ, performing the MOV instruction directly

TABLE 2-6   Jump-Condition Codes

CC	CONDITION	INSTRUCTION
000	not zero	JNZ
001	zero	JZ
010	no carry	JNC
011	carry	JC
100	odd parity	JPO
101	even parity	JPE
110	positive	JP
111	minus	JM

EXAMPLE 2-3

Hex Address	Hex Op Code	Mnemonic	Comments	Octal Address	Octal Op Code
	C2	JNZ			302
		LO			
		HI			
	78	MOV A, B			170

underneath. Example 2-3 indicates that the JNZ instruction is 3 bytes long. This is true of all the jump instructions, including the unconditional JMP. Each of these instructions contains a second and third byte used for addressing. The second byte of the instruction is the low-order part of the address. It is used to designate the location to which program execution will jump. The third byte of the instruction is the high-order byte of the address. It is used to denote the page of memory to which program execution will transfer.

2-14 FLAG CONTROL

The explanation of the branch instructions is not complete. So far we have introduced instructions in three of the instruction groups. These groups are the data movement group, the I/O group, and the branch group. None of these groups is capable of changing the flags or the condition codes. The flags are stored in a volatile register. When power is applied, the flags come up random.

As we know from Chapter 1, when the computer chips we are studying are reset, the program counter is cleared to page zero, location zero. Example 2-4 depicts a section of code that begins at 0000 hex. The first instruction is MVI A. It places a zero into the accumulator. Many beginning programmers will then attempt to have the computer jump elsewhere, using the JZ instruction. This is wrong. The MVI A instruction is part of the data-transfer group. As part of this group, it does not change flags. Consequently, the flag register remains as it was prior to the MVI instruction being performed. It is important to understand that the flags do not change unless changed by an instruction. When changed, the flags remains as is until another instruction that can affect flags comes along. Where does this leave us in Example 2-4? The flags came up random. The MVI cannot change any flags. Therefore, the flags remain as they powered up: random. Since the zero flag is powered up random, the results of the first JZ execution will be random.

Suppose we move the block of code found in Example 2-4 to page 03. The computer has a control program that allows us to start a program at this location. The GO

EXAMPLE 2-4

Hex Address	Hex Op Code	Mnemonic	Comments	Octal Address	Octal Op Code
00 00	3E	MVI A	Set A to 0	000 000	076
01		00		001	
02	CA	JZ		002	312
03		LO	Address bytes	003	
04		HI	"	004	

button is pressed. The control program transfers control of the machine to our program as explained in Chapter 1. Do we still have the problem with the flags being random? Most likely not. The control program will have performed some instructions that have set or cleared flags. So far, so good. Along comes our program. The MVI still does not change flags. (It never will.) The JZ statement is next. The jump will take place if the control program left the zero flag set. It will be ignored if, when we pressed GO, the flag was cleared. This is no better than before. *In order to function properly, a program must be written so the flag conditions reflect the task being performed.* We can only control the flags by using the proper instructions within our programs. The first group of instructions that will allow us to control flags, the counting instructions, is explained next.

2-15 COUNTING INSTRUCTIONS

The counting instructions are listed in Table 2-7. These instructions will either add or subtract from the operand specified. The first instruction listed in the table is INR r. This instruction will add 1 to the contents of the accumulator or any general-purpose register. It works like a simple arithmetic statement that might be written C = C + 1. So if the C register contains 5 before the instruction is performed, the C register will have a 6 stored in it after the increment instruction is carried out.

TABLE 2-7   Counting Instructions

INR r	d = A, B, C, D E, H, L, M
DCR r	
INX rp	rp = B, D, H, SP
DCX rp	

The DCR r instruction subtracts 1 from the contents of the register. It also operates on the accumulator and any of the general-purpose registers. In this case the decrement instruction performs like $D = D - 1$. If the D register contained a 9, it will have an 8 when the instruction is completed.

The increment and decrement instructions can also be written using the memory operand. It is possible to count up or down by ones using a memory location specified by the H register pair.

The counting instructions that operate on 8-bit operands can change every flag but the carry. This means when a counting instruction is performed by a program, the sign, zero, parity, and auxiliary flags change in response to the outcome of the increment or decrement. Of the four flags that will change, two are really usable. In this case the sign and zero flags can be tested, with the appropriate conditional jump statement letting the programmer make branching decisions.

Example 2-5 shows how a counting instruction can be used in a program. The first instruction in the program is the second example of the move immediate within a listing. In this case the number 7 is placed into the C register. The function of the C register will be to count the number of times the program will loop or branch back.

The decrement register instruction at 03 02 subtracts 1 from C. The first time this instruction is performed, 6 is left in the C register. This is a not-zero result. This result is indicated by the zero flag because the single-register counting instructions can change the contents of the flag register.

Since the first pass yields a 6, the JNZ instruction will be performed. In fact, it will continue to be performed, each time jumping back to the decrement instruction until the C register reaches zero. When the decrement instruction finally changes the contents of the C register to zero, the zero flag will be set. At this time, the JNZ instruction will

EXAMPLE 2-5

HEX ADDRESS	HEX OP CODE	MNEMONIC	COMMENTS	OCTAL ADDRESS	OCTAL OP CODE
03 00	OE	MVI C		003 000	016
01		07		001	
02	OD	DCR C		002	015
03	C2	JNZ		003	302
04		02		004	
05		03		005	
06	76	HLT		006	166

no longer agree with the condition of the flag it tests. Consequently, it will be ignored. The program flow will fall through the JNZ, moving to the HALT directly beneath it.

If the sign flag had been used to test the condition of the C register in Example 2-5, the most likely choice of a conditional jump would have been the jump on positive, JP.

An interesting thing occurs when the JP instruction is used. The computer copies the MSB of the result and then places the copy into the sign flag. When the C register reaches zero, the MSB is a binary 0. This result copied into the sign flag indicates a positive result. *The computer considers zero to be positive.* This means the JP instruction will jump one time more than the JNZ under the conditions of Example 2-5. The C register will have a -1 when the program reaches the halt.

This program illustrates a very simple loop. The body of the loop—that is, the instructions that are repeated—consists of the single-decrement instruction. The foot of the loop is marked by the conditional jump statement. Admittedly, the program is not complicated, but it demonstrates something very important. The concept is that of the *loop counter.* The body of the loop could have been a series of very complicated instructions needed to perform some task. Somewhere within the body of the loop, regardless of the complexity, there must exist an instruction that counts the number of times the loop is performed. This instruction is frequently a decrement or increment. Used with a register, this is a common way to implement loop counters.

When a loop counter is formed using a DCR or INR instruction, the operand is of course a single register. This means that a loop constructed using this technique can loop a maximum of 256 (base 10) times. In many cases this is not enough iterations of the loop. The programmer can elect to construct longer loops either through nesting or through the use of extended decrement or increment instructions.

2-16 PROGRAMMING LONGER LOOPS (NESTING)

Suppose it was necessary to construct a loop that needed to repeat 512 (base 10) times. A single register, as already indicated, could handle up to 256 iterations before it rolled over (counted the same numbers over). One way to extend a loop to repetitions greater than 256 is through *nesting*.

Nesting actually involves the creation of more than one loop. Furthermore, each loop used will be totally inside another loop. Figure 2-2 shows in block diagram form

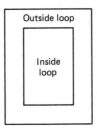

FIGURE 2-2
Nesting.

how this will work. Suppose the section labeled *inside loop* is formed by using a single-register loop counter. The counter is set to zero before the loop is entered. Each pass through the loop will subtract 1 from the loop counter. This can be done by using a decrement instruction. The zero flag will be tested after each decrement. The register will have to roll over before it reaches zero. This means the loop will be performed 256 times. Example 2-5 would operate this way if the C register had been initialized to zero.

Once this inside loop is exited—that is, the conditional jump statement is ignored—control will pass to the instruction below the conditional jump. In our discussion this will be an instruction found in the section of Figure 2-2 labeled *outside loop*. If the outside loop had its own loop counter, this counter could now be decremented. After decrementing it could then be tested to see if the conditions for exiting the outside loop were correct. If so, the program would proceed; if not, control would pass back to the instruction that would allow the inside loop to be repeated completely again. This means that for each pass through the outside loop, the inside loop is set to operate as if it were just starting.

Example 2-6 shows how a coded section of program might be implemented so nesting will cause looping to occur 512 times. In this listing, two loop counters are initialized with an LXI instruction. Even though the B and C registers will not be used as a 16-bit operand, loading them in this manner saves a byte when compared to the MVI sequence listed in Example 2-7. The highlighted section of Example 2-6 indicates the working section of the inside loop. The instructions within this section of the program carry out the tasks that need to be performed 512 times. At line 1B, the foot of the inside loop is encountered. The C register is decremented. After the first pass, the contents of the C register change from 00 hex to FF hex. Since this is not zero, the loop will be repeated. Eventually the C register will again contain 00 hex. At this time, control drops through the JNZ instruction at 1C, passing to the outside loop.

The outside loop serves no other function in this example than to extend the number of times the inside loop is to be performed. Consequently, there are no instructions between the foot of the inside loop and the foot of the outside loop. The B register is decremented. The original value placed into the B register was 2. After the first pass through the outside loop, it will be 1. Of course this is not zero, so the JNZ instruction at line 20 will branch back up to line 03 03. This is the first instruction of the inside loop! The inside loop will again be performed. Once? No! When we exited the inside loop the contents of the C register was 00 hex. We have just reentered the inside loop at the command of the outside loop. The outside loop did not in this case alter the contents of the C register. Therefore, the loop counter is still 00 hex. This means the inside loop will repeat 256 (base 10) times before again reaching the outside loop. The second time the outside loop is reached, the B register will be decremented to 00 hex. Control will pass to the remainder of the program because the JNZ instruction at line 03 20 will be ignored. Altogether, the inside loop will have repeated 512 times. This is what we wanted.

Nesting can, of course, be extended to include more than just one loop inside another. Figure 2-3 shows three loops nested together. In this case, each rectangle represents a loop with its own loop counter and an instruction or group of instructions that

EXAMPLE 2-6

HEX ADDRESS	HEX OP CODE	MNEMONIC	COMMENTS	OCTAL ADDRESS	OCTAL OP CODE
03 00	01	LX1 B	Set up loop counters	003 000	001
01		00		001	
02		02		002	
03			Loop		
			Instructions		
1B	OD	DCR C	Inside loop counter		015
1C	C2	JNZ			302
1D		03			
1E		03			
1F	05	DCR B	Outside loop counter		005
20	C2	JNZ			302
21		03			
22		03			
		·	Continue with program		
		·			
		·			
		·			
		·			

EXAMPLE 2-7

HEX ADDRESS	HEX OP CODE	MNEMONIC	COMMENTS	OCTAL ADDRESS	OCTAL OP CODE
03 00	OE	MVI C	Set up the loop counters	003 000	016
01		00		001	
02	06	MVI B		002	006
03		02		003	

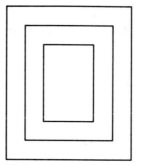

FIGURE 2-3 Three-loop nesting.

form the decision to loop or pass to the next outermost loop. When nesting loops, it is important to exit the loop only through the set of instructions designed to make the decision to exit. Branching out of a loop in any other manner is referred to as *crossing loop boundaries,* something most programmers avoid. When a loop is exited incorrectly, the program is of course not operating properly. In many cases this problem is difficult to find and correct. The problem is compounded when nested loops are used.

2-17 PROGRAMMING LONGER LOOPS (EXTENDED LOOP COUNTERS)

If the total number of times a loop must be performed is less than 65,536 (base 10), then a loop can be constructed using a register pair as a loop counter. The overall structure of the program will be easier to implement when compared to nested loops. Furthermore, if something goes wrong, a loop constructed using a register pair as a loop counter is easier to debug than nested loops.

Example 2-6 began by loading a register pair. After the initial values were loaded, these registers were used as 8-bit operands. The counting instructions contain instructions that allow the programmer to increment and decrement register pairs. The DCX instruction will subtract 1 from the register pair. Suppose register pair B was loaded with 04 00 hex. The C register is the lower-order part of this operand. The actual decrement takes place by subtracting 1 from its contents. Since C was set to 00 hex, decrementing the register results in FF hex. Every time the C register rolls under, the contents of the B register will be decremented by 1. The overall result of performing the DCX instruction once on the initial value 04 00 leaves 03 FF hex in the register-pair operand. The B register will not change again until the C register again rolls under. If the register pair was originally loaded with 00 00 hex, it would take 65,536 (base 10) times before the register pair was again at 00 00 hex. (The first DCX results in FF FF hex.)

The INX instruction will increment a register pair by 1. If LXI D entered 05 06 hex into the D register pair, INX D would change this pair's contents to 05 07. Not until the E register rolled over, changing from FF to 00 hex, would the contents of the D

EXAMPLE 2-8

HEX ADDRESS	HEX OP CODE	MNEMONIC	COMMENTS	OCTAL ADDRESS	OCTAL OP CODE
03 00	01	LXI B		003 000	001
01		00		001	
02		02		002	
03			Inside loop code	003 003	
1B	0D	DCR C	Foot of inside loop	033	015
1C	C2	JNZ		034	302
1D		03		035	
1E		03		036	
			Outside loop code		
30	05	DCR B	Foot of outside loop	060	005
31	C2	JNZ		061	302
32		03		062	
33		03			
		.	Continue with program		
		.			
		.			
		.			
		.			

register be incremented. The INX instruction and the DCX instruction *do not* change the contents of the flag register. Therefore, the results of these instructions cannot be tested directly by any of the branch instructions. When the logical instructions have been explained, a standard technique used to determine if the register pair is at zero will be explained.

You may now be wondering which way is better for building longer loops. In Example 2-6, the outside loop did nothing but extend the number of times the inside loop was performed. When this is the case, if the total number of times to loop can be handled by a register pair, using a register pair is usually easier than nesting. If in Example 2-6 there is a section of code between the foot of the inside loop and the foot of the outside loop, then nesting is necessary.

Example 2-8 shows a situation where nesting is necessary. The code that performs the task of the inside loop will still be performed 512 times, as in Example 2-6. This time, however, there is code between the foot of the inside loop and the foot of the outside loop. This code will not be performed 512 times. The number of times the task is performed is controlled by the loop counter for the outside loop. In Example 2-8 this code will be performed twice. Consequently, anytime you write a program where different blocks of code are performed a different number of times, you should think about using nested loops.

2-18 LOGICAL INSTRUCTIONS

In our discussion we will break the logicals into three subgroups. The first subgroup will consist of the instructions that perform functions that simulate gates. This group will include the AND, OR, XOR, and INVERT functions. The second subgroup of logicals will be used to test for equality. This subgroup will consist of the COMPARE instructions. The last subgroup consists of the rotate instructions.

The first group, those functions that simulate gate operations, operate on two operands, *one of which must be the accumulator*. The *result* of the logical operation is *stored in the accumulator* when the instruction is done. If the original contents of the accumulator were important, then that value must be moved somewhere else prior to performing the logical instruction. This can be done easily enough by preceding the logical with a data-transfer instruction.

Program Example 2-9 shows a section of code beginning at 05 04. The contents of the A register are moved into the B register for temporary storage. The contents of the C register are then ANDed to the contents of the A register with the ANA instruction. Notice that when using the ANA instruction only one operand is specified. This is because the second operand is, by default, the accumulator, as indicated earlier. Table 2-8 indicates the starting values in each register as well as the result of the operation.

Each bit pair, that is bit pair D0, D1, and so on is treated as if it were a separate gate with two inputs. The ANA C instruction will AND D0 of the C register with D0 of the A register. The result of this ANDing will not affect what happens to the other bit pairs. Next, the bit pair located at D1 will be ANDed together. This process will

EXAMPLE 2-9

HEX ADDRESS	HEX OP CODE	MNEMONIC	COMMENTS	OCTAL ADDRESS	OCTAL OP CODE
05 04	47	MOV B, A	Save the value	005 004	107
05	A1	ANA C	Perform AND	005	241
06	77	MOV M, A	Store result	006	167
07	78	MOV A, B	Restore A	007	170

TABLE 2-8   ANA C

```
        7 6 5 4 3 2 1 0   ← bit position
A =     0 1 1 0 1 1 0 1
C =     1 1 0 1 1 0 1 1
        0 1 0 0 1 0 0 1   ← result
```

take place for all 8-bit pairs. The result will then be placed into the accumulator, overwriting the original value in the accumulator. This is hardwired into the microprocessor chip (thus the need to save the contents of the accumulator prior to performing the logical).

After the ANDing has taken place, the listing of Example 2-9 continues by placing the result in a memory location. The original contents of the A register are then moved back into the accumulator at line 05 07.

The mnemonic for the OR operation is ORA. Table 2-9 shows the results of ORing the contents of the D and E registers. The ORA instruction uses the A register by default. This means that the D and E register cannot be ORed directly together. Example 2-10 shows how to OR the two registers together. First, at line 04 CO, the value in the D register is placed into the accumulator. Then the ORA E instruction is executed. The

TABLE 2-9   MOV A,D ORA E

```
        7 6 5 4 3 2 1 0   ← bit position
D =     0 1 1 1 0 0 1 1
E =     1 0 1 0 0 0 0 1
        1 1 1 1 0 0 1 1   ← result
```

EXAMPLE 2-10

HEX ADDRESS	HEX OP CODE	MNEMONIC	COMMENTS	OCTAL ADDRESS	OCTAL OP CODE
04 C0	7A	MOV A, D		004 300	172
C1	B3	ORA E		301	263

result, indicated in Table 2-9, is now stored in the accumulator. Once again, if the value in the A register was important, it would have to be moved somewhere else prior to performing the OR operation. In this example, the E register could be placed into the accumulator. Then the ORA D instruction could have been performed, with the same result.

The exclusive or operation is performed using the XRA instruction. Suppose we wanted to exclusive or the contents of memory location 10 00 with the contents of the B register. Since one of the operands is found in memory, the M operator will be used. As before, the second operand used by this instruction is the A register. Example 2-11 demonstrates how this is accomplished.

EXAMPLE 2-11

HEX ADDRESS	HEX OP CODE	MNEMONIC	COMMENTS	OCTAL ADDRESS	OCTAL OP CODE
02 00	21	LXI H	Point to memory location	002 000	041
01		00	to be used	001	
02		10		002	
03	78	MOV A, B	Transfer B to A	003	170
04	AE	XRA M	Perform exclusive OR	004	256
05	77	MOV M, A	Save result	005	167

The first line of the listing at 02 00 points to the memory location to be used in the coming operation. The second instruction in the listing moves the contents of the B register into the accumulator. Finally, the exclusive or operation takes place when the XRA M instruction is executed. The result of the operation is placed back into the memory location specified for future use.

An operand can be inverted by first placing its contents into the A register. After this is done, the CMA instruction is performed. The CMA instruction complements the contents of the A register. This instruction works by inverting each bit within the accumulator, resulting in forming the one's complement of the number. The result can then be placed back into the source of the information. Example 2-12 shows how to invert the contents of the C register.

The instructions discussed so far are listed in Table 2-10. These instructions, as

Example 2-12

HEX ADDRESS	HEX OP CODE	MNEMONIC	COMMENTS	OCTAL ADDRESS	OCTAL OP CODE
04 00	79	MOV A, C		004 000	171
01	2F	CMA	Invert	001	057
02	4F	MOV C, A	and replace	002	117

TABLE 2-10

LOGICAL INSTRUCTIONS	FLAGS AFFECTED
ANA d	all flags, C set to 0
XRA d	all flags, C set to 0
ORA d	all flags, C set to 0
CMP d	all flags
LOGICAL IMMEDIATES	
ANI	all flags, C set to 0
XRI	all flags, C set to 0
ORI	all flags, C set to 0
CPI	all flags
ROTATES	
RLC	only the carry
RRC	only the carry
RAL	only the carry
RAR	only the carry
COMPLEMENTS	
CMC	only the carry
CMA	no flags affected

d = A, B, C, D, E, H, L

we already know, affect the contents of the accumulator. With the exception of the CMA instruction, they also affect the flags. This means that the result stored in the A register is testable by using one of the branch instructions.

The zero flag is the most useful flag for testing purposes when using these instructions. The carry flag goes to a predetermined condition hardwired into the microprocessor. This makes this flag unusable for testing these operations.

The sign flag will respond to the result of what happened in the D7 bit pair. The other seven bit pairs, D6 through D0, will not affect the sign flag. Consequently, the sign flag is not useful when you wish to test the entire result.

The parity flag can be useful in data communication operations, but with support chips now handling most of the error checking, including parity testing, in data communication operations, the parity flag has little use here. Later, when discussing masking, a way in which the parity flag can be used is explained.

The auxiliary carry flag (the half-carry flag in the Z80) takes on predetermined states in some of the processors and can be used to test bit-3 results in other processors. Since it is not consistent from one processor to another, a program that might work in one hardware environment might not work in another environment. Since one of our objectives is to write software that will work identically in the 8080, 8085, and Z80, the aux carry and half-carry flags should be avoided when using these instructions.

EXAMPLE 2-13

HEX ADDRESS	HEX OP CODE	MNEMONIC	COMMENTS	OCTAL ADDRESS	OCTAL OP CODE
03 00	01	LXI B		003 000	001
1		00		001	
2		02		002	
03			Working section of the loop	003	
1B	0B	DCX B		033	013
1C	78	MOV A, B		034	170
1D	B1	ORA C		035	261
1E	C2	JNZ		036	302
1F		03		037	
20		03		040	

The listing of Example 2-13 shows how to construct a loop using a register pair as the loop counter. You will recall that the DCX and INX instructions do not change the flags. This means that another instruction or instructions must be used to test whether both registers in the pair are at zero. The code that begins at line 03 1B begins the sequence that tests to see if both registers are at zero. Notice that one of the registers is moved into the A register; it does not matter which. The other register is then ORed to the copy of the first, now residing in the accumulator. The ORA instruction does change the flags. The zero flag will be set if and only if the two registers are both zero. If a bit position in either is a logic 1, then that bit position will remain a logic 1 when the ORing is complete. This will result in a not-zero condition. In the case of Example 2-13, the JNZ instruction will be performed unless both registers are zero. This is exactly what is required to build a loop using a register-pair loop counter. The technique used in Example 2-13 is a commonly seen technique. You should study it until you are satisfied that you understand it.

2-19 MASKING

The logical instructions discussed so far, except for the CMA instruction, can operate with immediate operands. The mnemonics take the form of ANI, ORI, and XRI for *and immediate, or immediate,* and *exclusive or immediate* respectively. These instructions are 2-byte instructions, with the second byte being the immediate operand. The other operand is, of course, the accumulator (again by default).

The second byte of these instructions is most often used as a *mask byte.* A mask byte will be used to test the contents of the accumulator or what was moved into the accumulator against some predetermined pattern. In many cases the mask byte will be used to test a single bit. Consider the information in Table 2-11. Here an operand under test is masked against a pattern of all zeroes *except for bit position DO.* This means that if the ANI instruction is used, the only possible bit position that can be a logic 1 is bit position DO. All other bit positions will be masked out by ANDing them to a zero in the mask byte. Moving the single logic 1 to another bit position in the mask will allow the programmer to test any bit position within the byte. The result of the bit position where the mask had a logic 1 can then be tested using the zero flag. If the operand under test had a zero in the bit position being tested, then the ANI instruction and the mask will force all bit positions to zero. If the bit position under test had a logic 1 in the operand at the correct place, then the result of the operation would be not zero.

TABLE 2-11   **Masking by ANDing**

7 6 5 4 3 2 1 0	← bit position
0 0 0 0 0 0 0 1	← mask byte
0 1 1 0 1 0 1 0	← operand under test
0 0 0 0 0 0 0 0	← result

A mask byte with all highs in every bit position but one is useful when coupled with the ORI instruction. Consider BF hex. This byte breaks down into 1011 1111. All bit positions with the possible exception of D6 will have logic 1s in the result. In this case, if D6 in the operand under test were a logic 1, the result would contain all highs. This would be even parity. If D6 were a logic zero, the result would contain seven logic 1s or odd parity. Therefore, the JPE and JPO conditional jumps could be used. The hex mask bytes used with the ANI and ORI instructions when testing just a single bit position are listed in Table 2-12. Example 2-14 shows how the ORI instruction can be used to test if D7 is high. If the D7 bit in the B register is high, then the code given in Example 2-14 will produce even parity after masking it to 7F. The even-parity result will cause

TABLE 2-12   Mask Bytes

ANI	TESTS	ORI
01	D0	FE
02	D1	FD
04	D2	FB
08	D3	F7
10	D4	EF
20	D5	DF
40	D6	BF
80	D7	7F

EXAMPLE 2-14

HEX ADDRESS	HEX OP CODE	MNEMONIC	COMMENTS	OCTAL ADDRESS	OCTAL OP CODE
01 00	78	MOV A, B	Get operand under test	001 000	170
01	F6	ORI		001	366
02		7F	Test D7	002	
03	EA	JPE		003	352
04		20		004	
05		01		005	
			Perform if D7 is low		
20			Continue		

the JPE instruction to be performed. This in turn will skip the section of the program that has been highlighted.

To test several bit positions at once, form mask bytes that have more than just a single bit low or a single bit high. For example, suppose that D5 and D4 are to be tested for logic 1's. Some tasks will only be performed if both are high. The ANI instruction, coupled with a mask byte of 0011 0000, will leave every bit position low with the possible exception of the two bits under test. The use of the parity flag will not work here. If both D5 and D4 are low, this is even parity, but even parity will result if both D5 and D4 are high! Since the parity flag cannot exclude all possibilities except the one being tested, the parity flag alone is insufficient. Example 2-15 illustrates this situation.

EXAMPLE 2-15

HEX ADDRESS	HEX OP CODE	MNEMONIC	COMMENTS	OCTAL ADDRESS	OCTAL OP CODE
03 00	79	MOV A, C		003 000	171
01	E6	ANI	Mask all bits except D5	001	346
02		30	and D4	002	
03	E2	JPO		003	342
04		50		004	
05		03		005	
06	CA	JZ		006	312
07		50		007	
08		03		010	
			Do this code if D5		
			and D4 are HIGH		
03 50		.	Continue	003 120	
		.			
		.			
		.			

In this case D5 and D4 of the C register are to be tested. The mask byte is set in the immediate operand of the ANI instruction to 30 hex. All bit positions except the desired bits under test are masked out. The first of two consecutive conditional jump statements is found at line 03 03. If parity is odd, then one of the bits under test must be zero. If both were zero or if both were high, even parity would result. Since odd parity would indicate a situation in which the two bits under test did not meet the specified requirements, the JPO instruction is used to branch around the code that handles the situation if both bits are high.

If parity is even, the JPO instruction will be ignored. Control will pass to the JZ instruction at 03 06. The JZ instruction catches the possibility of both bits being zero. If they are both zero, the section of code that responds to both bits being high will again be skipped. Two consecutive jump statements can be used like this because the branch instructions, while testing the flags, do not alter the flags. This means that the ANI instruction sets the conditions for both the JPO and JZ branches.

In the next discussion, we will see how to use the compare subgroup of the logicals. These instructions will simplify multibit testing by operating on bytes.

2-20 COMPARE INSTRUCTIONS

Compare instructions can be used when you wish to test the contents of entire bytes. Like the logicals already discussed, one of the operands must be the accumulator. This means that if you wish to compare the contents of the D register to the contents of the E register, a copy of one register's contents must be moved into the A register prior to the compare instruction being performed.

The CMP r instruction will allow the programmer to test the contents of register r against the contents of the accumulator. In the paragraph above, the objective was to test the contents of D by comparing it to the contents of E. Example 2-16 shows how this can be done.

The compare statements operate by performing what is called an *invisible subtraction*. In the CMP r instruction, the contents of the register specified in the instruction are subtracted from the contents of the accumulator. *The contents of the accumulator are not changed.* The compare instructions do not store the answer of the invisible sub-

EXAMPLE 2-16

HEX ADDRESS	HEX OP CODE	MNEMONIC	COMMENTS	OCTAL ADDRESS	OCTAL OP CODE
03 00	7B	MOV A, E		003 000	173
01	BA	CMP D		001	272

traction. This is unlike the logical instructions discussed so far, such as ANA, where the answer was stored in the A register. The compare instructions do alter the flags. This makes it possible to make decisions using the compare instructions.

If the 2 bytes compared by the CMP r instruction are equal, the zero flag will be set. If the 2 bytes are not equal, the zero flag will be cleared. If the byte placed into the A register is less than the byte specified by the operand, then the carry flag will be set. If A is greater than the operand specified, the carry flag will be cleared.

The compare statements have two other forms besides the CMP r representation. The other two compares are CPI and CMP M. The CPI instruction is a 2-byte instruction. The second byte is an immediate byte. This byte will be subtracted from the contents of the accumulator. The flags will respond as indicated for the CMP r instruction. The CMP M instruction will compare the contents of a memory location to the contents of the accumulator. This compare operates the same as CMP r and CPI—that is, the operand specified, in this case a memory location, will be subtracted from the contents of the A register. Remember that when using the CPI and CMP M instructions this subtraction is invisible. The contents of the A register are not altered and no answer is stored.

2-21 ROTATE INSTRUCTIONS

The rotate instructions operate like circular shift registers. The only register that can be rotated is the accumulator. To rotate the C register requires that a copy of the C register be placed in the accumulator; the rotate is then performed. The results of the rotate can then be placed back into the C register with one of the data-transfer instructions.

Figure 2-4 shows the four rotate instructions. There are two left-shifting rotates and two right-shifting rotates. To shift left, use either the RLC or RAL instructions. The RLC instruction shifts every bit one position to the left. The most significant bit position, D7, is transferred into DO. At the same time, a copy of D7 is placed into the carry flag. The RAL instruction also rotates every bit position to the left one place. This instruction, however, treats the carry flag as a position within the register. This means that D7 transfers into the carry flag. The contents of the carry flag, before the shift, will move into DO. In this situation, you can think of the RAL instruction as clocking a 9-bit circular shift register.

The RRC and RAR instructions work like the left-shifting instructions except for the direction of the shift. The RRC instruction places D0 into D7 and copies this bit into the carry flag. Of course, all other bits are also shifting right at the same time. The RAR instruction operates as if it were clocking a 9-bit circular shift register.

The only flag affected by any of the shifts is the carry flag. Decisions to branch based upon the rotate instructions will be carried out using the JC and JNC conditional jumps. If a shift places a logic 1 into the carry flag, a JC instruction would be performed and the JNC instruction would be ignored. If the shift moved a logic 0 into the carry flag, the JNC instruction would be performed while the JC instruction would be ignored.

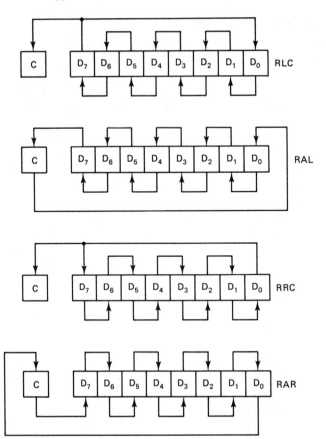

FIGURE 2-4 Effect of rotates on the accumulator.

2-22 UNDERSTANDING FLAG RESPONSE

The importance of understanding flag response was indicated earlier in this chapter. The program you write must use instructions that set or reset the flags. Then decisions made on the flag settings will be based upon events that happen within the program you write.

At this point in our discussion there are a large number of instructions that will alter the condition of the flags. It is important that the responses of the flags to the instructions chosen be understood.

Branching decisions are made based upon the conditions of the flags. As we have already seen, the decision to continue looping is based upon testing a flag with a conditional jump statement. If the code prior to the conditional jump statement is wrong, the loop may not repeat enough times. Worse, the loop may repeat too many times or never stop. If the code in the loop is controlling some industrial process, serious problems can arise.

The programmer can also fail to write correct code by testing the wrong flag. Consider the rotate instructions. These instructions only change the carry flag. If a JNZ instruction were to follow a rotate, the decision to jump would not be based on the rotate.

The flags will remain set or reset until another instruction that can alter them is executed. So in the preceding paragraph, the zero flag would indicate the result of the last instruction that affected the zero flag. The rotate instruction could just as easily have been a data movement instruction as far as the zero flag is concerned. *It is very important to know which flags are affected by which instructions.*

Another mistake that is often made involves the use of a false condition when the true condition is the one that is appropriate. If a section of code should only be performed if a flag is set, an instruction such as JNC or JNZ could be used to bypass the code. This jump statement would be ignored if the flag tested were set. Control would then pass to the code under the conditional jump statement, performing the code associated with a true condition. Example 2-17 shows a section of code from 04 50 through 04 80. The code starting at line 04 54 to 04 80 should only be performed if the RRC instruction at 04 50 sets the carry flag. If the carry flag is a logic zero, the JNC instruction will force control of the program around this section. If a JC instruction had been coded at 04 51, the opposite of what was desired would have occurred.

EXAMPLE 2-17

HEX ADDRESS	HEX OP CODE	MNEMONIC	COMMENTS	OCTAL ADDRESS	OCTAL OP CODE
04 50	0F	RRC		004 120	017
51	D2	JNC		121	322
52		80		122	
53		04		123	
			Perform this code if carry		
			flag is set		
04 80		.	Continue	004 200	
		.			
		.			

Of course, there are situations where using the true conditional branch instructions, such as JZ and JC, can result in program failure if the JNZ and JNC statements were needed.

To illustrate how to predict which flags and which conditions to use when setting up branching, the following examples will be explained.

Suppose that at some point in a program, it becomes necessary to see if the value

TABLE 2-13   Test Situation 1

D = 5
B = 3

MOV A, D
CMP B   operation 5 − 3

Flag response

carry	cleared	0
zero	cleared	0
sign	cleared	0

in the D register is larger than the value in the B register. The information in Table 2-13 shows one possible way in which this question can be answered.

First a copy of the value in the D register is moved into the accumulator. This is the first step in using the compare instruction that follows. The CMP B instruction then compares the B register value by performing an invisible subtraction. For purposes of illustration, suppose the D register contains a 5. The B register will be assigned a value of 3. Then the order of the code will cause the computer chip to perform 5 − 3. The carry flag will be cleared because the contents of A are not less than the contents of B. The zero flag will be cleared because the two numbers are not equal. Finally, the sign flag will be cleared because 5 − 3 yields a positive result. Now, if you wish to jump if in fact D is larger than B, the sample situation can be used to determine which flag and which condition to use.

The carry flag would be cleared even if the two numbers were equal. Since equality is not a condition on which we wish to jump, this flag is not appropriate for use in this situation. The zero flag is cleared. Can it be used? No, because the flag would be cleared even if D were less than B. The sign flag will be cleared if D is greater than B. Remember, though, that *zero is considered a positive result*. This flag would also be cleared if D were equal to B. Analysis indicates that no single flag is adequate to make the decision to jump. The solution is a combination of conditional jump statements. See Example 2-18 for a solution.

Example 2-18 shows how the JZ jump can be used to bypass the JP instruction. If the two numbers under test are not equal, the JZ instruction will be ignored. Control will fall through the JZ instruction, passing to the JP instruction at line 01 05. At this point, the result of the compare must have been greater than zero or less than zero. If D is greater than B, the result of the invisible subtraction yields a positive result. The JP operation will only be performed under the conditions specified by this example. In this circumstance the conditional jump will send program execution to page 00 line D0. Should D not be greater than zero, program flow will continue at line 01 08.

The last statement indicates that other ways exist to test if D is greater than zero. Specifically, if D is *not equal* to B and is *not less* than B, then it must be greater than

EXAMPLE 2-18

Hex Address	Hex Op Code	Mnemonic	Comments	Octal Address	Octal Op Code
01 00	7A	MOV A, D		001 000	172
01	B8	CMP B	Check D > B	001	270
02	CA	JZ	If numbers are equal, bypass	002	312
03		08	the JP	003	
04		01		004	
05	F2	JP		005	362
06		DO		006	
07		00		007	

TABLE 2-14   Test Situation 2

D = 5
B = 3
MOV A, B
CMP D   operation 3 − 5

Flag response

carry	set	1
zero	cleared	0
sign	set	1

B. The test situation outlined in Table 2-14 shows what happens if a copy of the B register's contents are moved into the accumulator before the compare statement is performed. In this case the CMP D instruction results in a 3 − 5 operation being performed. This operation results in a different flag outcome than the method used in Table 2-13. Consider the carry flag. The carry flag will be cleared if the numbers are equal; it will also be cleared if B is larger than D. It will only be set if B is less than D. *If B is less than D, then D must be greater than B.* In this situation the carry flag is sufficient to solve the problem. See Example 2-19 for the code that can replace 2-18.

What insights should you remember from this discussion? First, the decision as to which operand to place into the accumulator prior to a compare instruction is not arbitrary. The flags can be different. Second, there will be times when testing just a single flag is not adequate to solve the problem presented. Third, some foresight gained through the creation of sample problems can simplify coding. Example 2-19 not only operates

EXAMPLE 2-19

HEX ADDRESS	HEX OP CODE	MNEMONIC	COMMENTS	OCTAL ADDRESS	OCTAL OP CODE
01 00	78	MOV A, B	Check D > B	001 000	170
01	BA	CMP D		001	272
02	DA	JC	If so, branch up the program	002	332
03		DO		003	
04		00		004	

faster (fewer instructions), but it saved 3 bytes of memory. This savings in memory can be critical when working with small systems and limited amounts of memory. It is not uncommon to find a microprocessor that controls an industrial process with as little as 2 K of memory. Programs must be made to fit. *Code compacting* is a process where a program is reduced in size and still performs the same logic functions. Examples 2-18 and 2-19 show how code can be compacted by analyzing flag response. Other methods of code compacting will be discussed later in the text.

2-23 ARITHMETIC INSTRUCTIONS

The arithmetic instructions can be used for addition and subtraction. Multiplication and division are not available in the instruction sets of the 8080, 8085, and Z80. The multiplication and division operations must be implemented with addition and subtraction instructions included in a multiplication or division algorithm.

At this time we will concentrate on those instructions in the arithmetic subgroup that operate directly on 8-bit operands.

The ADD r instruction is used to add the contents of the register specified to the contents of the accumulator. The result is stored in the accumulator. The register specified in the operand field does not have its contents altered. ADD A adds the contents of the A register to itself. This in effect is like multiplying by 2.

The ADD M instruction adds the contents of the memory location specified by register pair H with the contents of the accumulator. The answer is stored in the accumulator. The memory location does not have its contents altered.

The ADI instruction is a 2-byte instruction. The second byte is an immediate operand. The value of this byte is added to the contents of the accumulator, and the result is stored in the accumulator. At this point, you should understand that the accumulator is used to store just about all the results of arithmetic or logical operations. One major exception is the compare instructions that perform invisible subtractions. Furthermore, the contents of the operands used in these calculations are not destroyed.

EXAMPLE 2-20

HEX ADDRESS	HEX OP CODE	MNEMONIC	COMMENTS	OCTAL ADDRESS	OCTAL OP CODE
03 00	01	LXI B		003 000	001
01		LO	DATA	001	
02		HI	DATA	002	
03	11	LXI D		003	021
04		LO	DATA	004	
05		HI	DATA	005	
06	79	MOV A, C		006	171
07	83	ADD E		007	203
08	6F	MOV L, A		010	157
09	78	MOV A, B		011	170
0A	8A	ADC D		012	212
0B	67	MOV H, A		013	147

The next three add instructions use the carry flag in the addition. Example 2-20 shows how to make use of this characteristic. Two register pairs are loaded with data. In this example we will treat these pairs as 16-bit operands. The low-order byte of the B pair is moved into the A register. The low-order byte of the D pair is added to this number. The arithmetic statement at line 03 07 will alter the flags. In particular, the carry flag will be set if this operation results in an overflow. The move instruction at 03 08 saves the low-order result in the L register. Since it is part of the data-transfer group, the flags remain as determined by the addition at 03 07. The high-order bytes are now added together. First the high-order byte of the B pair is transferred into the accumulator. The flags are not affected by this instruction either. Finally, at line 03 0A an ADC instruction is performed. The ADC instruction adds the 2 high-order bytes and includes any carry that might have been generated by the addition of the low-order bytes. The operation would have been B + D + 0 if no carry had been generated and B + D + 1 if a carry had been created by the low-order byte addition. In this way, 16-bit arithmetic has been performed even though we operated on 8-bit operands in each addition. It is important not to disturb the carry flag between the first add and the add with carry. If you do, the answer will not be correct for the full 16 bits. There are two other add instructions that make use of the carry flag in their calculations. These are the ADC M and ACI instructions.

The subtract instructions are similar in form to the addition instructions already discussed. SUB r subtracts the value in the specified register from the value placed in the A register. Unlike the addition instruction, it does matter which of two registers to be subtracted is placed in the accumulator. Addition is commutative, that is, 6 + 7 = 7 + 6. Subtraction is not. (6 − 7 ≠ 7 − 6, for example). Think about what you wish to accomplish before moving information when subtracting.

SUB M and SUI are two other subtract instructions that do not work with the carry flag. The first uses a value located in memory. The SUI uses an immediate byte.

SBB r, SBB M, and SBI will perform subtraction and take into account the carry flag. When subtractions are performed, the carry flag acts as a borrow flag. It will be set if a larger number is subtracted from a smaller number. The problem 5 − 7 will set the borrow (carry) flag. These instructions will allow subtractions to be extended over 16 bits.

2-24 TERMINATING PROGRAM EXECUTION

All programs should end with the HALT instruction. This will stop the execution of instructions and place the CPU in a halt state until the reset button is pressed (or until an interrupt is recognized; more about this later). Without the HALT statement the CPU would continue to fetch information from memory. This information would be interpreted as op codes. It does not matter if valid information or codes are present. Consequently, just about anything can happen if this occurs. All the previous work done by a program can be destroyed if the HALT statement is missing. Be sure to include one at the end of your program!

2-25 CLOSING THOUGHTS

A large subset of the 8080/8085 instruction set has been explained in this chapter. Remember that these instructions will work in a Z80 once they have been converted to op code form. (The mnemonics are not the same.) In addition to instruction explanations, examples of looping, nested looping, flag control, flag response, and masking were given and explained. This information was provided to illustrate instruction usage and build programming tools that can be used in the construction of programs.

Masking, as we have seen, is very useful for bit operations. The Z80 instructions set includes many instructions that allow the testing and control of individual bits. Since we are restricting ourselves to instructions that work on all three processors, these bit instructions were not explained. The student is encouraged, however, to study these instructions. They are very useful and eliminate the need for most masking procedures.

SUMMARY

1. The MOV instructions are part of the data-transfer group. They are used to move information from one register to another register or between registers and memory.

2. The CPUs studied in this text operate on binary information. This information is arranged in bytes. Certain bytes represent instructions. These bytes are referred to as *op codes*.

3. Register pair H is the CPU's pointer in operations involving the M operator.

4. The IN and OUT instructions are used to transfer information between the accumulator and I/O ports.

5. The conditional JMP instructions are used by a programmer when he or she wishes a program to test the outcome of an operation. If the conditions of the flags match the JMP, the branch will be performed; if the condition of the JMP does not match the flag condition, the branch will be ignored.

6. The counting instructions are very useful when a register or register pair will be used as a loop counter.

7. Masking operations allow a programmer to test the condition of a single bit.

8. Nested loops are preferred to loops controlled by a register-pair loop counter when there is code that will be performed by the outside loop but not by the inside loop.

9. The arithmetic and logical instructions allow a programmer to manipulate data.

QUESTIONS

1. What is the difference between a mnemonic and an op code?

2. What is the maximum number of bytes in an 8080/8085 instruction?

3. Do the contents of the source register change when using a MOV instruction?

4. Which register pair is used by the CPU as a memory pointer when instructions involving the M operand are performed?

5. Determine the op codes for the following instructions:

    LXI SP

    ORI

    CMP C

6. What binary value is represented by the hex number 5E?

7. A value of 50 hex is loaded into the accumulator. If an RRC instruction is performed repeatedly by a program, how many RRC instructions will be performed before the carry flag is set?

8. Using just 3 bytes, load the D and E registers with 76 hex and 89 hex, respectively.

9. What is the function of the second byte in an MVI instruction?

10. What is the function of the second byte in an OUT instruction?

11. List a single-byte instruction that increases the contents of the D register by 1.

12. What is the maximum number of loop iterations that can be performed by a loop that is using a register pair as a loop counter?

13. Explain why nested loops might be preferred to a loop controlled by a register-pair loop counter.

14. Which flag is affected by a rotate instruction?

15. Explain what is meant by *invisible subtraction*.

16. What is the difference between the ADD and ADC instructions?

The following program is performed:

03 00	LXI B
03 01	CF
03 02	DE
03 03	MOV A, C
03 04	ANI
03 05	F1
03 06	ADD B
03 07	HLT

17. What value is in the accumulator after the ANI is performed?

18. What is the state of the zero, carry, and sign flags after the ANI instruction is performed?

19. What value is in the accumulator after the ADD B instruction is performed?

20. What is the state of the zero, carry, and sign flags after the ADD B instruction is performed?

21. What values are in the B and C registers when this program halts?

LAB ASSIGNMENTS

Explanations of how things happen or operate are seldom enough. Practice is an important part of the learning process. It is important that at this time you attempt to use the information presented in Chapter 2.

1. Write at least six looping programs that repeat 25 times and then halt. Each program should make use of at least one new instruction. Furthermore, the decision to loop

or halt should be made with a different branch instruction each time. JZ, JNZ, JC, JNC, JP, and JM should all be used. Suggestions:

Count up by ones

Count down by ones

Add by ones

Subtract by ones

Start from a negative and count toward zero (two's complement)

If you have a computer that allows single-instruction stepping, step through these loops. The number of iterations (repetitions) is not so great as to cause finger fatigue. After each instruction is performed, monitor the loop counter and the flag register. Make sure you understand all the information presented.

2. Build a nested loop program that will cycle through an inner loop 200 times. The outer loop will be used to extend the looping. The loop counter for the outer loop will be set to 100. If your computer allows you to set a breakpoint (see Chapter 1), set one at an instruction that is part of the outer loop. Each time the breakpoint is reached, monitor the flags and the loop counters. Be sure you understand the information presented.

LAB QUESTIONS

1. List three ways in which a program can be made to count up by ones.
2. What is the hex representation of 25? The octal representation?
3. Can you construct a program that counts up by ones, stopping at 25, without using the A register?
4. Can you construct a program that starts at 25, counts down by ones, stopping at zero, without using the A register?
5. Assuming you perform the loops using a step button, what else must be done if you wish to see the loop counter change each time through the loop?
6. What is the hex representation of 100? The octal representation?
7. With a breakpoint set at the jump instruction that controls the outside loop in assignment 2, record register and flag information each time the breakpoint is set. In a short paragraph, explain your findings. Note: If your trainer does not have the breakpoint feature, predict what you would see. Turn in this prediction to your instructor along with your program listing.

3

PROJECT DEVELOPMENT

At the end of this chapter you should be familiar with:
1. flowchart uses and rules
2. the importance of documentation
3. documentation methods
4. logical constructs and how to code them
5. the rules of structured programming
6. modular program design
7. top-down coding
8. a preliminary analysis of the stack
9. common software debugging techniques

INTRODUCTION

At first many technicians do not understand the need to learn a computer language. This is even more true when the language is not as easy as the BASIC many people use in their home computers. Then, after it becomes evident that an ability to program will improve their understanding of computer systems, these beginning technicians approach programming in a haphazard manner with little forethought.

This chapter will teach the fundamentals needed to develop techniques that will lead to quickly solved problems and at the same time enhance the technician's understanding of the interdependence between software and hardware.

3-1 COMPUTER SCIENCE TECHNIQUES

Let's divide the computer world into two areas. The first area is that of information processing. This would include items such as payroll, accounts receivable, mailing lists, and games. Any application with an end product that is a report or display would be included in this area.

The second area is that of control. Items in this area would include a computer-controlled conveyor belt, control of heating and lighting, robotic control, and operation of a computer-controlled security system.

It might seem, at first, that these two areas are very different. There are skills used in the first area, that of information processing, that lend themselves to the development of control algorithms. In some cases the preparation of computer software for control applications requires more forethought than that for information processing. If a computer program compiling data goes wrong, the print out of the information, while useless, hardly presents a danger to anyone. A control program that goes wrong could prove very dangerous.

Let's briefly outline in this text some of the items that will be used to develop projects and why they are important before explaining them in greater detail.

Flowcharting

Many technicians are trained on small computer systems. These systems typically have very little support when it comes to finding errors in a program. Sometimes, because something important has been left out, an entire routine will have to be rekeyed into the computer trainer, which usually takes a considerable amount of time. A little forethought may save hours. A flowchart is an easy way of checking a solution before the program is entered into the computer.

The techniques and methods of developing flowcharts for projects in this text will be explained in detail in the sections on logical constructs, structured algorithms, and top-down design.

Documentation

Good documentation, the paperwork that explains what a project accomplishes and how to use it, is often hard to find. Not only that, but when it does exist, it frequently happens that the documentation is written after the project software is completed. Properly developed, the documentation can serve as an aid to the creation of software routines. As the software is written, an interaction should take place between the program and its documentation. The documentation should lead to solutions, cut down mistakes, and be updated as the software is written. Ideally, the final documentation and software routines should comprise a package that will make the project easy to modify and update.

A *list of variables* should be included in the documentation package. As with all good documentation, it should be written before the software is created. How many pieces of information will be stored? Which section of the computer will be used to store this information? If these questions seem pointless, consider the plight of a student assigned a project that will take three weeks. At the end of the second week, the student discovers that the small system being used does not have enough memory. If the variables list had been developed first, this could have been discovered in advance. The scope of the project could have been reduced or an alternate solution developed.

A *description of what should happen once the project is complete* should be in the documentation. Do not think that you are the only technician who will ever be responsible for the maintenance of the final product. It is possible that at some future time another technician might need to understand the program. Another consideration: Six months or a year later something may go wrong.

Perhaps the project is working fine, but management wants to add a new feature to the software. What happens if you are called back to fix the problem or provide the update? If enough time has elapsed, you may not remember all the details. An accurate description of the program or process will save maintenance time. Studies have been done that indicate many programs that need to be modified or have failed somehow need to be rewritten completely because no one can understand what was done originally.

The second function that a description of the project will yield is that of a self-test. After the software is complete, go back and reread the project objective. Does the software accomplish everything that was required? If so, fine. If not, more work needs to be done before the software is installed. It will cut down debug time if a project is as complete as possible when installed. Patches, or corrections to problems after the software is running, frequently lead to more problems, which then have to be corrected. Try to be as complete as possible the first time the software is tested.

A *description of the hardware or ICs necessary to make the software operate* is a vital part of the documentation package. This section of the documentation should include hardware that is not normally found in the system being used.

Hardware and software must be used together correctly. This is the area where the computer technician/programmer will be most important. When a system fails that involves both software and hardware, a person who understands both will probably be assigned to correct the problem. The documentation should inform this person of how the software and hardware interact. It should also point out clearly any hardware not normally found on such systems.

Special codes or binary patterns needed to turn on certain ICs, especially those used as I/O ports, should be listed. The programmable support chips studied in this text can be properly wired but not work because the code necessary to turn them on is never generated. It is unreasonable to expect a technician to be familiar with every IC manufactured. List the codes necessary to activate the ICs. Then the technician can investigate to see if these codes are present at the proper time.

3-2 PROJECT DEVELOPMENT

Each good hardware/software technician will create a method of solving problems, but until you have gained enough experience to outline your own solution methods, it is recommended that you follow the procedures given below. It is important to develop a method of solving problems professionally and quickly. Do not sit down to each new project and try things until you hit upon a solution. This is not time-effective, nor is it likely to lead to good solutions.

The first task to perform when assigned a new project is the project layout sheet detailed below. This sheet uses ideas from the computer science field laid out in such a way as to be useful to the hardware/software technician.

The Project Layout Sheet

The project layout sheet shown in Layout Sheet 3-1 will be used to organize the information of the documentation package used in projects discussed in this text.

The first section lists the project's overall objective. It should explain what the software is doing and note any special techniques that might not be understood by others.

The next major section of the project layout sheet defines the hardware environment. Immediately below the major heading Hardware Environment, the type of CPU used and the I/O structure will be listed.

After completing the above, a subsection of the Hardware Environment section will be used to list Support Chips. These ICs are not normally included in the computer system. In most cases, the ICs listed here will be the ICs wired to the computer's bus system specifically to accomplish the goals of the project.

An important part of this section will list the ports added to the computer's bus. If one of the support ICs is wired to respond to port 056, then that information should be listed.

The Software Environment is the next major section; it is subdivided into further sections. The first section under Software Environment is Memory Allocations. This section is used to show where the main program will be stored, where subroutines will be stored, where data and data tables will be stored, and where the stack will be located.

Layout Sheet 3-1

7432 PROJECT LAYOUT SHEET

OBJECTIVE:

To test a 7432 quad dual input or gate under software control

HARDWARE ENVIRONMENT:

8080-based CPU
Isolated I/O

Support Chips

1. 8212 — wired as an output latch. Responds to port 004. Pin connections are detailed in hardware/software interface section.
2. 8212 — wired as an input buffer. Responds to port 004. High order input nibble tied to pullup resistors. Low-order nibble connections detailed in hardware/software interface section.
3. 7432 quad dual input or gates — this is the IC under test

SOFTWARE ENVIRONMENT

Memory Allocations

1. main program — 003 000
2. error subroutine — 003 050
3. test pattern data table — 003 100

Register Allocations

1. A — I/O, arithmetic, logic
2. B — loop counter
3. C — test mask
4. D — test mask
5. E — error register. All lows indicate no errors have occurred. Any bit position left high indicates a faulty gate.
6. H&L — memory pointer for test patterns sent to the 7432

Port Allocations

1. 001 — output latched LEDs
2. 004 — 8212 input buffer
3. 004 — 8212 output latch

Layout Sheet 3-1 (*continued*)

Special Codes

None

HARDWARE/SOFTWARE INTERFACE

Input

Bit Positions	7432 output pins
D0	pin 3
D1	pin 6
D2	pin 8
D3	pin 11

Output

Data Bus — Output latch
D7 D6 D5 D4 D3 D2 D1 D0

7432 input pins
13 12 10   9   5   4   2   1

The stack and its importance will be explained later in this chapter in the section covering top-down design.

The next subsection under Software Environment is the Register Allocations table. This table will list the functions each register will have in the software to be written. If a project is very complicated—that is, it has many subroutines—then this section should be subdivided. The functions of the registers in each subroutine should be given. It is possible that some of the registers are global in nature. A *global register* has the same function everywhere within the program. A register which is used locally will have different functions in different subroutines.

The Port Allocations table is the next section of the documentation. It is a repeat of information that can be found in the Hardware Environment section. This information is repeated to facilitate the hardware/software interfacing that must be done. It is not unusual for a project to be developed by both a software technician and a hardware technician. For a time they may be working independently of each other. It is very important, then, that each works with the same information. If the programmer expects an additional I/O port to be wired to respond to 034, then the hardware technician should wire an I/O port for this number. The duplication of this information helps to insure that this is done.

Special Codes contains the information needed to turn on programmable ICs. It can also include information that the programmer expects to receive from machinery that the software will monitor. As an example, suppose a three-speed motor is being monitored by a computer. Each speed might have a circuit that generates a particular binary pattern. This pattern could then be read by the program to determine the speed of the motor.

The Hardware/Software Interface section is the last major section of the project layout sheet. Here the programmer and hardware technician work together to insure that the software will interact properly with the hardware. The hardware technician may have wired a keyboard in such a way that D7 is the status bit of the keyboard. This means that the software has to monitor bit position D7 to see if a key closure has been made. Without this information, the program would not be able to monitor the keyboard.

The I/O Loop

Once the project layout sheet has been completed, the construction of the I/O loop begins. In the control and diagnostic applications discussed in this text, the computer will be used to operate and/or monitor devices external to it.

The output part of the I/O loop is built first. The connections are then tested by running simple test programs to insure proper operation. Not only is information passed to the output ports, the ports are also tested to insure that they turn on only when "ordered" to do so by the port number.

The input buffers are built next. All control signals to the input buffers are connected *before* data bus connections are made. The input buffers' outputs are then checked to insure that they are in the tristate condition. If so, then the data bus connections are made. Once the input buffer is connected to the computer, simple input test programs are run, checking to see if the input buffers are sending information to the computer.

Once the input and output sections of the I/O loop are wired and operational, the loop is closed. This will allow the testing of a complete input/output cycle.

The methods of wiring additional circuitry to the computer and testing its operation are covered in detail in the chapters on digital interfacing and analog interfacing later in the text.

3-3 SOFTWARE DEVELOPMENT

Flowcharts

The first task in developing a new software routine is to organize the logic that will solve the problem. There are several ways in which this is done (pseudocode, flowcharts, outlines), but the most common way is with the flowchart. A flowchart is a pictorial representation of the logic of a software routine.

In this text the flowchart is restricted to seven symbols. A typical flowchart template has 22 symbols. Many of these symbols are used in software applications, such as system programming, that do not concern us here.

FIGURE 3-1 Terminal interrupt.

The first symbol used in flowcharts in this text is found in Figure 3-1. This is the symbol for terminal interrupt. It will be used to mark the beginning and end of a section of code. Notice that the top symbol in Figure 3-1 has "name" printed inside it. This marks the start of a section of code; the name would be the name for the section of code to follow. The bottom symbol has "stop" printed within it. This marks the end of a section of code. If the section of code had been a subroutine, "return" would have been used instead of "stop."

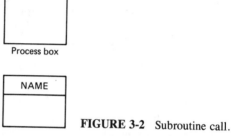

Process box

NAME

FIGURE 3-2 Subroutine call.

Figure 3-2 shows the two rectangles used in our flowcharts. The top rectangle is a process box. It will be used to indicate simple commands. The second rectangle is a subroutine call. Here the name within the box represents the name of the subroutine to be called.

FIGURE 3-3 Decision.

The diamond symbol of Figure 3-3 marks a decision point within a computer program. It will ask the computer to make a decision such as yes/no, true/false, or on/off. In the layout of software in this text, this decision point will have only two possible outcomes.

On page   Off page   FIGURE 3-4 Connectors.

The connectors of Figure 3-4 are used when it is inconvenient to link two sections of a flowchart with lines and arrows. The circle represents the on-page connector. The symbol that looks like home plate directs the reader of the flowchart to another page. It is the off-page connector.

General Flowchart Rules

Flowcharts not only help in the layout of the logic when the project is being developed, they serve to explain software code to others apart from the programmer. The following general rules should be used when drawing flowcharts to facilitate this second function.

    1. *Each flowchart symbol should restrict itself to one idea, command, or decision.* A single box with countless instructions is not the way to build flowcharts.

    2. *Flowcharts are written independent of computer code.* This means a flowchart is written in English and perhaps arithmetic equations. There are several reasons for this. First, a program may be transferred to another machine at some future date. This second machine may use a different language than the language of the first machine. A programmer assigned to make this transfer may not read the code of the first machine. If such is the case, the flowchart is almost useless. Second, an Englishlike flowchart allows management to read the flowchart to determine if a routine will perform the goals they have set for the project. It is unreasonable to expect all managers and supervisors to read code.

    3. *A flowchart should be independent of the architecture associated with the computer.* In other words, a flowchart should not refer to hardware features that are unique to a particular type of computer. The reasons for this are much the same as given for rule 2. As an example, suppose a flowchart refers to a special-purpose register found inside one CPU and not another. The solution to a particular section of code may be handled by that special-purpose register. If it does not exist in a second computer, a programmer assigned to make the program transfer to the new machine must start over.

    Certain hardware features, though, are so common as to be almost universal. Such a case involves the use of the stack, explained later in this chapter. It would not be inappropriate to have a box within a flowchart which said ''set up the stack.'' In most cases, however, it is wise not to refer to hardware features in a computer flowchart.

Logical Constructs

In basic digital classes the prospective technician learns that any combinational circuit can be solved using just a NAND gate (also NOR gates). The final solution to the circuit may not be as easy or cost effective as a circuit without the restriction of building exclusively with NAND gates, but it can be done. Some instructors may even assign such a problem. After the project has been completed the student is convinced that yes, it can be done, but why do it this way when there are other, easier solutions.

    The answer is patterns of solutions. If the student were forced to build many combinational circuits using only NAND gates, certain methods of solutions would present themselves again and again. Eventually, the student would begin to arrive more quickly at solutions to the circuitry required. This could save money in a business situation where labor is expensive and where the time required to design a new product can make or break some companies.

Computer programs, like combinational circuitry, can be written using certain building blocks known as *logical constructs*. These building blocks may seem restrictive at first. In fact, there are situations where other more "elegant" solutions may exist that do not use these logical constructs. Still, the logical constructs and the rules governing their use, the rules of *structured programming,* are considered so important that new computer languages have been created to make structured programming easier. Structured programming also leads to standardized algorithms that are easy for many programmers to understand.

In this text, logical constructs will be used in the development of all software. The student is asked to program following the rules given here. It is hoped that after gaining experience with this type of programming, certain techniques (patterns) to solving problems will become apparent. If so, the end result is a quicker solution.

After each logical construct is introduced and the rules for connecting them together are explained, examples will be given of how to build them with code.

FIGURE 3-5 The command logical construct.

The first logical construct is depicted in Figure 3-5. It should look familiar to the reader. It is the *command* box. This logical construct is used when the programmer wants the computer to carry out some instruction without having to make a decision.

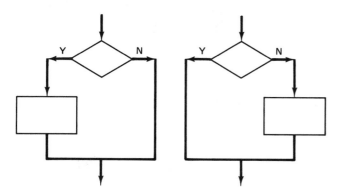

FIGURE 3-6 IF-THEN logical constructs.

The diagram in Figure 3-6 shows the IF-THEN logical construct. In this case, the computer must make a decision. If the results of that decision match the condition leading to the command box, then the command is performed. Otherwise, the computer software will bypass the command and proceed to the next logical construct in the program. Please note that the decision symbol is not considered to be a logical construct by itself.

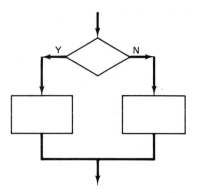

FIGURE 3-7   IF-THEN-ELSE.

The IF-THEN-ELSE is shown in Figure 3-7. Here there are commands in both paths leading from the decision symbol. If a condition is true, one command is performed; if a condition is false, the other command is performed. The commands within the IF-THEN-ELSE are exclusive to each other. If one is performed, the other will not be performed.

Remember that the decision symbol will have only two pathways leading from it. It is used to decide such things as true/false, on/off, and yes/no. The code must be set up to handle this type of decision making.

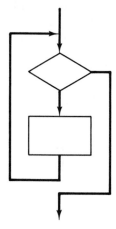

FIGURE 3-8   DO-WHILE.

The two types of loops—that is, repeating code—are found in Figures 3-8 and 3-9. The first of these is the DO-WHILE. It is a top-driven loop, which means the decision to perform or exit the loop is located before the body of the loop. It has as an advantage the ability to bypass the body of the loop if, upon reaching the decision point, the condition for entering the loop is wrong.

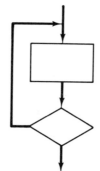

FIGURE 3-9 DO-UNTIL.

The DO-UNTIL loop is shown in Figure 3-9. It is a bottom-driven loop. The decision to repeat the loop or exit is under the body of the loop. This means that the body of the loop must be performed at least once. At the machine level, this type of loop generally produces less code than a top-driven loop.

Structured Programming

The rules that follow govern the way in which the logical constructs listed above may be connected and used.

1. There is one and only one entry to a logical construct.

2. There is one and only one exit from a logical construct.

3. A logical construct may be replaced by any other logical construct.

4. A logical construct may be replaced by any number of logical constructs.

5. There is one and only one HALT in a program.

6. There is one and only one way to reach the HALT.

In industrial control applications where the program is not supposed to stop, there can be one never-ending loop—that is, it repeats constantly. This loop will most likely will break rule 1, and should be the only case in which that rule is broken.

Rule 1 will prevent the programmer from jumping back to a section of code from many different places within the algorithm unless there is a logical connection such as a DO-UNTIL. Thus, if the program fails upon reaching a section of code, there is only one path to check for the error. In many cases, the error will immediately precede the location where the program aborted.

Rule 2 will prevent the use of decisions that have more than two possible outcomes. There is a logical construct known as a case structure that allows for this type of decision, but it will not be used here.

Rules 3 and 4 state what is allowed. Examine the flowchart section of Figure 3-10. The command box inside the IF-THEN has been replaced by an IF-THEN-ELSE. This

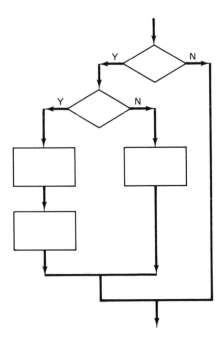

FIGURE 3-10 Logical construct expansion.

is rule 3. The command box to the left of the IF-THEN-ELSE has been replaced by two command boxes. This is rule 4.

The type of expansion allowed by the rules of structured software and shown briefly in Figure 3-10 make it possible to solve any logical problem using just the logical constructs listed in this text. As indicated earlier, this style of programming will seem restrictive at first, but with practice, the hardware/software technician will write code much faster.

Coding Logical Constructs

The command is a straightforward use of the op codes. For example, a flowchart might call for the addition of two numbers. This would involve the use of the ADD instruction. Sometimes a command will generate several lines of code. It should not be difficult for any student having completed the assignment at the end of Chapter 2 to write code for a command logical construct.

Example 3-1 shows a section of code beginning at 003 040. This code represents an IF-THEN situation. The first six lines blocked together represent the diamond of the IF-THEN. The INR C instruction underneath is the command box of the IF-THEN. Finally, the INR E instruction is another logical construct following the IF-THEN. Please notice that regardless of which pathway the IF-THEN performs, the next instruction to be performed is INR E. This follows the rule of having one and only one exit from a logical construct. All IF-THENs will follow the pattern of having one conditional jump

EXAMPLE 3-1

HEX ADDRESS	HEX OP CODE	MNEMONIC	COMMENTS	OCTAL ADDRESS	OCTAL OP CODE
03 20	79	MOV A, C	Code for a typical	003 040	171
21	FE	CPI	IF-THEN	041	376
22		00		042	
23	C2	JNZ		043	302
24		LO		044	
25		HI		045	
26	0C	INR C		046	014
27	1C	INR E		047	034

instruction. This conditional jump instruction will bypass the command(s) of the IF-THEN and proceed to the next logical construct.

The IF-THEN-ELSE is built using one conditional jump and one unconditional jump. A listing for this logical construct is found in Example 3-2. This section of code again checks to see if the C register is at 0. If it is not, then this time the code will jump to 005 032. Once again, the conditional jump is used to bypass one of the command paths of the logical construct. If C is at 0, then the conditional jump is ignored. If this is the case, the C register will be incremented. Below the INR C instruction is the unconditional jump instruction. It is absolutely necessary for this JUMP to be here. If it were left out of the code, it is possible that both the INR E and INR C instructions could be performed. The pathways of the IF-THEN-ELSE are exclusive to each other. This means that if one is performed, the other is not. The JUMP command makes this possible.

Example 3-3 is a complete program which adds 1 to D each time through the loop. When D reaches 8, the loop is exited by jumping (conditionally) to the HALT command. The unconditional JMP below the INR D instruction marks the foot of the loop. The instructions between the conditional jump at 003 005-007 and 003 011-013 form the body of the loop. The decision to loop or not to loop is before the body of the loop; this makes this example a DO-WHILE.

The DO-UNTIL is shown in Example 3-4. Again, this example is a complete program, much like the programs that were assigned at the end of Chapter 2. Here the E register is set to 16 and decremented each pass through the loop. Finally, when the E register reaches 0, the JNZ instruction is ignored and the loop is exited. The conditional

EXAMPLE 3-2

Hex Address	Hex Op Code	Mnemonic	Comments	Octal Address	Octal Op Code
05 10	79	MOV A,C		005 020	171
11	FE	CPI	Code for a typical	021	376
12		000	IF-THEN-ELSE	022	
13	C2	JNZ		023	302
14		032		024	
15		005		025	
16	0C	INR C		026	014
17	C3	JMP		027	303
18		033		030	
19		005		031	
1A	1C	INR E		032	034
		·	continue	033	
		·			
		·			
		·			

jump marks the bottom of the loop. The first instruction within the loop can be found by looking at the location to which the conditional jump jumps.

In all these examples, the method of making the decision—that is, whether a CPI, a CMP, or a DCR was used to set flags—is immaterial to the layout of the code.

Top-Down Design and Modular Programming

Even with careful preparation and documentation, sometimes a project becomes so large that a programmer has a hard time putting all the pieces together. When this is the case, modular design can greatly simplify the task.

This method of constructing a computer algorithm does not forgo the use of the techniques listed so far. Rather it combines with these techniques to form a powerful method of developing large, complex programs. The method of modular design makes extensive use of subroutines.

EXAMPLE 3-3

Hex Address	Hex Op Code	Mnemonic	Comments	Octal Address	Octal Op Code
03 00	16	MVI D	Set loop counter to zero	003 000	026
01		000		001	
02	7A	MOV A, D	Test loop counter	002	172
03	FE	CPI		003	376
04		010		004	
05	CA	JZ	If done go to halt	005	312
06		014		006	
07		003		007	
08	14	INR D	Continue: D = D + 1	010	024
09	C3	JMP	Go to top of loop	011	303
0A		002		012	
0B		003		013	
0C	76	HLT		014	166

A subroutine is a section of code that is tied together by some common purpose. The student is probably aware by now that the 8080/8085 architectures do not support a multiply instruction. A section of code can be written that will produce the answer for a multiplication, then return the answer to another section of code, usually the main program.

The main program in modular design will organize and access the subroutines that make up the program. It will be referred to as a *level-one routine* in this text. The subroutines that are called by the main program will be referred to as *level-two routines* in this text. If one of these subroutines calls a subroutine itself, then the subroutine called by the subroutine is a *level-three routine*. This progression is continued until the bottom is reached. The bottom would be a subroutine that does not call another subroutine.

What is the point of this division of the program into sections known as subroutines? First, it is a method of organizing large projects. Second, it will allow parts of the program to operate without all the parts having been coded. This is similar to a

EXAMPLE 3-4

HEX ADDRESS	HEX OP CODE	MNEMONIC	COMMENTS	OCTAL ADDRESS	OCTAL OP CODE
			Bottom driven		
03 00	1E	MVI E	Set loop counter	003 000	036
01		020		001	
02	1D	DCRE	Tally a pass through	002	035
03	C2	JNZ	the loop	003	302
04		002		004	
05		003		005	
06	76	HLT		006	166

situation involving the purchase of a stereo. The buyer of the stereo can usually save money by buying all the units housed in one cabinet. The problem with this choice is that if the record player malfunctions, then during the time the stereo is in the shop, none of the other sections can be used. If the stereo had components in different cabinets, it would have been possible to use the radio. Sometimes this is possible in software: If one subroutine fails, the others might still be usable.

Third, if a programmer is not sure how to code a particular section of the program, this section can be packaged as a subroutine, then coded later when the solution is determined. While waiting for the solution to the baffling section of code, the programmer can continue to code the remaining portions of the program.

Fourth, a large project is often divided into smaller sections, with each section assigned to a different programmer. Each programmer will be responsible for a particular section of code.

Fifth, a subroutine may be used many times. Different sections of the main program may need a multiplication to be performed. Why code this many times when it can be used again and again by writing it as a subroutine? This last reason is the one given most often for writing subroutines.

The preceding arguments are points in favor of *modular programming,* the partitioning of large, complicated projects into smaller, more easily understood modules known as subroutines.

Top-down design becomes evident when it is time to test the program. In top-down design the main program is written first. All subroutines are written as *dummy subroutines.* A dummy subroutine will contain a very simple output (or print) command that generates a code, which is used to indicate that the call to the subroutine has occurred. The main program is then coded. It is entered along with the dummy subroutines. The program is run, testing the logic of the main program. Once the logic of the main program is known to be good, the level-two subroutines are coded. If necessary, subroutines called by level two are dummied out. This process is continued until the lowest level of the program has been tested.

The advantage of this procedure lies in the time needed to find errors in the code. If the entire project is loaded and tested at once, a large amount of time may be required to find the mistake. If small sections are added and tested, the time required to find the error is minimized.

To make modular programming and top-down design integrate with the rules on structured programming, several new rules should be followed.

1. Each subroutine will perform a single specific task. A multiply subroutine, for example, would not also perform a seven-segment display update. What constitutes a single specific task is a judgment call on the part of the programmer. Clearly, though, the above tasks have nothing in common, and should be separate subroutines.

2. A subroutine can replace any command box found in a higher-level routine.

3. There is one and only one exit from the subroutine. This is known as the *return*.

4. There is one and only one path to the return.

3-4 8080/8085/Z80 SUBROUTINE SUPPORT

The 8080/8085 CPUs support subroutines through the use of the CALL instruction, the RETURN instruction, and the stack.

The CALL instruction is a 3-byte instruction. The first byte of the instruction is the op code representing the call. The next 2 bytes are address bytes in the usual low-high sequence. These 2 bytes form a 16-bit address that points to the first instruction of the subroutine. When it is executed, control transfers to the subroutine by placing the address in the program counter. Example 3-5 shows a section of code starting from 004 020. The CALL instruction at 004 021 calls a subroutine which is stored in page 5, beginning at line 000.

When the subroutine is finished, it performs the RET instruction as its last instruction. This will transfer control back to the calling routine. In this case, the calling routine will resume operation at 004 024. How can the subroutine know where to return? The answer is the stack.

The Stack

The stack is a data structure supported by the 8080/8085/Z80 architecture. A data structure is a collection of data with some common usage. It must also follow some specific means of retrieval. In the case of the stack, this method of retrieval is "last in, first

EXAMPLE 3-5

Hex Address	Hex Op Code	Mnemonic	Comments	Octal Address	Octal Op Code
04 10	83	ADD E		004 020	203
11	CD	CALL		021	315
12		000		022	
13		005		023	
		→		024	
05 00		·	Subroutine start	005 000	
		·			
		·			
		·			
		·			
		·			
	C9	RET			311

out." This means that the last item stored on the stack is the first item removed from the stack.

The CALL instruction places information on the stack. When the call is performed, the location of the next instruction following the call is stored as the last item on the stack. When the subroutine reaches RET, this instruction takes the last item on the stack and places it in the program counter. In this way, control can be transferred between sections of code using CALL and RET instructions.

What happens if a subroutine calls a subroutine? The second CALL instruction (located within the first subroutine) places a return address on the stack. It then transfers control to the second subroutine. When this subroutine reaches RET, it removes the last

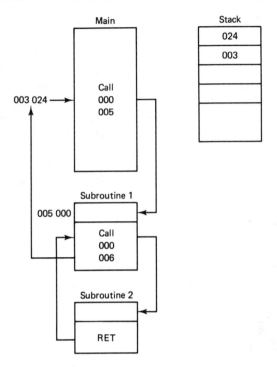

FIGURE 3-11   Stack operations.

address from the stack. This just happens to be the address of the next instruction below the CALL in the first subroutine. When the first subroutine reaches its RET, it also removes two items from the stack. These two items form the 16-bit address that will return control back to the main program. See Figure 3-11 to visualize what is happening. The stack supports top-down design!

The Stack Pointer

The stack is located in memory. The starting location is determined by the use of the LXI SP instruction. This instruction loads a special-purpose register known as the *stack pointer*. The contents of this register should always point to the last item stored on the stack.

   If proper care is taken so that for every instruction placing information on the stack, another instruction removes that information, then the stack pointer will take care of itself. What this means is that the CALLS and RETurns are paired so that they operate correctly with each other.

Register Storage

The stack can also be used to store information. There is a group of instructions known as the PUSH commands. These commands take register pairs and place copies of the register pairs' contents on the stack. To retrieve this information, a POP instruction is performed. If more than one register pair is stored on the stack, the pushes and pops must be written in inverse order. Example 3-6 shows how this is done. Note in this listing that for every PUSH, there is a POP. If this were not the case, the RET address would not be correct. As an example, suppose the last POP instruction, POP PSW, was omitted. Then when the RET instruction removed the last two items stored on the stack, it would place the contents of the A register and the flag register into the program counter. This type of error is very difficult to debug. Extreme care must be used when operating with the stack.

A final note: Definitions for global and local registers were given earlier. In Example 3-6 all the registers saved on the stack are local. This must be the case because

EXAMPLE 3-6

HEX ADDRESS	HEX OP CODE	MNEMONIC	COMMENTS	OCTAL ADDRESS	OCTAL OP CODE
		PUSH PSW			
		PUSH B			
		PUSH D			
		PUSH H			
			Body of		
			subroutine		
		POP H			
		POP D			
		POP B			
		POP PSW			
		RET			

whatever changes the subroutine made when using the registers was erased when the POP commands restored the registers to the value they had upon entering the subroutine.

3-5 AN ORDER-FILLING ROUTINE

The following discussion involves a program example that illustrates the concepts with which this chapter has dealt. It includes a discussion of the program's objectives, an analysis of the software used to meet these objectives, and a general overview of the hardware the computer controls. A detailed examination of the computer circuitry and interface electronics will not be done at this time.

The Situation

A distributor of breakfast cereals has several customers that frequently call in rush orders at the end of the business day. To satisfy these customers, the manager of the firm has been paying overtime to several employees to fill the orders manually. The manager would like to automate the process so that one employee can tell a computer how many boxes must be sent. The computer will then operate a conveyor system to fill the order automatically.

End-of-the-day orders are filled from the overrun bin. This bin contains boxes of both breakfast flakes and breakfast pops. The boxes will be dropped onto the conveyor belt in a random fashion. (See Fig. 3-12.) A sensing station is able to read the product

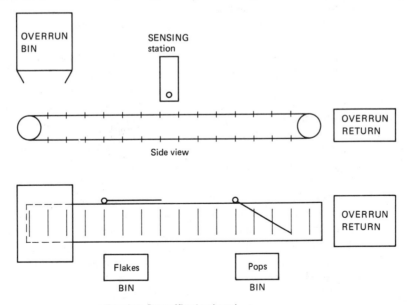

FIGURE 3-12   Breakfast order pictorial.

bar code, thus identifying which box is moving past the sensor. If a flakes box is identified, the flakes chute will be opened by a pulse from a oneshot controlled by the computer. The chute will return to the closed position after the oneshot pulse times out. If a pops box is identified, the pops chute will be opened. An operator can tell the computer how many of each box are required to fill the order.

There is one problem. The boxes are dropped onto the conveyor system from the overrun bin in a random order. This means that the flakes part of the order may be filled well before the pops part of the order, or the opposite can happen. The computer system must be able to ignore boxes from the filled part of the order while waiting to detect the second type of box. Boxes that are ignored will travel past both off-loading stations and be returned to the overrun bin automatically without any need of further computer intervention.

The Project

The hardware involved in this project is already wired and known to be operational. The programmer therefore concentrates on the software environment section of the project layout sheet found in Layout Sheet 3-2. The main program will be coded and stored in the computer starting at address 03 00. A subroutine that allows the operator to input the order requirements will be located at 06 00. This subroutine will be written by another programmer. The subroutine will return the number of boxes of flakes required in register B; the C register will contain the number of pops boxes needed. The person coding the subroutine will protect all other registers by saving copies on the stack. Upon returning to the main program, the registers, other than B and C, will be restored. This is the proper way to handle the subroutine. It will perform its task without disturbing any other part of the software environment.

The main program flowchart is found in Figure 3-13 (Flowchart 3-1). The boxes in the flowchart have been numbered for discussion purposes. Please take a moment to study this flowchart. Notice that diamond 5 marks the beginning of an IF-THEN-ELSE logical construct. Diamonds 6 and 9 mark the beginnings of IF-THEN logical constructs inside the logical construct started by diamond 5. The program fills an order by repeating its tasks using a bottom-driven loop. The DO-UNTIL will be exited when the condition in diamond 12 is satisfied. Finally, after exiting the loop, the computer will shut down the conveyor system before halting the program.

This flowchart follows the rules as given in this chapter regarding logical constructs and flowcharts. It makes no references to computer architecture other than referring to a stack. Port numbers and register are not indicated in the flowchart. It is the function of the project layout sheet to connect the hardware to the software.

The listing of the main program is found in Example 3-7. The first block of code establishes the stack. This allows the computer to make subroutine calls. The CALL instruction at 03 03 gets the input from the operator. When the subroutine returns to the main program, the B and C registers will contain the numbers of flakes and pops boxes to be loaded respectively. The OUT instruction at 03 06 turns on the conveyor.

The next block of code monitors the sensing station looking for boxes. If no box

SINGLE ORDER LAYOUT SHEET

OBJECTIVE:

To allow an operator to fill an order automatically. The operator will tell the computer how many boxes to load — the computer system will do the rest.

HARDWARE ENVIRONMENT:

8085 based CPU
Accumalator I/O

Support Chips:

1. 74121 oneshot triggered from port 02 — conveyor on
2. 74121 oneshot triggered from port 04 — flake chute open
3. 74121 oneshot triggered from port 06 — pops chute open
4. 74121 oneshot triggered from port 03 — conveyor off
5. 8212 wired as an input buffer; port 04 — box code sensor

SOFTWARE ENVIRONMENT:

1. main program — 03 00
2. operator input subroutine — 06 00

Register Allocation:

1. A — input/output; arithmetic; logical
2. B — flake box counter—global
3. C — breakfast pops counter—global

Port Allocations:

1. 02 — output—conveyor on
2. 03 — output—conveyor off
3. 04 — output—flake chute opens
4. 04 — input from box sensor
5. 06 — output—pops chute opens

Special Codes:

1. 00 — no box sensed
2. 1A — breakfast flakes sensed
3. 15 — breakfast pops sensed

HARDWARE/SOFTWARE INTERFACE

Wiring connections other than assigned port numbers have no bearing on the software.

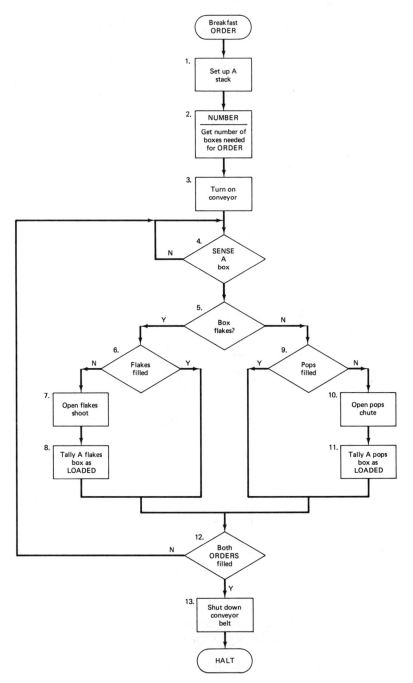

FIGURE 3-13 Flowchart 3-1.

EXAMPLE 3-7

HEX ADDRESS	HEX OP CODE	MNEMONIC	COMMENTS	OCTAL ADDRESS	OCTAL OP CODE
03 00	31	LX1 SP	Set up a stack	003 000	061
01		00		001	
02		10		002	
03	CD	CALL	Allow operator to input	003	315
04		00	number of boxes needed	004	
05		06		005	
06	D3	OUT	Turn conveyor on	006	323
07		02		007	
08	DB	IN	Check for a box	010	333
09		04		011	
0A	FE	CP1		012	376
0B		00		013	
0C	CA	JZ	If no box, check again	014	312
0D		08		015	
0E		03		016	
0F	FE	CPI	Is box sensed a flakes box	017	376
10		1A		020	
11	CZ	JNZ	If not, check if pops box	021	302
12		20		022	
13		03		023	
14	78	MOV A, B	If so, check if flakes order is	024	170
15	FE	CPI	filled	025	376
16		00		026	
17	CA	JZ	If so, see if entire order is	027	312
18		2E	filled	030	
19		03		031	
1A	D3	OUT	If not, offload a flakes box	032	323
1B		04		033	

EXAMPLE 3-7 (*continued*)

HEX ADDRESS	HEX OP CODE	MNEMONIC	COMMENTS	OCTAL ADDRESS	OCTAL OP CODE
03 1C	05	DCR B	Record A flakes	003 034	005
1D	C3	JMP	Go check to see if order is	035	303
1E		2E	filled	036	
1F		03		037	
20	FE	CPI	Check to see if box was pops	040	376
21		15		041	
22	CZ	JNZ	If not, ignore box	042	302
23		2E		043	
24		03		044	
25	79	MOV A, C	If so, check to see if pops	045	171
26	FE	CPI	box order is filled	046	376
27		00		047	
28	CA	JZ	If so, go check on entire	050	312
29		2E	order	051	
2A		03		052	
2B	D3	OUT	If not, offload a pops box	053	323
2C		06		054	
2D	0D	DCR C	Record A pops	055	015
2E	78	MOV A, B	Is entire order filled	056	170
2F	B1	ORA C		057	261
30	C2	JNZ	If not, continue processing	060	302
31		08		061	
32		03		062	
33	D3	out	If so, stop conveyor system	063	323
34		03		064	
35	76	HLT		065	166

passes the sensor, the code generated by the sensor will remain 00. This will make the program loop back up to 03 08, once again checking the input from the sensor. When the sensor inputs a code other than zero, a box has been sensed. The program will then fall out of this short loop.

Line 03 0F is a block of code that asks if the box detected was a flakes box. If so, the program falls through to line 03 14. This section of code determines if the flakes part of the order is filled. If is isn't, the flakes chute is opened. The flakes counter is also updated to record another off-loaded box. If the flakes part of the order is filled, the program will jump to 03 20.

At 03 20 the program repeats the process just described, but this time it is looking for pops boxes. If for some reason the sensor inputs a code that was neither flakes nor pops, the box would simply be ignored and returned to the overrun bin. If in fact the box detected was a pops box, then lines 03 2B to 03 2D would offload a pops box and update the pops counter.

The block of code starting at 03 2E is used to determine if the entire order has been filled. This section of code illustrates a frequently used technique to determine if two registers are both zero. The flakes counter is moved into the accumulator. The pops counter is then logically ORed to the value in the accumulator. The accumulator will contain a zero only if both registers involved in the operation were zero. Since the program tallies boxes by decrementing the counters involved, the order will be filled when both registers reach zero.

Finally, the OUT instruction at 03 33 shuts down the system.

3-6 SOFTWARE DEBUGGING

The information presented so far in this chapter has dealt with the techniques useful when developing a microprocessor project. These techniques have two major goals. First, if applied correctly, the organization and documentation will lead to quicker solutions. Second, the number of errors that are likely to occur as a project is developed will be reduced. Despite everything, organization and documentation do not guarantee that errors will not happen. This section deals with the skills and methods for finding and correcting errors.

Software error correction, commonly known as *debugging,* is in some ways more art than science. This can be very frustrating to an electronics technician who is attempting to become a microprocessor programmer. Electronics as an applied science deals with situations where values can be assigned to certain situations. Consider a simple series circuit powered by a battery. Through the use of Ohm's Law, the current that should be flowing in the circuit can be calculated. This specific value can then be checked by inserting an ammeter into the circuit. If the meter reading is significantly different from the calculated value, something is wrong with the circuit.

In software situations, problems are not always as clear. Even though a considerable effort is being made to standardize coding through the use of structured algorithms, style still plays an important part in software development. This difference in style makes it very difficult to teach debugging. Each programmer's style may cause certain types of errors to be made repeatedly. Another programmer may rarely make those errors, but might have another set of errors to which his code is susceptible.

In addition to problems with style, many different solutions may be possible for a single problem. With different solutions, different types of errors might be encountered.

With so many variables, it is difficult to predict what errors might happen, how often they might happen, and what specific steps should be taken to correct a problem when it does occur. Despite this, some standard debugging techniques have been developed. Those techniques, applicable in a microprocessor environment, will be discussed with examples on how to use them.

Error Prevention

The best way to correct an error is not to make one. As already indicated, error prevention is one objective of this chapter. To reemphasize this point, let's take another look at flowchart usage, this time as an error-prevention tool. (The previous discussion focused on the flowchart as a developmental tool.)

1. Run through the logic of the flowchart with some data that might be expected to occur in the program. Determine if the logic is sound. When you are finished, ask yourself if the results of this run meet the goals assigned to the program. When you are satisfied with this preliminary trace, proceed to the coding of the program.

2. As the program is developed, changes may be introduced in the original logic, often caused by oversights. Update the flowchart as the changes are made. The flowchart will have little use in debugging code that it does not represent correctly.

3. Use the flowchart to organize the code into readable sections. A continuous line-after-line, poorly commented program is difficult to debug. Each flowchart symbol represents a concrete idea or operation. Partition the coding into blocks separated either by blank lines or, if you are using an assembler, blank comment lines. If you have kept your flowchart as Englishlike as possible, the statements within the symbols of the flowchart make appropriate comments in a listing.

The other documentation procedures stressed earlier in the chapter, especially the project layout sheet, are useful tools for error prevention. Once you become comfortable with good documentation methods, this phase of the project goes quickly. When good documentation is available it is easier to spot differences in the code that do not match the plan. Consequently, the time spent looking for errors will be reduced.

Error Detection

This section will detail some commonly used methods for finding errors in malfunctioning programs. The first method relies on a visual inspection of the program. The next three methods explained in this section rely on the computer to help solve the problem. Most microcomputer trainers have the ability to support these three debug methods. An alternative will be mentioned for those times when a program must be debugged without the support of the features mentioned here. The last method discussed is essentially a paper-and-pencil method. It is time-consuming process, but often solves the problem simply by being very thorough. This method is called a *trace*.

When troubleshooting a circuit, the first step is to look for burned or broken parts. When troubleshooting a program, a visual inspection is also a good starting point. If a program has been hand assembled, check to see that the op codes chosen match the mnemonic used. Check the op codes for transposed numbers. Use the flowchart to determine if any task has been omitted or put in the incorrect place. Examine all multibyte instructions carefully. If a byte has been omitted, instruction boundaries will be off. The computer will end up trying to execute data and address bytes. Make sure the instructions that specify addresses follow the low-high sequence. If possible, have a second person look through the program too. Sometimes another person will quickly spot a problem that you have overlooked.

A *breakpoint* is a location in the program where execution is temporarily stopped. Those microcomputer trainers that support breakpoints will usually replace the instruction at the address you specify with a jump instruction that transfers control back to the monitor. When a breakpoint is reached, the monitor saves a copy of the registers including the flags, stack pointer, and program counter. These registers are then available for inspection, which means you can insert a breakpoint in the program at a spot where you suspect trouble, then run the program. The monitor will tell you when you have reached the breakpoint. At that time you can check the contents of the registers. If the values stored in the registers are not as expected, the code preceding the breakpoint has some problem. If everything seems to be in order, the program can be resumed from the breakpoint. Remember, the monitor stored a copy of the program counter so it will know where to resume. This makes it easy to place breakpoints inside loops. Each pass through the loop will encounter the breakpoint, so if necessary you can monitor registers as they are altered in each pass of the loop. This can be very useful. If you have no inkling of where the problem is located in the program, the following suggestions should help. Place breakpoints:

1. At branch points in a program. Check the flags that will be tested by the branch instruction. Do the conditions of the flags match the conditional branch instruction? Should they?

2. At the start of subroutines. Examine the registers. If data is passed to the subroutine, verify that it is present and correct. Examine the stack. Use the stack pointer value to obtain the address of the last item on the stack. Is the return address correct?

3. At the end of subroutines. Examine the registers. Have the registers that are to be restored with POP instructions been restored correctly? If the RET is the only instruction left to perform in the subroutine, is the return address the next item on the stack?

4. In the middle of a routine. This will allow you to start a binary search. If you do not reach the breakpoint, then there is a fault in the code prior to the breakpoint.

This is useful information. If you do reach the breakpoint, is the information correct? The information of this first breakpoint allows you to partition the program into two sections. The results should indicate which half of the routine is causing the problem. If the breakpoint is reached and the data is correct, the problem must be in the second half of the routine. Proceed by placing a breakpoint midway in the section that is bad. Continue in this fashion, each time dividing the remaining code by half. This process is called a *binary search;* if used properly, it will eventually point to the instruction or instructions that are causing the problem.

Forcing is a debug technique that allows you to test the construction of a branch point. Insert a breakpoint just prior to the branch. When control is transferred to the monitor, alter the contents of the registers or flags that affect the branch. Resume the program. Did the branch respond correctly? If not, examine the instructions that set up the branch. Did you compare with the right value? Did the instruction you use affect the flag being tested? If the branch sequence responds correctly under these circumstances, but not when run under program conditions, look for incorrect data prior to the branch.

Single stepping through branch points can be very useful. Insert a breakpoint just before a branch sequence. Then use a single-step feature to perform the branch. Check the contents of the program counter after the branch has occurred. Did the branch jump to the correct place? If not, check the low-high order of the address. Check to see if the jump corresponds to the jumps indicated in the flowchart.

The last debug technique is called a *trace*. A preliminary trace was already performed using the flowchart and some projected data. Traces are time-consuming. Essentially you will be playing computer by hand. As each instruction is encountered, you will update the contents of the flags, memory locations used, and registers on paper. The registers that must be included in the trace include the general-purpose registers, the stack pointer, and the program counter. In Z80 systems, the index registers should be included. A trace can be a very slow process. Therefore, before deciding to do a trace, try the other suggestions we have discussed. If you decide to do the trace, perform the trace using the flowchart, then the code. For each step in the flowchart trace, perform the corresponding step in the code. Do the results match instruction by instruction? When there is a difference, a problem has been found. This process will detect implementation errors. An implementation error occurs when the code does not produce the logic required by the flowchart.

To detect logic errors, you must ask yourself after each step if the results are as desired. Do they match the goal of the program at this point? This is a very difficult thing to do. Why? Because it questions decisions you made earlier, decisions that at the time seemed correct. If you refuse to admit the possibility of mistakes, you will have a very difficult time finding mistakes. Keep an open mind!

Error Detection Examples

The five short programs in Examples 3-8 through 3-12 all have faults. The programs are short and conceptually simple. This will allow us to highlight the debug process without getting bogged down in finding subtle logic errors. Furthermore, your programming skills are probably just developing. The types of errors you are likely to make will be similar to those found in the following examples. Even after you become a proficient programmer, bugs will still plague your code. Experience has shown that certain types of errors are quite common. These errors are:

> incorrect branching
>
> bad loop construction
>
> bad initialization
>
> stack errors
>
> memory pointer problems
>
> IF-THEN-ELSE constructs coded wrong

Stack errors fall into two major categories. The first is an unbalanced stack. Somehow more pushes were performed than pops. When this happens, return addresses are not available at the proper time. The second area is a failure to use the stack when it is required to protect registers and other variables from changes that might occur in a subroutine.

The concept of a memory pointer was introduced in Chapter 2. Later sections of this text deal with more sophisticated uses of memory pointers, including the use of multiple pointers within a program. A frequent error in handling multiple pointers happens when the wrong one is used.

Example 3-8 is meant to loop from 00 to 08 hex. The program is loaded into the machine and the "go" button is pressed. The halt light never comes on. After waiting a bit, the operator presses the reset button, then checks the codes stored in the computer. The codes turn out to be correct. Since this is a short looping program, two debug methods suggest themselves: single stepping through the program or inserting breakpoints. Single stepping gathers more information, so this method should be chosen when convenient.

After pushing the step button once, the A register is examined. It is cleared to 00 hex. This instruction worked. Another press of the step button executes the INR instruction. A is again examined. It contains a 01. So far, so good. The CPI instruction performs an invisible subtraction, which should not affect the contents of A. The step button is pressed a third time. A is examined. It still contains 01, which is good. What about the flags? The flag that matters in this application is the zero flag.

The flag register is brought to the displays. The zero flag is cleared. This is correct. If a zero had occurred, this flag would have been set. The step button is pressed and the JNZ instruction is performed. The step button is pressed again and again. The A register is repeating 00 01 00 01 00, which indicates that something is clearing A. The only instruction in the program that can do this is the initialization instruction at 03 00. This leads to an examination of the jump address. Sure enough, it branches back to the top of the program. Changing the byte at line 06 from 00 to 02 corrects the problem.

The next program, Example 3-9, has a longer loop. After correcting the previous

EXAMPLE 3-8

HEX ADDRESS	HEX OP CODE	MNEMONIC	COMMENTS	OCTAL ADDRESS	OCTAL OP CODE
03 00	3E	MVI A	Initialize loop counter		076
01		00			
02	3C	INR A	Add 1 to the loop counter		074
03	FE	CPI			376
04		08	Are we at 8?		
05	C2	JNZ	If not, continue		302
06		00			
07		03			
08	76	HLT			166

EXAMPLE 3-9

HEX ADDRESS	HEX OP CODE	MNEMONIC	COMMENTS	OCTAL ADDRESS	OCTAL OP CODE
03 00	06	MVI B		003 000	006
01		15		001	
02	05	DCR B		002	005
03	D2	JNC		003	322
04		02		004	
05		03		005	
06	76	HLT		006	166

problem with the step button we are suffering from finger fatigue. This time we choose to use breakpoints to solve the problem, which seems to be erratic. Sometimes when the program halts, 14 is in the B register. Other times the value in the B register is well outside the loop parameters of 15 to 00. The 14 result seems to indicate that the DCR B instruction is being performed. A breakpoint is inserted in the program at 03 03. The program is run and the breakpoint is reached. B is inspected. Yes, it is 14 hex. We are not yet to zero. The flags are brought out for inspection. The carry flag, which is the flag tested by the conditional branch, is set. Wait a minute—15-01 should not have needed to borrow. Why is the carry flag set? Ah, the DCR instruction does not alter the condition of the carry flag. The random results must have happened when the carry flag was cleared when we pressed "go." If so, then the program would never halt. The contents of B would depend on when we pressed reset. The conditional branch is changed to JNZ and the program works.

Example 3-10 is another loop which is meant to loop from 06 to FF, which is -1 in two's-complement arithmetic. This time, the CPI instruction used will alter the contents of the carry flag, yet we seem to get much the same results as we did in the last example. A breakpoint is set at 03 05. Each time through the loop, the breakpoint temporarily stops execution. The C register is examined. It is being decremented. The flags are brought out for inspection. The carry flag is always the same. This does not make sense. The op code information regarding CPI says that the carry flag is affected. It also says that one of the operands must be the accumulator. Our program does not change the A register. The MVI C and DCR C instructions are changed to MVI A and DCR A.

EXAMPLE 3-10

HEX ADDRESS	HEX OP CODE	MNEMONIC	COMMENTS	OCTAL ADDRESS	OCTAL OP CODE
03 00	OE	MVI C	Objective: to count from 6	003 000	016
01		06	to -1	001	
02	OD	DCR C		002	015
03	FE	CPI		003	376
04		00		004	
05	D2	JNC		005	322
06		02		006	
07		03		007	
08	76	HLT		010	166

The program is again tested. It still malfunctions. Once again, the program is run with a breakpoint at 03 05. A is now changing. Good. That corrects one problem, but the carry flag is the same each time through the loop. At this time it is decided to force the issue—the carry flag is set, then stored. This should cause the JNC instruction to be ignored, thus halting the program. The program is resumed and the program halts. Therefore the JNC instruction is working, but is receiving the wrong information.

Logically, we want to terminate the program when the computer performs the subtraction $(-1) - (0)$. Since zero is to the right of -1 on the number line, this should cause a borrow and trip the carry flag. Unfortunately, when we interpret FF as -1, the computer simply sees FF. The computer is actually performing this binary subtraction:

$$1111\ 1111$$

$$0000\ 0000$$

This will not generate a borrow. In fact, using 00 hex in a compare will never cause a borrow. What we have here is an implementation error.

Examining the final result desired, we see that D7 is set when we wish to terminate the program. D7 happens to be the sign flag. The CPI and the immediate byte are converted to NOPs. The JNC is changed to JP. The program is run with the previous changes—remember, we are now using A—and the final result is correct.

Example 3-11 is an event counter. This program will count the number of times loops are performed. The program is set to loop until it receives a termination code of 50 from input port 02. When this code is received, the program will terminate. B should contain the number of passes. Every time the program is used, the B register contains 00 hex when the halt light comes on. A breakpoint is placed at 03 07. Register B is incremented. The input port is set to 50. This should force the program to halt at the next pass. The program is resumed. The breakpoint is reached with B now containing 02. The A register has received the 50 from the input port. The program is resumed but the halt light did not come on. Another pass is performed. This time the flags are inspected. The A register still has 50, but the zero flag is cleared. The CPI 50 should have set the zero flag. The breakpoint is then set to 03 06. When it is reached, the zero flag is inspected. With a 50 in the A register, the zero flag is set. This is the correct condition. Since the flag is correct after the CPI and not correct at the JNZ, the intervening instruction must be causing a problem.

The INR B affects the flags and alters the conditions set by the CPI. This program demonstrates a very common error made by beginning programmers. *Do not place* intervening instructions between the setup and the conditional branch. The CPI and the INR B instructions are reordered, with the INR B placed at 03 04. The CPI follows at 03 05. The program is run and responds correctly to 50 from port 02.

One last point about this example. The B register was incrementing, yet the value in B was always zero when the program halted. This happened because after 256 passes B rolled over and was again zero. When this happened, the JNZ instruction was ignored and the program halted.

EXAMPLE 3-11

Hex Address	Hex Op Code	Mnemonic	Comments	Octal Address	Octal Op Code
03 00	06	MVI B		003 000	006
01		00		001	
02	DB	IN		002	333
03		02		003	
04	FE	CPI		004	376
05		50		005	
06	04	INR B		006	004
07	C2	JNZ		007	302
08		02		010	
09		03		011	
0A	76	HLT		012	166

The last example, Example 3-12, involves the use of a subroutine. The main program is set to count from 15 to 24 hex and then terminate. Each time through the loop, the program will display the loop counter. A time delay will be used to slow the computer. In this example, the delay will not slow the program enough for us to see the display changing. To set the delay to a precise value involves techniques explained in Chapter 4. In any case, it is not pertinent to the discussion at hand.

When this program is run, the halt light never comes on. The information at port 04 does change to 15 but never alters after that. Since this example uses a subroutine, a breakpoint is inserted at the first instruction of the subroutine. The program is run again. The breakpoint is reached, therefore the CALL worked. The stack pointer is examined so the return address can be located and checked. The stack pointer has a strange address that points to a location in the memory map where no memory chip exists. The stack pointer has never been initialized. An LXI SP instruction is added and the program is tested again. Once more, the breakpoint is reached. This time the stack contains an address that is just 2 less than the address set by the LXI SP instruction. Things are looking good. The return address is located. It is correct. The program execution is

EXAMPLE 3-12

HEX ADDRESS	HEX OP CODE	MNEMONIC	COMMENTS	OCTAL ADDRESS	OCTAL OP CODE
03 00	3E	MVI A		003 000	076
01		15		001	
02	D3	OUT		002	323
03		04		003	
04	3C	INR A		004	074
05	CD	CALL	Time delay	005	315
06		00		006	
07		04		007	
08	FE	CPI		010	376
09		24		011	
0A	C2	JNZ		012	302
0B		02		013	
0C		03		014	
0D	76	HLT		015	166
04 00	3E	MVI A		004 000	076
01		10		001	
02	3D	DCR A		002	075
03	C2	JNZ		003	302
04		02		004	
05		04		005	
06	C9	RET		006	311

resumed but the halt light never comes on. This indicates a problem with the decision point that handles whether to continue looping or to quit. The breakpoint is set to 03 0A. The tests begin again. The first pass through the loop reaches the breakpoint with the A register containing 00 hex. The port, however, is showing 15. Something somehow changed A. Looking through the program, we find instructions in the subroutine that alter the contents of A. In fact, the only way in which this subroutine can be exited is when the A register is at zero. This explains what we found in A at the breakpoint.

There are two possible solutions. The first is not to use A in the subroutine. Due to the shortness of the program, this is a viable alternative. In a longer program, though, it is possible that any register chosen would interfere with some function of the main program. A solution that would work in either situation is to save the register or registers on the stack. A PUSH PSW is added to the subroutine at its start and a POP PSW is placed just before the return. The program, when run with these changes, works properly.

3-7 CLOSING THOUGHTS

This chapter has dealt mainly with the development of software. Many concepts not usually presented to the prospective electronics technician but taught to the computer science student have been explained. It is the feeling of the author that an electronic technician working on computer circuitry cannot be fully effective unless he or she has an understanding of the hardware and software.

The order-filling example in this chapter did not investigate the relationships between hardware and software. The chapter on digital interfacing will take a close look at how circuitry is interfaced to the computer. After you have an understanding of how a computer is connected to external circuitry, this relationship can then be examined in further project examples.

SUMMARY

1. Flowcharts are used to organize and document the logic that will be used to solve software problems.
2. Careful and complete documentation can lead to quick solutions to problems. When something does go wrong in a project, the documentation can be an important tool in analyzing and correcting the problem.
3. Program logic can be implemented using logical constructs. The use of logical constructs helps to standardize code, making it easier for many programmers to understand the software techniques used to solve a problem.

4. Modular programming is a technique of subdividing large complicated tasks into smaller, more easily understood and managed tasks.

5. The stack is a special architectural feature found in many microprocessors. It makes it possible for a programmer to implement subroutine usage. This in turn makes it possible to use modular design.

6. The ability to find and correct software problems is as important as the ability to develop software. Common techniques used to find software problems include: breakpoints, forcing, performing a trace, and single stepping through a routine.

QUESTIONS

1. List two functions performed by a flowchart.
2. List the sections of a project layout sheet.
3. What is a special code? Where might it be used?
4. List the procedure for building an I/O loop.
5. How many ideas should be associated with a flowchart symbol?
6. List three logical constructs.
7. How many pathways can there be to a logical construct? How many exits?
8. What is the difference between an IF-THEN and an IF-THEN-ELSE?
9. What is the maximum number of HALTS in a structured program?
10. List at least three advantages of modular programming.
11. How many tasks may be performed by a subroutine in a structured program?
12. List at least three places where it would be appropriate to place breakpoints in a program that was being debugged.
13. What is a dummy subroutine?
14. How many bytes does a POP instruction remove from the stack?
15. A program contains the following instruction:

CALL

00

08

Which section of the CPU receives the address bytes of the CALL when the instruction is performed?

16. What is the access method used by the stack?
17. Explain what is meant by a *binary search*.
18. List at least three common software mistakes.

19. A program performs the following section of code:

IN

07

JZ

02

03

This section of code checks the status of an input port. If the port senses a zero, the JZ instruction directs control to page 03 location 02. When the code is tested, it does not work correctly. Why?

20. The following short looping program is loaded into a microcomputer. When it is run, it does not work correctly. Why?

03 00	MVI C
03 01	00
03 02	INR C
03 03	CPI
03 04	09
03 05	JNZ
03 06	02
03 07	03
03 08	HLT

LAB ASSIGNMENT

This assignment will test the student's ability to divide large projects into smaller, more manageable sections.

1. Program the microcomputer so it operates as a real time clock. No external hardware should be needed if the trainer has LEDs or displays. At this time, timing loops have not been discussed. One-second timing loops based on master clock frequencies of 750 kHz, 1 MHz, and 2 MHz are available in the appendices.

   Possible subroutines that can be developed with this project are:

   (a) a display routine
   (b) an AM/PM subroutine
   (c) a subroutine to handle an alarm

(d) a subroutine that might handle a snooze feature

(e) if the trainer has seven-segment displays, a subroutine to display messages

(f) a BCD-to-decimal display code conversion subroutine

(g) a time set subroutine that allows the time to be entered from the computer's keyboard

It is not necessary to code every possible suggestion. A clock works perfectly well without an alarm. Perhaps you will have other ideas. With proper modular design, it is possible to have a working clock, with the exception of the alarm. If the alarm subroutine is not complete by the time the project is due, stub it out by replacing it with a one-line subroutine—the return.

LAB QUESTIONS

1. Explain why it is necessary to adjust the one-second delays found in the appendices as you add more features to the clock project.

2. The AM/PM decision in the clock project can be implemented by an IF-THEN. Draw the flowchart for the IF-THEN that would handle this situation. Treat the AM/PM feature as if it were a toggle flip-flop. That is, each time HRS = 12, toggle between two different codes used to represent AM and PM.

3. Code the logic from the flowchart drawn in 2.

4. If the computer could track the clock time in BCD, explain how this would make the clock project easier. (Later we will investigate BCD operation within the microprocessor.)

5. If you elect not to implement a keyboard entry feature in your clock, explain how you can use the monitor program of your computer to alter the clock program so different starting times can be set.

6. Explain the changes that would be needed in the logic of your clock program to make it function as a stopwatch.

4

TIMING

At the end of this chapter you should be familiar with:

1. master clock requirements for the 8080, 8085, and Z80
2. the power-up timing requirements of the 8080, 8085, and Z80
3. the differences between cold and warm resets
4. clock state definitions
5. machine cycle functions
6. machine cycle timing
7. instruction cycle timing
8. the construction of software delay loops
9. the operation of an 8253 programmable interval timer

INTRODUCTION

The central processing units we are studying perform operations based upon a precisely controlled clock signal. The clock signal is a free-running oscillator that provides square waves compatible with the computer circuitry. The timing source for these waveforms originates from a crystal oscillator. The interval between pulses is considered to be a *clock period.*

We will investigate the timing needed to operate a computer starting from the basic clock period, progress to CPU timing, defining states, machine cycles, and instruction cycles; then we will present the first detailed analysis of a machine cycle in this chapter.

This knowledge will be used in the formulation of software timing loops. The program logic and timing calculations necessary to write the delays in the timing loops will be explained.

Finally, we will compare software timing, its advantages and disadvantages, with hardware timing. The first programmable support chip, the 8253, a programmable interval timer, will be introduced. Appropriate sections of the 8253's documentation will be included and analyzed. The chapter will conclude with a project centered around the 8253 demonstrating how it can be used in timing applications.

4-1 MASTER CLOCKS

8080 Master Clock

The 8080 requires a two-phase nonoverlapping clock. All operations are based on this timing. Figure 4-1 shows the timing relationships between the two clock signals. A *clock state* is considered to be the smallest unit of processor activity. The interval between two positive-going transitions of the phase-one clock mark the time of a clock state. These clock signals must be provided by external circuitry. In 8080 systems this is usually the 8224.

The 8224 is designed to produce the clock signals needed by the 8080. The 8224 pin-out and internal block diagram are shown in Figure 4-2. The frequency of oscilla-

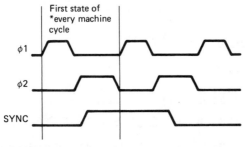

*SYNC does not occur in the second and third machine cycles of a DAD instruction, since these machine cycles are used for an internal register-pair add.

FIGURE 4-1 ϕ_1, ϕ_2, and sync timing. (Courtesy of Intel Corporation.)

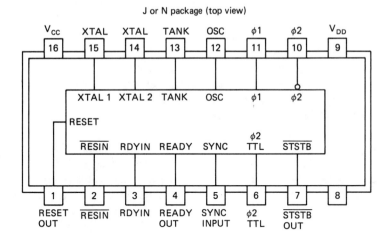

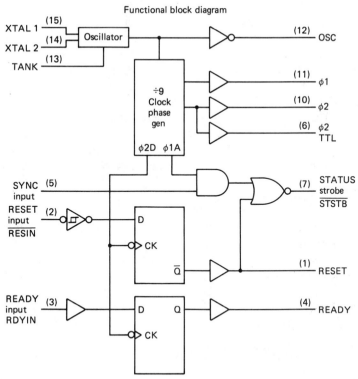

FIGURE 4-2 8224 clock driver. (Courtesy of Texas Instruments Incorporated.)

tions is determined by a series-resonant fundamental mode crystal connected between pins 14 and 15. The $\phi1$ and $\phi2$ outputs are designed for direct interfacing to the 8080. These signals are not TTL compatible. The 8224 does provide a $\phi2$ TTL compatible output at pin 6.

Referring once more to Figure 4-1, you should observe a waveform labeled SYNC. This waveform is generated by the 8080 at the rising edge of the phase-two clock. This sync pulse marks the start of every machine cycle.

A *machine cycle* consists of three, four, or five clock states. The 8080 will perform a machine cycle every time it accesses an I/O port or a memory location. This means that every time data is transferred over the I/O bus, a machine cycle is controlling that data transfer.

Now back to Figure 4-2. The SYNC pin on the 8224 can be connected to the SYNC waveform generated by the 8080. This pulse will then help to create another signal at the output of the 8224. This signal is the *status strobe,* a logical combination of the $\phi1$ signal and SYNC. It marks the time when the status bits are placed on the data bus (at the start of every machine cycle). These bits identify the machine cycle about to take place.

8080 Master Clock Limitations

The version of the 8080 that is most often encountered is the 8080A. This processor has a minimum clock period of .48 μs. This computes to a maximum frequency just over 2 MHz. The maximum clock period is listed as 2.0 μs. This means the clock frequency must be at least 500 KHz. The 8080A-1 can have a minimum clock period of .32 μs. The clock frequency for this IC can be as high as 3.12 MHz. It also must be clocked no slower than 500 KHz.

The frequency chosen within the acceptable ranges is a function of the support chips. The most important consideration is the speed of the memory chips. If the memory chips cannot keep up—that is, deliver information fast enough for the processor—the processor must wait. This would negate the reason for choosing a fast clock frequency.

8085 Master Clock

As indicated earlier, the 8085 has an in-chip clock generator. All this internal generator needs is a parallel resonant crystal connected between X1 and X2. See the 8085 pin-out diagram in the appendices. This clock will generate a two-phase nonoverlapping clock. These clock signals, $\phi1$ and $\phi2$, are used by the 8085 for internal timing. They are not available on the outside of the chip. The 8085 does provide a clock signal for external circuitry. This clock signal is present at the CLK pin of the 8085. It is an inverted version of $\phi1$. It is also one half the frequency of the crystal input.

Alternate 8085 Clock Sources

An RC network can be placed across the crystal inputs X1 and X2. The external capacitor in Figure 4-3 combines with the internal capacitance, which is approximately 15

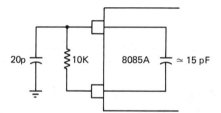

FIGURE 4-3 8085 RC clock source.

pF. The total capacitance is then multiplied by the external timing resistance value to obtain an RC time constant. The RC circuit of Figure 4-3 has an RC time constant equal to 350 ns. Inverted, this yields a frequency of 2.8 MHz.

This clock circuit is not recommended. First, the internal capacitance varies from chip to chip. Secondly, as capacitors and resistors age, their values tend to change. If the processor will be used in critical timing applications, this can present a problem.

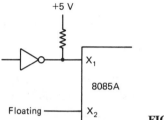

FIGURE 4-4 8085 TTL clock source.

The 8085A will accept a TTL clock input at X1. (See Fig. 4-4.) This circuit can be used in an attempt to synchronize 8085A operations with TTL circuitry not under control of the CPU. This can be very difficult, however, for as program length varies, the synchronization may be lost despite the TTL clock input.

Whichever clock arrangement is used, the 8085 also operates with machine cycles based upon the clock state. As in the 8080, whenever a data transfer is in progress, a machine cycle is controlling the transfer.

Unlike the 8080, the status bits are not time-multiplexed onto the data bus. The 8085 has three output pins, which indicate the machine cycle in progress. This will be discussed in more detail when we start analyzing machine cycles.

8085A Clock Limitations

The 8085A data sheets in the appendices list three versions of the 8085A. The crystal input must be at least 1 MHz for all three versions. Additionally, the crystal frequency must be twice the desired internal clock frequency. Therefore, if an internal clock frequency of 1 MHz is desired, the crystal frequency must be 2 MHz. The fastest of the three versions listed can accept a maximum crystal frequency of 12 MHz. This means internal operations will occur at 6 MHz.

Z80 Master Clock

The Z80 will accept a standard TTL-compatible clock signal. A clock generating circuit is shown in Figure 4-5. The output is TTL compatible, while the frequency is precisely controlled by the crystal.

Like the 8080 and the 8085, the Z80 builds machine cycles based on the frequency of the clock. Three or more clock states will be used to build machine cycles which, as before, are used to control the flow of information on the data bus.

The control signals are monitored if it becomes necessary to determine which machine cycle is in progress. Special status bits are not part of the Z80 architecture.

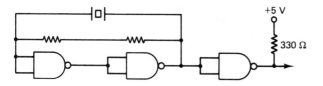

FIGURE 4-5   Z80 crystal clock source.

Z80 Clock Limitations

The frequency goes down to DC. Although the CPU may work at low speeds, certain devices such as dynamic RAM may force the CPU to operate at a certain minimum frequency. Dynamic RAM is discussed in Chapter 8. The upper frequency depends on which version of the Z80 is being used. The Z80H will clock at a frequency of 8 MHz. Slower versions of the computer chip are available.

4-2 POWER-UP TIMING

8080

The 8080 will begin to operate as soon as power is applied. The registers will power up randomly, therefore a power-up reset should occur. An external reset of three clock durations will clear the program counter. Program execution consequently begins at location 00 00 hex. The other registers are not affected by the reset. They will remain random until program instructions dictate their contents.

8085

Due to internal electrical characteristics, the 8085 is not guaranteed to operate until 10 ms after the power supply voltage reaches 4.75 V. The *reset in* control line should be kept low during this period. This control line is latched every time the clock pulse goes

TABLE 4-1   8085 Reset In Functions

RESETS	SETS
Program counter	RST 5.5 mask
Instruction register	RST 6.5 mask
INTE FF	RST 7.5 mask
TRAP FF	
SOD FF	
Machine state FF	
Machine cycle FF	
HOLD FF	
INTR FF	
READY FF	

high. When the 8085 detects the reset in line high, the CPU will enter the first clock state of the next instruction cycle. The functions performed by bringing the reset in line low are shown in Table 4-1. As with the 8080, this CPU will vector to 00 00 hex to begin program execution.

Z80

The Z80 CPU requires a minimum of three clock cycles for the reset function. After this period, the Z80 will begin to fetch instructions from 00 00 hex. It might seem from this discussion that all processors start at 00 00 hex, but such is not the case. The 6502 and the 6800 processors do not begin at 00 00 hex when reset. The 00 00 hex address is merely a convenient starting location for startup programs chosen by the designers of the CPUs we are studying.

The other Z80 functions affected by reset and power-up timing are listed in Table 4-2. These functions are explained elsewhere in the text. For now, realize that two special function registers I and R are cleared, and that the Z80 powers up or resets so that it handles interrupts like the 8080 and 8085 until instructed to operate otherwise.

TABLE 4-2   Z80 Reset Functions

Program counter	cleared to 00 00 hex
Interrupt register	cleared to 00 hex
Refresh register	cleared to 00 hex
Interrupt FF	disabled
Interrupt mode	defaults to mode 0

4-3 COLD/WARM RESETS

The above discussion used the word *reset* interchangeably with *power-up reset*. At this time, it is appropriate to make a distinction between cold resets and warm resets. A simple RC circuit such as the one depicted in Figure 4-6(a) can be used to achieve the delays necessary when the computer is first turned on. The RC time constant is set so the capacitor does not charge to a logic 1 prior to the time required by the CPU for turn on. This arrangement provides the automatic resetting of the computer when power is first applied. Turning power off, then back on again to reset the computer is called a *cold reset*. With all three processors, the general-purpose registers are randomized when this form of a reset is used.

A *warm reset* happens when the microprocessor is reset without turning power off. The RC circuit shown in Figure 4-6(b) shows a normally open push button across the capacitor. When the push button is closed it provides a direct short across the capacitor. This lowers the logic level to zero, resetting the CPU. When the push button is released, the capacitor begins to charge. When the capacitor reaches logic 1, the CPU is free to begin operations. The general-purpose registers retain the information that was stored prior to the warm reset. Of course, if a new program or application is to begin, new values must be inserted into these registers.

Finally, the special reset functions listed in the tables for all three processors, such as clearing the program counter to 00 00 hex, occur anytime the CPU is reset either by a cold reset or a warm reset.

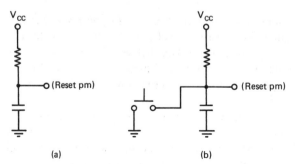

(a)   (b)   **FIGURE 4-6** Reset circuitry.

4-4 STATE DEFINITIONS

8080 State Definitions

The importance of the clock signal to the CPU should be clear. It limits how fast and how slow the computer chip can operate. The clock signal also determines the basic unit of processor activity, the clock state. During each clock state the CPU will be performing some task. Even if that task is to do nothing, the amount of time the CPU does nothing will be controlled precisely by the clock. The importance of the clock state and its use in building machine cycles and eventually the instruction cycle warrants a separate discussion on state activity.

Table 4-3 is a state definition table of the various clock states usable by the 8080. A clock state is denoted by T. A subscript further identifies which clock state is being discussed.

TABLE 4-3   8080 State Definitions

T_1	valid addresses placed on bus
	status bits placed on data bus
T_2	sample ready and hold inputs
T_w	optional wait states
T_3	data transfers take place
T_4	internal operations
T_5	internal operations

The first clock state listed in the table is T_1. During this time, addresses are placed onto the address bus. If a port number is being used, this port number will appear on the address bus in lieu of an address for a memory operation. Notice also that during this time the status bits will appear on the data bus.

T_2 is the time at which the CPU samples the ready and the hold inputs. The ready input is associated with memory operations. Slow memory devices can, in effect, place the CPU in an idle condition. The CPU will then idle or wait until memory is ready to deliver the information requested. The hold request is generally created by some type of direct memory access request. After the CPU acknowledges the hold request, until the requesting device finishes its task, the CPU's address and data bus will be in the tristate condition. This will be explained in greater detail when direct memory access controllers are explained in Chapter 8. The halt state can be entered if at this time the halt signal is asserted. This means the processor will only acknowledge halt requests during T_2.

T_w is an optional wait state. It will be entered if the CPU has been instructed to halt or if information from a slow memory device is not ready to be transmitted to the CPU.

T_3 is the time used by the computer system to transfer information into or out of the CPU. Op codes, data bytes, inputs from I/O ports, or interrupt instruction can enter the CPU at this time. Memory write operations and outputs to I/O ports can take place during T_3.

T_4 and T_5 are used by the processor for internal operations. These clock states may not occur, depending on the op code fetched during T_3. If an instruction requires some internal function to be performed, then T_4 and perhaps T_5 will be needed. For example, a move instruction that transfers information from one general-purpose register to another general-purpose register will use T_4 and T_5 to perform this operation.

8085 State Definitions

The 10 clock states used by the 8085 are shown in Table 4-4. This table shows the level of control lines, status lines, and bus lines during each clock state.

TABLE 4-4   8085A Machine State Chart (Courtesy of Intel Corporation.)

Machine state	STATUS & BUSES				CONTROL		
	S1, S0	IO/$\overline{\text{M}}$	A_8–A_{15}	AD_0–AD_7	$\overline{\text{RD}}$, $\overline{\text{WR}}$	$\overline{\text{INTA}}$	ALE
T_1	X	X	X	X	1	1	1[†]
T_2	X	X	X	X	X	X	0
T_{WAIT}	X	X	X	X	X	X	0
T_3	X	X	X	X	X	X	0
T_4	1	0*	X	TS	1	1	0
T_5	1	0*	X	TS	1	1	0
T_6	1	0*	X	TS	1	1	0
T_{RESET}	X	TS	TS	TS	TS	1	0
T_{HALT}	0	TS	TS	TS	TS	1	0
T_{HOLD}	X	TS	TS	TS	TS	1	0

0 = Logic "0"   1 = Logic "1"   TS = High Impedance   X = Unspecified

[†]ALE not generated during 2nd and 3rd machine cycles of DAD instruction.

*IO/$\overline{\text{M}}$ = 1 during T_4–T_6 states of RST and INA cycles.

During T_1, the 8085 activates the address latch enable. Addressing information appears on address pins that handle the high-order address byte. The low-order address byte is placed on the data bus. An external circuit using the address latch enable signal must latch this addressing information at this time.

T_2 and T_3 are used by the bus system for the actual transfer of information. Addressing information must be held constant during these clock states.

If an op code is being fetched, the 8085 will enter T_4. This clock state is used to decode the instruction.

Clock states T_5 and T_6 are used by certain instructions to carry out operations internal to the CPU. These states are optional; they do not occur on every instruction.

There are four T states with names. The first is T wait. This is used as in the 8080 to interface to slower memory devices. The processor samples the ready line during T_2. If the ready line is low, the 8085 will not proceed to T_3 but will enter the wait state. Once ready goes high, the processor will proceed to T_3 and complete the machine cycle.

T_{reset} are clock states used by the 8085 for power-up timing, which has already been discussed.

T_{halt} causes the CPU to stop execution of instructions. The processor tristates the address and data bus lines. Internal processor activity does not stop, however. The processor samples the hold line and unmasked interrupts during the time the clock is high.

If a hold request is active, the processor will temporarily leave the halt state and enter a hold state. Once the hold states have been completed, the 8085 will reenter the halt state. There are only two ways in which the processor can completely leave the halt state. The first way is through system reset; the second way occurs when the processor accepts an unmasked interrupt.

T_{hold} tristates the bus system. During this time, external devices can gain control of the I/O bus. Hold states are used most often for direct memory access operations. See Chapter 8 for more information on DMA operations.

Z80 State Definitions

T_1 and T_2 are used by the Z80 to place an address onto the address bus. Refer to Table 4-5. During this time the address must remain stable.

TABLE 4-5   Z80 State Table

T_1	output address
T_2	output address, sample wait
T_3	data transfers, dynamic refresh
T_4	dynamic refresh, internal operations
T_5	internal operations
T_6	internal operations
T_w	wait state
T_x	bus available state

Timing diagrams indicate that T_3 is used by the Z80 to sample data that is on the data bus. The rising edge of the T_3 state is used if an instruction is being fetched from memory.

Should an instruction be fetched from memory, T_3 and T_4 are used to decode the instruction and carry out any internal operations needed by the instruction fetched. This is very similar to the other two processors already discussed. The Z80 does perform an operation during these clock states that the other processors do not perform. The Z80 will place the contents of a special-purpose register, R, onto the address bus. This addressing information can be used by dynamic RAM for refresh cycles. If the CPU is connected to static RAM, this process is ignored.

T_5 and T_6 are optional clock states that may occur if the instruction fetched requires more time to carry out internal operations. A perusal of the Z80 instruction set shows that most of the instructions involving register-pair operations require these additional clock states.

T_w is a wait state. The Z80 samples the wait line during T_2 and every subsequent wait state. The sampling is done on the falling edge of the clock. Should the wait line be active low, the CPU will enter wait states. It is important to point out that if the Z80 is supporting dynamic RAM through the use of its R register, excessive wait states interfere with the refresh cycle during T_3 and T_4. Therefore, *excessive wait states can cause information in dynamic RAM to be lost.*

T_x is a state used by the CPU when it is in a bus idle machine cycle. During this time the Z80 tristates its bus lines. This clock state is used most often when direct memory access controllers are operating the bus systems. Information on DMA controllers is found later in this text.

4-5 MACHINE CYCLES

Each of the computer chips we study in this text perform data transfers under the control of machine cycles. As we already know, the basic unit of processor activity is the clock state. Clock states are used to build the various machine cycles used by the 8080, 8085, and Z80. What we have not yet done is investigate machine cycles in detail.

The machine cycle analyzed in detail in this chapter is the op code fetch. This machine cycle is used by the processor to get an instruction stored in memory onto the data bus and then into the instruction register. The instruction register will decode the instruction and then generate other machine cycles as needed.

Prior to analyzing an op code fetch in detail, an overview of the machine cycles used by the 8080, 8085, and Z80 will be presented. Throughout the remainder of the text other machine cycles will be examined in detail where appropriate. For example, an interrupt machine cycle will be explained in the chapter on interrupts.

Overview of 8080 Machine Cycles

Table 4-6 lists the machine cycles used by the 8080. We will go through each of these, giving a brief definition.

TABLE 4-6   8080 Machine Cycles

Instruction fetch	Memory read
Memory write	Stack read
Stack write	Input read
Output write	Interrupt acknowledge
Halt acknowledge	Interrupt acknowledge while halted

The *instruction fetch* is used by the 8080 to retrieve op codes from memory. The data-byte input during this machine cycle will be gated into the instruction register.

A *memory read* will take place when the computer needs information from memory that is not an instruction. MOV B,M, which moves a data byte from memory into the B register, will generate a memory read machine cycle.

The *memory write* machine cycle occurs when the computer transfers information from an internal register into memory. MOV M,C will use a memory write.

Stack read occurs when the 8080 takes information from the stack. POP instructions and the RETURN require the 8080 to perform a stack read.

Stack write transfers data to the stack from the CPU. The PUSH and CALL instructions cause a stack write to happen.

Information sent to the 8080 from an input port will be placed on the data bus during an *input read* machine cycle. The IN instruction is the only instruction that causes this machine cycle.

Information in the accumulator can be output using isolated I/O when the 8080 performs an *output write*. Like the input read, the output write has just one instruction, the OUT, that causes it to be generated.

Interrupt acknowledge is the 8080's response to an interrupt request. Interrupts were briefly mentioned when the overviews of the 8085 and Z80 were presented in Chapter 1. This machine cycle will be explained in detail in the chapter on interrupts.

The *halt acknowledge* machine cycle takes place when the 8080 executes a halt instruction.

The last 8080 machine cycle is the *Interrupt acknowledge while halted*. It is one of the ways available for restarting the system when the computer chip is in the halt state.

Overview of 8085 Machine Cycles

Table 4-7 lists the 8085 machine cycles for quick reference.

TABLE 4-7   8085 Machine Cycles

Op code fetch	Memory read
Memory write	I/O read
I/O write	Interrupt acknowledge
Bus idle*	

*BI: DAD, INA (RST, TRAP), HALT

The *op code fetch* begins the list of 8085 machine cycles. This is similar to the instruction fetch in the 8080.

Memory read is used to obtain information from memory other than op codes.

Memory write performs the same function in the 8085 that it did in the 8080.

I/O read is the name the 8085 uses for input read. Information is transferred into the CPU from an I/O port.

I/O write takes the place of output write. Information is transferred out of the 8085 to an I/O port during this machine cycle.

Interrupt acknowledge is still present in the 8085.

Bus idle and *halt* are grouped together in the Intel 8085 literature. The halt condition is treated as a subcondition of the bus idle machine cycle. The bus idle cycle handles special processing that takes place during a DAD instruction, is active when internal interrupt vectors are generated (more about this in the chapter on interrupts) and, as already mentioned, during a halt condition.

Notice that the stack machine cycles found in the 8080 set of machine cycles are missing from the 8085 set. The 8085 will handle operations to and from the stack with the memory read and memory write machine cycles. This means that the 8085 does not generate any special stack control signals. This presents no problem because the stack is located in memory anyway.

Overview of Z80 Machine Cycles

The list of Z80 machine cycles is found in Table 4-8. A brief rundown of these cycles follows.

TABLE 4-8   Z80 Machine Cycles

Instruction fetch	Memory read
Memory write	Input (IO RD)
Output (IO WR)	Interrupt acknowledge
Non-maskable interrupt	Bus request/acknowledge

Instruction fetch is used to retrieve op codes from memory.

Memory read is used to obtain information from memory other than op codes.

Memory write transfers information inside the Z80 to a memory device.

Input machine cycles retrieve information from input port circuitry. Unlike the 8080 and 8085, which had just one instruction that generated this machine cycle, the Z80 has an entire subset of I/O instructions.

Output machine cycles are used to transfer information inside the Z80 to output port circuitry. As mentioned above, there are many instructions in the Z80 instruction set that can use the output machine cycle.

The Z80 has an *interrupt request/acknowledge* cycle. The interrupt architecture of the Z80 is definitely more complex than that of the 8080 and is different from the 8085. This machine cycle will be explained in detail in the chapter on interrupts.

A *non-maskable interrupt* machine cycle exits in the Z80 architecture. This cycle handles interrupts that are requested through the NMI (non-maskable interrupt) pin.

Bus request/acknowledge machine cycles are used by the Z80 to handle requests from devices that wish to take control of the bus system. During this machine cycle the bus lines from the Z80 are placed in the tristate condition. The Intel processors handle this situation with hold states and hold acknowledge.

When a Z80 encounters a halt instruction, the processor starts to execute NOP instructions. This allows the Z80 to continue to support dynamic RAM refresh even while halted. The Z80 can be removed from this state by the acceptance of an interrupt or system reset (cold or warm).

Stack operations are handled by the Z80 through the use of memory read and memory write machine cycles. This is similar to the 8085 and different from the 8080.

A Detailed Look at An Instruction Fetch

The timing diagram of Figure 4-7 shows the waveforms of the Z80 instruction fetch machine cycle. The top waveform represents the master clock. Each pulse of the master clock marks a T state in the machine cycle. The diagram is divided into four T states.

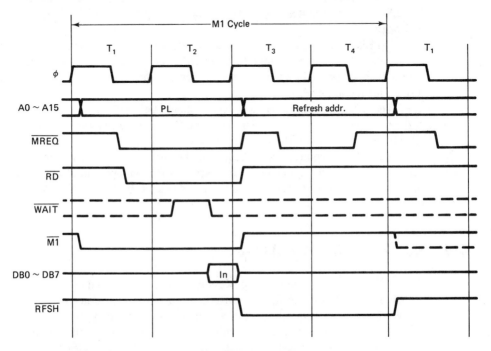

FIGURE 4-7   Z80 op code fetch. (Reproduced by permission. © 1986 Zilog, Inc. This material shall not be reproduced without the written consent of Zilog, Inc.)

The waveform just under the clock waveform represents what is happening on the 16 address lines. At the start of T_1 the contents of the program counter are placed onto the address bus. This addressing information is used to select the location in memory that holds the op code to be fetched. The address bus information is held constant during T_2 and is released just at the start of T_3. At T_3 the address bus is turned over to the R register so that it can place information on the bus for dynamic refresh. The refresh address is held constant during T_3 and T_4.

The next waveform in the timing diagram represents the memory request control line. Notice that this line pulses twice during the op code fetch. The MEMRQ* control line is activated (goes low) one-half clock cycle into T_1. The delay in asserting the MEMRQ* line allows the address bus setup time to stabilize. The RD* control line is asserted just once during this machine cycle. When both the MEMRQ* and the RD* are low, data from memory should be placed onto the bus. If the MEMRQ* line is low by itself, memory will not place any information on the bus; but if dynamic in nature, it can perform refresh operations. Static memory would ignore the MEMRQ* pulse during T_3 and T_4.

If a WAIT* pulse is sent to the CPU, it will be sampled at the falling edge of T_2. If the WAIT* line is not asserted, the processor will proceed to T_3; otherwise wait states will begin.

M1* is a control signal that marks the instruction fetch machine cycle. It will only be low if the computer is attempting to find an op code. Since each instruction cycle begins with an op code fetch, M1* indicates the start of instruction cycles. We will discuss instruction cycles shortly.

The data, hopefully a valid op code, should be present and valid on the data bus at the rising edge of T_3. At the same time the CPU is sampling the data bus, the control signals MEMRQ* and RD* are being deactivated.

The RFSH* control line indicates the beginning of the dynamic refresh process. The Z80 uses T_3 and T_4 to decode and carry out internal operations associated with the instruction that has just been fetched. Please note that this control line does not exist in the 8080 and the 8085.

4-6 INSTRUCTION CYCLES

An *instruction cycle* is the time a processor requires to fetch and execute an instruction. As we already know, the first machine cycle of any instruction cycle is the op code fetch. The code fetched will determine which processor activity will follow. The 8080 and 8085 use from one to five machine cycles, depending on the complexity of the instruction to be performed. The types of possible machine cycles have already been discussed. The Z80 has some instructions that take six machine cycles to complete, although most of its instructions are performed in one to five machine cycles.

The chart found in Table 4-9 is an excellent breakdown of the instruction cycles possible in an 8080 system. Although it lacks specific timing information, such as which edge of a signal to use, the information presented allows the user to determine what processor activity is occurring during each T state of an instruction cycle.

Consider the very first entry, a MOV r1, r2. This instruction is one machine cycle long. It is completed in five clock states. The contents of r2 will be copied into r1 where r1 and r2 are any general-purpose register. At T_1 the contents of the program counter are placed onto the address bus. The status bits, indicating which machine cycle is underway, are placed on the data bus. During T_2 the contents of the program counter are incremented to the next memory location as indicated by PC = PC + 1. While this internal operation is underway, the 8080 is sampling the READY line. Should it be asserted, the CPU will enter wait states beginning at the next clock. If not, execution proceeds to T_3. T_3 is used to move the instruction fetched into the temporary register and into the instruction register.

T_4 is used to carry out part of the instruction. The contents of the source register, in this case r2, are copied into the temporary register. SSS indicates the source register. Parentheses around the SSS—that is, (SSS)—indicate the contents of the operand. T_5 is used to complete the process. The contents of the temporary register are moved into the destination register, indicated by (TMP) $\rightarrow$ (DDD). The arrow indicates data flow.

Notice that the chart of Table 4-9 (column M1) does not indicate what is happening on the external address bus and data bus during T_4 and T_5. For this information a waveform diagram such as 4-7 would have to be consulted.

One last point about this example. You might wonder why the contents of the source register were not moved directly into the destination register. If you refer to the 8080 block diagram in Chapter 1, you will see there is no direct connection between any of the general-purpose registers. Information is moved from point to point internally over a data bus that is buffered from the external data bus. Like the external bus, only one operand can use this bus at a time. The register-select circuitry selects which of the registers in the register array will have access to the internal data bus. Information flows out of the array from the selected register, is stored temporarily, then the register-select circuitry is changed to select the destination register. When the destination register has access to the internal data bus, the information from the temporary register flows back into the register array, where it is gated into the selected register.

All of this is, of course, handled by internal electronics inside the CPU. If the internal electronics were to fail, the chip would have to be replaced. Consequently, many texts gloss over internal operations. It is hoped that a study of this facet of the computer will lead to a better understanding of the computer circuitry, provide the opportunity to practice reading computer documentation (an important skill), plus give you a source of information about instruction operations. Sometimes the charts found in Table 4-9 clear up a point that might not be understood when reading the description of an instruction in English.

The CPI instruction explained in Chapter 2 is located 10 lines down on Table 4-9 (c). The instruction cycle for this instruction is three machine cycles long. The first machine cycle is the op code fetch. T_1 through T_3 are duplicates of what happened in the MOV instruction just examined. T_4 is used to copy the contents of the accumulator into the accumulator latch. This is indicated by (A) $\rightarrow$ ACT. T_5 is not used.

The second machine cycle of this instruction is a memory read machine cycle. Footnote 6, Table 4-9(e), indicates this. T_1 of M2 places the address of the immediate byte onto the address bus. The status bits are dumped to the data bus, indicating that a memory read is about to take place. T_2 increments the program counter. This is done internally and does not affect the address on the external address bus, which is already latched into the address buffer of the CPU during T_1. At the edge of T_2 and T_3 the immediate byte is brought into the CPU and stored in the temporary register, B2 $\rightarrow$ TMP.

TABLE 4-9(a)   8080 Instruction Cycle Table (Courtesy of Intel Corporation.)

MNEMONIC	OP CODE		M1[1]					M2		
	$D_7 D_6 D_5 D_4$	$D_3 D_2 D_1 D_0$	T1	T2[2]	T3	T4	T5	T1	T2[2]	T3
MOV r1,r2	0 1 D D	D S S S	PC OUT STATUS	PC = PC +1	INST→TMP/IR	(SSS)→TMP	(TMP)→DDD			
MOV r, M	0 1 D D	D 1 1 0				X[3]		HL OUT STATUS[6]		DATA→DDD
MOV M, r	0 1 1 1	0 S S S				(SSS)→TMP		HL OUT STATUS[7]		(TMP)→DATA BUS
SPHL	1 1 1 1	1 0 0 1				(HL) ———→SP				
MVI r, data	0 0 D D	D 1 1 0				X		PC OUT STATUS[6]		B2→DDDD
MVI M, data	0 0 1 1	0 1 1 0				X				B2→TMP
LXI rp, data	0 0 R P	0 0 0 1				X		PC = PC + 1		B2→r1
LDA addr	0 0 1 1	1 0 1 0				X		PC = PC + 1		B2→Z
STA addr	0 0 1 1	0 0 1 0				X		PC = PC + 1		B2→Z
LHLD addr	0 0 1 0	1 0 1 0				X		PC = PC + 1		B2→Z
SHLD addr	0 0 1 0	0 0 1 0				X		PC OUT STATUS[6]	PC = PC + 1	B2→Z
LDAX rp[4]	0 0 R P	1 0 1 0				X		rp OUT STATUS[6]		DATA→A
STAX rp[4]	0 0 R P	0 0 1 0				X		rp OUT STATUS[7]		(A)→DATA BUS
XCHG	1 1 1 0	1 0 1 1				(HL)←→(DE)				
ADD r	1 0 0 0	0 S S S				(SSS)→TMP (A)→ACT		[9]	(ACT)+(TMP)→A	
ADD M	1 0 0 0	0 1 1 0				(A)→ACT		HL OUT STATUS[6]		DATA→TMP
ADI data	1 1 0 0	0 1 1 0				(A)→ACT		PC OUT STATUS[6]	PC = PC + 1	B2→TMP
ADC r	1 0 0 0	1 S S S				(SSS)→TMP (A)→ACT		[9]	(ACT)+(TMP)+CY→A	
ADC M	1 0 0 0	1 1 1 0				(A)→ACT		HL OUT STATUS[6]		DATA→TMP
ACI data	1 1 0 0	1 1 1 0				(A)→ACT		PC OUT STATUS[6]	PC = PC + 1	B2→TMP
SUB r	1 0 0 1	0 S S S				(SSS)→TMP (A)→ACT		[9]	(ACT)-(TMP)→A	
SUB M	1 0 0 1	0 1 1 0				(A)→ACT		HL OUT STATUS[6]		DATA→TMP
SUI data	1 1 0 1	0 1 1 0				(A)→ACT		PC OUT STATUS[6]	PC = PC + 1	B2→TMP
SBB r	1 0 0 1	1 S S S				(SSS)→TMP (A)→ACT		[9]	(ACT)-(TMP)-CY→A	
SBB M	1 0 0 1	1 1 1 0				(A)→ACT		HL OUT STATUS[6]		DATA→TMP
SBI data	1 1 0 1	1 1 1 0				(A)→ACT		PC OUT STATUS[6]	PC = PC + 1	B2→TMP
INR r	0 0 D D	D 1 0 0				(DDD)→TMP (TMP) + 1→ALU	ALU→DDD			
INR M	0 0 1 1	0 1 0 0				X		HL OUT STATUS[6]		DATA→TMP (TMP)+1→ALU
DCR r	0 0 D D	D 1 0 1				(DDD)→TMP (TMP)+1→ALU	ALU→DDD			
DCR M	0 0 1 1	0 1 0 1				X		HL OUT STATUS[6]		DATA→TMP (TMP)-1→ALU
INX rp	0 0 R P	0 0 1 1				(RP) + 1 ———→RP				
DCX rp	0 0 R P	1 0 1 1				(RP) - 1 ———→RP				
DAD rp[8]	0 0 R P	1 0 0 1				X		(rl)→ACT	(L)→TMP, (ACT)+(TMP)→ALU	ALU→L, CY
DAA	0 0 1 0	0 1 1 1				DAA→A, FLAGS[10]				
ANA r	1 0 1 0	0 S S S				(SSS)→TMP (A)→ACT		[9]	(ACT)+(TMP)→A	
ANA M	1 0 1 0	0 1 1 0	PC OUT STATUS	PC = PC +1	INST→TMP/IR	(A)→ACT		HL OUT STATUS[6]		DATA→TMP

TABLE 4-9(b)

	M3			M4			M5				
T1	T2[2]	T3	T1	T2[2]	T3	T1	T2[2]	T3	T4	T5	
HL OUT STATUS[7]	(TMP) → DATA BUS										
PC OUT STATUS[6]	PC = PC + 1 B3 → rh										
	PC = PC + 1 B3 → W		WZ OUT STATUS[6]	DATA → A							
	PC = PC + 1 B3 → W		WZ OUT STATUS[7]	(A) → DATA BUS							
	PC = PC + 1 B3 → W		WZ OUT STATUS[6]	DATA → L WZ = WZ + 1		WZ OUT STATUS[6]	DATA → H				
PC OUT STATUS[6]	PC = PC + 1 B3 → W		WZ OUT STATUS[7]	(L) → DATA BUS WZ = WZ + 1		WZ OUT STATUS[7]	(H) → DATA BUS				
[9]	(ACT)+(TMP)→A										
[9]	(ACT)+(TMP)→A										
[9]	(ACT)+(TMP)+CY→A										
[9]	(ACT)+(TMP)+CY→A										
[9]	(ACT)-(TMP)→A										
[9]	(ACT)-(TMP)→A										
[9]	(ACT)-(TMP)-CY→A										
[9]	(ACT)-(TMP)-CY→A										
HL OUT STATUS[7]	ALU → DATA BUS										
HL OUT STATUS[7]	ALU → DATA BUS										
(rh)→ACT	(H)→TMP (ACT)+(TMP)+CY→ALU	ALU→H, CY									
[9]	(ACT)+(TMP)→A										

TABLE 4-9(c)

MNEMONIC	OP CODE		M1[1]					M2		
	$D_7 D_6 D_5 D_4$	$D_3 D_2 D_1 D_0$	T1	T2[2]	T3	T4	T5	T1	T2[2]	T3
ANI data	1 1 1 0	0 1 1 0	PC OUT STATUS	PC = PC + 1	INST→TMP/IR	(A)→ACT		PC OUT STATUS[6]	PC = PC + 1 B2	→TMP
XRA r	1 0 1 0	1 S S S				(A)→ACT (SSS)→TMP		[9]	(ACT)+(TPM)→A	
XRA M	1 0 1 0	1 1 1 0				(A)→ACT		HL OUT STATUS[6]	DATA	→TMP
XRI data	1 1 1 0	1 1 1 0				(A)→ACT		PC OUT STATUS[6]	PC = PC + 1 B2	→TMP
ORA r	1 0 1 1	0 S S S				(A)→ACT (SSS)→TMP		[9]	(ACT)+(TMP)→A	
ORA M	1 0 1 1	0 1 1 0				(A)→ACT		HL OUT STATUS[6]	DATA	→TMP
ORI data	1 1 1 1	0 1 1 0				(A)→ACT		PC OUT STATUS[6]	PC = PC + 1 B2	→TMP
CMP r	1 0 1 1	1 S S S				(A)→ACT (SSS)→TMP		[9]	(ACT)-(TMP), FLAGS	
CMP M	1 0 1 1	1 1 1 0				(A)→ACT		HL OUT STATUS[6]	DATA	→TMP
CPI data	1 1 1 1	1 1 1 0				(A)→ACT		PC OUT STATUS[6]	PC = PC + 1 B2	→TMP
RLC	0 0 0 0	0 1 1 1				(A)→ALU ROTATE		[9]	ALU→A, CY	
RRC	0 0 0 0	1 1 1 1				(A)→ALU ROTATE		[9]	ALU→A, CY	
RAL	0 0 0 1	0 1 1 1				(A), CY→ALU ROTATE		[9]	ALU→A, CY	
RAR	0 0 0 1	1 1 1 1				(A), CY→ALU ROTATE		[9]	ALU→A, CY	
CMA	0 0 1 0	1 1 1 1				(Ā)→A				
CMC	0 0 1 1	1 1 1 1				C̄Y→CY				
STC	0 0 1 1	0 1 1 1				1→CY				
JMP addr	1 1 0 0	0 0 1 1					X	PC OUT STATUS[6]	PC = PC + 1 B2	→Z
J cond addr[17]	1 1 C C	C 0 1 0				JUDGE CONDITION		PC OUT STATUS[6]	PC = PC + 1 B2	→Z
CALL addr	1 1 0 0	1 1 0 1				SP = SP - 1		PC OUT STATUS[6]	PC = PC + 1 B2	→Z
C cond addr[17]	1 1 C C	C 1 0 0				JUDGE CONDITION IF TRUE, SP = SP - 1		PC OUT STATUS[6]	PC = PC + 1 B2	→Z
RET	1 1 0 0	1 0 0 1					X	SP OUT STATUS[15]	SP = SP + 1 DATA	→Z
R cond addr[17]	1 1 C C	C 0 0 0			INST→TMP/IR	JUDGE CONDITION[14]		SP OUT STATUS[15]	SP = SP + 1 DATA	→Z
RST n	1 1 N N	N 1 1 1			φ→W INST→TMP/IR	SP = SP - 1		SP OUT STATUS[16]	SP = SP - 1 (PCH)	→DATA BUS
PCHL	1 1 1 0	1 0 0 1			INST→TMP/IR	(HL) ──────→ PC				
PUSH rp	1 1 R P	0 1 0 1				SP = SP - 1		SP OUT STATUS[16]	SP = SP - 1 (rh)	→DATA BUS
PUSH PSW	1 1 1 1	0 1 0 1				SP = SP - 1		SP OUT STATUS[16]	SP = SP - 1 (A)	→DATA BUS
POP rp	1 1 R P	0 0 0 1					X	SP OUT STATUS[15]	SP = SP + 1 DATA	→r1
POP PSW	1 1 1 1	0 0 0 1					X	SP OUT STATUS[15]	SP = SP + 1 DATA	→FLAGS
XTHL	1 1 1 0	0 0 1 1					X	SP OUT STATUS[15]	SP = SP + 1 DATA	→Z
IN port	1 1 0 1	1 0 1 1					X	PC OUT STATUS[6]	PC = PC + 1 B2	→Z, W
OUT port	1 1 0 1	0 0 1 1					X	PC OUT STATUS[6]	PC = PC + 1 B2	→Z, W
EI	1 1 1 1	1 0 1 1				SET INTE F/F				
DI	1 1 1 1	0 0 1 1				RESET INTE F/F				
HLT	0 1 1 1	0 1 1 0					X	PC OUT STATUS	HALT MODE[20]	
NOP	0 0 0 0	0 0 0 0	PC OUT STATUS	PC = PC + 1	INST→TMP/IR		X			

118

TABLE 4-9(d)

M3			M4			M5						
T1	T2[2]	T3	T1	T2[2]	T3	T1	T2[2]	T3	T4	T5		
[9]	(ACT)+(TMP)→A											
[9]	(ACT)+(TMP)→A											
[9]	(ACT)+(TMP)→A											
[9]	(ACT)+(TMP)→A											
[9]	(ACT)+(TMP)→A											
[9]	(ACT)-(TMP); FLAGS											
[9]	(ACT)-(TMP); FLAGS											
PC OUT STATUS[6]	PC = PC + 1	B3──►W									WZ OUT STATUS[11]	(WZ) + 1 → PC
PC OUT STATUS[6]	PC = PC + 1	B3──►W									WZ OUT STATUS[11,12]	(WZ) + 1 → PC
PC OUT STATUS[6]	PC = PC + 1	B3──►W	SP OUT STATUS[16]	(PCH)──────►DATA BUS SP = SP - 1		SP OUT STATUS[16]		(PCL)──►DATA BUS			WZ OUT STATUS[11]	(WZ) + 1 → PC
PC OUT STATUS[6]	PC = PC + 1	B3──►W[13]	SP OUT STATUS[16]	(PCH)──────►DATA BUS SP = SP - 1		SP OUT STATUS[16]		(PCL)──►DATA BUS			WZ OUT STATUS[11,12]	(WZ) + 1 → PC
SP OUT STATUS[15]	SP = SP + 1	DATA──►W									WZ OUT STATUS[11]	(WZ) + 1 → PC
SP OUT STATUS[15]	SP = SP + 1	DATA──►W									WZ OUT STATUS[11,12]	(WZ) + 1 → PC
SP OUT STATUS[16]	(TMP = 00NNN000)──►Z (PCL)──►DATA BUS										WZ OUT STATUS[11]	(WZ) + 1 → PC
SP OUT STATUS[16]		(rl)──►DATA BUS										
SP OUT STATUS[16]		FLAGS──►DATA BUS										
SP OUT STATUS[15]	SP = SP + 1	DATA──►rh										
SP OUT STATUS[15]	SP = SP + 1	DATA──►A										
SP OUT STATUS[15]		DATA──►W	SP OUT STATUS[16]	(H)──────►DATA BUS		SP OUT STATUS[16]		(L)──►DATA BUS	(WZ)──►HL			
WZ OUT STATUS[18]		DATA──►A										
WZ OUT STATUS[18]		(A)──►DATA BUS										

119

TABLE 4-9(e)

NOTES:

1. The first memory cycle (M1) is always an instruction fetch; the first (or only) byte, containing the op code, is fetched during this cycle.

2. If the READY input from memory is not high during T2 of each memory cycle, the processor will enter a wait state (TW) until READY is sampled as high.

3. States T4 and T5 are present, as required, for operations which are completely internal to the CPU. The contents of the internal bus during T4 and T5 are available at the data bus; this is designed for testing purposes only. An "X" denotes that the state is present, but is only used for such internal operations as instruction decoding.

4. Only register pairs rp = B (registers B and C) or rp = D (registers D and E) may be specified.

5. These states are skipped.

6. Memory read sub-cycles; an instruction or data word will be read.

7. Memory write sub-cycle.

8. The READY signal is not required during the second and third sub-cycles (M2 and M3). The HOLD signal is accepted during M2 and M3. The SYNC signal is not generated during M2 and M3. During the execution of DAD, M2 and M3 are required for an internal register-pair add; memory is not referenced.

9. The results of these arithmetic, logical or rotate instructions are not moved into the accumulator (A) until state T2 of the next instruction cycle. That is, A is loaded while the next instruction is being fetched; this overlapping of operations allows for faster processing.

10. If the value of the least significant 4-bits of the accumulator is greater than 9 or if the auxiliary carry bit is set, 6 is added to the accumulator. If the value of the most significant 4-bits of the accumulator is now greater than 9, or if the carry bit is set, 6 is added to the most significant 4-bits of the accumulator.

11. This represents the first sub-cycle (the instruction fetch) of the next instruction cycle.

12. If the condition was met, the contents of the register pair WZ are output on the address lines (A_{0-15}) instead of the contents of the program counter (PC).

13. If the condition was not met, sub-cycles M4 and M5 are skipped; the processor instead proceeds immediately to the instruction fetch (M1) of the next instruction cycle.

14. If the condition was not met, sub-cycles M2 and M3 are skipped; the processor instead proceeds immediately to the instruction fetch (M1) of the next instruction cycle.

15. Stack read sub-cycle.

16. Stack write sub-cycle.

17. CONDITION   CCC

		CCC
NZ	— not zero (Z = 0)	000
Z	— zero (Z = 1)	001
NC	— no carry (CY = 0)	010
C	— carry (CY = 1)	011
PO	— parity odd (P = 0)	100
PE	— parity even (P = 1)	101
P	— plus (S = 0)	110
M	— minus (S = 1)	111

18. I/O sub-cycle: the I/O port's 8-bit select code is duplicated on address lines 0-7 (A_{0-7}) and 8-15 (A_{8-15}).

19. Output sub-cycle.

20. The processor will remain idle in the halt state until an interrupt, a reset or a hold is accepted. When a hold request is accepted, the CPU enters the hold mode; after the hold mode is terminated, the processor returns to the halt state. After a reset is accepted, the processor begins execution at memory location zero. After an interrupt is accepted, the processor executes the instruction forced onto the data bus (usually a restart instruction).

SSS or DDD	Value	rp	Value
A	111	B	00
B	000	D	01
C	001	H	10
D	010	SP	11
E	011		
H	100		
L	101		

The third machine cycle performs the comparison. T_2 of M3 performs the invisible subtraction (ACT) − (TMP). A copy of byte 2, the immediate byte, is subtracted from the copy of the accumulator. The results of this operation change the flags, setting condition codes that can be used by conditional jump instructions. T_3 of M3 does not occur.

Footnote 9 is interesting. A listing of the CPI instruction states that it requires seven clock states. These are, of course, the clock states used for the op code fetch and memory read. The M3 shown in the chart for CPI is an an example of what is often called an *invisible machine cycle*. M3 overlaps the op code fetch of the next instruction. The overlapping allows faster program execution, since parts of two instructions are happening simultaneously.

The information beginning with the clock states, continuing with machine cycles, and finishing with a discussion on instruction cycles has had two purposes. The first and most obvious is to develop an understanding of how a CPU chip functions. A knowledge of what is happening at all times is invaluable when repair of a computer system becomes necessary. The second purpose leads into our next topic, that of software timing.

4-7 Software Timing

Software timing involves the construction of programs that produce specific delays tailored for certain situations. Suppose we have a microcomputer operating at a master clock frequency of 1 MHz. This computer is to control a circuit that must be pulsed once every second. An OUT instruction can be used to produce pulses. This instruction, however, takes 10 clock states or a total of 10 μs to complete. A program consisting of just OUT instructions would pulse the circuit we wish to control much too often. Somehow the computer must be instructed to output a pulse just once a second, every second.

One way this can be accomplished is through the use of *software delay loops*. The information about clock states, machine cycles, and instruction cycles can be used to calculate how long a section of code will take to perform. Furthermore, it is possible to tailor a program to last a certain length of time by the proper selection of instructions included in the code to be executed.

The information presented in Table 4-10 is a condensed version of the information presented in the instruction cycle charts of Table 4-9. This new chart highlights the number of bytes used in each instruction, the number of T states used by each instruction, and which machine cycles will occur. For the purposes of calculating execution times and building software delay loops, we will concentrate on the number of clock cycles used by each instruction.

Example 4-1 is a straight-line program. This means that the program proceeds toward the halt without looping back toward the beginning of the program. The program of Example 4-1 loads two numbers into the computer; the first number is placed in the A register, the second is placed into the B register. At line 03 04 the two numbers are added together. The next instruction, at 03 05, displays the answer at an output port. The program is terminated at 03 06. The comment column indicates the number of T

Instruction		Code	Bytes	T States 8085A	T States 8080A	Machine Cycles
ACI	DATA	CE data	2	7	7	F R
ADC	REG	1000 1SSS	1	4	4	F
ADC	M	8E	1	7	7	F R
ADD	REG	1000 0SSS	1	4	4	F
ADD	M	86	1	7	7	F R
ADI	DATA	C6 data	2	7	7	F R
ANA	REG	1010 0SSS	1	4	4	F
ANA	M	A6	1	7	7	F R
ANI	DATA	E6 data	2	7	7	F R
CALL	LABEL	CD addr	3	18	17	S R R W W*
CC	LABEL	DC addr	3	9/18	11/17	S R•/S R R W W*
CM	LABEL	FC addr	3	9/18	11/17	S R•/S R R W W*
CMA		2F	1	4	4	F
CMC		3F	1	4	4	F
CMP	REG	1011 1SSS	1	4	4	F
CMP	M	BE	1	7	7	F R
CNC	LABEL	D4 addr	3	9/18	11/17	S R•/S R R W W*
CNZ	LABEL	C4 addr	3	9/18	11/17	S R•/S R R W W*
CP	LABEL	F4 addr	3	9/18	11/17	S R•/S R R W W*
CPE	LABEL	EC addr	3	9/18	11/17	S R•/S R R W W*
CPI	DATA	FE data	2	7	7	F R
CPO	LABEL	E4 addr	3	9/18	11/17	S R•/S R R W W*
CZ	LABEL	CC addr	3	9/18	11/17	S R•/S R R W W*
DAA		27	1	4	4	F
DAD	RP	00RP 1001	1	10	10	F B B
DCR	REG	00SS S101	1	4	5	F*
DCR	M	35	1	10	10	F R W
DCX	RP	00RP 1011	1	6	5	S*
DI		F3	1	4	4	F
EI		FB	1	4	4	F
HLT		76	1	5	7	F B
IN	PORT	DB data	2	10	10	F R I
INR	REG	00SS S100	1	4	5	F*
INR	M	34	1	10	10	F R W
INX	RP	00RP 0011	1	6	5	S*
JC	LABEL	DA addr	3	7/10	10	F R/F R R†
JM	LABEL	FA addr	3	7/10	10	F R/F R R†
JMP	LABEL	C3 addr	3	10	10	F R R
JNC	LABEL	D2 addr	3	7/10	10	F R/F R R†
JNZ	LABEL	C2 addr	3	7/10	10	F R/F R R†
JP	LABEL	F2 addr	3	7/10	10	F R/F R R†
JPE	LABEL	EA addr	3	7/10	10	F R/F R R†
JPO	LABEL	E2 addr	3	7/10	10	F R/F R R†
JZ	LABEL	CA addr	3	7/10	10	F R/F R R†
LDA	ADDR	3A addr	3	13	13	F R R R
LDAX	RP	000X 1010	1	7	7	F R
LHLD	ADDR	2A addr	3	16	16	F R R R R
LXI	RP,DATA16	00RP 0001 data16	3	10	10	F R R
MOV	REG,REG	01DD DSSS	1	4	5	F*
MOV	M,REG	0111 0SSS	1	7	7	F W
MOV	REG,M	01DD D110	1	7	7	F R
MVI	REG,DATA	00DD D110 data	2	7	7	F R
MVI	M,DATA	36 data	2	10	10	F R W
NOP		00	1	4	4	F
ORA	REG	1011 0SSS	1	4	4	F
ORA	M	B6	1	7	7	F R
ORI	DATA	F6 data	2	7	7	F R
OUT	PORT	D3 data	2	10	10	F R O
PCHL		E9	1	6	5	S*
POP	RP	11RP 0001	1	10	10	F R R
PUSH	RP	11RP 0101	1	12	11	S W W*
RAL		17	1	4	4	F
RAR		1F	1	4	4	F
RC		D8	1	6/12	5/11	S/S R R*
RET		C9	1	10	10	F R R
RIM (8085A only)		20	1	4	—	F
RLC		07	1	4	4	F
RM		F8	1	6/12	5/11	S/S R R*
RNC		D0	1	6/12	5/11	S/S R R*
RNZ		C0	1	6/12	5/11	S/S R R*
RP		F0	1	6/12	5/11	S/S R R*
RPE		E8	1	6/12	5/11	S/S R R*
RPO		E0	1	6/12	5/11	F
RRC		0F	1	4	4	F
RST	N	11XX X111	1	12	11	S W W*
RZ		C8	1	6/12	5/11	S/S R R*
SBB	REG	1001 1SSS	1	4	4	F
SBB	M	9E	1	7	7	F R
SBI	DATA	DE data	2	7	7	F R
SHLD	ADDR	22 addr	3	16	16	F R R W W
SIM (8085A only)		30	1	4	—	F
SPHL		F9	1	6	5	S*
STA	ADDR	32 addr	3	13	13	F R R W
STAX	RP	000X 0010	1	7	7	F W
STC		37	1	4	4	F
SUB	REG	1001 0SSS	1	4	4	F
SUB	M	96	1	7	7	F R
SUI	DATA	D6 data	2	7	7	F R
XCHG		EB	1	4	4	F
XRA	REG	1010 1SSS	1	4	4	F
XRA	M	AE	1	7	7	F R
XRI	DATA	EE data	2	7	7	F R
XTHL		E3	1	16	18	F R R W W

Machine cycle types:

F   Four clock period instr fetch
S   Six clock period instr fetch
R   Memory read
I   I/O read
W   Memory write
O   I/O write
B   Bus idle
X   Variable or optional binary digit
DDD Binary digits identifying a destination register
SSS Binary digits identifying a source register
RP   Register Pair   BC = 00, HL = 10
                      DE = 01, SP = 11

B = 000, C = 001, D = 010 Memory = 110
E = 011, H = 100, L = 101 A = 111

*Five clock period instruction fetch with 8080A.

†The longer machine cycle sequence applies regardless of condition evaluation with 8080A.

•An extra READ cycle (R) will occur for this condition with 8080A.

EXAMPLE 4-1

HEX ADDRESS	HEX OP CODE	MNEMONIC	COMMENTS	OCTAL ADDRESS	OCTAL OP CODE
03 00	3E	MVI A	7 states	003 000	076
01			06		001
02	06	MVI B	7 states	002	006
03			05		003
04	80	ADD B	4 states	004	200
05	D3	out	10 states	005	323
06			03		006
07	76	HLT	7 states 8080	007	166
			5 states 8085		

states used by each instruction. This information was obtained from Table 4-10. If an 8080A processor performs this program, the total number of T states used is 35. An 8085A processor uses 33. The difference is the number of T states used in executing the HLT command. Most but not all of the instructions in the 8080A instruction set use the same number of T states when performed by an 8085A. Careful perusal of Table 4-10 is important.

If an 8080A is driven by a 1 MHz master clock, then each T state or clock period lasts 1 μs. This means that the program of Example 4-1 takes 35 μs to perform. The 8085A would perform the program in 33 μs.

The program of Example 4-2 includes a loop. To determine how long this type of program will take, first divide the program into the group of instructions that is part of the loop. This will include the conditional jump statement that makes the loop possible. In Example 4-2 the loop contains two instructions. The total number of T states in the loop is 15 when performed by the 8080A. This means that each pass through the loop takes 15 μs when the master clock oscillates at 1 MHz. A 2 MHz clock would reduce the time for each pass to 7.5 μs. During the remainder of the explanations given here, it is assumed that the master clock will cycle in 1 μs.

Given that we now know how long it takes to complete a pass through the loop, we must determine how many times the loop is to be performed. The loop counter is register B. This register has 05 hex placed into it by the MVI instruction at line 03 00.

EXAMPLE 4-2

Hex Address	Hex Op Code	Mnemonic	Comments	Octal Address	Octal Op Code
03 00	06	MVI B	7 states	003 000	006
01		05		001	
02	05	DCR B	5 states	002	005
03	C2	JNZ	10 states	003	302
04		02		004	
05		03		005	
06	76	HLT	7 states	006	166

When this number reaches zero, the JNZ instruction will be ignored and the program will reach HLT.

The loop is set to iterate five times. So 5 × 15 T states yields a total of 75 T states to complete the loop. This means 75 μs have elapsed.

After determining the time required to perform the loop, total the number of T states used by instructions not in the loop. In Example 4-2 there are two instructions not in the loop. Together these instructions use a total of 14 T states. This means that an 8080A will take 75 + 14 = 89 μs to complete Example 4-2.

At this point, with the information presented in Table 4-10 and the examples given so far, you should be able to calculate how long it will take to execute a program. Suppose, though, that you wish to design a program to take a predetermined amount of time?

The first thing that must be done is to determine the needed delay. For our first example we will require a 200 μs delay. Let us see if the structure of Example 4-2 can be used to produce this delay. The program takes 89 μs to perform as written. The loop itself takes 15 μs per pass. If just the loop is considered, 200/15 yields 13.333. If we set the loop counter to 13, then the loop would eat up 195 μs, five μs short of the desired delay. The setup instructions, those outside the loop, use 14 μs. This would total 195 + 14 = 213 μs. Adjusting the loop counter to 12 gives a total of 180 μs. The program with a loop counter value of 12 would take 194 μs to complete. This is closer but not yet exactly what we want.

If an instruction that does nothing, such as NOP, is inserted into the program outside the loop, another 4 μs would be added to execution time, which would now be 198 μs in length. Example 4-3 shows how this program would look. Scanning through

EXAMPLE 4-3

HEX ADDRESS	HEX OP CODE	MNEMONIC	COMMENTS	OCTAL ADDRESS	OCTAL OP CODE
03 00	06	MVI B	≈ 200 μs	003 000	006
01		OC		001	
02	05	DCR B		002	005
03	C2	JNZ		003	302
04		02		004	
05		03		005	
06	00	NOP		006	000
07	76	HLT		007	166

the T states listed in Table 4-10 shows no instructions taking just 2 μs to complete. Does this mean that we cannot get any closer to 200 μs than 198? In some cases it will be very difficult to get exactly the delay required. This is one disadvantage of software delays. Even when it is possible to get exactly the delay desired, the programmer's time is so expensive to an employer that fine tuning a delay is not worth it.

The use of the NOP, an instruction that does nothing, is an example of fine tuning. In our example, the NOP was inserted into the program outside the loop. Sometimes it is necessary to extend a loop when fine tuning a delay program. If so, then NOPs can be written in the body of the loop.

At some point the delay desired will exceed the ability of a program's structure. Suppose that Example 4-3 had the loop counter set to maximum. This means that the loop will perform 256 passes. Register B was initially loaded with 00 hex. The loop would then use 256 × 15 T states, consuming a total of 3840 μs. The instructions outside the loop cause the program to take a total of 3858 μs to complete. If a 10 ms delay was required, Example 4-3 would fall far short of the goal; 3840 μs is 3.84 ms.

More do-nothing instructions can be added, of course, but in this case the required delay is more than triple the time already used by Example 4-3. In this case, a loop that could repeat a larger number of times would solve the problem.

Example 4-4 shows a register pair used as a loop counter. This loop counter can be a maximum of 65,536 decimal. Will it suffice for a 10 ms delay? The body of the loop contains four instructions. Together they use a total of 24 T states. Twenty-four μs will be used in each pass. The delay required, 10 ms divided by 24 μs, results in 416.66

EXAMPLE 4-4

Hex Address	Hex Op Code	Mnemonic	Comments	Octal Address	Octal Op Code
03 00	01	LXI B	10 states	003 000	001
01		AO		001	
02		01		002	
03	0B	DCX B	5 states	003	013
04	78	MOV A, B	5 states	004	170
05	B1	ORA C	4 states	005	261
06	C2	JNZ	10 states	006	302
07		03		007	
08		03		010	
09	76	HLT	7 states	011	166

decimal. This is clearly within the ability of the loop counter. A time of 9.984 ms will be used by the loop if the loop counter is set to 416 decimal. An additional 17 μs are used by the LXI and HLT instructions. This totals 10.001 ms. Just a reminder here, the DCX instruction used in Example 4-4 does not alter the flags; this is why the ORA instruction is included in the loop.

We did fairly well in creating a 10 ms delay. It would certainly be a shame if every time we wanted such a delay we had to rewrite the program. Changing the HLT to a return would add 3 μs to the program, allowing us to use the program as a subroutine whenever a delay of 10 ms was required. In fact, this delay could be so useful it might be included as part of the programs stored permanently in the computer's ROM (see the chapter on memory).

There is a drawback to using Example 4-4 as written when it is changed to a subroutine. It destroys the contents of registers A, B, and C. It also changes the contents of the flags. The convenience of the subroutine is diminished because of these drawbacks. The subroutine shown in Example 4-5 is the solution. Here the loop counter is set to 01 9E hex, which is 414 decimal. The loop now takes 9.936 ms. The instructions outside the loop use up a total of 66 μs. This subroutine uses a total of 10.002 ms with a master clock of 1 MHz. The PUSH and POP instructions save and then restore the registers and flags by using the stack as a temporary holding place for the calling program's values. This makes the subroutine transparent to the calling program. The calling

EXAMPLE 4-5

HEX ADDRESS	HEX OP CODE	MNEMONIC	COMMENTS	OCTAL ADDRESS	OCTAL OP CODE
LA 00	F5	PUSH PSW	11 states	032 000	365
01	C5	PUSH B	11 states	001	305
02	01	LXI B	10 states	002	001
03		9E		003	
04		01		004	
05	0B	DCX B	5 states	005	013
06	78	MOV A, B	5 states	006	170
07	B1	ORAC	4 states	007	261
08	C2	JNZ	10 states	010	302
09		05		011	
0A		1A		012	
0B	C1	POP B	10 states	013	301
0C	F1	POP PSW	10 states	014	361
0D	00	NOP	4 states	015	000
0E	C9	RET	10 states	016	311

program calls the time-delay subroutine. Ten ms elapse. When control of the computer is returned to the calling program, nothing has changed except the time.

Now that we have a workable fixed time-delay subroutine, let's investigate how to use it. A 1 s delay would require that the 10 ms delay be called 100 times. The calling program, though, will use up some time that must be incorporated into the calculations.

Consider Example 4-6. It will make use of the 10 ms delay by calling the subroutine at 1A 00. To meet the 1 s delay it must perform this call 100 times. If so, then the instructions of 4-6 take up a total of 3.2014 ms. The loop in Example 4-6 uses 32 μs per pass. If the 3 ms inaccuracy is acceptable, then you are done. If not, some fine tuning is in order. If the subroutine is used 99 times, then .99 s are used. The calling program adds another 3.2 ms to this total for a combined .9932 s. This is further away than before.

EXAMPLE 4-6

HEX ADDRESS	HEX OP CODE	MNEMONIC	COMMENTS	OCTAL ADDRESS	OCTAL OP CODE
			1 minute delay		
03 00	06	MVI B	7 states	003 000	006
01		64		001	
02	CD	CALL	17 states	002	315
03		00		003	
04		1A		004	
05	05	DCR B	5 states	005	005
06	C2	JNZ	10 states	006	302
07		02		007	
08		03		010	
09	76	HLT	7 states	011	166

Example 4-7 shows the main program with a padded loop. In this case, 12 do-nothing instructions have been placed inside the loop. The total number of states in each pass is now 92. Multiply this by 99 for a total of 9108, equivalent to 9108 μs. Tack on the 14 μs for the instructions not inside the loop and you get a grand total of 9122 μs. Adding this total to the .99 created by calling the delay subroutine 99 times, the delay becomes .99912 seconds. We are now .88 ms away. How much has this extra work improved the accuracy of the delay? In Example 4-6 the percentage of error was 3.2 ms/1 s × 100 = .32%. With a lot of additional calculations we are now within .088%. The time spent in reducing the error was significant. It might also be fruitless if the timing circuitry of the master clock is not very exact. What is even worse, a very important commodity in microcomputer programming was lost: memory. In many small systems memory is at a premium. Example 4-7 did not gain a significant amount of accuracy for the memory lost. Suppose someone says to replace the 12 do-nothing instructions with a loop, so you go at it again. At some point someone must decide how close is close. Less than one percent error can be considered good, especially when you realize that most electronic components do not have that kind of accuracy.

One last word about the do-nothings used in Example 4-7. MOV A,A does actually move information along the internal data bus, but when the instruction is finished, the internal values stored in A are unchanged. MOV B,B could also have been used.

EXAMPLE 4-7

HEX ADDRESS	HEX OP CODE	MNEMONIC	COMMENTS	OCTAL ADDRESS	OCTAL OP CODE
			1 minute delay		
03 00	06	MVI B		003 000	006
01		63		001	
02	CD	CALL	17 states	002	315
03		00		003	
04		1A		004	
05	7F	MOV A, A	5 states	005	177
06	7F	MOV A, A	"	006	177
07	7F	MOV A, A	"	007	177
08	7F	MOV A, A	"	010	177
09	7F	MOV A, A	"	011	177
0A	7F	MOV A, A	"	012	177
0B	7F	MOV A, A	"	013	177
0C	7F	MOV A, A	"	014	177
0D	7F	MOV A, A	"	015	177
0E	7F	MOV A, A	"	016	177
0F	7F	MOV A, A	"	017	177
10	7F	MOV A, A	"	020	177
11	05	DCR B	5 states	021	005
12	C2	JNZ	10 states	022	302
13		02		023	
14		03		024	
15	76	HLT	7 states	025	166

4-8 HARDWARE TIMING SUPPORT

There is an alternative to using software to produce delays needed by the computer to interface to slower devices. That alternative is to use support circuitry to produce the delays for the computer chip. We will call this alternative *hardware timing support.* To amplify, any support circuitry that aids the computer in a timing application—and as we will see in just a moment, this includes more than just delay functions—will be providing hardware timing functions for the CPU.

Before we begin the discussion on hardware timing support it is appropriate to look at the strengths and weaknesses of software timing. These strengths and weaknesses must be known if an intelligent decision to switch or not to switch to hardware timing support is to be made.

Software timing requires the addition of no extra chips in the computer circuitry. This is a tremendous advantage. Not only does it reduce chip count when the final product is made, it reduces PC board space. Consequently, software delay loops can save a lot of money. This advantage is in itself enough to warrant the consideration of using software delays. In many instances it can override all other concerns. Second, software delay loops, when stored in RAM, can be changed when needed. This provides a great deal of flexibility. With the advent of programmable timing chips, this flexibility is now equaled by hardware timing chips.

Software timing loops have two major disadvantages. First, they take up memory. If the memory map is fully implemented and in use, there may be no place to put a software delay loop. A memory map that is not fully implemented allows for the expansion of memory. If the software delay loop requires additional memory to be added to the computer circuitry, then you have added hardware as well as software when the loop is added to the system. To be truly cost effective, the loop must make use of memory already available without forcing additional memory to be added to the system.

Second, as was pointed out in Chapter 1, the processors we are studying perform one program at a time. Therefore, when the computer must wait through the use of a software delay, it is doing nothing else except, in effect, twiddling its thumbs. This can be valuable time lost.

Hardware timing support requires the addition of extra circuitry and more PC board space. This cost is realized every time a new unit is produced. The software delay is paid for once in programmer salary. If the timing function is extremely complicated, it may take a programmer a long time to implement. If a date has been set when a product goes into production, it may be necessary to use hardware circuitry that produces the timing function required. Thus, available hardware timing circuitry can make it possible to meet a deadline that could not be met by the software department. This is an advantage of hardware.

If the CPU has a support chip that will handle timing functions for it, the CPU does not have to produce those functions through software. This has two advantages. The first is the reduction in memory chips required. If the cost of adding a timing chip is less than the price of memory chips removed (or freed for other uses), then the timing chip has served its purpose. The second point in favor of hardware timing circuitry is that the computer chip does not have to be directly responsible for producing that function. In the case of a software delay, replaced by a hardware delay, the computer chip no longer has to run the delay loop. This means the computer chip is now free to do other things.

Certain tasks occur frequently within a computer architecture. Timing functions are an example. Handling input and output circuitry, such as keyboards and displays, is another area. Many manufacturers have produced a line of programmable support chips to handle these tasks. These chips are capable of performing support tasks under minimal directions from the CPU. Once these tasks are shifted away from the CPU, it can spend more time computing and less time monitoring circuit operations. Throughout the rest of this text we will introduce, explain, and use different types of support chips when their functions are required. Since this section is on timing functions, the 8253 programmable interval timer will be discussed first.

8253 Programmable Interval Timer

The 8253 is designed to provide a computer system with a variety of timing functions. One of these functions is the creation of accurate delays using the programmable features of the 8253. Rather than set up delay loops in software, a programmer can configure the 8253 to match the requirements of the application. Software is kept to a minimum, while at the same time great flexibility can be achieved by using different modes of operation provided by the 8253 counters/timers. In addition to delays, the 8253 has found uses in the following areas:

> programmable rate generator
> binary rate multiplier
> digital oneshot
> real time clock
> event counter
> motor controller

The pin out and the internal block diagram of the 8253 are shown in Figure 4-8. Functionally, the 8253 is divided into six internal blocks. The data bus buffer passes information into and out of the 8253 under the direction of the read/write control section. The control word register block receives instructions from the CPU in the form of control words. These control words are then used to direct the operation of the three counters that are inside the 8253.

Let's consider each section in more detail.

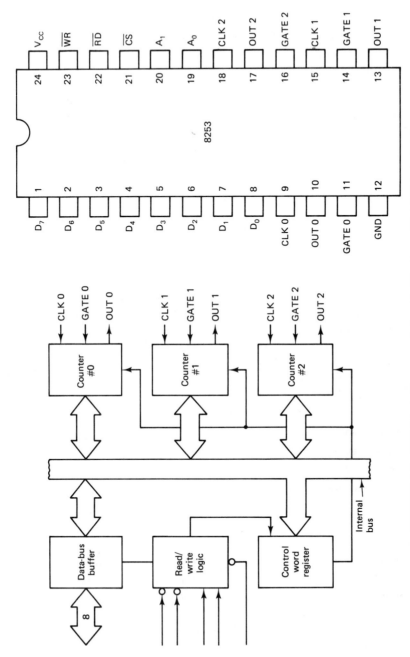

FIGURE 4-8 8253 block diagram and pin out. (Courtesy of Intel Corporation.)

Data bus buffer.   This buffer is bidirectional and tristate. It can connect directly to the data bus lines. The buffer serves three purposes:

loading count values into the counters/timers
accepting programming mode words
reading count values for the CPU

Read/write logic.   This section accepts control line information from the system bus. From these signals it generates control signals for overall device operation. This section will only be enabled when CS is low. When CS* is low, the other control signals—RD*, WR*, A1, and A0—can affect the 8253. When the WR* line is active low, information will be flowing out of the CPU and into the 8253. When the RD* line is active low, information from one of the counters will be transferred into the CPU. A1 and A0 are used as select lines. They will direct information into or out of the three counters or select the control word register to receive a mode word from the CPU.

Control word register.   The control word register is selected when A1 and A0 are both high. When this is the case, information from the CPU can be gated into this register. The information stored in the control register will determine the operational mode of each counter. It will also determine if the counter will operate in binary or BCD. This register is unidirectional. It will accept information from the CPU. The CPU cannot read its contents.

Counters.   Each of the three counters is identical to the others. They are 16-bit presettable down counters. As already indicated, they can operate on regular binary or BCD. Each can operate fully independent of the others. This means that the 8253 can perform three timing functions at the same time, each function handled by a different counter. It is also possible to cascade the counters to produce longer count sequences. Finally, the counters are bidirectional. They will accept information from the CPU, and their internal count value can be ascertained by the CPU through a read operation.

System interface.   The connections from the 8253 to the CPU bus used in the program examples to follow is shown in Figure 4-9. The concept of digital interfacing to computer bus systems will be examined in detail in the next chapter. At this time, if you wire the 8253 as shown, you will be able to duplicate the program examples and perform the tasks at the end of the chapter. What you must know now are the port numbers that the 8253 will respond to as wired in Figure 4-9. These port numbers are:

octal	hex
port 200	80—counter 0
port 201	81—counter 1
port 202	82—counter 2
port 203	83—control register

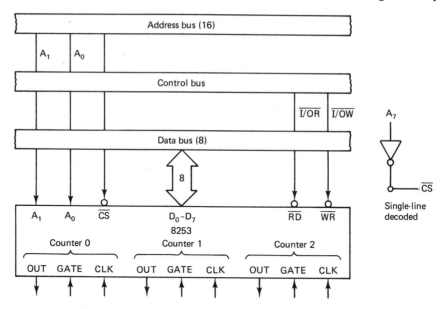

FIGURE 4-9   8253 system interface. (Courtesy of Intel Corporation.)

If you are using a small microcomputer system, it is very unlikely that these port numbers will interfere with anything already wired to the computer. If they do, your instructor will have to change the wiring on chip select. After completing the next chapter, you should be able to change the chip select wiring yourself, as needed.

Programming the 8253.   A set of control words must be sent to the 8253 to set up each counter to the desired mode of operation. The specified count must also be loaded into the correct counter. If you fail to send this information, be aware that the mode, output, and count of all counters are undefined.

Mode control words.   All the modes of operation for each counter are programmed by software from the CPU through simple I/O operations. Each counter can be individually programmed by writing a control word into the control register. The first thing to understand, then, is the format of the control word and the way it determines how the counter will operate.

The charts in Table 4-11 define the control word format. The bit functions of the control word are shown in Table 4-11(a). The first 2 bits determine which counter will be addressed. The breakdown of the patterns possible is given in Table 4-11(b). D5 and D4 determine the read/load sequence for the counter chosen. From Table 4-11(c), it is clear that a counter can be read or loaded depending on the pattern chosen for these 2 bits. It is important to point out that the counters, while 16-bit devices, receive their information from an 8-bit data bus. This means that to fully load a counter, two output operations must be performed. When using the full 16 bits, a counter expects to receive

TABLE 4-11   8253 Control Word (Courtesy of Intel Corporation.)

Control Word Format

D$_7$	D$_6$	D$_5$	D$_4$	D$_3$	D$_2$	D$_1$	D$_0$
SC1	SC0	RL1	RL0	M2	M1	M0	BCD

(a)

Definition of Control

SC — Select Counter:

SC1	SC0	
0	0	Select Counter 0
0	1	Select Counter 1
1	0	Select Counter 2
1	1	Illegal

(b)

RL — Read/Load:

RL1	RL0	
0	0	Counter Latching operation (see READ/WRITE Procedure Section)
1	0	Read/Load most significant byte only.
0	1	Read/Load least significant byte only.
1	1	Read/Load least significant byte first, then most significant byte.

(c)

M — MODE:

M2	M1	M0	
0	0	0	Mode 0
0	0	1	Mode 1
X	1	0	Mode 2
X	1	1	Mode 3
1	0	0	Mode 4
1	0	1	Mode 5

(d)

BCD:

0	Binary Counter 16-bits
1	Binary Coded Decimal (BCD) Counter (4 Decades)

(e)

the lower byte first; the higher byte will be sent last. You should also note that it is possible to send just 1 byte to the counter. When this is done, the byte not used is zeroed when the counter is loaded.

The next 3 bytes in the control word determine which mode of operation will be used. There is a total of six modes of operation, numbered 0 through 5. This is shown in Table 4-11(d). The modes of operation will be explained in detail when we finish the control word format.

The last bit of the control word determines whether the counter will operate in a binary or BCD. This is shown in 4-11(e).

The counter will not respond to its instructions until the count value is written (1 or 2 bytes) and one complete clock cycle has elapsed. Any reading of the counter prior to this time might yield invalid data.

Modes of operation

Mode 0: Interrupt on terminal count.   The output of the counter will be low after the mode word is sent to the control register. Once the count is loaded, counting will begin. When the counter has timed out—that is, reached terminal count—the output will

**TABLE 4-12 8253 Gate Pin Summary
(Courtesy of Intel Corporation.)**

Modes \ Signal Status	Low Or Going Low	Rising	High
0	Disables counting	——	Enables counting
1	——	1) Initiates counting 2) Resets output after next clock	——
2	1) Disables counting 2) Sets output immediately high	1) Reloads counter 2) Initiates counting	Enables counting
3	1) Disables counting 2) Sets output immediately high	Initiates counting	Enables counting
4	Disables counting	——	Enables counting
5	——	Initiates counting	——

go high and remain high. A new mode word or a new count for the counter in question will cause the output to go low. In this mode the counter will continue to decrement after terminal count is reached. Table 4-12 shows how the gate control affects a counter in this mode of operation. When the gate input to a counter is low, counting is suspended. Counting will occur only when the gate is high. This information is also conveyed in the waveforms of Figure 4-10. The CPU can use this mode of operation as a delay, performing a task only when a counter has timed out and signaled the CPU that terminal count has been reached. This mode of operation will be used later in the text in the chapter on interrupts.

Mode 1: Programmable oneshot.   Once the counter has been programmed and sent a count value it is ready to respond to gate control. In this mode of operation the gate control acts as a oneshot trigger. On the rising edge of a gate pulse, the counter output will go low. The duration of the low pulse is determined by the count value loaded into the counter. When the counter has timed out, the output will go high. The high output is the stable state of this mode. The low output is the quasi-stable state. New counts sent to the 8253 while in the low state will not affect the output until the next time the counter is triggered. This oneshot is retriggerable. The waveforms for mode 1 operation show that the count will remain low for the full count sequence after any rising trigger. As Table 4-12 indicates, a rising edge on the gate pin of a counter using this mode of operation initiates counting. Consequently, if triggers are delivered faster than

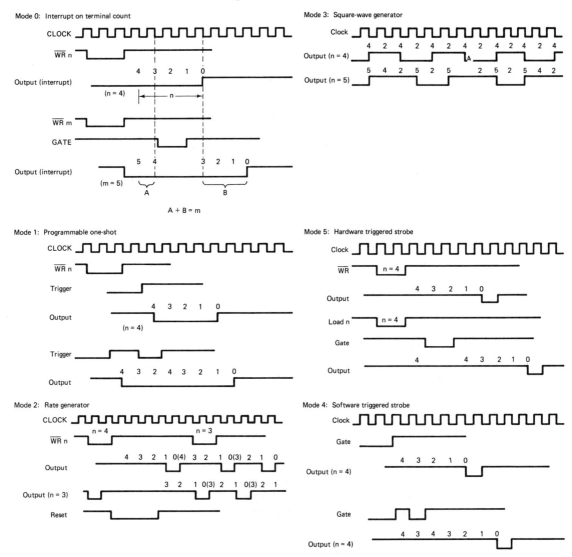

FIGURE 4-10 8253 timing diagrams. (Courtesy of Intel Corporation.)

the counter can time out, the output can be kept low indefinitely. An example of this mode of operation will be found later in this chapter.

Mode 2: Rate generator.   This mode produces a rectangular waveform. The mark is determined by the count loaded into the counter. The space is set by the 8253 to be one clock cycle in duration. The 8253 will continue to produce waveforms at the counter output unless it is instructed to change. If a new count is loaded during countdown, it will not be implemented until the following countdown sequence. The gate control can be used to temporarily stop the countdown sequence. This has the effect of lengthening the mark. See the waveforms of Figure 4-10. This chapter also includes an example of this mode of operation.

   Mode 3: Square-wave generator.   If you load an even number into a counter configured in this mode, the output will be a square wave. The square wave is created by decrementing the count by 2 at each falling edge of the counter's clock input. When the terminal count is reached, the logic level of the output is switched. The count sequence is then reloaded and the process begins again. The output frequency is a combination of the input clock frequency and the value loaded into the counter. Should you decide to load an odd number into the counter, the output will cycle between $(N + 1)/2$ and $(N - 1)/2$ timing intervals. See the waveforms for mode 3. Odd numbers do not produce 50 percent duty cycle waveforms. The last thing to note about this mode of operation is the function of the gate control. If the gate input is low or going low, the output from the counter will stop. When the gate input is high, the 8253 will produce square waves at its output. This mode of operation will be left as an exercise at the end of the chapter.

   Mode 4: Software triggered strobe.   When the mode word is sent to the control register, the output will go high. After the counter is loaded, the count will begin. The output will go low for one clock cycle when the terminal count is reached. Pulling the gate input low will inhibit the counting. Loading a new count value into the counter while it is counting will not affect the current sequence. The new value will be used on the following sequence. The waveforms for mode 4 show that the count sequence resumes from the starting value when the gate is returned high.

   Mode 5: Hardware triggered strobe.   Once the counter is set to this mode and loaded with a count sequence, counting will commence at the rising edge of a gate signal. Steady-state logic at the gate input has no effect on this mode of operation. See Table 4-12. The waveforms for mode 5 depict a continuation of the count even when the gate input is pulled low. If a rising edge should occur before the terminal count is reached, the count sequence will start over. Once terminal count is reached, the output will go low for one clock cycle, then return high. This mode of operation will be used to create an on-delay control in an example later in this chapter.

Clocking the 8253

The 8253 will accept TTL-compatible waveforms from DC up to 2 MHz. Frequently the clock inputs to the three counters will be tied together and driven from one clock source. This clock source can be taken from the master clock circuitry driving the computer chip.

Reading 8253 Counters

In many counting applications it is useful if the CPU can determine the value in a counter at any given time. The CPU can then make decisions based upon the count value it receives from the 8253. Event counters are the most likely instance of this situation. There are two ways in which a value in an 8253 counter can be read. The first way is through the use of simple input or I/O read operations. The counter to be read is selected using A1 and A0. Table 4-13(a) shows the proper combinations of A1 and A0. Note that A1 and A0 both being high during an input results in an illegal state. As mentioned earlier, the control register cannot be read. When using this approach to reading the counter values, the count sequence must be inhibited. This can be done through the use of the gate or by disabling the clock input to the counter. Failure to meet this restriction

TABLE 4-13   8253 Read Operations (Courtesy of Intel Corporation.)

Read Operation Chart

A1	A0	RD	
0	0	0	Read Counter No. 0
0	1	0	Read Counter No. 1
1	0	0	Read Counter No. 2
1	1	0	Illegal

(a)

Reading While Counting

In order for the programmer to read the contents of any counter without effecting or disturbing the counting operation the 8253 has special internal logic that can be accessed using simple WR commands to the MODE register. Basically, when the programmer wishes to read the contents of a selected counter "on the fly" he loads the MODE register with a special code which latches the present count value into a storage register so that its contents contain an accurate, stable quantity. The programmer then issues a normal read command to the selected counter and the contents of the latched register is available.

MODE Register for Latching Count

A0, A1 = 11

D7	D6	D5	D4	D3	D2	D1	D0
SC1	SC0	0	0	X	X	X	X

(b)

SC1,SC0 — specify counter to be latched.

D5,D4   — 00 designates counter latching operation.

X   — don't care.

The same limitation applies to this mode of reading the counter as the previous method. That is, it is mandatory to complete the entire read operation as programmed. This command has no effect on the counter's mode.

may lead to reading a count value when the counter is in transition, resulting in erroneous information. *It is important to remember that a counter set up to operate as a 16-bit counter must be read completely.* The first byte received is the low byte; the second byte is the high byte of the counter.

The second method of reading a counter value allows the counter to be read without interfering with the count sequence. A mode word is sent to the 8253 as depicted in

Layout Sheet 4-1

8253 PROJECT LAYOUT SHEET ONE

OBJECTIVE:

To use the 8253 as a programmable oneshot. The active low output will be set for 5 s.

HARDWARE ENVIRONMENT:

8085-based CPU
Accumulator I/O

Support Chips:

8253 programmable interval timer clocked from a 1 s TTL-compatible pulse

SOFTWARE ENVIRONMENT

Memory Allocations:

Main program starts at 03 00 hex.

Register Allocation:

A — basic I/O and 8253 setup

Port Allocations:

   1. 80 hex — counter 0 8253
   2. 83 hex — control register 8253

Special Codes:

12 hex — 8253 counter 0 mode 1 operation

HARDWARE/SOFTWARE INTERFACE

Other than port numbers, hardware connections have no effect on the software.

Figure 4-13(b). This mode word will select the counter to be read by using the first 2 bits of the mode word for addressing. D5 and D4 both low indicate that a latching operation is to be performed. Upon receipt of the latch word, a counter's value is placed into a storage register inside the 8253. The programmer then sends normal input or I/O reads to the 8253 and receives the latched information. This type of read operation also requires the entire counter to be read if it is set up as a 16-bit counter.

4-9 8253 PROJECT DISCUSSIONS

The layout sheet for project one is shown in Layout Sheet 4-1. The program is a straight-line program without any looping. (See Example 4-8.) It establishes the control word for counter 0 in mode 1 operation in the accumulator. Convert this hex number to binary and cross it to the control word breakdown given in Table 4-11. This should help you practice control word setup. This information is then sent to the 8253 control register via the system interface wiring shown in Figure 4-9. The A register is then reloaded with the duration of the low pulse, which in this case is five clock cycles. The layout sheet informs us that the 8253 will be clocked with a 1s TTL waveform. Therefore, the

EXAMPLE 4-8

HEX ADDRESS	HEX OP CODE	MNEMONIC	COMMENTS	OCTAL ADDRESS	OCTAL OP CODE
			8253-1		
03 00	3E	MVI A	Control word for mode 1	003 000	076
01		12		001	
02	D3	OUT	Initialize counter for mode 1	002	323
03		83		003	
04	3E	MVI A	Set duration of output pulse	004	076
05		05		005	
06	D3	OUT	Send duration to counter 0	006	323
07		80		007	
08	76	HLT		010	166

output will remain low for 5 s after counter 0 has been triggered. There are many possible applications for oneshots, but for purposes of this discussion, assume the 8253 counter 0 output is inverted. This inverted output can then be used to activate a device for 5 s after a trigger has been applied to the gate of counter zero.

The program for the second 8253 project is shown in Example 4-9. This program is also straight line. The control word is different and the port number selecting the counter has been changed to 81 to allow communications with counter 1. The output pulse will be high for 4 s and low for 1 s. This corresponds to the waveform shown for mode 1 operation shown in Figure 4-10. The layout sheet is almost identical to that for the first project and is left as an optional exercise.

EXAMPLE 4-9

HEX ADDRESS	HEX OP CODE	MNEMONIC	COMMENTS	OCTAL ADDRESS	OCTAL OP CODE
			8253-2		
03 00	3E	MVI A	Set up control word for	003 000	076
01		54	mode 2	001	
02	D3	OUT	Initialize counter 1 to mode 2	002	323
03		83		003	
04	3E	MVI A	Establish mark duration	004	076
05		04		005	
06	D3	OUT	Send duration interval to	006	323
07		81	counter 1	007	
08	76	HLT		010	

Mode 5 operation is established by Example 4-10. The mode word is now 9A hex and the port number selecting the counter has been changed to 82. After the program is run, counter 2 will act like an on-delay switch. A trigger into the gate of counter 2 will result in an output 3 s later. This means that a device attached to counter 2 will not turn on until 3 s after the trigger. On-delay applications are very common in control situations involving machinery. In some respects on-delay logic is like a fuse on a bomb; instant

EXAMPLE 4-10

Hex Address	Hex Op Code	Mnemonic	Comments	Octal Address	Octal Op Code
			8253-3		
03 00	3E	MVI A	Control word for modes	003 000	076
01		9A		001	
02	D3	OUT	Initialize counter 2	002	323
03		83		003	
04	3E	MVI A	Set up delay after trigger	004	076
05		03		005	
06	D3	OUT	Transmit delay to counter 2	006	323
07		82		007	
08	76	HLT		010	166

on is certainly not wanted when using explosives. The layout sheet for this project is also left as an optional exercise.

All three programs were short, straight-line logical constructions. As indicated in the discussion of the 8253, the amount of software needed to initialize the 8253 is insignificant. This is an advantage. The computer chip is now free to perform other tasks while the 8253 is handling timing functions.

4-10 CLOSING THOUGHTS

This chapter has presented the foundation of computer timing. The basic timing cycles of a computer were investigated starting with the clock cycle, proceeding to the machine cycle, and ending with the instruction cycle. This information can be used to predict what will be on the bus system at any given time. This can be vital in troubleshooting applications.

The timing information was then used to explain how to develop software delay loops. Software delays allow the CPU to interface to slower mechanical devices. An alternative to software delays was then discussed, culminating in a discussion on the 8253 programmable interval timer.

SUMMARY

1. The microprocessors covered in this chapter perform operations based on a precisely controlled clock signal.
2. The basic unit of processor activity is the clock state.
3. Machine cycles comprise multiple clock states. Machine cycles are used by the processors covered in this chapter to control the flow of data over the bus.
4. Machine cycles are combined together to form instruction cycles. An instruction cycle comprises the activity associated with an instruction that is being performed by the CPU.
5. Software delay loops can be constructed to meet various timing delay requirements associated with tasks that will be performed by the processor. A software delay can be calculated by determining the number of clock states required to complete a section of code, then multiplying this information by the time required to complete one clock state.
6. Hardware support timing is available to the processor from support chips such as the 8253 programmable interval timer.

QUESTIONS

1. What is the smallest unit of processor activity?
2. What is the significance of the SYNC pulse?
3. What processor activity is controlled by machine cycles?
4. In a system based on an 8085, what problems can occur if the master clock is derived from an RC network?
5. How many clock cycles are needed to reset an 8080?
6. How many clock cycles are needed to reset a Z80?
7. Explain the difference between a cold and warm reset.
8. What activities are carried out by an 8080 during T_1?
9. What does a Z80 do at the rising edge of T_3?
10. What is a common usage for a hold state?
11. What activity is carried out by a Z80 when halted?
12. What information is present on a Z80 address bus during T_3 of an op code fetch?
13. When does the Z80 sample the WAIT* control line?
14. What is the significance of the M1* control line in a Z80 system?

15. When does the 8080 place status bits on the data bus?

16. Explain the following:

$$(A) \rightarrow TMP$$

17. Explain what is meant by *overlapping cycles*.

18. How many T states are required by an 8080 to execute an LHLD instruction?

19. What section of the CPU receives the data when an instruction fetch is performed?

20. If an 8080 has a master clock frequency of 1 MHz, how long does it take to complete the following program?

    LXI B

    08

    04

    MOV A, C

    ADD B

    OUT

    06

    HLT

21. The 8253 will use counter 2 as a 16-bit counter. The mode of operation will be mode 4. Determine the mode control word when the counter operates in binary.

22. The 8253 counters, when operating in mode 1, are referred to as programmable oneshots. Explain what happens if a trigger pulses the gate while the counter is timing down.

ASSIGNMENTS

1. Write a software delay loop for .5 s. Package it as a subroutine. Then use it from a calling program.

2. Wire the 8253 as shown in Figure 4-9. Clock the 8253 from a 4 KHz signal. Set up the 8253 mode 3 to produce a 1 KHz output at the output of counter 1. Verify circuit operation and frequency using an oscilloscope.

LAB QUESTIONS

1. If a single-byte register is used for a loop counter when programming a 500 ms delay, how many T states would have to be in the loop if the master clock operates at 1 MHz?

2. What control word was used in assignment 2?

3. If counter 0 had been used rather than counter 1, what would the control word be?

4. How was the gate control of counter 1 wired in the 8253 assignment? Why? Explain what would have happened if it had been wired at a different logic level.

5. What value was loaded into the counter in assignment 2?

6. If the counter has been told to count down in BCD, would this have affected the output frequency in the 8253 assignment?

5

DIGITAL INTERFACING

At the end of this chapter you should be familiar with:
1. how port numbers are decoded
2. how a computer generates a device-select pulse
3. the IN and OUT instruction cycles
4. memory-mapped concepts
5. the advantages and disadvantages of memory-mapped I/O
6. how memory-mapped addresses are decoded
7. how the CPU generates an address-select pulse
8. how select pulses can be used as control pulses
9. the 8212
10. the 8255, mode 0 operation

INTRODUCTION

This chapter deals with the subject of digital interfacing, the connection of digital circuitry to the computer's I/O bus. The method of data transfer between the CPU and the I/O devices attached to the bus will be explored as four additional machine cycles are explained. Decoding circuitry, which allows multiple numbers of devices to share the same signals, will be examined. The method in which the decoders allow only the addressed device to respond to control and data information is detailed. The two major methods of transferring information to the I/O ports, isolated I/O and memory-mapped I/O, will be explored. The chapter ends in the study of two chips specifically designed to interface to a computer bus, the 8212 and the 8255. From the discussion of these last two chips you should be able to understand the system interface and chip-select circuitry used in Chapter 4 when we used the 8253.

5-1 BUS STANDARDS

The pin outs of the three microprocessor chips shown in Figure 5-1 show a great deal of similarity. A careful examination also shows some important differences. The 8085, for example, does not have 16 address pins. As was pointed out in Chapter 1, the lower address bus and the data bus share the same pins. An address latch had to be connected to these pins, then turned on by address latch enable to capture the lower address while it was present. Once latched, the lower address could be presented to the bus at a later time.

The Z80 has two pins that it uses to distinguish between I/O and memory operations, namely, IORQ* and MREQ*. The 8085 uses the IO/M* pin to handle this function. The 8080 has a pin labeled DBIN which, when active, indicates data flow into the CPU. The WR* line, when active, indicates data flow out of the CPU. There are no pins on the 8080 that indicate if a transfer is I/O or memory in nature. This is because the 8080 dumps additional information onto the data bus, in the form of status bits, about what will be happening during a machine cycle. Like the 8085, which required a latch for the lower address byte, the 8080 requires a latch or bus controller to capture this information, which is then used to create additional control signals.

The processor chips are also incapable of driving the bus themselves, except in very small systems. Each usually requires some type of current buffer to handle the currents necessary to operate the bus. Therefore, from the preceding discussion, you should realize that the information at the pin outs of the computer chips will not be presented to the bus in exactly the same format.

To complicate matters further, the support circuitry that delivers the pin-out information to the bus system can be different from one computer to the next. Sometimes the way in which a bus is implemented is unique to a particular manufacturer. Other times a bus standard such as S − 100 is used. Unfortunately or fortunately, depending upon your perspective, there are many bus standards in existence. This means it is possible to purchase two computers that are centered around an 8085A, with each having a

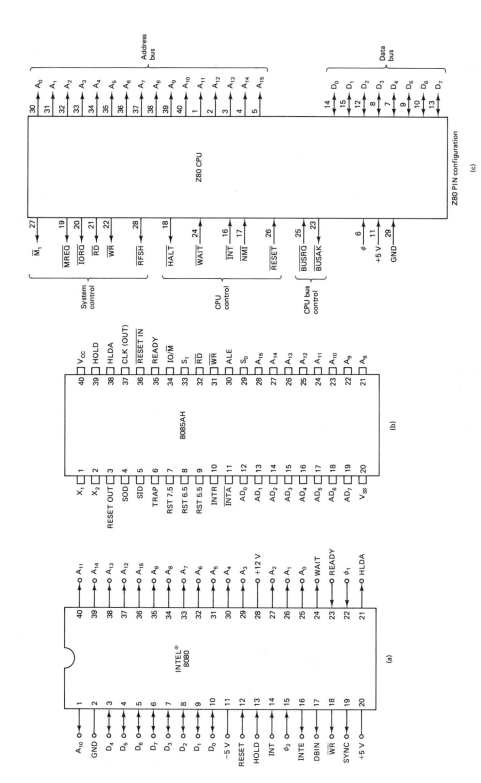

FIGURE 5-1 Pin outs of three microprocessor chips [(a) and (b)] Courtesy of Intel Corporation.(c) Reproduced by permission, © 1986 Zilog, Inc.; this material shall not be reproduced without the written consent of Zilog, Inc.]

different bus structure. Bus standards and the ways in which computer buses are implemented will be explained in more detail later in this text in the chapter on system operation. One of the tenets of this text, however, is that there is enough similarity from system to system to quickly understand differences that may exist. Consequently, it should not be necessary to study every processor currently on the market to become adept in microcomputer electronics. The 8080A, 8085A, and Z80 are presented together to help foster this idea and give you the confidence needed to learn a processor not discussed within these pages when it becomes necessary to do so.

For now, we need to set some standards for the experiments and computer inter-

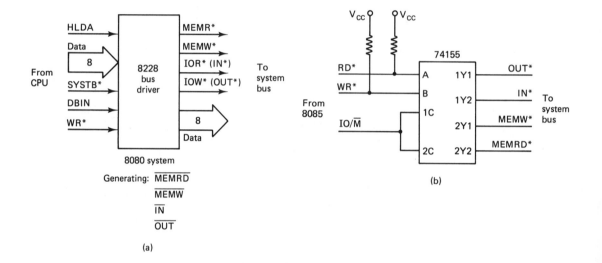

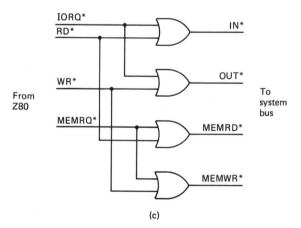

FIGURE 5-2 Control signal generation.

facing that follow. These standards will help you in connecting devices to your computer system despite differences in bus structure and signal nomenclature.

In all three cases, the data lines from the processors will be labeled D7 through D0. The address lines, whether latched or not, will be labeled A15 through A0. Power and ground will be labeled Vcc and ground. That is the easy part. Now for the control signals. IN* and OUT* will be used during I/O operations. It is very likely that your system refers to these signals as IOR* (replacing IN*) and IOW* (replacing OUT*). The primary memory-control signals will be labeled MEMR* and MEMW*. INT will be used for interrupt requests. This signal is active high on the 8080 and 8085; it is active low on the Z80. We will use this signal later. Direct memory access operations will be started on the 8080 and the 8085 through the use of the HOLD control line. On a Z80 system, this signal is labeled BUSRQ*. See Figure 5-2 for a quick reference of the signals we will be using in the interfacing and experiments in this text.

5-2 ISOLATED I/O

Isolated I/O uses the accumulator as the section of the computer chip that receives information from or transmits information to the I/O bus during input and output operations. No other register is usable for data transfer during input or output operations. For this reason isolated I/O is often called *accumulator I/O*. This concept has an important impact on computer programs. First, the instructions we will use in this text have just two op codes that can initiate an I/O operation, the IN and the OUT. The Z80 has a much larger set of I/O instructions, but since we will be writing programs that will work on all three processors, we will limit ourselves to the IN and the OUT. Second, any information that is in the accumulator prior to an I/O operation must be moved from the accumulator to a temporary storage location. This generates extra instructions in a program. To help make this clearer, consider a program that needs to receive information from a keyboard. This information will be transferred from the keyboard via the I/O bus and into the A register. If the A register contained the result of an important calculation, the data from the keyboard would overwrite this information once the input operation was completed. This means that the calculation result had to be moved and stored elsewhere prior to the IN instruction being executed. Consequently, extra instructions have been added to the program. Once the I/O operation is completed, it might be necessary to restore the calculation result in the accumulator. More move instructions will have to be added to the program. One will place the keyboard value somewhere other than the A register, a second will return a copy of the calculation result to the accumulator. The program has become longer without performing any computations directly related to the task. These extra instructions were added because of the architecture of I/O operations, not because of additional logic. This slows down program execution.

The advantage in isolated I/O can be seen when it is realized that the computer can transfer information into and out of the processor without having to use memory. This retains memory locations (addresses) for memory circuitry and not for I/O operations. We will come back to this concept when we discuss memory-mapped I/O.

5-3 BUS WIRING

In most instances the peripherals attached to a computer bus will share the same set of address and data lines. Some of the control signals will also be wired to every device on the bus. This bus configuration is used to cut down on wiring. This of course reduces the amount of PC board space needed and saves money. If you visualize every peripheral with its own dedicated lines, you should see the advantage of using common lines. Figure 5-3 shows a bus with three peripherals. Each peripheral consists of an interface card, often called a controller card, and a device attached to the controller card. The computer ''talks'' to each through the common lines. Special control signals called de-vice-select pulses insure that only one peripheral will turn on at a time. This is necessary for several reasons. First, electrical damage can result if more than one output circuit is on at the same time. Second, information can become garbled when more than one peripheral tries to use the bus at the same time. Finally, information or instructions that might be appropriate for a disk drive should not be accepted by a printer or other pe-ripherals on the bus. The next major section discusses how device-select pulses are created and sent to the peripherals on the bus.

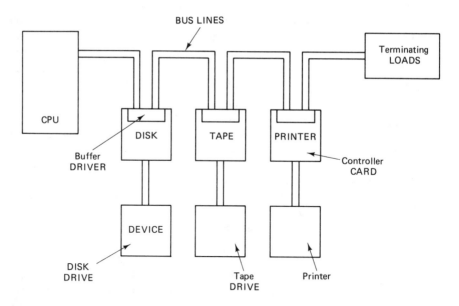

FIGURE 5-3   A daisy-chained bus.

5-4 DEVICE-SELECT PULSES

A device-select pulse is a pulse generated by the CPU and the CPU subsystem in re-sponse to a software instruction, in our case, the IN and OUT instructions. The pulse can be either active high or low depending on the circuitry used to create it.

This pulse, once created, will be used to turn on a device or integrated circuit attached to the I/O bus. The pulse should be ignored by all but the device or IC intended to respond. That is, every device *not selected* should remain electrically isolated from the bus. Electrical isolation is possible through the use of tristate or open collector circuitry. Only the selected device will turn on and place information on the bus when the computer wants information inputted. Only the selected device will accept information from the processor chip. All other devices, although wired to the same lines, should ignore the data transfers.

Port Numbers

As we saw in Chapter 2, the IN and OUT instructions are 2-byte instructions. The first byte is, as always, the op code. The second byte is the port number. This port number will be used by the CPU to select or address a particular device attached to the bus. When we examine the OUT and IN machine cycles, we will see how the port number is transferred to the I/O bus. A decoded port number is one part of a device-select pulse. Decoders will be examined in detail in this chapter.

IN* and OUT* Control Signals

The IN* and OUT* control signals are the second part of a device-select pulse. A decoded port number will be logically combined with one of these two control signals to tell the selected device the direction of data flow. Sometimes a device or IC might receive the decoded port number and control signals on different pins. At other times, the device will receive the information already logically combined as a device-select pulse.

Figure 5-4 shows how a device-select pulse could be created. In this diagram the decoder is shown as a block diagram. It is wired to the I/O bus in such a way that it receives all the port numbers generated by the CPU. It will produce an active low on line 07 only in response to port number 07. All other port numbers will leave this line high. Later we will take a look at decoder circuitry in greater detail. The output of the decoder is logically combined with the OUT control signal with an OR gate. The only time the output of the OR gate will be low is when the decoder output is low and the OUT* control line is asserted. The device attached to the output of the OR gate will be set to respond only when the ODS07* signal is low.

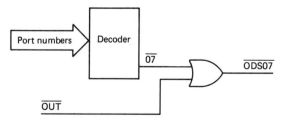

FIGURE 5-4   Device-select pulse circuit.

OUT Instruction Cycle

The waveforms for the OUT instruction cycle as performed by the 8080A are shown in Figure 5-5. During the first machine cycle, the op code is fetched. The sync pulse marks the beginning of each machine cycle and indicates when status bits are placed on the data bus. The sync pulse can be used to latch the status bits for use later in the machine cycle. The status bits and their position on the data bus are found in Figure 5-6. The footnote near the status waveform indicates which column of status bits will be dumped onto the data bus. During M1, the pattern representing the instruction fetch is output. The address bus is used by the program counter at this time to locate the OUT instruction in memory. The OUT op code will be placed onto the data bus. The time the information is valid is marked as byte one on the data bus waveforms. Since information is flowing into the 8080A at this time, DBIN goes active high. The op code is sent to the instruction register and decoded.

M2 is used to fetch the port number of the device to be selected. The sync pulse once again goes active high, marking the start of a new machine cycle. This time the status bits will follow the pattern of column 2 from the status bit chart found in Figure 5-6. This pattern represents a memory read operation. The port number will be trans-

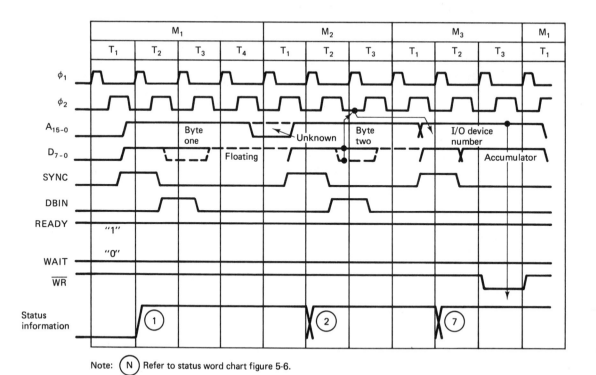

Note: (N) Refer to status word chart figure 5-6.

FIGURE 5-5   Output instruction cycle. (Courtesy of Intel Corporation.)

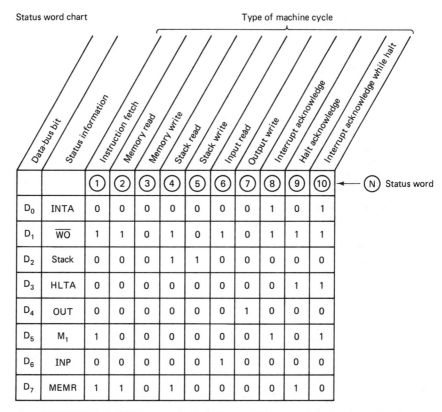

FIGURE 5-6   8080 status bit definitions. (Courtesy of Intel Corporation.)

ferred into the CPU over the data bus at the time the data bus waveform is marked byte two. The address bus contains the value of the program counter that pointed to the port number stored in memory.

OUT machine cycle.   The third machine cycle is the OUT machine cycle. The sync pulse goes high once more, marking the start of the actual I/O operation. This time a status bit pattern from column 7 of the status bit chart is dumped onto the data bus. The OUT status bit is now high. It will have to be latched for use later in the machine cycle. The CPU then transfers the port number it received in M2 onto the address bus. This port number is an 8-bit operand. In the 8080 the port number is duplicated on the lower and upper half of the address bus. This means that a port decoder could be attached to either half of the address bus. The 8085 places port numbers on the upper half of the address bus only. The OUT* signal can be generated from a circuit as shown in Figure 5-2(b).

The Z80 presents port numbers on the lower half of the address bus. Port decoders will be wired to the low address bus on 8080 and Z80 systems, with port decoders wired to the upper address byte on 8085 systems.

The port number is also placed onto the bus system prior to the information from the A register being placed onto the data bus. This gives the decoders time to decode the port number and present a stable control signal when the actual data transfer takes place. Finally, look at the WR* waveform. This waveform goes active low, indicating information is flowing out of the CPU. It does not indicate whether this information is to be delivered to memory or to an I/O device. When logically combined with the out status bit that was latched earlier, it creates an OUT* control signal that when combined with the decoded port number produces a device-select pulse. This pulse, as we already know, will activate the addressed device, which will then accept information.

IN Instruction Cycle

The waveforms for this instruction cycle are shown in Figure 5-7. The first two machine cycles of the IN instruction are identical to those discussed in the OUT instruction cycle. Therefore, we will concentrate on the IN machine cycle.

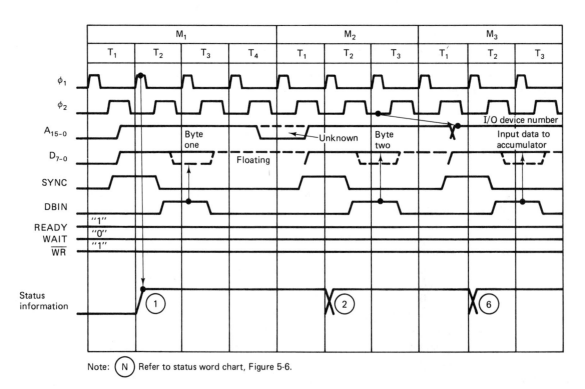

Note: (N) Refer to status word chart, Figure 5-6.

FIGURE 5-7 Input instruction cycle. (Courtesy of Intel Corporation.)

IN machine cycle.   The M3 cycle of the IN instruction controls the data transfer of information from an input port to the CPU. The status bits that are placed onto the data bus at the start of this machine cycle follow the pattern of column 6 in the status bit chart in Figure 5-6. Please note that the IN status bit is high. The port number is placed on the address bus prior to the actual data transfer. Once again, this is done to give the port decoders time to function. The control signal DBIN goes high, indicating that the data bus will accept information that is being input to the CPU. By itself the DBIN signal does not differentiate between inputs from memory or from an I/O port. When logically combined with the IN status bit, the IN control signal is created. This signal is then combined with the decoded port number to produce a device-select pulse that will gate information onto the data bus.

Port Decoders

Since a port number is 8 bits wide, it can differentiate between 256 possible combinations. Couple these combinations with an OUT* signal and 256 output ports can exist. Combine the port numbers with the IN* signal and another 256 ports, this time input ports, can exist. This indicates that the 8080A, 8085A, and Z80 can interact with a maximum of 512 ports. Many times a single device will respond to both an IN and an OUT when its port number is placed onto the bus. Such a port is bidirectional. Even if every port on the bus is bidirectional, which would be very unusual, the processors can still access 256 different devices. This may seem limited, but it isn't. Think about a typical home computer. There may be two disk drives, a printer, perhaps a modem, and a display terminal. This is a total of five devices. Toss in a couple of game paddles, a joystick, a cassette interface, and a speaker—we are still far short of the 256 possibilities. Even if we persisted in adding devices just to tax the CPU's ability to handle the bus system, there is a way around this restriction. It is called *memory-mapped I/O*. At the moment, though, we are concentrating on isolated I/O. From the above discussion it should be clear that this form of I/O is sufficient in many applications. It is now time to see how the port decoders that make this I/O possible work.

Figure 5-8 shows an eight-input AND gate connected to the lower half of the address bus. TTL inputs can be connected directly to the bus lines, provided they do not cause the fan out of the bus drivers to be exceeded. This particular gate will produce a high out when the input is B7 hex. Placement of the inverters on different lines would

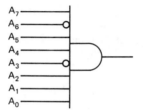

FIGURE 5-8 Absolute port number decoder.

result in the gate responding to different port addresses. This circuit depicts what is known as *absolute decoding*. An absolutely decoded port number is one that was produced by using all the address lines carrying the port number. In the case of isolated I/O this is a total of eight lines. When all port numbers are absolutely decoded there are no ambiguities in the I/O port structure. An ambiguity exists when two or more port numbers activate the same decoder and thus the same device.

The drawback of an absolutely decoded system lies in the amount of hardware it requires. If each of the 256 port numbers were decoded by AND gates and inverters, a very large PC board would have to be created. This is much too expensive. Remember the home computer example? Most systems do not have a large number of peripherals attached to the bus. This makes partial decoding and even linear decoding possible. *Partial decoding* does not use all the address lines to form a decoded port address. *Linear decoding* uses just one line to activate the port decoder or circuitry connected to the bus system.

In Chapter 4 the 8253 has CS* asserted when A7 goes low. The port numbers listed for the 8253 were 80, 81, 82, and 83 hex. These numbers all have A7 high. CS* is controlled by a single line from the address bus. This is an example of linear decoding. Any hex number greater than 80 will also activate CS* on the 8253. Consider 92. In binary this becomes 1001 0010. Since A7 is high, CS* will go low. Counter 2 of the 8253 could be accessed if 92 is placed on the bus during an I/O operation. Since there are two or more port numbers that can turn on the 8253, there are ambiguities in the port structure. Will this create problems? Only if port 92 already exits in the system! A small system having only a few ports is not likely to have port numbers in excess of 80. Most designers start from 00 hex when decoding and work up to FF hex. If the computer trainer you are using decodes from 00 hex to 0F hex (a very common arrangement), the linear decoding used to activate the 8253 will not interfere with the ports already wired to the computer.

Linear decoding uses up a large amount of the available port numbers. Using A7 takes numbers from 80 to FF hex out of use. This means 128 port numbers are no longer available for expansion at a later time. They have already been committed to a single port. This is the drawback of linear decoding. The advantage is the simplicity of the hardware required to implement the port decoder.

Partial decoding is a compromise between the absolute decoders and the linear decoders. The greater the number of address lines used in a decoder, the fewer the ambiguities. To understand this better, suppose we build a partial decoder using A7 and A6. The circuit of Figure 5-9 produces an active low output only when A7 and A6 are high. The port numbers that can bring the output line low must be above CO hex. Compared to the linear decoder used to activate the 8253, we have 64 fewer ambiguities. The port numbers 80 through BF will no longer activate this decoder.

FIGURE 5-9 Partial decoding.

Partial decoding can easily be implemented through the use of decoding chips. The next few examples show how this type of decoding is accomplished. Study this section carefully until you understand all the examples. Many small systems use the types of circuits found in the examples that follow.

Decoding circuitry analysis.   The 74154 is a 4-line to 16-line decoder. The function table and pin out and block diagram are shown in Figure 5-10. Only one output pin will be low at a time. That output will correspond to the pattern input on select lines D through A. If the input nibble is 1001, then output 9, which is pin 10, will be low. Verify chip operation for other input combinations with the function table. If either strobe, G1, or G2 is high, the 74154 is disabled. All outputs will be high and the chip will ignore any input patterns it might receive.

Figure 5-11(a) shows a common way in which the 74154 is interfaced to the address bus. Here the lower nibble of the port number is applied to the inputs of the 74154. A3, the most significant bit of the address lines used, is connected to D, the most significant input of the 74154. This sequence is carried out until all four 74154 select lines are connected to the address bus. With both strobes grounded, the 74154 can produce up to 16 decoded port numbers. These port numbers are usually designated 00 to 0F hex. Due to the ambiguities, not all 8 bits of the port number are used; other port numbers can activate this decoder. Ten to 1F hex would work, as would 20 to 2F hex and so on. The entire upper hex digit can cycle from 0 to F because, as wired, this high-order nibble is a ''don't care.''

A slight modification in the wiring of the 74154 is shown in Figure 5-11(b). Here one of the strobes is connected to the OUT* pulse. In this configuration, the 74154 will only pull the selected line low if an out machine cycle is taking place. This makes the 74154 a device-select pulse generator. The IN* pulse could have been wired to G2 in Figure 5-11(b). Then it would produce 16 device-select pulses for input devices.

The circuits of Figure 5-11 cycle through 16 port numbers, then accept repeats where the high-order nibble has been incremented. This makes it very difficult to expand the port structure at a later time should it be necessary.

The circuit in Figure 5-12 shows an absolute decoder that avoids this problem. The G1 strobe is driven by a four-input NAND gate connected to A7 through A4. Since all 8 bits of the port number are in use, this device-select pulse generator is absolutely decoded. This means that no ambiguities are introduced into the port structure when this circuit setup is used. The port numbers that activate the 74154 are F0 through FF hex. The decoder will only operate when the high-order nibble is F and the IN* control signal is low. To select port numbers with high-order nibbles other than F, place inverters on the inputs of the NAND gate in a fashion similar to that in Figure 5-8.

An F placed on A7 through A4 during a memory operation will not activate the decoder because *both* strobes must be low to produce an active low out on one of the output lines. This situation highlights why it is convenient to sometimes have chips with two strobes rather than one.

The circuit of Figure 5-13 shows how to wire 74154s to generate 256 device-select

Function Table

Inputs						Outputs															
G1	G2	D	C	B	A	0	1	2	3	4	5	6	7	8	9	10	11	12	13	14	15
L	L	L	L	L	L	L	H	H	H	H	H	H	H	H	H	H	H	H	H	H	H
L	L	L	L	L	H	H	L	H	H	H	H	H	H	H	H	H	H	H	H	H	H
L	L	L	L	H	L	H	H	L	H	H	H	H	H	H	H	H	H	H	H	H	H
L	L	L	L	H	H	H	H	H	L	H	H	H	H	H	H	H	H	H	H	H	H
L	L	L	H	L	L	H	H	H	H	L	H	H	H	H	H	H	H	H	H	H	H
L	L	L	H	L	H	H	H	H	H	H	L	H	H	H	H	H	H	H	H	H	H
L	L	L	H	H	L	H	H	H	H	H	H	L	H	H	H	H	H	H	H	H	H
L	L	L	H	H	H	H	H	H	H	H.	H	H	L	H	H	H	H	H	H	H	H
L	L	H	L	L	L	H	H	H	H	H	H	H	H	L	H	H	H	H	H	H	H
L	L	H	L	L	H	H	H	H	H	H	H	H	H	H	L	H	H	H	H	H	H
L	L	H	L	H	L	H	H	H	H	H	H	H	H	H	H	L	H	H	H	H	H
L	L	H	L	H	H	H	H	H	H	H	H	H	H	H	H	H	L	H	H	H	H
L	L	H	H	L	L	H	H	H	H	H	H	H	H	H	H	H	H	L	H	H	H
L	L	H	H	L	H	H	H	H	H	H	H	H	H	H	H	H	H	H	L	H	H
L	L	H	H	H	L	H	H	H	H	H	H	H	H	H	H	H	H	H	H	L	H
L	L	H	H	H	H	H	H	H	H	H	H	H	H	H	H	H	H	H	H	H	L
L	H	X	X	X	X	H	H	H	H	H	H	H	H	H	H	H	H	H	H	H	H
H	L	X	X	X	X	H	H	H	H	H	H	H	H	H	H	H	H	H	H	H	H
H	H	X	X	X	X	H	H	H	H	H	H	H	H	H	H	H	H	H	H	H	H

H = high level, L = low level, X = irrelevant

SN54154 . . . J or W package
SN54L154 . . . J package
SN74154, SN74L154 . . . J or
N package (top view)

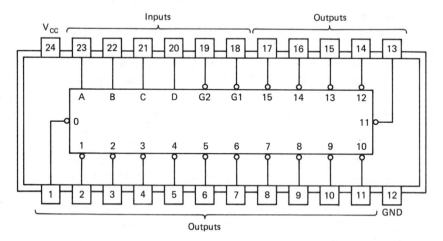

Positive logic: see function table

FIGURE 5-10 74154 function table, pin out and block diagram. (Courtesy of Texas Instruments Incorporated.)

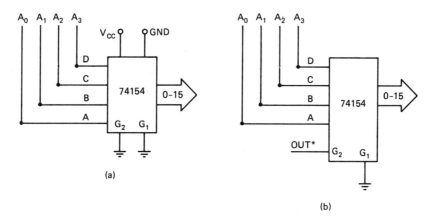

FIGURE 5-11   Device-select decoders.

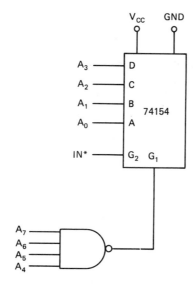

FIGURE 5-12   Device-select generator for FO to FF.

pulses. The high-order nibble is wired to the 74154 at the left of the circuit. This 74154 serves to select one of the 74154s found in the second tier of the logic. The top 74154 in the column on the right of the circuit will only have its G2 strobe go low if output 15, located on pin 17, of the first 74154 goes low. For this to happen, the input to the 74154 on the left of the circuit must be F. Consequently, the top chip in the column on the left produces device-select pulses for FO through FF. When this top chip is activated, all the other decoders in the column on the left are disabled because their G1 strobes are high. This prevents any ambiguities. All port numbers are absolutely decoded because the high nibble selects which chip to activate and the low-order nibble, which is wired

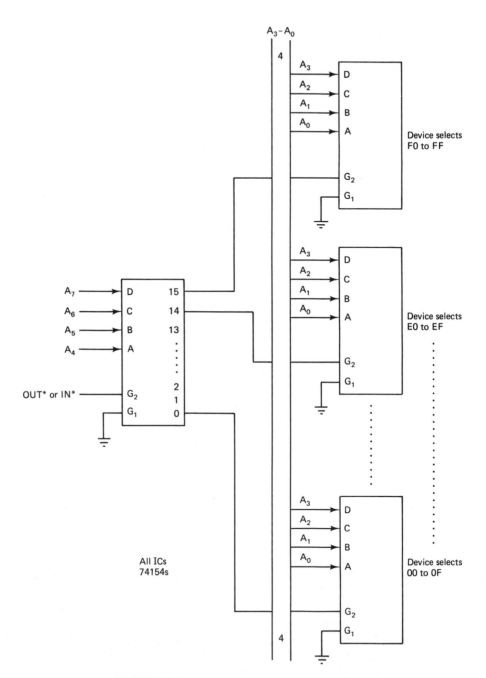

FIGURE 5-13 Generating 256 device-select pulses.

to every 74154 in the second column, activates the correct output line on the chip that is allowed to turn on.

The circuit of Figure 5-13 generates device-select pulses, because the controlling 74154 will not turn on unless it receives an IN* or an OUT* signal. Please do not think that this means the IN* and OUT* signals are ORed together and connected to G2. One or the other signal will be connected to G2, not both.

To understand why, think about the functions of these control signals. They indicate the direction that data is to flow on the data bus. In a properly working computer, at least one of these lines is always high. Consequently, ORing the two signals together would lock the OR gate output high. The device-select pulse circuit would never turn on. Additionally, the device-select pulse must convey the direction that data will flow on the bus. Think about a bidirectional port that receives a device-select pulse from the circuit of Figure 5-13. If the pulse really indicated IN or OUT, the port circuitry would not know if it should latch information found on the bus or activate its outputs and dump information onto the bus lines.

The implication of this leads to the realization that to fully implement a port structure as shown in Figure 5-13, two circuits must be built. One circuit would produce pulses when it was activated by the IN* signal; the other circuit would produce pulses when it was activated by the OUT* signal. Together the two circuits would produce 512 device-select pulses, the maximum possible under isolated I/O.

There is an advantage in letting the port circuitry respond directly to the IN* and OUT* control signals. Consider Figures 5-14(a) and (b). Figures (a) and (b) are set up as unidirectional ports. The circuitry in these ports will either accept information from the CPU, making it an output port, or send information to the CPU, making it an input port. The circuitry of (a) would respond to device-select pulses from a circuit such as the one in Figure 5-13. The pulse not only activates the port, but through the logic of how it was created indicated the direction of data flow on the bus. Remember that a device-select pulse is comprised of a decoded port number and a control signal. Figure (b) is a unidirectional port with two control lines. G2 would be activated upon receiving

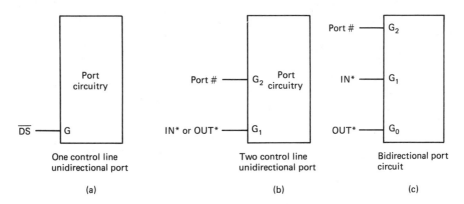

FIGURE 5-14 Typical port architecture.

a decoded port number. G1 would be activated when it received the correct control signal, which could be IN* or OUT* depending on the type of port figure (b) was. The advantage to the situation in Figure (b) is understood when you realize that it allows for the removal of one of the two circuits found in Figure 5-13 that produce the 512 device-select pulses.

When G2 of the 74154 on the left of the circuit (Fig. 5-13) is removed from a control signal and grounded, the circuit changes from a device-select pulse generator to a port decoder. The information out of the circuit in Figure 5-13 no longer indicates direction of data flow on the bus. The G2 strobe of 5-14(b) is now connected to the output of the port decoder. When G1 of Figure 5-14(b) is pulled low by the control signal, the port responds. Thus, by grounding one line and wiring a control signal so it reaches every port, the 17 ICs of Figure 5-13 needed to create a second 256 device-select pulses are eliminated.

Figure 5-14(c) depicts a bidirectional port that has three control inputs. The first input, G2, is activated when it receives the decoded port number. The two control signals IN* and OUT* are connected to G1 and G0 respectively. If either are asserted when the port strobe is active, the port will respond, either placing data on the bus or taking data from the bus.

The circuit shown in Figure 5-15 indicates how a bidirectional port might be set up. The 7430 NAND gate is wired with inverters on the inputs to produce a low out only when it receives 54 hex. The 7430 is acting as the port decoder. The outputs of the OR gates are the actual device-select pulses. The top OR gate is wired to the OUT* control signal. The output of this gate can be low only when the port decoder outputs a low when the control signal is low. The bottom OR gate generates the device-select pulse needed for input operations.

Two last points before we close the discussion on port decoding circuitry. First, do not think that the 74154 is the only decoder used for port decoding. A 74155 wired as a 3-line to 8-line decoder can also be used. In fact, this is an assignment at the end of the chapter. Second, when a port decoder produces many decoded addresses, it is likely to be a part of the central computer, probably located on the mother board. When a port decoder produces a single unique pulse, such as the decoder in Figure 5-15, it is likely to be on the controller card. See Figure 5-3 to visualize this.

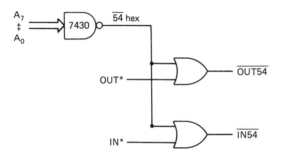

FIGURE 5-15 Device-select decoder.

5-5 MEMORY-MAPPED I/O

In a memory-mapped system, every device or chip attached to the I/O bus is treated as if it were a memory location. Therefore, memory chips, I/O ports, and interface chips are all wired to the computer bus as if they were memory. This design philosophy is used by such processor chips as the 6502 and the 6800.

The 8080, 8085, and Z80 are designed around a general-purpose register set with the bulk of I/O operations handled by isolated I/O. These processors can also be wired to support memory-mapped operations. The techniques used in memory-mapped operations, and the advantages and disadvantages of doing so, will be discussed in this section.

Memory-Mapped Considerations

When a memory operation occurs, the contents of the program counter or another memory pointer are placed on the address bus. This address is a full 16 bits wide. This means that a total of 65,536 addresses are available. This is much larger than the 256 addresses that are available when using isolated I/O. At first this seems like a tremendous advantage for memory-mapped operations. At closer look, this advantage is not as important as it seems; in fact, there are some drawbacks.

From our previous discussion on isolated I/O we learned that many typical computer systems do not need a large port structure. This means that isolated I/O is satisfactory for many computer systems when performing I/O operations. If 256 addresses are plenty, then 65,536 is overkill. This is a minor point. What follows next is not.

Every time a memory address is reserved for a memory-mapped I/O port, one less cell can be addressed in the memory system. As we know, the computer chip should control the I/O bus so only one device or chip at a time is using the common lines. Since a memory-mapped port will be treated as if it were memory, the memory control signals will be used to activate the port. Should a memory chip be wired with the same address as the memory-mapped port, both would turn on when the memory control signals were asserted. This would load down the bus lines, garble information, and possibly damage some of the components attached to the bus. Should we decide to create memory-mapped ports for the processors we are studying, we must sacrifice some memory locations for this function.

Decoding is a second area of concern. In isolated I/O it was possible to absolutely decode a port address using just eight lines. In a memory-mapped system, it will be necessary to use 16 lines when absolutely decoding. Of course, we could always build partial address decoders, as we did in isolated I/O. Say we elect to use four lines to construct a decoder. In isolated I/O that leaves four lines as "don't cares." In memory-mapped I/O that leaves 12 lines as "don't cares." In the isolated I/O situation, there are 16 sets of port numbers that will produce the same results. In the memory-mapped situation, there are 4096 sets of port numbers that would activate the decoder. These values were calculated by taking the numbers of "don't cares" and using them as a power of base 2. The end result is that large blocks of memory become unusable, as memory, when partial decoding is used to wire memory-mapped ports. The discussion on linear decoding that follows will make this clearer.

At one time, before many of the processors came with fully expanded memory systems, it was popular to use A15 as a control signal to differentiate between memory operations and memory-mapped I/O operations. If A15 was low, then a memory operation was in progress. If A15 was high, then a memory-mapped I/O operation was in progress. The use of this single line divided the memory map into two blocks of 32K. The upper 32K were reserved for memory-mapped operations, while the lower 32K were reserved for memory. The use of this single line as a control signal caused 32K to be removed from regular memory! Choosing another address line as the control signal would not have improved the situation. Suppose AO had been chosen: AO low—memory operation; AO high—memory-mapped operation. Now all 32K even locations are reserved for memory, while 32K odd cells are reserved for memory mapping. We have the same situation as before, but now programs can not be stored in contiguous locations. Since the processor increments the program counter by 1, this fails to satisfy the architecture requirements of the CPU.

From the preceding discussion you should be wary of partial and linear decoding when using memory-mapped I/O. The more lines used, the better. It is also very important to know the memory map. It is vital that memory-mapped ports be located in holes, with the port address decoded sufficiently to avoid any interference with normal memory operations. We will pursue these points when we investigate memory address decoders.

So far, it seems that the one advantage listed is a two-edged sword. What, then, makes memory mapping a viable consideration when using the 8080, 8085, and Z80? In isolated I/O the only register that can access the bus was the accumulator. This was pointed out when we discussed the software problems that can arise when preparing the accumulator for I/O. Table 5-1 indicates instructions that interact with memory. If an I/O port was memory-mapped, it would be possible to send information to and from any register to that port. MOV B,M would load information into the B register from a memory-mapped port. This is just one possibility with the list shown in Table 5-1.

This eliminates the bottleneck that developed when only the A register could gain access to the bus. The additional instructions also give the programmer greater flexibility in register usage and program layout.

The advantage gained is not as significant when the Z80 is used as it is when the 8080 and 8085 are used. The Z80 has two instructions—IN r,(C) and OUT(C),r—that allow the processor to transfer registers to the bus using the IO/W and IO/R control signals. In these instructions, the register specified is moved into or out of the CPU while a port address taken from the C register is placed on the lower address bus.

Memory Machine Cycles

To help solidify the discussion on memory-mapped I/O we will look at the machine cycles used by the 8085 to perform memory operations. Later in the text, when regular memory operations are discussed, the Z80 memory machine cycles will be discussed.

TABLE 5-1   Instructions Usable for
Memory-Mapped Transfers

MOV B, M	MOV C, M
MOV D, M	MOV E, M
MOV H, M	MOV L, M
MOV A, M	MOV M, B
MOV M, C	MOV M, D
MOV M, E	MOV M, H
MOV M, L	MOV M, A
STAX B	STAX D
LDAX B	LDAX D
ADD M	ADC M
SUB M	SBB M
ANA M	XRA M
ORA M	CMP M
INR M	DCR M
MVI M	
STA	LDA
SHLD	LHLD

The memory-read machine cycle used by the 8085 is shown in Figure 5-16. This machine cycle takes three clock cycles to complete, unless wait states are added at the request of external circuitry. During T_1, the 8085 pulls the status line IO/M low to indicate that a memory read is in progress. If this line were left high, the 8085 would be performing an IO/R, equivalent to the IN machine cycle performed by the 8080 which has already been explained. The other two status lines, S1 and S0, are equal to 1 and 0 respectively. The high-order address bus information is placed onto the bus and held constant throughout the rest of the machine cycle. The data bus is used to handle the low-order half of the address during T_1. The address latch enable is asserted high, signaling an external latch to capture this information. At T_2, the address bus has a complete address because the latching operation was complete by the end of T_1. This frees up the data bus for data transfers. The read pulse goes low, indicating that the bus is now ready to accept inputted information. The external device responds to this pulse by placing the information onto the bus. The inputted information is then gated to the part of the CPU indicated by the op code currently in the instruction register.

The timing diagram for a memory-write machine cycle as performed by the 8085

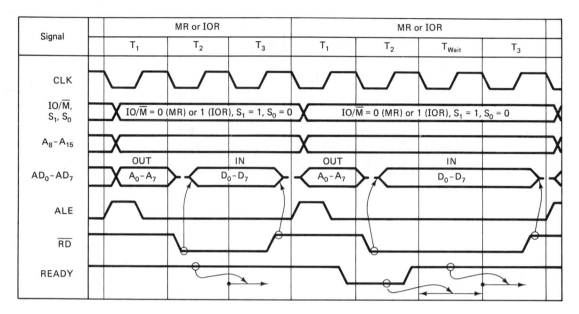

FIGURE 5-16   8085 memory-read machine cycle. (Courtesy of Intel Corporation.)

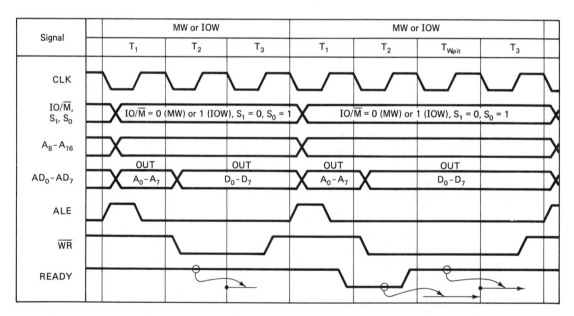

FIGURE 5-17   8085 memory-write machine cycle. (Courtesy of Intel Corporation.)

is shown in Figure 5-17. T_1, with the exception of the status lines S1 and S0, is identical to the timing used in the memory-read cycle just explained. The logic levels on S1 and S0 are now 0 and 1 respectively. At the start of T_2, the write pulse is asserted. This signals the external device that the CPU has placed valid information onto the bus. This signal therefore can be used to strobe the external device so it can capture the information on the bus.

Memory-Mapped Circuitry

The function of the memory-mapped decoder is to produce a decoded address or address-select pulse. When working with memory-mapped ports, we use address-select pulse rather than device-select pulse. An *address-select pulse* is the combination of a decoded address and a control signal used in memory machine cycles.

Figure 5-18 shows a circuit that should look very familiar. The 74154 is still used to decode the low-order nibble from the address bus. This will produce 16 different address-select pulses when the decoder is activated. This time, the strobes are controlled by a MEMW* pulse and A15. When A15 is high, a memory-mapped I/O operation is underway. This decoder sets up the situation that was described earlier, when we explained how A15 could be used as a control signal. The upper 32K of memory has been reserved for memory-mapped I/O. The decoder is partially decoding the address, so a lot of ambiguities will exist in the upper 32K of memory.

The circuit of Figure 5-19(a) shows a decoder that uses more than just A15 to indicate memory-mapped operations. Here the high-order nibble of the address bus is driving the inputs of a NAND gate which controls G2 on the decoder. G1 is activated

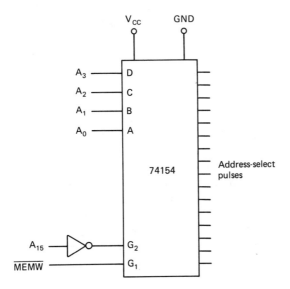

FIGURE 5-18 Memory-mapped decoder, active when $A_{15} = 1$.

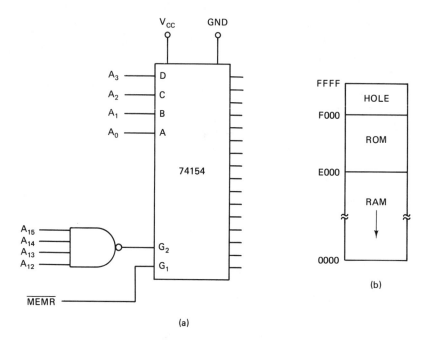

FIGURE 5-19   Memory-mapped decoder, active with high nibble = F.

when the MEMR* signal is low. A corresponding memory map for this situation is found in Figure 5-19(b). Since the high-order nibble was used, the hole in the memory map is now set aside for memory-mapped operations. This hole is a block of 4096 bytes. The greater number of lines in the decoder reduces the amount of memory lost to memory-mapped operations.

A Short Program Example

The program listing of Example 5-1 will activate the circuit of Figure 5-20.

   The objective here is to transfer the information in the B register to the memory-mapped port located at F0 04 hex. The first instruction in the program loads the value to be transferred into the B register. The H register pair is then set to point to address F0 04. The MOV M,B instruction will cause the processor to perform a memory-write machine cycle. This cycle will activate the control signals needed to turn on the decoder. When the decoder is selected, the output line marked 4 will go low. This will turn on the 8-bit latch connected to the data bus. The processor will then send the contents of the B register to the bus, where the activated latch captures the information. Refer back to the memory-write machine cycle waveforms to see the timing sequence.

EXAMPLE 5-1

Hex Address	Hex Op Code	Mnemonic	Comments	Octal Address	Octal Op Code
03 00	06	MVIB	This program	003 000	006
01		05		001	
02	21	LXIH	will activate the decoder	002	041
03		04		003	
04		FO		004	
05	70	MOV M, B	in Figure 5-20	005	160
06	76	HLT		006	166

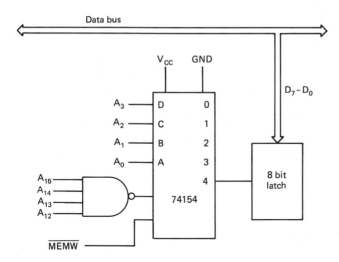

FIGURE 5-20 An output port.

5-6 USING SELECT PULSES AS CONTROL PULSES

In the preceding discussions involving memory-mapped I/O and isolated I/O, we analyzed machine cycles that transferred information to and from ports under the control of the CPU. If we ignore any transferred data, then the pulses we have been discussing can be used for control of devices hooked up to the computer.

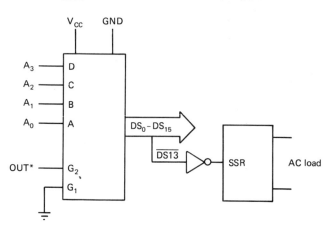

FIGURE 5-21 Control-pulse generation.

Consider the situation depicted in Figure 5-21. Here we have a circuit that will generate device-select pulses when OUT machine cycles are performed using port number 0 through 15. Example 5-2 shows an OUT instruction, part of a larger program, that uses port OD hex. Notice that the information in the A register is not indicated. This is because the contents of the A register are immaterial to this situation. The device attached to the port does not have the capability of receiving digital information. In fact, the data lines are not even wired to this port. The sole purpose of the OUT instruction is to generate a device-select pulse at the appropriate output pin. This pulse is then inverted and applied to the input side of a solid-state relay. The pulse activates the relay, which then closes its output contacts, activating the AC load. The computer still sent the A register information onto the bus, but since there was nothing connected to D7–D0 that was activated, this information appeared briefly and was not latched by any device connected to the bus.

What happens to the contents of the A register when the OUT instruction is used like this? Nothing. A copy of the accumulator is placed onto the bus, but the internal

EXAMPLE 5-2

HEX ADDRESS	HEX OP CODE	MNEMONIC	COMMENTS	OCTAL ADDRESS	OCTAL OP CODE
		OUT	Activate part 13 (dec) and		
		OD	turn on device		

value of A is undisturbed. If we had generated a device-select pulse with an IN instruction simply to activate some circuitry, there would have been a problem. The IN instruction indicates that the processor expects information to be placed onto the bus. The circuit of Figure 5-21 is not capable of doing this. Consequently, the bus information is undetermined when the processor is in the input mode. The value of A would be erased by random information. If the bus lines are pulled up to Vcc by resistors, then the contents of the A register would have been overwritten by FF hex. So when using device-select pulses as control lines, use the OUT instruction to generate the correct signals.

Figure 5-21 should generate some questions in your mind about interfacing analog devices to the computer bus and about solid-state relays. These questions will be answered later in the text.

5-7 THE 8212

The 8212 is an 8-bit input/output port that is capable of latching information off the data bus or placing data onto the bus. The outputs of the 8212 are tristate so interfacing to a computer bus is possible. Control lines are available for the CPU to direct information into or out of the 8212 when the appropriate machine cycles are generated.

The internal logic of the 8212 is shown in Figure 5-22(a). There are 8 D latches available. This makes the 8212 compatible with the data buses we are learning. The outputs of the latches are isolated by eight tristate buffer/drivers. The buffer/drivers provide isolation when tristated and current driver capability when active. They are controlled from an internal enable line that responds to combinations of input control signals.

The control signals into the 8212 number 4. They are the mode, labeled MD; the strobe, labeled STB; device select 1, labeled DS1*; and device select 2, labeled DS2. The function table in Figure 5-22(c) shows how these signals affect the operation of the 8212. There is also an additional clear line labeled CLR* that will zero out the latch.

To get the 8212 to latch information on its inputs, the common clock line must be activated. This clock line is driven by an internal OR gate. The OR gate's inputs in turn are driven by the outputs of two internal AND gates, which accept information from the MD and STB and the device-select AND gate.

When DS1* is active low and DS2 is high, the 8212 is selected and the output buffers are enabled. The clock to the 8212 D latches will then be controlled by the MD. Should the mode be high, the top AND gate will produce a high when the device is selected. If this is the case, the 8212 will immediately pass the information on its inputs through the output buffers. If the mode is low, then clocking pulses to the D latches will come through the lower AND gate. When the STB goes high, the information on the inputs will pass directly through the tristate buffers when the device select AND gate is active.

When the 8212 is not selected it is still possible to control the outputs from the

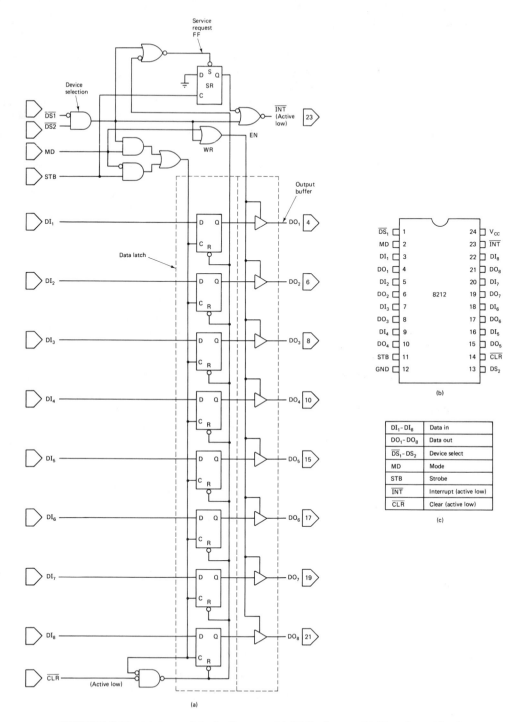

$\overline{DS}_1$	1	24	V_{CC}
MD	2	23	$\overline{INT}$
DI_1	3	22	DI_8
DO_1	4	21	DO_8
DI_2	5	20	DI_7
DO_2	6	19	DO_7
DI_3	7	18	DI_6
DO_3	8	17	DO_6
DI_4	9	16	DI_5
DO_4	10	15	DO_5
STB	11	14	$\overline{CLR}$
GND	12	13	DS_2

(b)

DI_1 – DI_8	Data in
DO_1 – DO_8	Data out
$\overline{DS}_1$ – DS_2	Device select
MD	Mode
STB	Strobe
$\overline{INT}$	Interrupt (active low)
$\overline{CLR}$	Clear (active low)

(c)

FIGURE 5-22 (a) Internal logic diagram. (b) 8212 pin out. (c) Function table. [(a), (b), and (c) courtesy of Intel Corporation.]

174

MD setting. If the MD is high, it will pass this status through the internal OR gate controlling the enable line. If the mode is not asserted, and the 8212 is not selected, the outputs will remain in the tristate condition.

As you can see, there is a set-reset flip-flop available for use inside the 8212. This flip-flop is very useful when the 8212 is connected as an interrupting port. This function will be discussed in the chapter on interrupts.

The circuit of Figure 5-23 shows one way in which the 8212 could be wired as a data latch. DS1* is grounded and DS2 is tied high by connecting it to Vcc. This means that the outputs of the 8212 are always on, presenting whatever information they have latched to the circuitry attached to the 8212's outputs. The mode is grounded. The top AND gate feeding the OR gate controlling the internal clock line of the 8212 is disabled. This means that the clock can only be generated from an STB pulse. The STB line is attached to an inverter. The inverter in turn is connected to a device-select pulse generator, such as the one shown in Figure 5-20. When the computer chip executes an OUT to port 04, the 8212 will be clocked and latch the information that it finds on the data bus. This information will be held at the 8212's outputs until the CPU generates another DS04* writing new information into the latch.

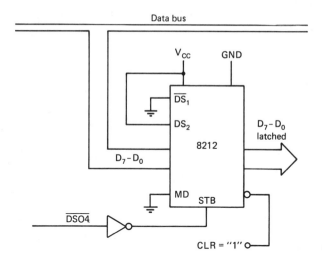

FIGURE 5-23 8212 output port = data latch.

The 8085 has a multiplexed data bus. The low-order address byte shares the data lines. This has been pointed out several times. See the 8085 memory machine cycle waveforms in this chapter for a quick review. The diagram of Figure 5-24 shows how the 8212 can be used to latch the low-order address byte at the correct time. In this schematic, the mode is tied high. Therefore, the output side of the 8212 is always on. The STB and CLR lines are tied high and have no real function in this circuit. With the mode tied high, the device-select AND gate determines when a clock will be delivered to the latches inside the 8212. DS1* is tied to ground, making DS2 the controlling input.

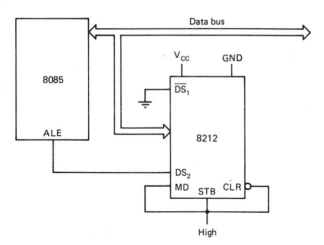

FIGURE 5-24 8085 low-order address latch.

At T1, the 8085 places the low-order byte of the address onto the data bus. At the same time ALE, address latch enable, goes high. When this signal goes high the 8212 is selected and the low address byte enters the latch. At T2 and T3 the ALE signal is low. This means that the low-order address byte will be held constant throughout the machine cycle even though the information on the data bus is changing.

The next 8212 circuit is Figure 5-25. Here the 8212 is wired as an input port. The clock to the latches is active at all times by tying the mode low and the strobe high. This means that whatever is placed on the D inputs of the latch immediately appears at the outputs of the D latches. At this point the information is blocked by the deactivated tristate buffers. When the computer is ready to accept information onto the data bus, it

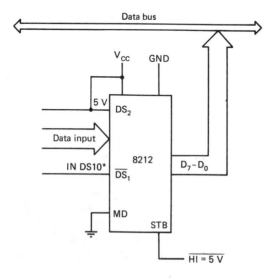

FIGURE 5-25 8212 input port.

generates a device-select pulse labeled INDS 10*. An IN instruction with a port number of 10 will activate this pulse. Since it is connected to DS1* and the 8212 already has DS2 tied high, the 8212 will be selected. This activates the buffers, and the information from the latches will be placed on the data bus.

5-8 THE 8255

The 8255 is a programmable peripheral interface chip. Like the 8212, it was designed to interface between a bus system and chips and devices that were not designed to interface to a computer bus. Like the 8253 programmable interval timer that was used in Chapter 4 to produce hardware timing functions, it is programmable. This gives the 8255 user a great deal of flexibility when it comes to interfacing. The 8255 system interface is very similar to the system interface found in the 8253.

The internal block diagram of the 8255 can be found in Figure 5-26(a). This chip has a bidirectional data bus buffer, which means that it can act as an input and an output port. The direction of data flow is determined by the read/write control-logic section. This section has six control inputs. The first two, RD* and WR*, determine the direction of data flow. Despite their names, these pins can be wired to IN* and OUT* or MEMRD* and MEMWR*. This means that the 8255 can be wired to respond to isolated I/O or memory-mapped I/O.

A1 and A0 are connected directly to A1 and A0 on the address bus. These lines select which of the sections of the 8255 will respond to the various commands sent to the chip by the computer. The 8253 had this feature also. The reset pin resets the 8255 to a default condition. This condition will be explained shortly. It is common to tie this line to the system reset. In the event that system reset is active low, an inverter must be inserted between the system reset and the 8255 reset. The last control line is CS*. The RD*, WR*, A1, and A0 lines will be ignored if CS* is high. Additionally, the data bus buffer will be in the tristate condition. No information can flow into or out of the 8255 unless chip select is low.

The 8255 has three ports, labeled A, B, and C. They can be configured as input or output ports depending on the control words sent to the 8255. Each of the ports is 8 bits wide, although port C can be divided into two 4-bit groups called port C upper and port C lower.

The way in which the ports are used is determined by the sections labeled control group A and control group B. Group A comprises port A and port C upper. Group B comprises port B and port C lower. The ports can be used in three ways: mode 0, mode 1, and mode 2.

Mode 0 is basic input/output. We will investigate two ways in which to use mode 0 in this chapter. The first is unconditional data transfer. In this situation the CPU does not bother to determine the status of the 8255. When the CPU is ready to transfer data, it does so without examining what is happening inside the 8255. The second mode 0 technique uses software programs that check the status of the 8255. This is referred to as status-driven I/O. The status of the 8255 and the devices it interfaces are determined

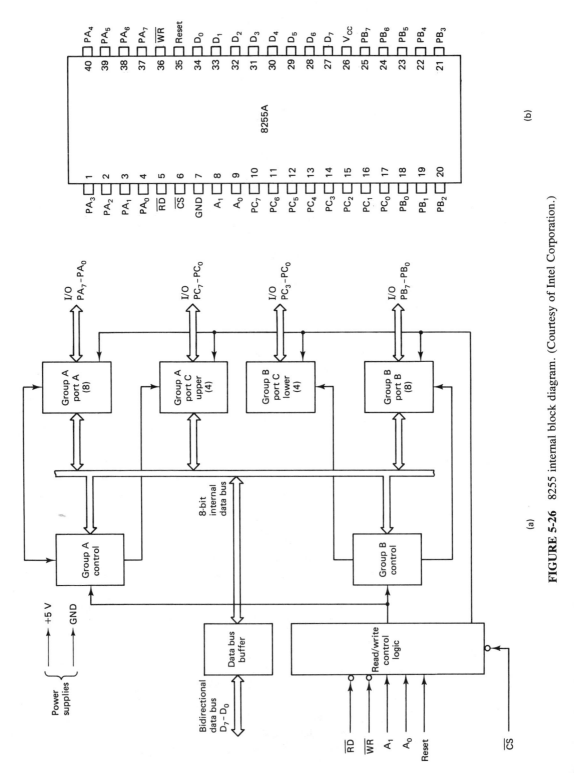

FIGURE 5-26 8255 internal block diagram. (Courtesy of Intel Corporation.)

(a)

(b)

178

through the use of handshaking signals that indicate what conditions or operations are present in the circuitry.

Mode 1 operation is interrupt-driven I/O. This mode of operation will be used in the chapter on interrupts, and will be explained in that chapter.

Mode 2 is used for bidirectional data transfer through port A. This mode of operation is used frequently in the control of sophisticated peripherals where the 8255 acts as an interface between the computer and such devices as a disk drive. Mode 2 will not be discussed in the text.

Programming the 8255

When the 8255 is reset, the control register and the three ports are cleared. At the same time, the ports are placed in the input mode. To alter this situation, the 8255 must be programmed; this is done by sending control words to the 8255 which configure the ports in the desired manner. These control words are unidirectional. The CPU can send information to this register, but cannot read its contents.

A typical 8255 system interface is shown in Figure 5-27. The data bus is connected to the 8255 bidirectional bus buffer. The reset function is taken from an inverter, which is connected to system reset. The IN* and OUT* lines drive the RD* and WR* pins. Chip select is single-line decoded from A7. This makes the ports appear as:

BUS PORT	8255 PORT
80	port A
81	port B
82	port C
83	control register

This correspondence holds only for the 8255 as wired in Figure 5-27.

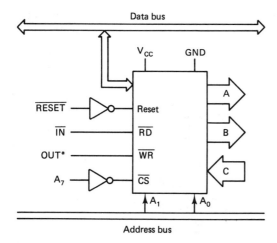

FIGURE 5-27 8255 system interface.

We will set up mode 0 operation for the 8255 with ports A and B configured as output ports, while port C is configured as an input port. In mode 0 operation, output ports are latched but input ports are not. This means that information input to a port in mode 0 must be held by the device connected to the 8255 until the CPU has read it. If not, information might be lost.

The first thing that must be done prior to using the ports is to program the 8255 control register. The control-register format is indicated in Figure 5-28. The first bit, D7, determines the type of control word being sent to the 8255. Since we are interested in establishing mode 0, this bit will be set high. D6 and D5 determine the mode of operation for group A. Notice that port C upper must have the same mode of operation as port A. Mode 0 being our objective, D6 and D5 are set to 00. D4 determines if port A will be an input or output port. We have decided that it will be an output port. D4 is set to 0. D3 controls port C upper. In our example, port C is being used as an 8-bit input port. At this time, we will set port C upper to input by setting D3. We must remember to set port C lower the same way, since we are treating it as an 8-bit port.

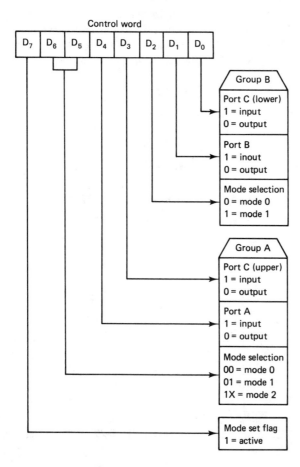

FIGURE 5-28 8255 mode definition format. (Courtesy of Intel Corporation.)

Group B is controlled by bits D2, D1, and D0. This group cannot be placed in mode 2 operation. This means that a single bit can be used to select the mode of operation. D2 will be reset, placing group B in mode 0 operation. Port B was designated as an output port by the schematic of Figure 5-27. D1 will be reset to meet this condition. Finally, port C lower will be made into an input port by setting D0. Collecting our bits, we assemble a binary 10001001, which is 89 hex. This information must be sent to the 8255 via port 83.

Example 5-3 shows a program that establishes the conditions required by the circuit in Figure 5-27. The control word is formatted and placed in the A register, which is then transferred to the 8255 control register via port 83. The program then enters a loop, checking to see if the input to port C matches a code specified by the CPI instruction at lines 06 and 07. If a match is not found, the program will continue to loop, polling port C. Once a match has been found, the JNZ instruction is ignored and control passes to the OUT instruction at line 0B. This instruction will simply echo back to the 8255 the valid code input from port C. This could be used to tell the person entering the code at port C that his information has been accepted. Then a control code is sent to initiate an operation by sending a 05 to port B via port 81.

This program illustrates how to initialize the 8255 mode word plus how to communicate with each of the ports. Additionally, the output ports were not sent information until port C sent the correct code to the CPU. This is an example of conditional data transfer that we will expand on next.

Status-Driven I/O

The way in which port C was used in the preceding example did not use all the flexibility available in the 8255. It is true that port C was used to determine if a data transfer should occur. This is certainly preferable to unconditional data transfers, but port C was used as a single 8-bit input port. As we will see in this section on status-driven I/O, it is often convenient to use port C as two nibble ports, where each individual line can be controlled or monitored through the programming features of the 8255.

There is a second type of control word that the 8255 will accept. This is the *set/reset control word*. The format for this kind of control word is pictured in Figure 5-29. The first bit tells the 8255 what type of control word it is receiving. Since we are now interested in the set/reset control word, D7 will be low. The next three bits positions are "don't cares." It is customary to take "don't cares" to logic 0. D3, D2, and D1 form a binary counter that specifies which of the eight pins of port C will be affected by this control word. The correspondence between the counter and the pin mnemonic is straightforward. Count 0 affects pin 0, count 1 affects pin 1, and so on. The last bit, D0, determines the status of the pin selected. If D0 is set, then the pin selected will be set. A reset D0 will clear the pin selected.

This control word is sent to the same control register as the other type of control word. The leading bit lets the 8255 know which control word it is receiving; consequently, no additional ports are needed, so A1 and A0 are sufficient to direct information into and out of the 8255. We are now in a position to control individual bits in port C.

EXAMPLE 5-3

HEX ADDRESS	HEX OP CODE	MNEMONIC	COMMENTS	OCTAL ADDRESS	OCTAL OP CODE
03 00	3E	MVI A		003 000	076
03 01	89		8255 control word	003 001	
03 02	D3	OUT	Send control word	003 002	323
03 03	83			003 003	
03 04	DB	IN	Monitor port C	003 004	333
03 05	82			003 005	
03 06	FE	CPI		003 006	376
03 07	02			003 007	
03 08	C2	JNZ		003 010	302
03 09	04			003 011	
03 0A	03			003 012	
03 0B	D3	OUT		003 013	323
03 0C	80			003 014	
03 0D	3E	MVI A		003 015	076
03 0E	05			003 016	
03 0F	D3	OUT		003 017	323
03 10	81			003 020	
03 11	76	HLT		003 021	166

These bits, when set to an output condition, can be used to control devices interfaced to the 8255. At the same time, we can monitor individual bits from port C through masking, as explained in Chapter 2.

With this as a background, let's take a look at a project that uses a lot of what we have learned about digital interfacing, the 8255, and, from Chapter 4, the 8253.

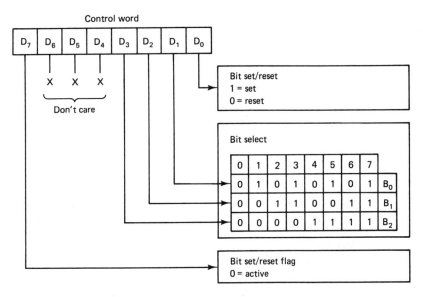

FIGURE 5-29   8255 bit set/reset format. (Courtesy of Intel Corporation.)

5-9 DATE CODE STAMP PROJECT

The computer has been assigned the task of monitoring two products as they come down a conveyor belt. The two products must be stamped with expiration dates. They are not to be sold after the expiration date. The computer will determine which product has passed a sensor by reading a bar code. Once the computer knows which product has passed the sensor, it will select the proper date code and stamp the product. The interface for the sensor, the bar code input, the date code output, the conveyor control, and the stamp control will be handled by an 8255.

The 8255 will be configured for mode 0 operation as detailed in the Layout Sheet 5-1. The mode control word will be 91 hex. Individual bits of port C will be used to activate and deactivate circuitry attached to the interface. In some cases, the connection is direct, as in the date stamp latch. In other cases, such as the conveyor control, the 8255 output will drive a relay. The system interface will be the same as shown in Figure 5-27. Once again, the 8255 will respond to ports 80 through 83.

An 8253 will be used as a shift timer. At the beginning of the day, counter 0 will be loaded with the number 8. Mode 5 will be used. The counter's clock will be driven by a one-hour TTL waveform. This counter will not begin counting until it receives a rising edge on the gate control. The gate control will be connected to PC6 of the 8255. Once the conveyor is turned on, the count sequence can begin. The computer will monitor the 8253 count value by latching and reading the value each time through the program. When the shift is over, the counter will have reached terminal count and the conveyor will be shut off.

Layout Sheet 5-1

DATE STAMP PROJECT LAYOUT SHEET

OBJECTIVE:

To monitor products traveling down a conveyor belt and stamp them with the correct expiration date

HARDWARE ENVIRONMENT:

8080-based CPU
Isolated I/O

Support Chips:

1. 8255 — single line decoded from A7 — mode 0 all ports
   port A — input — product code
   port B — output — expiration date
   port C lower — input — sensing
   port C upper — control
2. 8253 — single line decoded from A6
   counter 0 — mode 5 — 8-hour shift timer

SOFTWARE ENVIRONMENT

Memory Allocation:

1. main program — 03 00
2. time delay — system-dependent location
3. stack — 20 00

Register Allocation:

A — I/O — control word formatting

Port Allocations:

40 — 8253 counter 0
43 — 8253 control register
80 — 8255 port A
81 — 8255 port B
82 — 8255 port C
83 — 8255 control register

Layout Sheet 5-1 (*continued*)

Special Codes:

91 — 8255 control word
1A — 8253 control word
0D — turn conveyor on
0C — turn conveyor off
09 — transfer date to stamp
0B — stamp product
0A — release stamp

HARDWARE/SOFTWARE INTERFACE:

8255
PCO — set — box sensed
PC4 — stamp latch, 1 — latch; 0 — off
PC5 — stamp control, 1 — on; 0 — off
PC6 — conveyor control, 1 — on; 0 — off

The 8253 will be connected as shown in Figure 4-9, with the exception that chip select will be driven by A6. This means that the 8253 will respond to ports 40 through 43.

The flowchart for the project is located in Figure 5-30. Study the logic before proceeding to the code. It will give you an overall picture that will help in the code explanation that follows.

Example 5-4 begins with line 03 00, where a stack is set up. The next two instructions initialize the 8255 as indicated in the project layout sheet. This is followed by the initialization of the 8253 and the loading of counter 0 with the number 8. Up to this point there have been examples given on how to perform these functions. Verify the control words by using the documentation provided on the 8255 and 8253.

Line 03 0F begins a sequence that sets PC6 turning on the conveyor belt. The control word begins with a 0, indicating a set/reset control word. The binary counter and the last bit of the control word indicate that PC6 is to be set. The output from this pin will drive a relay, which in turn controls the power to the conveyor belt.

Lines 03 13 through 03 19 poll the sensor looking for a box. Remember that input ports are not latched in mode 0 operation. This means that after a box has passed the sensor, the input bit will not remain set. The masking operation at 03 15 is checking to see if PCO is set. If so, a box has been detected.

Once a box has been detected, the computer will activate port A on the 8255 to obtain the product code. This port is status driven in that it will not be activated until the correct status is seen at PCO.

The CPI at 03 1C checks for the kind of box detected. This code, along with the JNZ at 03 1E, selects the proper expiration code for the box just detected. The date code is sent to port B of the 8255 at line 03 29. The date code is then transferred to the stamp

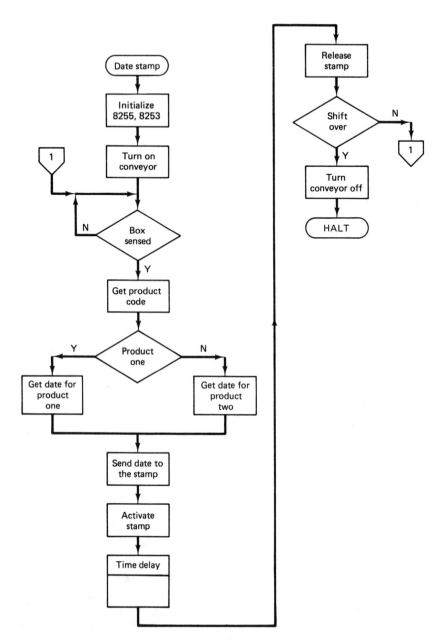

FIGURE 5-30 Flowchart for data stamp project layout sheet.

EXAMPLE 5-4

HEX ADDRESS	HEX OP CODE	MNEMONIC	COMMENTS	OCTAL ADDRESS	OCTAL OP CODE
03 00	31	LXI SP		003 000	061
03 01		00		003 001	
03 02		20		003 002	
03 03	3E	MVI A	8255 control	003 003	076
03 04		91	1001 0001	003 004	
03 05	D3	OUT	Initialize 8255	003 005	323
03 06		83		003 006	
03 07	3E	MVI A	8253 control	003 007	076
03 08		IA	0001 1010	003 010	
03 09	D3	OUT	Initialize 8253	003 011	323
03 0A		43		003 012	
03 0B	3E	MVI A	Load counter 0	003 013	076
03 0C		08		003 014	
03 0D	D3	OUT		003 015	323
03 0E		40		003 016	
03 0F	3E	MVI A	Turn on conveyor	003 017	076
03 10		0D	0000 1101	003 020	
03 11	D3	OUT		003 021	323
03 12		83		003 022	
03 13	DB	IN	Box sensed	003 023	333
03 14		82		003 024	
03 15	EG	ANI		003 025	346
03 16		01		003 026	
03 17	C2	JNZ	If not, check again	003 027	302
03 18		13		003 030	
03 19		03		003 031	

EXAMPLE 5-4 (*continued*)

HEX ADDRESS	HEX OP CODE	MNEMONIC	COMMENTS	OCTAL ADDRESS	OCTAL OP CODE
03 1A	DB	IN	If so, get product code	003 032	333
03 1B		80		003 033	
03 1C	FE	CPI	Product 1?	003 034	376
03 1D		01		003 035	
03 IE	C2	JNZ	If not	003 036	302
03 IF		26		003 037	
03 20		03		003 040	
03 21	3E	MVI A	If so, set date code for	003 041	076
03 22		10	product 1	003 042	
03 23	C3	JMP		003 043	303
03 24		28		003 044	
03 25		03		003 045	
03 26	3E	MVI A	Set date code for product 2	003 046	076
03 27		20		003 047	
03 28	D3	OUT	Transfer date code to port B	003 050	323
03 29		81		003 051	
03 2A	3E	MVI A	Transfer code to stamp	003 052	076
03 2B		09		003 053	
03 2C	D3	OUT		003 054	323
03 2D		83		003 055	
03 2E	3D	DCRA	Deactivate stamp latch	003 056	075
03 2F	D3	OUT		003 057	323
03 30		83		003 060	
03 31	3E	MVI A	Stamp product code	003 061	076
03 32		0B		003 062	
03 33	D3	OUT		003 063	323
03 34		83		003 064	

EXAMPLE 5-4 (*continued*)

HEX ADDRESS	HEX OP CODE	MNEMONIC	COMMENTS	OCTAL ADDRESS	OCTAL OP CODE
03 35	CD	CALL		003 065	315
03 36		LO	Delay till stamping done	003 066	
03 37		HI		003 067	
03 38	3D	DCRA	Release stamp	003 070	075
03 39	D3	OUT		003 071	323
03 3A		83		003 072	
03 3B	3E	MVI A	Latch counter 0	003 073	076
03 3C		00		003 074	
03 3D	D3	OUT		003 075	323
03 3E		43		003 076	
03 3F	DB	IN	Read counters	003 077	333
03 40		40		003 100	
03 41	FE	CPI	Shift over?	003 101	376
03 42		00		003 102	
03 43	C2	JNZ	If not, continue	003 103	302
03 44		013		003 104	
03 45		03		003 105	
03 46	3E	MVI A	If so, turn conveyor off	003 106	076
03 47		OC		003 107	
03 48	D3	OUT		003 110	323
03 49		83		003 111	
03 50	76	HLT		003 112	166

circuitry by pulsing PC4. First PC4 is set by the set/reset control word located at line 03 2C and sent to the 8255 at line 03 2D. The contents of the A register are then decremented. This is a common way of toggling set/reset control words. Decrementing A resets the LSBit in A and leaves the rest of the control word intact. This reset function is then sent to the 8255. The duration of the pulse can be determined by calculating the T states between the set and reset operations. This number can then be multiplied by the master clock period. If the pulse is too short to activate the electronics in the stamp circuitry, a software delay can be inserted into the program. This is not very likely, because pulses delivered through software are limited in frequency by the rate at which the program can be executed. This frequency is almost always lower than an IC input can handle.

The date is actually stamped by setting PC5 at lines 03 31 to 03 34. Since the stamp is a mechanical device, the computer must wait for it to finish stamping before turning off. A software delay is called at 03 35. The address of the time delay is immaterial to this discussion and was not designated. The length of the delay, though, should be tailored to the speed of the stamping process.

Line 03 38 deactivates the stamp by decrementing the control word, which resets PC5 when it is sent to the 8255.

At line 03 39 the value in counter 0 is latched, using a latch control word. Once latched, the information is transferred into the CPU, where it checks to see if the counter has timed out. If not, the program resumes checking for boxes. If so, the conveyor is shut off by resetting PC6, after which the program is terminated.

5-10 DATA COMMUNICATIONS

In the previous sections of this chapter we dealt with interfacing techniques where data was moved from one part of a computer system to another in parallel. Parallel interfacing can be defined as an operation in which a group of bits moves over several lines at the same time. In our case, the group of bits was equal to 8; consequently, the data bus was 8 bits wide. In this mode of transmission, each bit traveled over its own wire. Computers and digital systems that are close to each other use this mode of transmission.

In a data communication system the primary method of data transfer is over a serial interface. Usually the distance the data must travel between source and destination is significantly longer than the distance information is moved within a computer. Consequently, methods that eliminate the need for multiple data lines become important enough for us to investigate. In this section we will look at an overview of a data communication system and the way in which serial interfacing is used within such a system.

Organization of a Data Communication System

The block diagram of Figure 5-31 shows how a data communication system can be implemented. The system consists of a data source, referred to as *data terminal equipment* (*DTE* hereafter), an interface between the source and the *data communication*

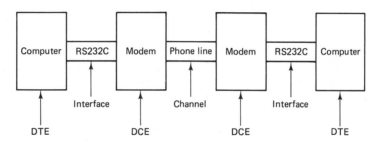

FIGURE 5-31 A typical data communications link.

equipment (*DCE* hereafter), the DCE that converts the data to a form suitable for transmission over the channel, a DCE at the receiving end that converts information back into a form suitable for the computer circuitry, and an interface between the DCE at the receiving end and the DTE receiver, usually another computer.

The DTE-DCE Interface

The most common interface between data terminal and data communication equipment is the RS-232C standard. Figure 5-32 shows the pin placements on a typical RS-232C female connector. A brief discussion of each of the lines follows.

Pins 1 and 7 are ground pins. Pin 1 is connected to the chassis of the equipment and should be connected at just one end of the interface. It will act as a shield ground when shielded cabling is used. Pin 7 is the common reference for all signals including data, timing, and control pulses. Pin 7 must be connected at both the DCE and DTE ends of the line for proper operations.

Pins 2 and 3 are used for transmitted data and received data. Pin 2 is the TD pin and pin 3 is the RD pin. You should be aware that the names are given to these lines from the point of view of the DTE. This means that the DTE places information to be transmitted to the DCE on pin 2. The DTE will receive data from the DCE on pin 3. Therefore, the DCE must transmit on pin 3 while receiving data from the DTE on pin 2.

Pin 4 is request to send (RTS) and pin 5 is clear to send (CTS). A DTE should query the DCE to see if it is ready to receive data. This can be accomplished by transmitting a request to send. The DTE should then wait until it receives a CTS before transmitting data.

Pin 6 and pin 20 are functionally grouped. Pin 6 is data set ready (DSR) and pin 20 is data terminal ready (DTR). The DSR signal is a status line that indicates that the DCE is powered and not in the test mode. In dial-data applications, the DTR signal can be used as an off-hook condition.

Pin 8 is designated DCD for data carrier detect. When a modem is functioning as the DCE it will assert this line when a signal on the telephone line is detected that meets

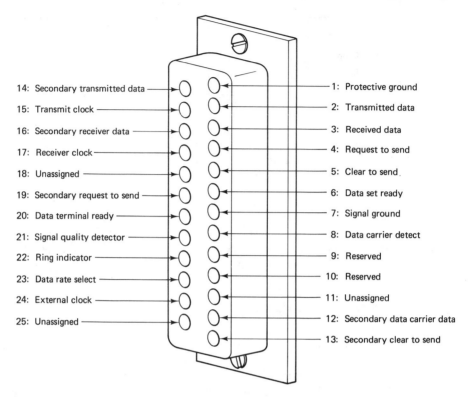

14: Secondary transmitted data
15: Transmit clock
16: Secondary receiver data
17: Receiver clock
18: Unassigned
19: Secondary request to send
20: Data terminal ready
21: Signal quality detector
22: Ring indicator
23: Data rate select
24: External clock
25: Unassigned

1: Protective ground
2: Transmitted data
3: Received data
4: Request to send
5: Clear to send
6: Data set ready
7: Signal ground
8: Data carrier detect
9: Reserved
10: Reserved
11: Unassigned
12: Secondary data carrier data
13: Secondary clear to send

FIGURE 5-32   A typical RS-232C female connector.

the conditions the modem circuitry can interpret as valid information. In other applications this pin will be jumpered to pin 20.

Pins 15, 17, 21, and 24 are used for synchronous data transmissions. In synchronous operations the transmitting modem must transmit a logic 1 or logic 0 at each bit time. The modem must then control the timing of the bits from the DTE. Pin 15—transmitter signal element timing—and pin 17—receiver signal element timing—are used for these purposes. In cases where the modem does not control the timing, pin 24 is used. Pin 21 is a status line that indicates the received information meets some quality criterion. It is called signal quality detector.

Pin 22 is the ring indicator. This pin can be used by the DCE to inform the DTE that the phone is ringing.

The remaining pins can be used if the DCE is equipped to transmit and receive information on a secondary channel at the same time data is being transferred over the pins already discussed. They have the same functions as the primary pins discussed and can be found in Figure 5-32. The pin numbers are 12, 13, 14, 16, and 19.

Serial Interfacing

From the discussion of the RS-232C standard, it should be obvious that there are not eight data lines. Since we are dealing with computers that transfer information in parallel, a technique must be found to convert the data to a form that can travel down a single wire. What follows is an explanation of how parallel data is converted into serial format.

In a serial data transfer, the bits would move over a single line one at a time, following each other over the single line until the entire data transfer was completed. This mode of data transfer is used when the distances the data is being transferred is longer than a few feet. The conversion between parallel and serial format can be accomplished through the use of shift registers.

In Figure 5-33, the computer connected to the 74165 will be used to transmit information to the computer connected to the 74164. When the transmitting computer is ready, it can activate the load control on the 74165. This will gate 8 bits into the shift register. Once the computer releases the load function, the 74165 is free to shift the information out of Qh onto the line between the shift registers. This information will be placed on the transmission line at the rate of the clock driving the 74165.

The 74164 will receive this information through its serial inputs. Once all 8 bits have been gated into the 74164, the receiving computer can sample the Q outputs of the 74164, reading the byte of information sent over the single line. The system as depicted in Figure 5-33 is simple. Unfortunately, it will not work without some control signals.

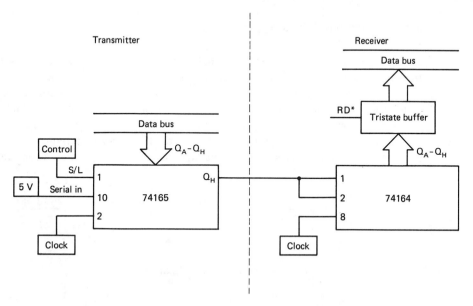

FIGURE 5-33 A "first step" parallel-to-serial communications link.

First, the transmitting computer should have some way in which to determine if the 74165 is ready to accept another byte. Such a control signal is frequently called transmitter ready (or T-ready). This signal would only go active after an entire byte had been transferred out of the 74165. The transmitting computer should monitor this line, and should only transfer a new byte when the T-ready line is active. Otherwise, it would overwrite valid information with a premature load signal to the 74165.

Likewise, the receiving computer should have access to a receiver ready (R-ready) signal. This signal should only become active after the 74164 has received 8 bits. When the receiving computer recognizes the R-ready line as active, it knows that a complete byte is within the 74164 and ready to be read into the computer. Thus, the R-ready line can be used to signal the receiving computer to sample the Q outputs of the 74164.

The transmitter circuit also needs to determine when the receiver is ready. Data should not be sent to the receiver if the receiver register contains data or if the receiver circuit is not operating. Prior to the start of a data transfer, the transmitter could send a request to send signal. If the receiver were powered up and did not contain data, the receiver could send a clear to send signal back to the transmitter. Once the transmitter received this signal, it could begin clocking the information that it contained onto the line.

Clocking is also an important part of this operation. If the transmitter clock and the receiver clock are not the same frequency, the transmitter might send 8 bits in the time that the receiver clocks in 1 bit. Of course, the opposite can happen. The receiver could sample the line eight times while the same bit is present, thus loading eight copies of the same bit into the register.

Asynchronous Transmission

The majority of serial data transfers takes place asynchronously. In such a system, the transmitter and receiver are clocked at the same rate. The clocks at the two ends of the system, however, can drift in and out of phase or be a slightly different frequency. This could cause problems if not corrected. The solution is the use of a *frame,* which consists of start and stop bits as well as the data to be transferred. A very common frame is the 11-bit start/stop pattern. Figure 5-34 shows an 11-bit start/stop frame. It is standard practice to take an inactive serial data line high. Thus, the line contains a constant stream

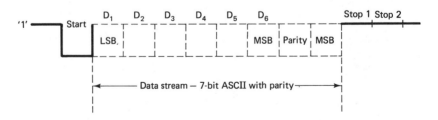

FIGURE 5-34 An 11-bit start/stop frame.

of 1s. In our previous example, this was implemented by tying the serial input of the 74165 high. When the line is activated, the data will be preceded by a start bit that will take the line low. This low-going pulse informs the receiver that a character will be transferred. The negative-going pulse is used by the receiver circuitry to synchronize its clock to the incoming data. The process involves a clock that can run at a rate 16 times that of the incoming data. This higher frequency is used to respond as rapidly as possible after the negative-going edge. After eight ticks of this clock, the line will again be sampled to see if it is still low. If so, a valid start bit is recognized. If the line is high, the transition is regarded as electrical noise on the line and no further action is taken. If the valid start bit is accepted, the 16X clock is divided down by 16 to create a sample clock. This clock will change near the middle of each data bit. The clock transition can then be used to sample the data. A slight difference between when the data is sampled and when the middle of the data bit actually occurs can now happen within the frame without causing problems.

Once the data has been transferred, the 11-bit start/stop frame must end with two successive stop bits. These bits take the transmission line high. After this, a new character can be transferred at any time. This means that the time between characters is indeterminate. The time within a frame is controlled by the 16X clock (which can be other multiples of the sample clock—64X is also used), which synchronizes the transmitter and receiver clock at the start of each frame. Why, then, is this type of transmission called *asynchronous*? Because no clocking information is within or accompanies the data.

From the preceding discussion you should see how the RS-232C interface can be used to handle many of the problems encountered. Fortunately, many of the tasks indicated can now be handled by a special-purpose chip known as a UART or USART (universal asynchronous receiver transmitter or universal synchronous asynchronous receiver transmitter). Unfortunately, the RS-232C standard was meant to be used as an interface between DTE and DCE. In many instances, manufacturers use this interface standard in nonstandard ways. We will first look at a typical UART, then take a look at some situations in which the RS-232C interface is used.

UARTS

The AY-3-1015 is a 40-pin dip IC that handles UART tasks. The pin out is shown in Figure 5-35. The functions of the pins are detailed in this section.

Pin 1. Vcc 5 V.

Pin 2. Not connected.

Pin 3. Ground.

Pin 4, RDE*.   A logic 0 on this line places the received data onto the output lines.

Pin configuration

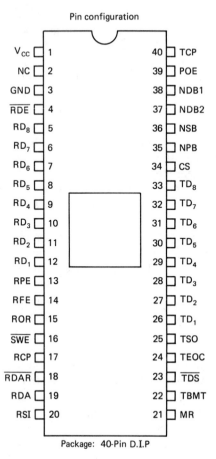

Package: 40-Pin D.I.P

FIGURE 5-35 An AY-3-1015 pin out.

Pins 5 through 12, pin mnemonics RD8 through RD1. These lines are the output data lines. RD1 contains the LSB. The lines can be tristated for connection to a computer bus.

Pin 13, PE (parity error). This line will go to a logic 1 if the received character does not agree with the selected parity. It can be tristated.

Pin 14, FE (framing error). This line goes high if the received character has no valid stop bit. A tristate line.

Pin 15, OR (overrun). This line goes high if the previously received character is not read before the next character is transferred to the receiver holding register. A tristate line.

Pin 16, SWE* (status word enable). A logic zero will place the status bits onto the output lines where they can then be sampled by the computer.

Pin 17, RCP (receiver clock).   This line should have a clock waveform with a frequency 16 times the desired receiver data rate.

Pin 18, RDAV*.   A logic 0 on this line will reset the DAV line.

Pin 19, DAV (data available).   This line will go to a logic 1 when an entire character has been received and stored in the receiver holding register. It has a tristate output.

Pin 20, SI (serial input).   This line is used to accept the serial input. A transition from a mark to a space is required to begin data reception.

Pin 21, XR (external reset).   This line can be used to reset the shift registers. It will also set SO, EOC, and TBMT. DAV is reset. The error flags are cleared as well as the input data buffer. The line must be pulled to a logic 0 when not in use.

Pin 22, TBMT (transmitter buffer empty).   This line will go high when the transmitter holding register is ready to accept another character. Tristate output.

Pin 23, DS* (data strobe).   An active low on this line will enter data into the data bits holding register. Initial data transmission is started at the rising edge of DS*. The data must be held stable during the entire strobe.

Pin 24, EOC (end of character).   This line will go high each time a complete character is transmitted, and will remain high until the start of the next transmission.

Pin 25, SO (serial output).   This line is used to output the data a bit at a time. When not in use, this line will output a constant stream of logic 1s.

Pins 26 through 33.   These are data lines used to input parallel data into the UART.

Pin 34, CS (control strobe).   A logic 1 on this pin will transfer the control bits into the control-bits holding register. The pin can be strobed or tied high.

Pin 35, NP (no parity).   When this line is high, no parity bit will be sent with the transmitted character. The stop bits will then immediately follow the data. When not used, this line should be tied low.

Pin 36, NSB (number of stop bits).   If the line is low, two stop bits will be included in the frame. If the line is high, one stop bit will be included in the frame.

Pins 37 and 38, NB2 and NB1.   These two leads are used to select the number of bits in the character.

NB2	NB1	
0	0	5 bits
0	1	6 bits
1	0	7 bits
1	1	8 bits

Pin 39, EPS (even-parity select).   When this pin is high, the parity bit added will establish even parity. When the line is low, odd parity will be used.

Pin 40, TCP (transmitter clock).   This input should have a clock signal 16 times the frequency of the desired transmitter data rate.

A UART interface.   Figure 5-36 shows one way in which the AY-3-1015 can be interfaced to a computer bus. A positive-going pulse taken from a system reset will start the UART in the conditions listed under XR in the pin-out discussion. The pro-

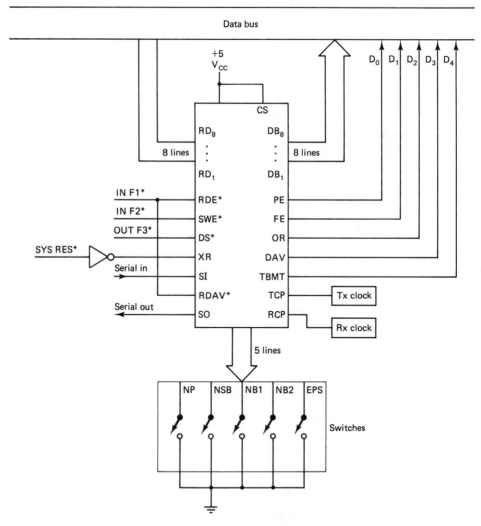

FIGURE 5-36   An AY-3-1015 bus interface.

grammable features of the UART are selected by a set of switches tied to pins 35 through 39. The condition of these control bits are placed into the UART's control-bits holding register because pin 34 CS is tied high.

To start a data transmission, the computer should generate a device-select pulse that will take SWE* low. This will gate the status bits onto the data bus and into the accumulator. Once in the accumulator, a masking operation can be used to eliminate all but the TBMT status bit. If the bit is high, then the CPU knows the transmitter is ready to accept another character. A character can then be transferred to the UART by generating a device-select pulse that takes the DS* line low. Initial data transmission will start on the rising edge of DS*.

The computer could continue to monitor the status bit TBMT by continuously pulsing the SWE*. Each time it found the TBMT bit high, another character could be transferred to the UART until the entire message was transmitted.

The destination point within the communications link would also have a UART acting as an interface between the serial line and the bus of the computer that was to receive the information. This computer could monitor the status bits of the receiving UART, but would mask out all status bits except DAV. When DAV went high, the receiving computer could then pulse the RDE* line, obtaining the byte within the receiving holding register.

The preceding discussion covers a one-way communications link. When data flow is in just one direction, the link is said to be in the *simplex* mode. If the communications link is bidirectional, the link is said to be *duplex*. There are two versions of duplex. *Half duplex* is two-way communications, with each end of the link taking turns as a transmitter; *full duplex* involves simultaneous two-way communications.

The interface of Figure 5-36 can also be used to implement a duplex link. The computers at each end of the link can poll the status bits, checking for either TBMT or DAV, then pulse DS* to transmit another byte or pulse RDE* to receive a byte.

RS-232C Uses

Modems.   As indicated earlier, the proper use for the RS-232C interface is the DTE to DCE part of the communications link. The most common form of DCE is a *mo*dulator/*dem*odulator or *modem*. The modem will take serial information from the interface and convert this information into a form that can be transmitted over the phone system.

A switched telephone system uses different transmission methods ranging from wire pairs to microwaves. A wire path between two different phones will probably exist only within a local area served by a central office. Consequently, it will be difficult to transmit data in pulse form much farther than the central office. A further problem arises when the local system is using loading coils. In such a case it might be impossible to transmit the pulsed information even as far as the local central office.

The function of the modem is to convert the digital information into a form suitable for transmission over the phone system. This means that the modem must have two interfaces. One interface is to the phone system. It is a simple interface consisting of just two wires, called the tip and the ring. The other interface is to the DTE. It is here that the RS-232C interface is used to establish standards.

The RS-232C interface is used with certain protocols, or procedures used to establish communication between the two ends of the communication link. The DTE and the modem at the transmitter must establish communication with each other. The DTE transmitter requests access to the transmission line, in this case the phone line. The DCE transmitter must then determine if the modem at the receiving end of the line is powered and ready to accept information. Since modems have very little, if any, capacity to store information, the receiving modem must determine if the DTE at the receiving end of the link is ready to accept information. If so, it signals the transmitter that it is ready and information can then be transmitted.

Protocols, in addition to setting procedures for how the link will be handled, establish ways in which errors can be detected and corrected. A thorough discussion of this facet of data communications would take us away from our primary objective, which is an introduction to microcomputers. It is probably a good idea for you to pursue this topic by obtaining a book on data communications after mastering the material presented in this text.

Computer to video terminal.   Many systems will use an RS-232C interface to hook a video terminal to a computer. In many such cases, the equipment at both ends of the line is treated as DTE. When this is the case, lines 2 and 3 will be crossed to eliminate the possibility of both devices attempting to transmit over the same line. Figure 5-37 highlights this idea. The remaining RS-232C signals are not shown because in many cases they are not used. Furthermore, since RS-232C signal definitions are based on the DTE point of view, confusion will exist over the proper use of signals when both ends of the DTE-DCE interface are DTE.

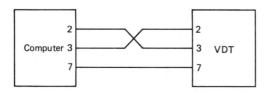

FIGURE 5-37 RS-232C data lines crossed for DTE-to-DTE communications.

Computer to serial printer.   Many computers interface to a printer through a serial I/O port. The port used is usually an RS-232C interface. The interfacing, however, can become quite complex. In some situations some signals may not be used; in others certain lines may not be connected; and in many cases the signals are being used in ways never intended when the RS-232C interface was adopted. This means that the printer interface cable might be unique to a particular type of printer and not work with another printer. Consequently, there really is no standard. Let's look at some ways in which a computer-to-printer interface might be accomplished. Keep in mind, though, that what we will investigate is not really the RS-232C interface at all, but an attempt to use this standard DTE-to-DCE output port as a general-purpose serial I/O port.

A major problem when attempting to connect a printer to a computer through the RS-232C interface is flow control. *Flow control* is the process of monitoring the data transfer rate. If the computer transmits characters faster than the printer can print, information will be lost or garbled.

An RTS-CTS method of flow control has been attempted. When a computer requests to send, it is asking for access to the transmission line. A DCE is supposed to respond with a clear to send when the line is available for use. The interface standards do not allow the DCE to drop the CTS signal. What happens then when a printer drops CTS, indicating that its print buffer is full? If the computer is transmitting a character, it has two choices. One, it stops transmitting. This will garble the information. Two, it waits until the present character has been completely transmitted before stopping transmission. In this case, the printer's buffer might overflow, causing information to be lost. In either case, problems arise.

Another method of flow control involves the use of the DTR-DSR signals. The signal chosen will depend on whether the manufacturer of the printer decides it is DTE or DCE. Suppose the printer is wired as DTE. In that case, the DTR signal can be dropped when the printer buffer is nearly full. When the buffer is nearly empty, the signal can be reasserted. Unfortunately, the computer on the other end might not interpret the signal in this manner, because neither DTR nor DSR was designed for flow control in the RS-232C standard.

The last and probably the best method of flow control involves the sending of special-purpose control signals to the computer over line 3, where the computer reads information from the printer. In most cases, these signals are XON and XOFF. The software operating the port must then take appropriate action.

Hopefully, after having completed this introduction to data communications and serial interfacing, you will have an idea how a typical communications link is set up, how a UART can be used to convert parallel data to serial format, how a computer can monitor the status bits of the UART to control data flow, and how the RS-232C interface is used, even when applied incorrectly. You should also have many questions. Questions about synchronous transmissions, modem modulation and demodulation techniques, and telephone electronics probably come to mind. Since this is not the main thrust of this text, you are again encouraged to explore these areas in other books dealing specifically with data communications.

5-11 CLOSING THOUGHTS

In this chapter we have examined the basis of digital interfacing. Although not every technique was covered, the foundation was laid for the digital interfacing techniques you will need as a technician. Two new chips were introduced in this chapter, the 8212 and the 8255. The 8212 is a good-purpose input/output chip that can be controlled by the CPU. The 8255 is a programmable support chip that can be very effective as an interface between the bus and external devices. The date stamp project showed the great flexibility this chip has, even though we have not yet touched on mode 1 and will not discuss mode 2. This chip is worth a considerable investment in study and lab time.

The system interface for the 8255 was seen to be very similar to the system interface used for the 8253. The layout of many programmable support chips is similar enough that you should understand the system interface. Study this once more if you are not yet sure how the connections are made.

SUMMARY

1. Isolated I/O uses the IN and OUT instructions to transfer data into and out of the CPU. The only register with access to the bus during the IN and OUT machine cycles is the accumulator.
2. Port numbers are used by the CPU to activate the appropriate I/O port. Decoder circuitry receives the port number and logically combines this number with an IN* or OUT* control signal to form a device-select pulse.
3. Memory-mapped I/O treats every device as if it were a memory location.
4. Memory-mapped decoder circuitry accepts an address and logically combines this with either the WR* or RD* control signal. This combination is then referred to as an address-select pulse. The address-select pulse is used to activate the correct memory-mapped port.
5. A device-select pulse can be used as a control pulse. When this technique is used, the OUT instruction should be used to create the pulse.
6. The 8212 is an 8-bit latch designed to interface to a computer bus. The 8212 can operate as an input buffer, an output latch, or an interrupting port.
7. The 8255 is a programmable peripheral interface designed to operate with a computer bus. The 8255 has three 8-bit ports; each port can be configured to operate as an input port or an output port. Other features, as well as input or output, can be selected through the control words sent to the 8255 from the CPU. Once programmed, the 8255 will continue its task until reset or reprogrammed.

QUESTIONS

1. Which two pins are used by the Z80 to distinguish between I/O operations and memory operations?
2. What control line is used by the 8085 to help form the IN* control signal?
3. What information and signals are required to form a device-select pulse?
4. What is meant by *absolute decoding*?

5. How many lines are needed to absolutely decode a port number? An address used in an address-select pulse?

6. Which machine cycle, M1, M2, or M3, of the OUT instruction cycle outputs the value in the accumulator?

7. An IN instruction cycle is performed. At what clock of M3 will the data bus information be sampled?

8. What is meant by *linear decoding*?

9. What is an ambiguity?

10. Using an AND gate and inverters, draw the logic diagram for a circuit that will absolutely decode 57 hex.

11. What is meant by an *address-select pulse*?

12. How many bidirectional ports are possible with memory-mapped I/O?

13. What is the set/reset control word that will set PC1?

14. What is the set/reset control word that will clear PC6?

15. When using isolated I/O, a software bottleneck can develop. Explain what is meant by this statement.

16. Explain why the IN instruction should not be used to generate control pulses.

17. An 8255 is configured for mode 0 operation. Port A will be set up as an input port, port B as an output port, port C upper will be an input port, and port C lower will be an output port. Determine the control word that establishes this format.

18. If an 8255 is wired to respond to ports 130, 131, 132, and 133 octal, which port number is used by port B?

19. What is the proper wiring procedure when interfacing an input port to the computer bus?

20. The 8255 has two pins labeled PA1 and PA0. It also has two pins labeled A1 and A0. What are the functional differences between these two sets of pins?

21. What is meant by *status-driven I/O*?

LAB ASSIGNMENTS

Remember, whenever you wire an input or bidirectional port, wire all control lines first. Then make sure the data pins of the port are tristate before hooking to the bus.

1. Wire a 74155 as a 3-line-to-8-line device-select generator for output ports B0 through B7. Use absolute decoding. Write a short test program that will then activate the circuit. Test to see if you have control of all device-select pulse outputs.

2. Wire an 8212 as an input port. Control the input through a set of dip switches. The dip switches will ground the inputs of the 8212 when closed. The inputs should be pulled up to Vcc so when the switches are open, there is a minimal chance of getting

erroneous data. Write a program that looks for a particular pattern from the 8212. When the computer receives the correct pattern, output a recognition code on your trainer's displays and halt the program.

3. Replace the 8212 with an 8255. Use mode 0 operation with the following configuration: port A input, port B output, and port C output. Connect the dip switches to port A as you did with the 8212. Instantly transfer the switch input back to the 8255 through port B. This process is known as echoing and is one way in which data transmissions are checked for errors. Monitor the outputs of port B with a logic probe and verify circuit operation.

4. With the 8255 wired as in assignment 3, change the program and practice setting and resetting individual pins of port C.

LAB QUESTIONS

1. Draw the scematic of the circuit for assignment 1.

2. Record the control line format you used in assignment 2. Account for DS1*, DS2, STB, MD, and CLR*.

3. Draw the flowchart used in assignment 2. Identify the logical constructs used within the program.

4. Record the control word used in assignment 3.

5. If your computer has breakpoint capability, set a breakpoint just before the IN activating port A. Change the dip switches to a setting or 305. Then set the dip switches to 203. With a new breakpoint just after the IN, resume the program. At the new breakpoint, inspect the contents of the accumulator. What value did the computer receive from the 8255? What does this tell you about the operation of an input port in mode 0?

6

DIAGNOSTICS

At the end of this chapter you should be familiar with:

1. the concept of how software can be written to test circuitry for correct operation
2. how data tables can be used to simplify programming
3. the use of multiple data tables within a program
4. indexed access as it applies to data tables
5. the concept of base addresses
6. software techniques used to form displacements into data tables

INTRODUCTION

The next two projects are examples of programs that perform diagnostics. In each of these projects an integrated circuit is tested for faults under software control. The software routines operate the hardware necessary to perform the tests, retrieve an answer or response from the IC being tested, and then compare that answer with a pattern prestored in the computer's memory. If the response from the hardware matches the pattern prestored in the computer's memory, then that test has been successfully completed. The programs in each case are structured as loops that keep testing various functions of the IC until all required tests have been completed. If all test sequences produce matches between the IC's response and the expected response already within the computer, then that IC has passed the diagnostics. If not, then the software should record in some fashion what type of error has occurred. This is done by an error subroutine. These error subroutines will be discussed when each project is analyzed in detail.

In addition to exposing the student to some diagnostic routines, the programs have several other important features the student should learn. These features include the use of data tables and memory pointers.

6-1 MEMORY POINTERS

The 8080/8085 and Z80 architectures allow the programmer to form register pairs so that a program can point to or indicate any specific memory location within the memory space. Unaided by specialized memory schemes such as bank select, these processors can access 64K of memory. This involves the use of 16 address lines, as discussed earlier in the section on bus structure. If a programmer is to take control of these lines, it must be possible for the programmer to send information to the address lines at the appropriate time.

Fortunately, the timing is handled by the hardware when the correct instructions are used. Most of these instructions involve the M operator. An example of such an instruction is MOV B,M. This instruction moves the contents of a memory location into the B register. As was indicated in the chapter on basic instructions, register pair H must first be loaded with the 16-bit address of the memory location to be accessed. This makes register pair H the memory pointer for this instruction. In the next two programs the idea of a memory pointer is extended to the use and manipulation of data tables. The register pairs B and D can also be used as memory pointers. An instruction such as STAX D stores the contents of the accumulator at the memory location pointed to by register pair D. In some cases it is convenient to have a memory pointer assigned to a specific data table while a second memory pointer handles another data table. Examples of this situation follow in one of the two diagnostic projects.

6-2 DATA TABLES

Data tables are data structures. Another data structure, the stack, was introduced in the section on top-down design. Recall that a data structure is a collection of data with some commonality, which must follow a specific means of access. The stack's main function was the storage of return addresses and registers. This provided the computer with a way to handle subroutine calls. The method of access for the stack was LIFO—last in, first out. The data table uses the indexed method of access.

When using data tables, it is often convenient to point to the first datum in the table. A programmer will assign a register pair to the table when laying out the register usage table. The location in memory of the first entry in the table is called the *base address*. This base address is the starting point for all manipulations of the data in the table when using an index.

The index is a number that has some correlation with an entry in the table. As an example, suppose a data table is filled with the ASCII representations of the numbers 0 through 9. The table could be constructed in such a way that the codes are stored in sequential order. Thus, location 3 in the table would contain the ASCII code for the digit 3. To obtain this code, the program would first point to the base address of the table. The index, in this case the number 3, is added to the base address to form a displacement. The results of this addition are moved back into the memory pointer for the table. Now the address in the memory pointer will select the memory cell containing the code for the number 3. When an instruction such as MOVA,M is executed, the code will be transferred to the A register. The end result of this process is that the code for the number 3 is now in the A register.

Example 6-1 performs this lookup process. The section of code is structured as a subroutine. It has a major weakness in that the index is a part of that subroutine. This means that each time the subroutine is used it returns the code for the number 3. Below the code section of Example 6-1, the data table for the codes 0–9 is shown. The base address for this table is located at 004 010 octal.

Example 6-2 shows a section of a main program that loads the index in a register before calling the lookup subroutine. The subroutine assumes that the index will be found in the C register. If the person coding the main routine fails to place the index in the C register prior to the call, the subroutine will return the wrong value. This may seem very restrictive, but it allows the main routine to obtain the code for any number by calling the subroutine of Example 6-2. This is very important when considering how much code has to be generated. In Example 6-1, 10 different subroutines would have to be coded. In Example 6-2, only one subroutine has to be coded. This advantage far outweighs the disadvantage of placing the index in the C register prior to the call instruction.

In the preceding discussion we looked up a code. This would be the same as

EXAMPLE 6-1

HEX ADDRESS	HEX OP CODE	MNEMONIC	COMMENTS	OCTAL ADDRESS	OCTAL OP CODE
-ANY-	21	LXI H	Base Address of lookup	-ANY-	041
		010	table		
		004			
					016
	OE	MVIC	Index		
		003			
	79	MOV A, C	Form displacement		171
	85	ADDL			205
	6F	MOV L, A	Update pointer		157
	7E	MOV A, M	Get code for #3		176
	C9	RET			311
			ASCII TABLE		
				004 010	

looking up a telephone number in an address book. In the address book the tabs indicating the letters of the alphabet serve as the index. The correlation is formed when *Smith* is stored on the page for names beginning with the letter *S*. It might seem as if the process of pointing to the first page of the address book—that is, forming a base address—is unnecessary. A person, however, knows where his or her address book is kept. The computer must be told where the data table is located. That is the function of the base address.

Now it is time to analyze the two diagnostic examples. The first tests the operation of a 7432 or gate. The second example tests the operation of a 74155 decoder. Each project follows the suggested outline for project development, documentation standards, and top-down design, as given earlier in the text.

EXAMPLE 6-2

HEX ADDRESS	HEX OP CODE	MNEMONIC	COMMENTS	OCTAL ADDRESS	OCTAL OP CODE
-ANY-	OE	MVIC		-ANY-	016
		003			
	CD	CALL			315
		LO			
		HI			
		.			
		.			
		.			
		.			
			Subroutine "lookup"		
-ANY-	21	LXIH	Base address	-ANY-	041
		010			
		004			
	79	MOV A, C	Get index form displacement		171
	85	ADD L			205
	6F	MOV L, A	Update pointer		157
	7E	MOV A, M	Get code		176
	C9	RET			311

6-3 THE 7432 DIAGNOSTIC PROJECT

Hardware Discussion

Layout Sheet 6-1 lists two 8212 eight-bit input-output ports as support chips. These ICs are wired using the techniques developed in the chapter on digital interfacing. As indi-

Layout Sheet 6-1

7432 PROJECT LAYOUT SHEET

OBJECTIVE:

To test a 7432 quad dual input or gate under software control

HARDWARE ENVIRONMENT:

8080-based CPU
Isolated I/O

Support Chips:

1. 8212 — wired as an output latch. Responds to port 004. Pin connections are detailed in hardware/software interface section.
2. 8212 — wired as an input buffer. Responds to port 004. High-order input nibble tied to pull-up resistors. Low-order nibble connections detailed in hardware/software interface section.
3. 7432 quad dual input or gates — this is the IC under test

SOFTWARE ENVIRONMENT

Memory Allocations:

1. main program — 003 000
2. error subroutine — 003 050
3. test pattern data table — 003 100

Register Allocations:

1. A — I/O, arithmetic, logic
2. B — loop counter
3. C — test mask
4. D — test mask
5. E — error register. All lows indicate no errors have occurred. Any bit position left high indicates a faulty gate.
6. H&L — memory pointer for test patterns sent to the 7432

Port Allocations:

1. 001 — output-latched LEDs
2. 004 — 8212 input buffer
3. 004 — 8212 output latch

Layout Sheet 6-1 (*continued*)
   Special Codes:

None

HARDWARE/SOFTWARE INTERFACE

Input:

Bit positions	7432 output pins
D0	pin 3
D1	pin 6
D2	pin 8
D3	pin 11

Output:

Data Bus — Output latch
D7 D6 D5 D4 D3 D2 D1 D0

7432 input pins
13   12   10   9   5   4   2   1

cated in the chapter on project development, the output latch was wired first, then tested, using a simple output program.

    The input latch was wired next. The computer used in this project already had a port 4 in use. Since the monitor program was strobing port 4, the input buffer was activating at the wrong time, disabling the data bus.

    The information on the layout sheet was compared to the computer documentation. The fact that port 4 was in use was overlooked. Normally, the circuitry producing the device-select pulse would have to be rewired to avoid the double use of port 4. This time, though, because the project was developed using the guidelines given in the chapter on project development, the software could still be modified to correct the problem. See the explanation of the use of the EI instruction in the software discussion of this project.

    The 7432 is wired into the output-input loop in such a way that the gate whose output is pin 3 is called gate 0. All the gates' outputs are wired to correspond to a bit position on the data bus. The gate number is taken from the bit position to which it is wired. Thus, at the end of the project, if D3 of the error register is high, then gate 3 has failed. This is the gate whose output is pin 11. See the section Hardware/Software Interface on the layout sheet.

    The schematic for the project can be found in Figure 6-1. The top 8212 is wired as an output latch. It is activated by device-select pulse Out 004*. The outputs of this latch drive the inputs of the 7432 to be tested. The bottom 8212 in Figure 6-1 is wired

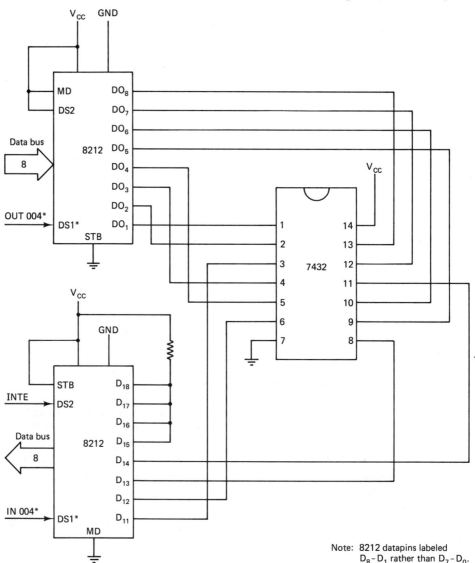

FIGURE 6-1 7432 project schematic.

as an input buffer. It is set to operate when it receives device-select pulse In 004*. Note that the device-select pulse cannot turn on this chip unless the computer control line INTE, attached to DS2, is set high. The high-order input to the bottom 8212 is wired high through a pull-up resistor. The low-order nibble input to this 8212 samples the outputs of the 7432.

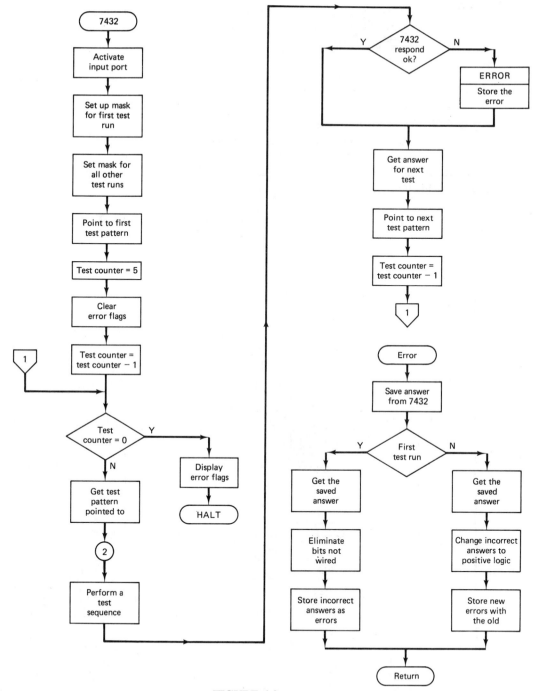

FIGURE 6-2

Software Discussion

Flowchart. The flowchart for the project can be found in Figure 6-2. The main routine logic can be found on sheets 1 and 2; the error subroutine logic is found on sheet 3. The main program is structured to perform the testing process by using a top-driven DO-WHILE logical construct. An IF-THEN logical construct within this loop will call the error subroutine should the 7432 under test be faulty. The error subroutine uses an IF-THEN-ELSE to determine which test run has failed. The first test run is treated differently than the other test runs. The discussion of the error subroutine code will explain this further.

Main routine. The first instruction of the main routine is EI. Refer to Example 6-3. EI is the mnemonic for *enable interrupt*. It activates the computer's interrupt ca-

EXAMPLE 6-3

HEX ADDRESS	HEX OP CODE	MNEMONIC	COMMENTS	OCTAL ADDRESS	OCTAL OP CODE
			7432 Tester		
03 00	FB	EI	Activate input	003 000	373
03 01	0E	MVIC	Mask for 1st test run	003 001	016
03 02		360		003 002	
03 03	16	MVID	Mask for remaining tests	003 003	026
03 04		377		003 004	
03 05	21	LXI H	Base address of test	003 005	041
03 06		100	pattern table	003 006	
03 07		003		003 007	
03 08	06	MVIB	Set up loop counter	003 010	006
03 09		005		003 011	
03 0A	1E	MVIE	Clear error register	003 012	036
03 0B		000		003 013	

EXAMPLE 6-3 (*continued*)

HEX ADDRESS	HEX OP CODE	MNEMONIC	COMMENTS	OCTAL ADDRESS	OCTAL OP CODE
03 0C	05	DCRB	Tests done?	003 014	005
03 0D	CA	JZ	If so, exit do-while	003 015	312
03 0E		037		003 016	
03 0F		003		003 017	
03 10	7E	MOV A, M	Get a test pattern	003 020	176
03 11	D3	OUT	Execute a test sequence	003 021	323
03 12		004		003 022	
03 13	DB	IN		003 023	333
03 14		004		003 024	
03 15	B9	CMP C	Valid operation?	003 025	271
03 16	C4	CNZ	If not, call error subroutine	003 026	304
03 17		050		003 027	
03 18		003		003 030	
03 19	4A	MOV C, D	Get mask for remaining tests	003 031	112
03 1A	2C	INRL	Paint to next test pattern	003 032	054
03 1B	05	DCR B	Record doing a test	003 033	005
03 1C	C3	JMP		003 034	303
03 1D		015	Foot of do-while	003 035	
03 1E		003		003 036	
03 IF	7B	MOV A, E	Get test results	003 037	173
03 20	D3	OUT	Display test results	003 040	323
03 21		001		003 041	

EXAMPLE 6-3 (*continued*)

HEX ADDRESS	HEX OP CODE	MNEMONIC	COMMENTS	OCTAL ADDRESS	OCTAL OP CODE
03 22	76	HLT		003 042	176
			Error		
			Subroutine		
03 28	F5	PUSH PSW	Save test results	003 050	365
03 29	7D	MOV A, L	Check to see if this is first	003 051	175
03 2A	F3	CPI	test run	003 052	376
03 2B		100		003 053	
03 2C	C2	JNZ	If not, go to other test run	003 054	302
03 2D		066		003 055	
03 2E		003	Error code	003 056	
03 2F	F1	POP PSW	Restore test results	003 057	361
03 30	E6	ANI	Mask to capture	003 060	346
03 31		017	test results	003 061	
03 32	5F	MOV E, A	Save errors	003 062	137
03 33	C3	JMP	Go to return	003 063	303
03 34		072		003 064	
03 35		003		003 065	
03 36	F1	POP PSW	Restore test results	003 066	361
03 37	2F	CMA	Set errors to logic 1	003 067	057
03 38	B3	ORA E	Mesh old, new	003 070	263
03 39	5F	MOV E, A	Save all errors	003 071	137

EXAMPLE 6-3 (*continued*)

HEX ADDRESS	HEX OP CODE	MNEMONIC	COMMENTS	OCTAL ADDRESS	OCTAL OP CODE
03 3A	C9	RET		003 072	311
			Test		
			Patterns		
03 40		000		003 100	
03 41		125		003 101	
03 42		252		003 102	
03 43		377		003 103	

pability. Interrupts will be discussed in a later chapter, but an interesting use for this instruction can be explained now.

There is a status line INTE on the computer bus. It is a flag indicating the condition of the interrupt mechanism. When INTE is high, the CPU can be interrupted. This line will stay high until an interrupt occurs. Since this application does not use interrupts, the INTE line is being used as a latched control line.

The INTE control line is wired to the 8212 input buffer. On start-up, the INTE line is set low. This means that the input buffer wired to the bus for this application cannot activate until EI is executed. This insures that the input buffer will not turn on before the program testing the 7432 is run. This little trick allowed the input buffer to be partially decoded, thus eliminating extra hardware.

The next instruction places a byte of 360 into the C register. During the first test sequence, all zeroes will be sent to the 7432's inputs. The proper response would be zeroes in the low-order nibble. The high-order nibble is not used. It is wired to pull-up resistors, making the high-order nibble all highs. In binary the total pattern would be 11110000. Grouping the bits for octal representation yields 360.

The second, third, and fourth test sequences should have a response of all highs. The low-order nibble will be 1111 if the OR gates are functional. Again, the high-order nibble is wired high, making the correct response 11111111. This groups into 377 octal. The D register has this value stored in it.

Next, the H and L register pair is set up as memory pointer. The value placed into these registers at line 003 005 is the base address of a data table that contains the test patterns that will operate the 7432. See Layout Sheet 6-1.

TABLE 6-1   OR Gate to Data Bus Interface

GATE 3		GATE 2		GATE 1		GATE 0		OCTAL EQUIVALENT
D7	D6	D5	D4	D3	D2	D1	D0	
0	0	0	0	0	0	0	0	000
0	1	0	1	0	1	0	1	125
1	0	1	0	1	0	1	0	252
1	1	1	1	1	1	1	1	377

The binary patterns in Table 6-1 are laid out so that each pair of bits (D0,D1–D2,D3, etc.) counts through a complete sequence of all possible states for an OR gate. In essence, each pair of bits represents the truth table inputs for one of the OR gates found within the 7432. The binary patterns found in Table 6-1 are converted to octal and stored in memory, located as specified in the memory map for the project.

The B register is the loop counter. It is set to 5 and decremented once before entering the DO-WHILE loop which starts at line 003 015.

The last initialization before entering the DO-WHILE loop is clearing the E register. In this program the E register will be used to store any errors that are found. If the contents of the E register remain zero, then the 7432 under test is functional. A high bit in D0, D1, D2, or D3 indicates that a gate has failed. Refer to Table 6-1 to determine which bit corresponds to which gate inside the 7432.

The first instruction inside the loop is found at line 003 020. It retrieves a test pattern from the data table pointed to by H and L. The next block of code performs the test sequence itself. This is done by outputting a test pattern, which is sent to the inputs of the OR gates through the output latch at port 004. A response is then read from the input buffer, also wired to respond to port 004.

The first pass through the loop compares 360, stored in the C register earlier, with the answer from the 7432. Since H and L are still pointing to the base address of the data table containing test patterns, all zeroes are transmitted to the inputs of the OR gates. A correct response, therefore, is 360.

The compare instruction at 003 025 checks for a match. If the response matches the value in the C register, the call to the error subroutine is not performed. If there is a discrepancy, the call is performed and the error subroutine records the fault.

At line 003 031, the correct answer for all remaining tests is placed into the C register. Thus, all remaining passes through the DO-WHILE loop will check for a response of 377.

After this the L register is incremented by 1, moving the displacement into the data table to the next entry. This way each pass through the loop will retrieve a different test pattern to be sent to the 7432. This process is known as updating the memory pointer. Whenever a data table is used to retrieve information in the same order in which it was stored, it is very easy to access the information by updating the memory pointer for the table each time through the loop. In some cases the memory pointer can also be used as the loop counter. In this way, when a memory pointer reaches a certain address, the loop is exited.

Line 003 033 subtracts 1 from the loop counter, marking a pass through the loop. The foot of the DO-WHILE is the jump instruction found at 003 034. It jumps the program back to the top of the loop, where the decision to exit from the loop is located, in this case 003 015.

Once all the tests have been performed, the program exits the loop by jumping to 003 037. Here a simple sequence of instructions obtains the test results from the error register E. The answer is moved to the accumulator and output to port 001, which is a set of latched LEDs that can be read to determine which gate, if any, failed.

Error subroutine.   The error subroutine begins at 003 050. The first instruction saves the process status word on the stack. This keeps a copy of the response from the 7432 intact. Now that a copy of the answer is saved on the stack, the accumulator is free to use for arithmetic and comparisons.

The block of code beginning at 003 051 is used to determine if the failure of the 7432 occurred during the first test run. This is necessary because on this test run incorrect responses will be highs, while on all other test runs incorrect responses will be low. If the L register is at 100, then the memory pointer has not been updated. This indicates that the main program has not yet made one complete pass of its main loop.

Lines 003 057 through 062 record any errors that might have happened on the first test run. The answer from the 7432 is returned to the accumulator from the stack by the POP instruction. The information is then masked with the binary pattern 00001111. This becomes 017 in octal. What happens here is simple. The high-order nibble, which is tied to pull up resistors, is ANDed with all zeroes, thus "erasing" the bits that have no meaning in this application. Finally, the low-order nibble is moved to the register. At this time, at least 1 bit in this nibble must be high. If not, the error subroutine should not have been called.

The jump instruction at 003 063 bypasses the code handling the storage of errors that happen on the remaining test runs by jumping to the return at the end of the subroutine.

Any errors that occur on any other test run are recorded by the section of code starting at 003 066. As before, the A register was used to determine if this was the first test as described above. Like before, the answer from the OR gates is placed back into the A register with the POP instruction. Unlike before, any errors that have happened will return lows to the computer. The second, third, and fourth test runs will place at least one high on the inputs of all the OR gates. A properly operating OR gate should return a high. Thus, if a failure has happened, a low will be recorded somewhere in the low-order nibble.

A decision was made when the program was first constructed. That decision cleared the E register, indicating that no errors had happened. Now an error is indicated by a low being placed in the accumulator. This is a contradiction. The CMA instruction removes this problem by complementing every bit position with the A register. Therefore, this section of code also indicates failures by placing bit positions high. The complement instruction has one other benefit. The high-order nibble which is tied to pull-up resistors is made low by the complementing. Thus, this section of code does not need to mask out the high-order nibble.

At 003 070 the results of the errors just detected are combined with any errors that might have happened before. The ORA instruction meshes the highs without erasing any highs that were already stored. The last instruction before the return places the results of the error detection in the E register so that later the results may be reviewed.

6-4 THE 74155 DIAGNOSTIC PROJECT

Hardware Discussion

This project also uses two 8212s to form the input-output loop. This time, the internal logic of the 8212 is used to simplify the decoding necessary to turn the chips on at the correct time. The OUT line from the control bus is connected to DS1 of the output latch. A7 from the address bus will be connected to DS2. When an OUT is performed with A7 high, the 8212 will clock the information on the data bus into the D flip-flops and then latch the information when OUT goes high. The mode was tied high and the strobe of the IC was tied low. This output latch will respond to any port number between 200 and 377. In this project, this presents no problem because the computer used did not have any ports in this range. This made single-line decoding possible.

The input buffer was also single-line decoded. The IN control line was tied to DS1. The DS2 pin of the input buffer was tied to A6. This buffer will activate for any port number in the range 100 to 177. Then any port number above 300 will also turn this buffer on. The software and hardware used in this project prevented any possibility of this IC turning on at the wrong time. To complete the control logic, the mode was tied low. The strobe was tied high.

The 74155 is wired as a 3-line-to-8-line decoder. Only one output at a time should be low. The hardware/software interface is set up so the low output will be at D0 when the select lines are 000, at D1 when the select lines are at 001, and so on. See Layout Sheet 6-2 for the rest of the sequence.

The strobes of the 74155 are wired to ground in this project. They are assumed to be operational and are not checked.

The Hardware Environment Section found within Layout Sheet 6-2 summarizes this information. The project schematic can be found in Figure 6-3.

Software Discussion

Flowchart.   The main flowchart logic is depicted on sheets 1 and 2 of Figure 6-4. Notice that the overall structure of this routine is almost identical to the logic structure used to test the 7432. The main testing loop is again a top-driven DO-WHILE.

Layout Sheet 6-2

74155 PROJECT LAYOUT SHEET

OBJECTIVE:

To test a 74155 3-line-to-8-line decoder under software control

HARDWARE ENVIRONMENT:

8080-based CPU
Isolated I/O

Support Chips:

1. 8212 wired as an output latch — single-line decoded from A7 responding to port 200
2. 8212 wired as an input buffer — single-line decoded from A6 responding to port 100
3. 74155 wired as a 3-line-to-8-line decoder. This is the IC under test.

SOFTWARE ENVIRONMENT

Memory Allocation:

1. page 003 000 — main program
2. page 003 100 — fill subroutine
3. page 003 200 — error subroutine
4. page 4, (0–7) — correct answer table
5. page 5, (0–7) — error table
6. page 7 — stack operations

Register Allocations:

1. A — I/O, logic, arithmetic
2. B and C — error table pointer
3. D — loop counter, test sequence driver
4. H and L — memory pointer for correct answer table, error table pointer in FILL subroutine

Port Allocations:

1. 200 — output latch — driving the inputs to the 74155
2. 100 — input buffer — reading the response from the 74155

Layout Sheet 6-2 (*continued*)

Special Codes:

None

HARDWARE/SOFTWARE INTERFACE

Input:

D7 D6 D5 D4 D3 D2 D1 D0 — data bus inputs
1Y3 1Y2 1Y1 1Y0 2Y3 2Y2 2Y1 2Y0 — 74155 outputs

Output:

D2 — wired to select line C of the 74155
D1 — wired to select line B of the 74155   through output latch
D0 — wired to select line A of the 74155

Once again, within the body of the loop, there is an IF-THEN logical construct that calls an error subroutine if a 74155 under test fails. Earlier in the text, one of the arguments in favor of structured programming was that it led to patterns in solutions. The similarity between the flowcharts should serve to reinforce that point. Similar projects should lead to similar solutions. Hopefully, if you make a serious effort to become a structured programmer, you will gain the advantage of quickly solving new problems using techniques developed before.

The FILL subroutine is a straight-line routine until it enters a bottom-driven loop. This DO-UNTIL will be performed until the error table locations have been nulled out.

The ERROR subroutine is a straight-line program. It is easily coded because the breakup of the logic into smaller parts made this task very simple and straightforward.

Main routine.   See Example 6-4. This project was run on a machine where the monitor program did not establish the stack. Accordingly, since subroutines are to be used, the first instruction of the program sets the stack pointer.

The second block of code establishes a memory pointer for the answer table, preloaded at 004 000. This data table contains responses that a functional 74155 would produce when tested as in this example.

The third block of code uses the B register pair as a second data table pointer. If any errors are located, the program will fill a data table entry with the number of the sequence that failed. This will be done in an error subroutine. The main program initializes the memory pointer to the base address of the error table.

Register D is used as the loop counter. It is cleared, so each pass through the test loop will find D being incremented.

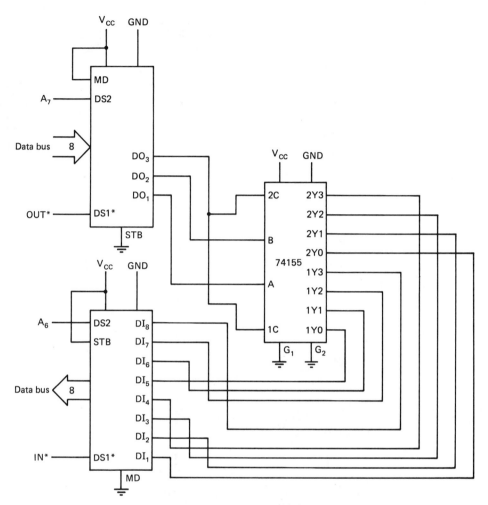

Note: 8212 $D_8 - D_1$ rather than
$D_7 - D_0$.

FIGURE 6-3 74155 project schematic.

Next, a CALL is performed at location 003 013. This CALL accesses a subroutine called FILL. The FILL SUBROUTINE will store a null pattern in the error table. This is done because, on power up, the contents of the error table are random. It is possible that one of these random numbers might equal an error value. Therefore, the null value is an octal pattern that cannot possibly be stored by the software performing the tests on the 74155. If the error table contains nothing but the null value after the tests have been completed, then the 74155 tested was functional. This CALL is also the last instruction in the initialization sequence.

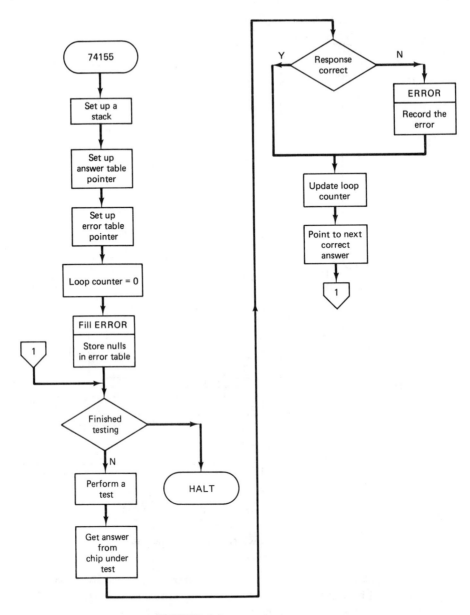

FIGURE 6-4

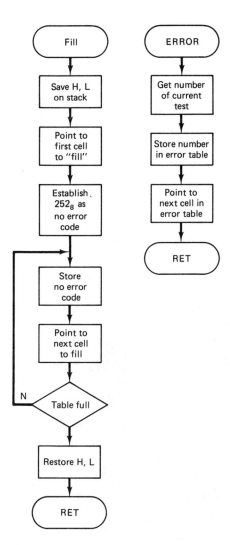

FIGURE 6-4 *(cont.)*

The block of code beginning at line 003 016 tests to see if all the tests have been performed. If the loop counter has reached 8, the jump on zero instruction within this block of code exits the DO-WHILE by jumping to the HALT command at 003 041.

If the loop counter has not reached 8, the jump on zero command is ignored and the algorithm enters the test loop. In this example, the loop counter is performing double duty. Not only is it the loop counter, it is also the test-sequence driver. The 74155 has been wired to respond as a 3-line-to-8-line decoder. This being the case, all eight output

EXAMPLE 6-4

HEX ADDRESS	HEX OP CODE	MNEMONIC	COMMENTS	OCTAL ADDRESS	OCTAL OP CODE
			74155 Test		
03 00	31	LXI SP	Set up a stack	003 000	061
03 01		000		003 001	
03 02		010		003 002	
03 03	21	LXI H	Answer table pointer	003 003	041
03 04		000		003 004	
03 05		004		003 005	
03 06	01	LXI B	Error table pointer	003 006	001
03 07		000		003 007	
03 08		005		003 010	
03 09	16	MVI D	Clear loop counter	003 011	026
03 0A		000		003 012	
03 0B	CD	CALL	Fill error table with nulls	003 013	315
03 0C		100		003 014	
03 0D		003		003 015	
03 0E	7A	MOV A, D	Check to see if testing is	003 016	172
03 0F	FE	CPI	finished	003 017	376
03 10		010		003 020	
03 11	CA	JZ	If so, go to halt	003 021	312
03 12		041		003 022	
03 13		003		003 023	
03 14	D3	OUT	Perform a test sequence	003 024	323
03 15		200		003 025	
03 16	DB	IN		003 026	333
03 17		100		003 027	

EXAMPLE 6-4 (*continued*)

Hex Address	Hex Op Code	Mnemonic	Comments	Octal Address	Octal Op Code
03 18	BE	CMP M	Is answer correct?	003 030	276
03 19	C4	CNZ		003 031	304
03 1A		200	If not, call error routine	003 032	
03 1B		003		003 033	
03 1C	14	INR D	Update loop counter	003 034	024
03 1D	23	INX H	Update correct answer pointer	003 035	043
03 1E	C3	JMP		003 036	303
03 1F		016	Foot of DO-WHILE	003 037	
03 20		003		003 040	
03 21	76	HLT		003 041	166
03 40	E1	PUSH H	Save H, L	003 100	345
03 41	21	LXI H	Point to error table	003 101	041
03 42		000		003 102	
03 43		005		003 103	
03 44	1E	MVIE	Set up null indicating no errors	003 104	036
03 45		252		003 105	
03 46	73	MOV M, E	Null an entry	003 106	163
03 47	23	INX H	Update error pointer	003 107	043
03 48	7D	MOV A, L	Is table nulled?	003 110	175
03 49	FE	CPI		003 111	376
03 4A		010	If so, go to exit and return	003 112	
03 4B	CA	JZ		003 113	312
03 4C		121		003 114	
03 4D		003		003 115	

EXAMPLE 6-4 (*continued*)

HEX ADDRESS	HEX OP CODE	MNEMONIC	COMMENTS	OCTAL ADDRESS	OCTAL OP CODE
03 4E	C3	JMP	If not, continue	003 116	303
03 4F		106		003 117	
03 50		003		003 120	
03 51	EI	POP H	Restore H, L	003 121	341
03 52		RET		003 122	311
03 80	7A	MOV A, D	Get test sequence	003 200	172
03 81	02	STAX B	Store in error table	003 201	002
03 82	03	INX B	Update error pointer	003 202	003
03 83	C9	RET		003 203	311
			Correct answers		
		DATA			
04 00		376		004 000	
04 01		375		004 001	
04 02		373		004 002	
04 03		367		004 003	
04 04		357		004 004	
04 05		337		004 005	
04 06		277		004 006	
04 07		177		004 007	

conditions can be tested simply by counting up from zero. The contents of the loop counter are moved into the A register, then outputted to the select lines of the 74155. The transfer of the loop counter to the A register takes place at location 003 016. The output instruction does not occur until 003 024; however, none of the intervening instructions change the contents of the A register. The CPI instruction at 003 017 does change the condition of the flags, but this instruction performs an invisible subtraction.

Therefore, at 003 024, the A register does contain the contents of the loop counter. The next instruction inputs the results of the test that has just been performed.

The CMP M instruction is interesting. In the 7432 example, there were only two correct responses possible. In this program there are eight correct answers that must be stored. If the answers had been stored in the registers, there would have been no registers available for use. The correct answers had to be stored in a data table. The correct answer table uses the H register pair as its memory pointer. This makes it necessary to compare the answer in the A register with the contents of memory pointed to by H and L. The first pass through the test loop has H and L pointing to the base address. So, in the first pass through the loop, the answer in the accumulator is compared to 376.

The contents of the data table located at 004 000 in Example 6-4 are stored in such a way that each time the memory pointer is updated, the position of the single low bit is shifted to the left. This makes an alternate solution possible to the storage of the correct answers. A single register could have started with the value 376. After the first test sequence, the contents of this register could have been placed in the A register, then shifted left using one of the rotate instructions. Each pass through the loop would shift the single low bit one additional place.

The above paragraph brings into focus the reason for data tables in these types of applications. In most cases it is easier to look up an answer than to write complicated software that duplicates the logic of the circuit being tested. It should be understood that in each of these examples, the logic being tested was of a relatively simple nature. In such cases the amount of code generated using lookup tables may be more than the code created to reproduce the logic of the circuit under test. If this is the case, the lookup table approach may not be the best. There is a second consideration, though.

The time it takes the programmer to reproduce the logic through software is a very important consideration. If the programmer already knows the correct responses from a circuit, it is much easier to write diagnostic software using standard data table techniques. This greatly reduces the amount of time needed to produce a working algorithm.

At location 003 030, the error subroutine will be called if the answer in the A register does not match the answer currently pointed to by H and L.

Lines 003 034 and 003 035 update the loop counter and the data table pointer for the correct answer table. This is the normal position for these instructions within such a loop.

Finally, the JUMP instruction at 003 036 forms the foot of the DO-WHILE. It jumps back to 003 016 where the decision to exit the loop is made.

A careful examination of the program at this point shows no display routine. The computer used in this project was not interfaced to a printer. The errors had to be read by stepping through the error table. A print subroutine, for those fortunate enough to have a process-control computer interfaced to a printer, would be an excellent addition to the program.

Subroutines.   The FILL subroutine which begins at 003 100 is a simple DO-UNTIL loop. It will continue to fill the error table with the null value 252 until all eight locations contain the null. It will then return back to the main program.

The error subroutine starting at location 003 200 is a straightforward storage routine. Each time an error is detected it is called by the main program. After the error is stored, the error table pointer is updated to point to the next slot in the error table. This will prevent the storage of errors on top of each other. This subroutine also returns to the main program. The development of a more complicated error subroutine is left as a possible assignment at the end of this chapter.

6-5 CLOSING THOUGHTS

The two projects of this chapter show simple diagnostic routines demonstrating the use of data tables. In most cases the data tables greatly simplify the code in the diagnostic routine. Even when the logic being tested is fairly simple, the use of data tables will save the programmer a lot of time. The concepts of base address, indexing, and displacement were presented. Although the 8080/8085 microprocessors do not directly support indexing, this concept is very widespread. In fact, certain other microprocessor architectures have a special-purpose index register located within the CPU chip. In these computers, the displacement is formed automatically when the indexed mode of addressing is used. The Z80, 6800, and 6502 are three such CPUs.

SUMMARY

1. Diagnostic routines are software programs designed to test circuitry for correct operation. When a computer checks its own subsystems it is said to be performing self-diagnostics.

2. Data tables are data structures that use an indexed method of access. Properly used, data tables can greatly simplify programming tasks.

3. A base address is the address of the first datum in a table.

4. When using multiple data tables, it is often convenient to use a memory pointer other than H and L. The STAX and LDAX instructions allow the B and D register pairs to serve as pointers to a data table.

5. Subroutines used to look up or retrieve data from a table are more flexible and useful if the index is passed to it from the calling routine.

QUESTIONS

1. In this chapter, data tables were used to simplify diagnostic routines. List at least three other areas where data tables could be used to simplify programming.

2. What is the first location in a data table called?

3. Which method of access is used with data tables?

4. Of the three processors covered in this text, which has an architectural feature that supports the method of access used with data tables?

5. What two items associated with a data table are added together to form a displacement?

6. Explain the drawbacks to a lookup routine as coded in Example 6-1.

7. Construct a data table that contains the correct responses from a properly functioning 74154. Record this information in octal as well as hex.

8. What operation is performed by a CMA instruction?

9. In applications where large data tables are used, it is better to use an INX rather than an INR to update the table pointer. Why?

10. In the 7432 project, errors were recorded using logic 1s. If errors had been recorded using logic 0s, what instruction would have to replace the ORA E instruction in the error subroutine?

11. What other ways could have been used by the error subroutine in the 7432 project to detect if the first test run was the test run that had failed?

12. In the 7432 project, a complete test sequence was performed by an OUT followed by an IN instruction. How much time is there between the IN machine cycle and the OUT machine cycle? Assume the processor was operating at 1 MHz.

13. Using manufacturer's data books, determine how long it takes the output of the 7432 to change once the OUT machine cycle takes place. The delay introduced by the output latch must also be considered. Using this information, how fast could a processor run before the correct answer was not available by the time the IN machine cycle took place?

14. In applications where the length of the data table can change or is unknown, the computer must have some means of checking to see if it has reached the end of the table. One method is to insert a dummy value at the end of the table. A dummy value is a datum that cannot possibly occur within the parameters of the project. With this in mind, consider the way in which errors are stored in the 74155 lab. Is it necessary to step through the entire table to check for errors? Explain why or why not.

15. If the 74155 routine were modified to test G1 and G2, how many times would the DO-WHILE loop have to be repeated?

16. If G2 were controlled from D4 and G1 controlled from D3, determine the new correct-answer table. The remaining select lines are wired as in the project.

17. In the situation where G2 and G1 were tested, would it still be all right to store a null of 252 in the error table?

18. Explain how you might test the general-purpose registers within the CPU using a self-diagnostic routine. What assumptions must be made when performing such a test? Do these assumptions apply to self-diagnostics in general?

19. The FILL subroutine is an example of how software can be written to create data tables. At times, writing a program to create a table might be preferable to entering

long sequences of data. Flowchart a routine that will store 9 through 0 (descending) in 10 consecutive memory locations.

20. In a regular memory operation, the CPU provides an address, then receives data in response. In content-addressable memory, CAM, the computer provides a datum and memory returns the address of where the value is stored. Flowchart a subroutine to implement a CAM function. The flowchart will have the datum passed to it by the calling routine. The subroutine will then search a page of memory looking for the value desired. Once found, the subroutine will record the address where the calling routine can find it. Control will then return to the calling program. If the value is not found, a code should be passed back to the calling routine indicating that the value was not present.

LAB ASSIGNMENTS

1. Using the 74155 project, modify the error subroutine so that it stores not only the test sequence that failed, but also the pin number that failed under that test. This is an excellent project because it forces you to work with documentation and logic developed by another person, not that unusual a situation. It will also help to insure that you have a good understanding of the 74155 project.

2. Test a 74181 arithmetic logic chip under diagnostic software. The 74181 will have six of its inputs driven from an output port. These inputs will be select lines 0–3, the mode input, and carry in. Construct a program that will loop 48 times, testing all the logic functions of the ALU. Hardwire the input nibbles A and B to a known binary pattern. Using these inputs, predict the proper response from the ALU. Store these answers in a correct-answer table. Monitor the outputs F3 to F0 and the carry out. If an error is detected store the test sequence that failed in an error table. For this project, ignore the propagate and generate output pins. It is suggested that the 8255 be used in mode 0 to operate the input and output port assignments. As a guideline, let port A of the 8255 operate the inputs of the ALU. Let port B of the 8255 monitor the outputs of the ALU. Careful analysis of the hardware/software interface will be important.

LAB QUESTIONS

1. Record the new error subroutine used in assignment 1.

2. Record the select line, mode, and carry in to data bus connections, that is, their logical positions. Do not wire the ALU directly to the data bus.

3. Does the way in which the ALU inputs were wired affect the program logic? Does it affect the correct-answer table?

4. Since F3–F0 and carry out are monitored in assignment 2, what must be done in the program logic when the input to the mode control on the ALU is high?

5. Is it useful to write a FILL routine for assignment 2? Explain your answer.

7

ADVANCED INSTRUCTIONS

At the end of this chapter you should be familiar with:

1. These additional instructions: STA, LDA, DAA, DAD, SPHL, PCHL, XCHG, SHLD, LHLD
2. how to handle multiple memory pointers
3. how the stack pointer and stack operate when storing registers and addresses
4. how multiple stacks are handled
5. how block transfers are performed
6. the use of address tables
7. code compression
8. skip-chain logic
9. memory-mapped pointers
10. addressing modes

INTRODUCTION

In this chapter we will examine most of the remaining instructions in the 8080/8085 instruction set. In a few cases, special Z80 instructions will be discussed. If you are working with a Z80 system you should try these instructions. Remember, though, that we are restricting our instruction usage to the 8080/8085 instruction set, so the programs in this text will work on all three processors.

The division between basic instructions as presented in Chapter 2 and the advanced instructions presented here is arbitrary. Most of the new instructions you will learn here are more powerful. This means, in general, that the instruction will perform more internal CPU functions than those instructions presented earlier. Additionally, these instructions are frequently found in software routines that make use of advanced software concepts. Some of these software functions are examined here, although this chapter is not meant to be a treatise on advanced software. Remember, the goal of this text is to help make you an integrated software/hardware technician with enough skills in both areas to progress to more difficult topics when called for in future courses and on the job.

After you have completed this chapter, you will know almost the entire 8080/8085 instruction set. The major area left undiscussed is the set of instructions that deal with interrupts. This set of instructions will be found in Chapter 11, Interrupts. Finally, this chapter will conclude with a discussion on addressing modes.

7-1 STA, LDA

The *store accumulator direct* and the *load accumulator direct* are 3-byte instructions. The second and third bytes form addresses in the usual low-high sequence. The value of these instructions can easily be understood when it is realized that the A register can be moved to and from memory, without having to place the memory location into the H register pair. This does several things for the programmer. First, register pair H is free for other uses. After you have completed this chapter, you should realize that this can be very important, as register pair H plays an important part in the architecture of the processors we are using. Second, if register pair H were being used for something, the STA and LDA instructions eliminate the need to transfer the register-pair value elsewhere, load the pair with the address where A is to be transferred, complete the transfer of A, and then restore the contents of H and L. If the sequence just described can be eliminated through the use of a 3-byte instruction, a savings in memory has been realized. Whenever the same logical function can be performed with instructions that use fewer bytes, then the code is said to be compressed. Code compression will be an important concept throughout this chapter.

Example 7-1 shows a section of code from a larger program. This section is responsible for obtaining information from an I/O port and saving this information in memory. At the start of the section, STA is used to store a copy of the contents of the accumulator at 06 00 hex. This is necessary because the IN instruction overwrites this

EXAMPLE 7-1

HEX ADDRESS	HEX OP CODE	MNEMONIC	COMMENTS	OCTAL ADDRESS	OCTAL OP CODE
04 05	32	STA		004 005	062
04 06		00	STA, LDA Example	004 006	
04 07		06		004 007	
04 08	DB	IN		004 010	333
04 09		30		004 011	
04 0A	32	STA		004 012	062
04 0B		00		004 013	
04 0C		05		004 014	
04 0D	3A	LDA		004 015	072
04 0E		00		004 016	
04 0F		06		004 017	

information. The code at lines 04 08 and 04 09 obtain information from port 30. This information is then transferred to 05 00 hex through the use of another STA instruction. Finally, the original contents of the accumulator are restored by the LDA instruction, which retrieves the information stored at 06 00 hex.

7-2 MORE ARITHMETIC INSTRUCTIONS

DAA

The *decimal adjust the accumulator* instruction is used when you want the processor to perform arithmetic in binary-coded decimal. This instruction can be very convenient to use when the results of an operation will be transferred to a port that uses seven-segment displays. In most cases the decoder/driver for the displays will accept BCD. This means that if the calculations have been carried out in BCD, a binary to BCD conversion does not have to be performed, prior to output for use, by a seven-segment display.

This instruction corrects illegal decades that result from the addition of BCD numbers. The DAA instruction will not work correctly with a counting instruction, nor does it check operands prior to the BCD addition. This means that it is the programmer's responsibility to use valid BCD numbers when performing BCD arithmetic.

Example 7-2 shows the first use of the DAA instruction. In this example the program will display the numbers 0 through 9 decimal at port 50 hex. This port will accept BCD inputs. The numbers will be displayed in one-second intervals, the timing controlled by the CALL to the software delay.

EXAMPLE 7-2

HEX ADDRESS	HEX OP CODE	MNEMONIC	COMMENTS	OCTAL ADDRESS	OCTAL OP CODE
03 00	3E	MVI A		003 000	076
03 01		00		003 001	
03 02	D3	OUT	Display seconds	003 002	323
03 03		50		003 003	
03 04	C6	ADI	Increment seconds	003 004	306
03 05		01		003 005	
03 06	27	DAA	Adjust for BCD	003 006	047
03 07	CD	CALL	1 second delay	003 007	315
03 08		LO		003 010	
03 09		H1		003 011	
03 0A	FE	CPI	Done with display	003 012	376
03 0B		10		003 013	
03 0C	C2	JNZ	No, continue	003 014	302
03 0D		02		003 015	
03 0E		03		003 016	
03 0F	76	HLT	Stop	003 017	166

There are four important ideas that this example should trigger. First, the DAA instruction follows immediately after the ADI. As soon as the calculation was performed, it was checked for illegal BCD decades. If any were detected, they are corrected. Second, the program began at 00 hex. This is the same number as 0000 0000 base 2. It also happens to be a legal BCD number. From your past work in digital, you should be aware that the first 10 numbers, 0 through 9, are the same in both binary and BCD. This means that the values used prior to the addition were valid BCD operands. This must be the case or calculations can wind up incorrect. Third, even though a loop was constructed that incremented by ones, a counting instruction was not used. The DAA, as was pointed out, does not work with counting instructions. There is a tendency to forget this when loops are being constructed using BCD loop counters. Stick to the add instructions. Finally, the loop termination is handled by a CPI instruction that checks for 10. This is a BCD operand. When the ADI instruction changed the count from 0000 1001 to 0000 1010, an illegal decade resulted. The DAA operation altered this value to 0001 0000. If the CPI immediate byte had checked for OA hex, the loop would not have terminated correctly.

EXAMPLE 7-3

HEX ADDRESS	HEX OP CODE	MNEMONIC	COMMENTS	OCTAL ADDRESS	OCTAL OP CODE
05 30	OE	MVI C		005 060	016
05 31		45	BCD operand	005 061	
05 32	16	MVI D		005 062	026
05 33		67	BCD operand	005 063	
05 34	7A	MOV A, D	Prepare to ADD	005 064	172
05 35	81	ADD C	BCD ADD	005 065	201
05 36	27	DAA	Correct illegal decades	005 066	047

Example 7-3 shows two BCD numbers being added together. The two operands are already in BCD form. When added together, illegal decades result. The DAA corrects these decades by checking for values greater than 9, the maximum BCD value. The lower decade will be corrected if the operation results in a decade greater than 9 or if the aux carry flag had been set. The high-order decade will be corrected if the decade has an answer greater than 9 or if the carry flag is set. The overall DAA operation is a two-step process. First, the lower decades are added together. In Example 7-3 this would look like:

$$
\begin{array}{r}
0101 \\
\underline{0111} \\
1100
\end{array}
$$

This is an illegal result and will be corrected by the following operation:

$$
\begin{array}{r}
1100 \\
\underline{0110} \\
0010
\end{array}
\text{ with the aux carry flag set}
$$

The illegal decade is added to a correcting factor of 6. The corrected decade is now 2 decimal. This is the correct value. The aux carry flag is set, indicating overflow from the lower decade. This information will be used in the next step of the DAA operation.

Once the DAA has inspected and, if necessary, corrected the lower decade, the higher decades are added together with any overflow from the lower decade. Following through with our example, we obtain:

$$
\begin{array}{r}
0100 \\
0110 \\
\underline{1\text{—aux carry}} \\
1011
\end{array}
$$

This is an illegal decade and must be corrected. The correction is as follows:

$$
\begin{array}{r}
1011 \\
\underline{0110} \\
0001\text{—with the carry flag set}
\end{array}
$$

The final result of 112 base 10 did not fit into the register. The maximum BCD value that will fit into a register is 99. This is smaller than the 256 possibilities a single register can handle in binary. Since 99 was exceeded, the carry flag was set. In this operation, the carry flag indicates a result greater than or equal to 100. If the answer had to be stored elsewhere in the computer, two registers or memory locations would have to be used.

When a register holds two BCD digits as the A register does after the BCD addition in Example 7-3, that register is said to be packed. Two 7-segment displays would have to be connected to a port to handle the complete number. In some cases, the number has to be unpacked, split into two separate decades, and transferred to an output port one at a time.

BCD subtraction is performed by using ten's-complement arithmetic. Subtraction is performed by adding the ten's complement. To see how this works in decimal, examine the following subtraction:

$$
\begin{array}{r}
53 \\
47 \\
\hline
6
\end{array}
$$

The above operation is how people normally perform subtraction. To do the same in ten's-complement form, convert the bottom number to its ten's-complement form and add.

$$
\begin{array}{r}
53 \\
53 \\
\hline
106
\end{array}
$$

The carry into the extra column is thrown out, resulting in 06, the same answer we obtained the normal way. Ten's-complement numbers are formed by changing a number to a nine's complement and adding 1. The following examples illustrate how this is done:

$$65 \text{ becomes } 34 + 1 = 35$$

$$18 \text{ becomes } 81 + 1 = 82$$

$$23 \text{ becomes } 76 + 1 = 77$$

Notice that a nine's complement is the difference between the digit to be converted and 9. For example, the nine's complement of 4 is 5, the nine's complement of 2 is 7, and so on.

The point of this discussion is not to teach number theory, but to show how we can continue to use the DAA instruction and perform subtraction. Example 7-4 shows how the preceding concepts can be used in a computer program.

The objective of this section of code is to subtract the BCD value stored in D from the BCD value stored in E. The first instruction places 99 BCD into the accumulator. The C register is subtracted from 99, resulting in the nine's complement being formed in the A register. The ADI instruction then creates the ten's complement. This E register is then added to this ten's complement with the ADD instruction. This allows us to use the DAA instruction to adjust for illegal decades.

To strengthen this example, suppose E had 65 and D had 32. The correct result should be 33 when the sequence is finished.

$$
\begin{array}{ll}
99 & \text{—in A} \\
32 & \text{—in D} \\
\hline
67 & \text{—nine's complement in A} \\
1 & \text{—form ten's complement} \\
68 & \text{—in A} \\
65 & \text{—in E}
\end{array}
$$

EXAMPLE 7-4

HEX ADDRESS	HEX OP CODE	MNEMONIC	COMMENTS	OCTAL ADDRESS	OCTAL OP CODE
04 18	3E	MVI A		004 030	076
04 19		99	BCD value	004 031	
04 20	92	SUB D	Form nine's complement	004 032	222
04 21	C6	ADI	Form ten's complement	004 033	306
04 22		001		004 034	
04 23	83	ADD E		004 035	203
04 24	27	DAA		004 036	047

Binary breakdown of 68 + 65 is:

$$0110\ 1000$$
$$0110\ 0101$$
$$1100\ 1101$$

Correction from DAA on lower decade:

$$1101$$
$$0110\text{—correction factor}$$
$$0011\ \text{with aux carry set}$$

Correction on upper decade:

$$1100$$
$$1\text{—aux carry}$$
$$0110\text{—correction factor}$$
$$0011\ \text{with carry set}$$

The result in the accumulator is 0011 0011 or 33 BCD, which is the correct value. The carry flag is set, indicating overflow, but in ten's complement arithmetic, carries beyond the columns set by the numbers to be added are ignored.

Multiplication and division of BCD numbers are even more complex and will not be discussed here. In most cases it will be easier to multiply and divide in binary, then convert the answer to BCD. We are almost back where we started—that is, the need to have a conversion routine that changes binary to BCD for display usage. This function might be so important that a routine to handle this is written and stored as a permanent part of the computer's software. The discussion later in this chapter on firmware utilities will examine this concept.

DAD

The DAD instructions can be used to perform 16-bit arithmetic without the need to use ADC and ACI. The DAD instructions perform this arithmetic by using register pairs, one of which must always be register pair H. Register pair H is used in 16-bit arithmetic like the accumulator is used in 8-bit arithmetic. One of the operands, by default, is the HL pair. The other operand can be any of the following register pairs:

> BC
> DE
> HL
> SP

When the 16-bit arithmetic operation is complete, the result is stored in the H and L registers. The only flag affected by this instruction is the carry flag. It will be set if the 16-bit addition cannot handle the result and an overflow results. Otherwise, this flag is reset.

Example 7-5 shows how register pairs H and D are added together. When the section of code is finished, the hex value of 12 OD is stored in the H register pair.

EXAMPLE 7-5

HEX ADDRESS	HEX OP CODE	MNEMONIC	COMMENTS	OCTAL ADDRESS	OCTAL OP CODE
03 00	21	LXI H	16-bit arithmetic	003 000	041
03 01		05		003 001	
03 02		02		003 002	
			Example		
03 03	11	LXI D		003 003	021
03 04		08		003 004	
03 05		10		003 005	
03 06	19	DAD D		003 006	031

Performing a DAD H doubles the value stored in this register pair. The DAD SP instruction has a very interesting use, which we will see in the next section.

7-3 STACK OPERATIONS

We were introduced to the stack when subroutine usage was first explained. At this time we are going to look at the stack in more detail in connection with some new instructions and software concepts.

Stack Architecture

We have discovered that the stack is a data structure that follows the access method of last in, first out. It can be used for storage of register values by performing PUSH instructions. When those values are to be restored to the registers, a POP instruction must be performed. The stack is also very important when subroutines are used. By storing return addresses, the stack allows the CPU to remember where to resume program flow after a subroutine has been completed. Nested subroutines are supported by the stack through the use of the last in, first out access method. The three processors implement the stack in the same fashion. It is this implementation method that we will now examine.

The stack is stored in memory. The starting point for the stack is determined by the programmer when he or she loads the stack pointer register. This pointer is loaded when the LXI SP instruction is performed. Figure 7-1 shows a map of the memory used by the stack in the discussion that follows.

This map shows three different stack sequences that illustrate how the stack is implemented. The stack pointer has been initialized to 20 00 hex just once in the program, most often at the start of the main routine. In our case, LSI SP 00 20 would perform the initialization.

The first sequence shows how the stack can be used to obtain a copy of the flags. A PUSH PSW instruction is performed in a program. A copy of the A register and the flags is placed in the stack. The value to be saved is stored at the next location lower than the stack pointer address. Since the stack pointer is set to 20 00, the first value stored is located at 19 FF. The second value, in this case the flags, is stored as SP-2 or 19 FE. When the storage operation is completed the stack pointer is decremented by 2. After the PUSH PSW is complete the stack pointer will contain 19 FE. Two things should be emphasized at this point. First, data transfers to and from the stack are done with 16-bit operands. Second, as items are added to the stack, the stack works its way *down* in memory and the stack pointer is decremented. The direction of stack flow for each instruction shown in Figure 7-1 is indicated by arrows pointing up or down.

Sequence 1 is completed when a POP H instruction is performed. The flags are placed in the L register, where they are then available for inspection, and the copy of A that was on the stack is placed into the H register. After the POP has been completed, the stack pointer is incremented by 2. This places the stack pointer back at 20 00, the

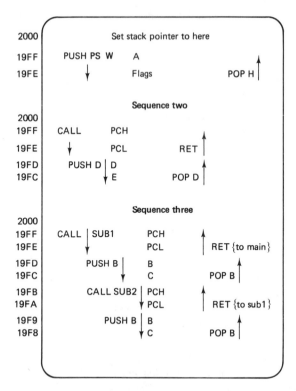

FIGURE 7-1 Storage sequences as stack is used.

original value loaded into the stack pointer by the LXI SP instruction. One last point about this example: The copies of the A register and the flags that were placed in the stack still reside at 19 FF and 19 FE. These copies will not be destroyed until the stack is used again and new values overwrite the old.

Sequence 2 illustrates a subroutine call with one set of registers saved. A call in the main program causes the address of the instruction after the call to be placed onto the stack at 19 FF. The order of the stored bytes is high byte first, then low byte. This order is followed for all register pairs. A PUSH D instruction is then performed in the subroutine to save the values in these registers. This means that when the subroutine is finished, the values of these registers prior to the call can be restored by a POP. The PUSH forces the stack pointer down two additional places in memory. If the subroutine then performed a RET, without popping D, the stack pointer would be pointing at the values from the D pair. This information would be placed into the program counter by the RET. Since it is not a valid return address, the program would bomb.

The POP D instruction keeps the stack operations balanced. For every PUSH there is a POP; for every CALL there is a RET. Without this balance, the stack loses track of where information is stored. Incorrect stack operations are a common reason why programs fail.

Sequence 3 shows how the stack can implement nested subroutines. The first CALL, located in the main program, forces a return address into the stack. Register pair B is then saved. The stack pointer has now decremented four places from the starting value. A second CALL located in subroutine 1 calls subroutine 2. This call places a second return address on the stack. This return address is used by the CPU to find its way back to subroutine 1. PUSH B is performed once more in subroutine 2. Do not think that this is a meaningless example. This second PUSH B is not saving a copy of the B pair from the main routine; it is saving the values placed into these registers by subroutine 1. When subroutine 2 finishes, it restores the B pair for subroutine 1 and returns. Subroutine 1 then resumes its execution with the values it expects in B and C. When it completes execution, it restores the B pair with a POP and returns to the main program with RET. At the end of this entire sequence the stack pointer is back at the original location and is once more ready for use.

Programs are stored in memory and the PC is incremented as the instructions are performed. Thus flow moves up in memory. The stack pointer moves down as it is used. It is vital that the stack never overlap a program, as it will erase instructions. If such happens, the program will bomb. Therefore, when setting the stack pointer, set it at the highest available RAM location. This will help prevent the stack from overwriting your programs.

Reading the Stack Pointer

There are times when it will be convenient to know the contents of the stack pointer. This information can be used to gauge how close the stack comes to a program or data table, as well as to track the flow of a program through the subroutines.

The 8080/8085 instruction set does not have an instruction that allows the stack pointer to be read directly. The section of code in Example 7-6 accomplishes the task

EXAMPLE 7-6

HEX ADDRESS	HEX OP CODE	MNEMONIC	COMMENTS	OCTAL ADDRESS	OCTAL OP CODE
03 00	21	LXI H	Determining the stack	003 000	041
03 01		00	pointer	003 001	
03 02		00		003 002	
03 03	39	DAD SP	Contents	003 003	071

of obtaining the value of the stack pointer. The first instruction clears the H register pair. The second instruction, the DAD SP, adds the contents of the stack pointer to the H pair. Since H was cleared prior to the DAD operation, the contents of H and L, where the answer is stored, is now a copy of the stack pointer. Register pair H can now be examined to find out where the stack pointer is located.

The drawback to Example 7-6 is the destruction of the H and L registers. We already know several important uses for this register pair. It acts as a memory pointer and is used in 16-bit arithmetic. Later in this chapter we will see more uses for H and L. It is quite likely that the pair is already in use when this section of code is used to determine the stack pointer contents. Fortunately, there is a quick, easy way to store the pair and save the contents for use later in a program.

Example 7-7 uses two new instructions: SHLD, store H and L direct, and LHLD, load H and L direct. Each of these instructions is a 3-byte instruction where the second and third bytes are address bytes. Example 7-7 begins with SHLD, which moves a copy of H and L into two addresses, beginning with the address specified in the instruction. Register L is moved to the address listed in the instruction. Register H is moved to the address + 1. All of this is done by the computer as part of the execution of the instruc-

EXAMPLE 7-7

HEX ADDRESS	HEX OP CODE	MNEMONIC	COMMENTS	OCTAL ADDRESS	OCTAL OP CODE
04 00	22	SHLD	Save H, L	004 000	042
04 01		00		004 001	
04 02		05		004 002	
04 03	21	LXI H	Get stack pointer	004 003	041
04 04		00		004 004	
04 05		00		004 005	
04 06	39	DAD SP	Contents	004 006	071
04 07	22	SHLD	Save stack pointer value	004 007	042
04 08		10		004 010	
04 09		05		004 011	
04 0A	2A	LHLD	Restore H, L	004 012	052
04 0B		00		004 013	
04 0C		05		004 014	

tion. As a programmer, you must remember to point to two consecutive bytes in memory that are free.

The code of Example 7-7 now places the stack pointer value in H and L through the DAD SP instruction. The stack pointer value is then transferred to two bytes in memory through the use of another SHLD instruction. After the program has finished, the stack pointer can be examined at 05 10 and 05 11 hex. The last instruction in the sequence restores the original value of register pair H by performing an LHLD instruction that addresses 05 00 hex.

Multiple Stacks

There may be times when it is convenient to have two or more stacks. One stack may be used for the usual storage of registers and handling of subroutine calls; the other stack may be used to handle data that has some special purpose and needs to be grouped in a last in, first out method. Since stack operations follow this access method, it would not be efficient to implement such a structure in code when the hardware has features that perform most of the functions involved in such a data structure.

Even when the user has just one stack in use by his routines, the computer may be using another stack for the monitor or control program that is operating the computer interfaces. If the system stack is set up correctly, the user may not even know this stack exists.

We have taken the first step in implementing more than one stack: locating the stack pointer value and then storing it for later use. In this case, later use would involve toggling between different stacks. With this in mind, let's examine some code that toggles between a system stack and a user stack.

When you work with a computer trainer, you will manipulate a memory pointer that tracks program and data entry. This memory pointer responds to keyboard commands and is updated by the computer's control program. At this point in the text, you should be thoroughly familiar with the functions of a computer trainer. If not, review the sections of Chapter 1 that deal with program entry and execution.

Examining Example 7-8, we see a listing that begins at 00 00 hex. This is the address where the 8080, 8085, and Z80 begin to fetch instructions when they are powered up. The first activity carried out by this program is to initialize a stack pointer for system use. After this the monitor continues to run, scanning a keyboard for data entry and updating displays as the operator enters data.

Once a user program has been entered, the operator will transfer control from the monitor to the user program. This is usually handled by setting the memory pointer to the start of the user program and pressing the "go" button.

Example 7-8 continues with a section of code that implements the "go" function. The starting address of the section is marked with a *. There is no way for us to know where this section of code is located without a monitor listing. The first task performed by this section of code stores the contents of the memory pointer that was kept in the H register pair. Then a sequence we have studied is performed. From 3 through 9 the stack pointer is read and saved for later use in locations FF 60 and FF 61. The next instruction

EXAMPLE 7-8

Hex Address	Hex Op Code	Mnemonic	Comments	Octal Address	Octal Op Code
			Cold Reset		
00 00	31	LXISP	Set up system stack	000 000	061
00 01		LO		000 001	
00 02		HI		000 002	
* 0	22	SHLD	"GO function"	0	042
1		50		1	
2		FF	Save memory pointer	2	
3	21	LXI H		3	041
4		00		4	
5		00		5	
6	39	DAD SP	Get system SP	6	071
7	22	SHLD	Save system SP	7	042
8		60		10	
9		FF		11	
A	2A	LHLD	Restore memory pointer	12	052
B		50		13	
C		FF		14	
D	E9	PCHL	Execute user routine	15	351

restores the memory pointer to H and L. Control of the computer is then transferred to this new address by a new instruction.

PCHL copies the contents of H and L into the program counter. Once this operation is completed, the computer begins to fetch instructions from this new address. In effect, the computer jumps to the address loaded from H and L.

The user can now initialize a stack of his own without disturbing the system stack.

When control of the computer is returned to the monitor, it can look up the stack pointer value that was just stored. The next example shows how this might be done.

At some point in time, control will be returned to the monitor. The most common method is for the user program to halt. The operator then presses the reset button and performs a warm reset. The warm reset returns execution to the monitor. A section of code listed in Example 7-9 indicates what might happen in a two-stack system.

The first block of code obtains the value of the user stack. This value is then stored for inspection. The instruction after this first block loads H and L from locations FF 60

EXAMPLE 7-9

Hex ADDRESS	Hex OP CODE	Mnemonic	Comments	Octal ADDRESS	Octal OP CODE
			Warm Reset		
-ANY-	22	SHLD	Save H, L	-ANY-	042
	50				
	FF				
	21	LXI H	Obtain user SP data		041
	00				
	00				
	39	DAD SP			071
	22	SHLD	Store user SP data		042
	62				
	FF				
	2A	LHLD	Get system SP data		052
	60				
	FF				
	F9	SP HL	Restore system stack		371
	2A	LHLD	Restore H, L		052
	50				
	FF				

and FF 61 hex. This was the location where the system stack pointer was stored in Example 7-8. The next instruction, SPHL, is one that has not yet been discussed. This instruction transfers the contents of the H pair into the stack pointer. In this case, it restored the system stack. Finally, the last instruction restores the value H and L had at the start of this sequence.

7-4 MULTIPLE MEMORY POINTERS

Chapter 6, Diagnostics, introduced how to handle data tables. Data tables are very useful in a wide variety of applications. This means that they are frequently used in many applications. A memory pointer might be used to handle a data table, another pointer might be used for memory-mapped I/O, and a third may be used for normal memory transfers. This section will highlight the use of multiple memory pointers by looking at some examples where they are used.

Block Transfers

Often it is necessary to move a data table or a block of code from one location in memory to another. There are many reasons why this might occur. A section of ROM may be moved to RAM where it can be edited, a block of memory representing a drawing may be moved into the RAM that handles the display memory for a CRT terminal, and a data table may have to be moved to make room for additional instructions at the end of a program. As you gain experience with computers, other applications will appear. What we will examine next should give you the techniques necessary to perform block transfers when necessary.

A block transfer program is listed in Example 7-10. The first two instructions set table pointers to the first entry of each location. Register pair H points to the data to be moved, while register pair D, acting as a second memory pointer, points to the destination of the information. Register C is used to count the bytes moved. When the block has been transferred, C will contain zero and the program will halt.

Each pass through the loop will transfer 1 byte. Line 03 08 obtains the byte to be moved, while the STAX D instruction at 03 09 moves the byte to its new location. After this transfer is complete, both memory pointers are updated so the next byte can be moved in the following pass.

Z80 Block Transfer

The Z80 has special instructions that handle block transfer very efficiently. The program shown in Example 7-11 performs the same block transfer that occurred in Example 7-10 through the use of the LDIR instruction. This instruction moves bytes pointed to by H and L to locations pointed to by D and E. Each time it is executed a byte is moved, both

EXAMPLE 7-10

Hex Address	Hex Op Code	Mnemonic	Comments	Octal Address	Octal Op Code
			Block Transfer		
03 00	21	LXI H		003 000	041
03 01		00		003 001	
03 02		05		003 002	
03 03	11	LXI D		003 003	021
03 04		00		003 004	
03 05		06		003 005	
03 06	0E	MVI C		003 006	016
03 07		4A		003 007	
03 08	7E	MOV A, M		003 010	176
03 09	12	STAX D		003 011	022
03 0A	23	INX H		003 012	043
03 0B	13	INX D		003 013	023
03 0C	0D	DCR C		003 014	015
03 0D	CZ	JNZ		003 015	302
03 0E		08		003 016	
03 0F		03		003 017	
03 10	76	HLT		003 020	166

memory pointers are incremented, and the byte counter BC is decremented. If BC is not zero, the instruction is repeated. The Z80 has other block transfer instructions, but they will not be discussed here. This section has been included to highlight an important difference in the instruction sets. Our programs and project examples will continue to be written so they will perform on all three processors.

EXAMPLE 7-11

HEX ADDRESS	HEX OP CODE	MNEMONIC	COMMENTS	OCTAL ADDRESS	OCTAL OP CODE
			Z80 Block Transfer		
03 00	21	LXI H		003 000	041
03 01		00		003 001	
03 02		05		003 002	
03 03	11	LXI D		003 003	021
03 04		00		003 004	
03 05		06		003 005	
03 06	01	LXI B		003 006	001
03 07		4A		003 007	
03 08		00		003 010	
03 09		LDIR	Z80 Instruction	003 011	
03 0A	76	HLT		003 012	

Memory-Mapped Pointers

There may be times when it is convenient to have a memory pointer for memory operations and another for memory-mapped I/O. Suppose we choose the H pair for memory and the B pair for memory-mapped I/O. All of the registers can be transferred into memory by using the M operator. However, the STAX and LDAX instructions only allow the A register to be moved. If this is the case, then the advantage of moving any register to a memory-mapped port is lost. Changing the functions of the two pointers does not improve the situation; instead, you simply change problems. Now all the registers can be transferred directly to a memory-mapped port, but only the A register can be moved into and out of memory through the STAX and LDAX instructions using B as a memory pointer.

There is an easy way around this problem. Place one memory pointer in the H pair and the other in the D pair. Select one pair to represent the pointer for memory and the other pointer to represent the pointer for memory-mapped I/O. Suppose we select H and L for memory operations and the D pair for memory-mapped operations. When performing memory operations, the H pair is left alone. Therefore, a MOV B, M would move a memory location into the B register. To toggle to a memory-mapped operation, use the XCHG instruction. This instruction swaps the values in H and L with the values in D and E. After the XCHG, register pair H is now pointing where D pointed. That happens to be a memory-mapped location. Now the instruction MOV B, M would move a value from a port into B. When you are ready to resume normal memory operations, perform the XCHG instruction again. Example 7-12 shows how this would be done.

EXAMPLE 7-12

HEX ADDRESS	HEX OP CODE	MNEMONIC	COMMENTS	OCTAL ADDRESS	OCTAL OP CODE
			(H, L)-memory		
			(D, E) MM I/O		
04 50	EB	XCHG		004 120	353
04 51	4E	MOV C, M	Port data into C	004 121	116
04 52	EB	XCHG		004 122	353
04 53	46	MOV B, M	Memory data	004 123	106
			Transfer to B		

7-5 ADDRESS TABLES

This chapter has discussed pointers, particularly where more than one was involved. We will continue this discussion, but with an important twist. In this section we will deal with pointers to pointers and an important application of this idea, the address table.

When an address points to a location where another address is located and that second address points to the data to be manipulated, *indirect addressing* is being used. Figure 7-2 highlights this idea graphically.

It might seem strange that such a method of obtaining the desired value exists. Why not point to the value directly? Direct addressing such as the LDA instruction uses is not as easy to change. Suppose LDA was included in a program located in PROM. If the location of the value was changed, the second and third bytes of the instruction would

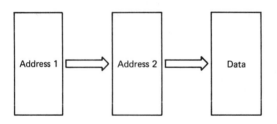

FIGURE 7-2   Concept of indirect addressing.

no longer point at the correct location. The PROM would now be useless. Indirect addressing could have avoided the problem.

Many of the instructions we have studied use indirect addressing. A MOV C,M instruction is an example. This instruction points to the HL pair, which points to the memory location. If MOV C,M were in a PROM, the address it used could be altered by changing HL prior to calling the PROM routine. Since HL are in the CPU, they are easily alterable.

There are many other advantages to indirect addressing that find applications in advanced computer programming. As an electronic technician one of these techniques, the address table, will be a useful tool in your software skills.

Code Compression

We have repeatedly emphasized that the electronic technician is likely to see microprocessors implemented with small amounts of memory. If the technician is involved in the development of programs that are to be fitted into ROM, PROM or EPROM techniques usable in compressing or compacting code will be important. Even in a repair situation where a process is to be tracked as it progresses through software, the ability to follow the code can be a skill that might make the difference between finding a problem and failing to solve the problem.

In several projects earlier in the text we had a computer monitoring a conveyor where a limited number of products were possible. Consider what would happen if we let just 20 different items pass a sensor and each different item sensed required a different action on the part of the computer. The logic of such a program might go like this:

Is it item 1

Yes—jump to code for item 1

No—go to next question

Is it item 2

Yes—jump to code for item 2

No—go to next question

Is it item 3

etc.

Such a sequence of code is often called a *skip chain*. It uses up a lot of memory and slows program execution. Each time the computer must make a decision, execution time suffers. The start of a skip-chain flowchart is shown in Figure 7-3. If each of the decision points is handled by a CPI, an immediate byte, and a 3-byte jump, each decision point will use 5 bytes of memory. In a 20-item skip chain, 100 bytes will be used just to direct the computer to the correct response.

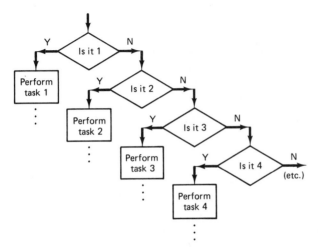

FIGURE 7-3 Start of a flowchart showing skip-chain logic.

A second drawback of skip-chain structures is response time. It is not equal. The time the computer takes to respond to task 20 will be longer than the time it takes to respond to task 1. This is due to the greater number of questions it must answer before it even reaches 20.

Example 7-13 shows how an address table can be used to improve on the skip-chain method just discussed. The setup for the address table begins at 04 02 after the product code has been entered from port 04. The LXI instruction points to the start of the address table. The RLC instruction forms an index from the product code entered. In this case, the product code is rotated to multiply it by 2. This keeps the index on even-byte boundaries, necessary due to the layout of the address table, which works with 16-bit addresses. The index is added to the base address to form a displacement into the address table. This displacement is then moved back into the pointer to the

EXAMPLE 7-13

HEX ADDRESS	HEX OP CODE	MNEMONIC	COMMENTS	OCTAL ADDRESS	OCTAL OP CODE
04 00	DB	IN	Get product code	004 000	333
04 01		04		004 001	
04 02	21	LXI H	Point to address table	004 002	041
04 03		00		004 003	
04 04		05		004 004	
04 05	07	RLC	Form index	004 005	007
04 06	85	ADD L	Form displacement	004 006	205
04 07	6F	MOV L, A	Point to address	004 007	157
04 08	5E	MOV E, M	Get low address	004 010	136
04 09	23	INX H	Get high address	004 011	043
04 0A	56	MOV D, M		004 012	126
04 0B	EB	XCHG	Transfer control to code for	004 013	353
04 0C	E9	PCHL	product sensed	004 014	351
05 00		LO	Product 1		
05 01		HI			
05 02		LO	Product 2		
05 03		HI			
05 04		LO	Product 3		
05 05		HI			
05 06		etc			
05 07					
05 08					

address table. The low byte of the address is transferred into the E register. The address table pointer is then incremented so that it points to the high byte of the address. This byte is then moved into the D register. The D pair now points to the code to be performed in response to the product code obtained from port 4. This code is moved into H and L with the XCHG instruction. Finally, control is transferred to the code that responds to the product code by PCHL.

The setup code that allowed us to use an address table was 11 bytes long. The IN is not counted because it is needed by the skip chain too. The address table is 40 bytes long if 20 products are to be handled. This means that a total of 51 bytes were used. Since the skip chain is 100 bytes long, a considerable savings in memory has been realized. Finally, the time to reach a block of code for any product is equal. The code for product 19 will be reached in the same time it takes the computer to reach the code for product 1.

Not all address tables are built the same way. Some only have 1-byte addresses. Others may contain some additional information associated with the process to be performed. Despite this, the basic idea of address tables has been explained. It is a powerful technique that should be studied carefully, especially if you ever plan to get into control programming, where the code must be compressed to fit into a given PROM. As can be seen from this example, an address table just might make the difference.

7-6 ADDRESSING MODES

In the software examples discussed to this point in the text, we have used indexed addressing, indirect addressing, direct addressing, register addressing, register indirect addressing, and implied addressing. In some situations, the program had to create the addressing technique used. In others, the CPU architecture supported the addressing mode used. In this section we will examine those addressing modes supported by the processors we are studying.

Immediate Addressing

The instruction contains the data to be manipulated. MVI is an example of such an instruction. All three processors support this mode.

Immediate Extended Addressing

The instruction contains 2 immediate bytes. An example would be LXI. All three processors support this mode of addressing, although the 8080/8085 documentation does not distinguish between immediate and immediate extended.

Zero-Page Addressing

This form of addressing uses the restart instructions associated with interrupts. The high-order byte of the address is page zero. The low-order byte of the address is determined by which restart instruction is used. There are eight of these instructions. All three processors support this addressing mode. See Chapter 11, Interrupts, for more details.

Direct Addressing

The second and third bytes of the instruction point to a specific memory cell. STA is an example of an instruction that supports direct addressing. Z80 documentation refers to this addressing mode as *extended.*

Register Addressing

The operation code specifies the register operands to be used. MOV A, B is an instruction that uses register addressing. This mode is available in all three processors.

Register Indirect Addressing

The instruction directs the CPU to a register pair, which then points to another operand. STAX D is an example. All three processors support this mode of addressing.

Implied Addressing

The op code will imply the use of one or more operands. ADD B implies that the A register will be used as one of the operands. While all three processors support this type of addressing, the 8080/8085 documentation does not make this distinction.

Relative Addressing

This form of addressing uses 1 byte of data after the op code as a displacement byte. The displacement byte tells the processor how far to jump from the instruction. JR, jump relative, is an example of such an instruction. The displacement byte is a signed two's-complement number. The range of the jump is + 129 base 10 to − 126 from the jump relative op code address. A positive number jumps forward in the program, while a negative number jumps back toward the start of the program. This mode of addressing is supported only by the Z80.

Indexed Addressing

The data byte following the op code is a signed two's-complement number. This byte is added to the contents of an index register, either IX or IY. The index register forms the base address. When manipulating data tables, the index register is frequently set to the address of the first datum. The data byte is then used as an index into the table. The instruction automatically forms the displacement itself. This process does not alter the contents of the index register. Of the three processors we are investigating, only the Z80 architecture supports this addressing mode; however, we have seen how to implement this mode through software when using the 8080/8085 processors.

Bit Addressing

This addressing mode allows any memory location or CPU register to be specified for bit operations. Three bits in the op code specify which bit will be the operand; the other bits specify which register or memory location. BIT 5,D will operate on bit 5 of the D register. This mode is available in the Z80. Bit testing, setting, and resetting can be done in 8080/8085 systems through masking operations.

Addressing Summary

Whenever selecting a processor to work with, consider the addressing modes available. If an application exists where an addressing mode is not supported by the CPU architecture, the mode will have to be supported through software. This uses up memory, which is a disadvantage. Like most things in life, additional features may cost more. It may be economically desirable to buy a lower-cost processor and implement some addressing modes yourself. Your software abilities, the application, and cost will determine which way to go.

7-7 CLOSING THOUGHTS

This chapter has introduced many new instructions. They were presented in the context of advanced software applications.

We learned in this chapter that the H register pair is very significant in the architecture of the processors we are working with. This is evident when you consider the special instructions that allow you to manipulate the H register pair.

The closer look at the way stacks are implemented will help you when you run into stack problems created by your software. Most programmers (I want to say *all*) will at one time or another have problems with the stack. The technique of obtaining the stack-pointer value can be very important. If you are fortunate, the system you use may have such a feature. If not, you should know how to implement it for yourself.

Software problems with multiple stacks can be difficult to correct. Unless the amount of work saved by using multiple stacks is immense, avoid this situation.

The concept of multiple memory pointers was explained. Their usefulness can be immense. Remember the suggestion about using the XCHG instruction—it can save a lot of work.

Addressing tables were explained. Their importance in code compression was illustrated through a program example. This technique also brought out in the open the concept of indirect addressing. We had been using a form of indirect addressing, register indirect addressing, without emphasizing it. This led into a discussion of addressing modes with which we closed the chapter.

One last point concerning the DAA instruction learned in this chapter. Enhanced versions of the 8080 will adjust BCD results with subtract instructions. This eliminates the need to form ten's-complement numbers. Consult the spec sheet for the version you are using. The Z80 will adjust on subtracts and increments when using the DAA instruction. This makes this instruction a potential trouble spot, since it will not work the same on all versions of the processors we are studying. If you stick to the techniques used in this chapter you will avoid problems.

SUMMARY

1. The STA and LDA instructions allow the CPU to transfer A register information into and out of memory without having to reference the HL register pair.

2. The DAA instruction is used in BCD operations.

3. The DAD instruction is used to perform 16-bit addition. The answer is stored in the HL pair.

4. A section of code was examined that allowed the programmer to determine the contents of the stack pointer. The key instruction in the sequence was DAD SP.

5. The XCHG instruction is very useful when it is necessary to use more than one memory pointer.

6. Code compression concerns methods of reducing the amount of code needed to perform a task. Address tables are an important technique used to compress code.

7. Addressing modes are ways in which the computer can calculate or determine the address of a variable, operand, and so on. The number of addressing modes available in a processor is an important consideration in its selection. Addressing modes not supported by a processor's architecture will have to be implemented in software, if needed.

QUESTIONS

1. What is the function of the STA instruction? What type of addressing does it use?

2. What is the function of the DAA instruction?

3. When BCD decades are corrected, what number is added to the decade to make the correction?

4. Which flag is used when the CPU tests for overflow from the low-order decade?

5. Determine the nine's complement of the following numbers: 103, 24, 63, and 72.

6. Determine the two's complement of the following numbers: 1101 0110 and 0111 0100.

7. In BCD arithmetic, what is the weight of the carry flag? That is, when set, what value does it represent?

8. Where is the answer stored when a DAD instruction is performed?

9. What register pairs can be used with the DAD instruction?

10. As items are added to the stack, what happens to the stack pointer?

11. How many bytes can be transferred to the stack in a single stack operation?

12. Where is the typical location of LXI SP within a program?

13. Explain why it is important to keep the PUSHes and the POPs balanced.

14. How many bytes of memory will be used by an SHLD instruction? (Do not include the bytes used to store the instruction itself in your answer.)

15. What is the function of PCHL?

16. What is the function of the SPHL instruction?

17. How can the XCHG instruction be used to ease handling multiple memory pointers?

18. Which of the processors studied in this text can perform an LDIR instruction? Explain how this instruction works.

19. What type of addressing mode is used when a program implements an address table?

20. Name two instances where an address table is useful.

21. What is meant by *code compression*?

22. Explain the term *skip chain*.

23. List two drawbacks of skip chains.

24. Which of the processors we have studied in this text support immediate addressing? Zero-page addressing? Bit addressing?

ASSIGNMENTS

1. Write a skip-chain program that handles 10 different codes. The code can be input through a port that you interface or you can load a value into a register prior to running this program.

2. Calculate at what point (how many codes, decisions) an address table is more memory efficient if the address table uses 2 bytes for each function and has 11 setup instructions. Remember, in a skip chain each decision will use at least 5 bytes per decision.

3. Write a block-transfer program that will copy the system monitor for your trainer

into RAM. Do not overwrite the block-transfer program. If the monitor will not fit into RAM, adjust the byte counters to transfer as much as possible.

LAB QUESTIONS

1. Each decision point in a skip chain corresponds to a _____ logical construct?
2. Record your answer to assignment 2.
3. How many memory pointers are required in assignment 3?
4. How can the block-transfer program be written so that bytes transferred from the monitor to RAM do not go through the accumulator?
5. What instructions were used to advance the byte counters in assignment 3? Explain why they were used.

8

MEMORY

At the end of this chapter you should be familiar with:

1. memory machine cycles
2. ROM [read only memory] principles, ROM types
3. decoder circuitry used for ROM chips
4. read/write memory principles
   a. static
   b. dynamic
5. RAM decoder circuitry
6. direct-memory access concepts
7. DMA controller Z8410

INTRODUCTION

One of the characteristics that marks a computer is the ability to perform a stored sequence of instructions without operator intervention. This does not mean that the computer will not accept input from an outside source once a program is underway. What it does imply is that a computer can act on previously recorded instructions as well as interact with instructions that require an immediate response.

A calculator, in contrast, operates on instructions that require an immediate response. It does not have the ability to remember instructions entered at an earlier time, nor does it have the ability to store instructions for a later use.

Admittedly, the boundary between calculator and computer has grown fuzzy with the advent of a programmable calculator. Strictly speaking, a calculator that accepts and acts on stored programs is a computer. The programmable calculator does have a limited amount of memory. It also has, as a rule, a much smaller instruction set.

This blurring of boundaries is an ongoing process in electronics. Our industry changes so rapidly, that standards, much less standard definitions, are constantly changing.

One of the areas of rapid change has been the area of memory technology. In the late 1970s, memory chips were costly by today's standards. A person purchasing a home computer often settled for a system with 4K of RAM. Upgrades to 16K were in the hundreds of dollars. Today, it is unusual to see a home computer sold with less than 64K. Memory expansions cards are available that increase memory size to 128K and beyond. One of the factors that has made this possible is the increase in packing densities. Chip manufacturers have succeeded in placing more and more bits into an IC. Consequently, the cost per bit has decreased, with the result that larger-capacity memory chips are finding their way into computer systems.

It is impossible for a text to keep up with this rapid change. While we cannot look at the very latest memory chips available, the chips selected for review are widely used, still found in current IC catalogs, and will illustrate the interaction between memory and the CPU.

The interaction between memory and the CPU starts with a memory machine cycle operation. The control signal information from these cycles will activate decoder circuitry that in turn selects a memory IC from the memory map. The selected IC will then respond by placing information onto the bus or, if capable, accepting information from the CPU.

This chapter focuses on this process. It concludes with a discussion of direct memory access and a study of a DMA controller.

8-1 MEMORY MACHINE CYCLES

Earlier in the text, the 8085 memory machine cycles were discussed in the section on memory-mapped I/O. For purposes of comparison and to refresh your memory (no pun intended), the Z80 memory machine cycles are examined here.

Z80 Memory-Read Machine Cycle

The memory-read cycle waveforms generated by the Z80 are shown in Figure 8-1. This machine cycle uses three clock states. The address information is placed onto the address bus just after the rising edge of T1. This information is held constant during the entire cycle. At the falling edge of T1, the MEMRQ* and RD* control signals are taken active low. The delay in generating the control signals allows the address time to stabilize; decoder circuits can also use this delay to decode the address. The CPU will sample the data bus during T3. The falling edge of T3 is used to deactivate the control signals. A MEMR* control signal can be created by logically combining MEMRQ* and RD*. See Figure 5-2 for one way in which this can be done.

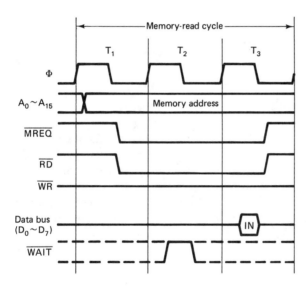

FIGURE 8-1   Z80 memory-read machine cycle. (Reproduced by permission. © 1986 Zilog, Inc. This material shall not be reproduced without the written consent of Zilog, Inc.)

Z80 Memory-Write Machine Cycle

The memory-write waveforms for a Z80 are depicted in Figure 8-2. The address is placed on the bus early in T1 and held stable during the entire machine cycle. At the falling edge of T1, the MEMRQ* signal goes low. At this time, the address is stable, which allows MEMRQ* to be used as a chip enable for dynamic memories. The WR* signal is not activated until the data on the data bus has had a chance to stabilize. The WR* pulse is deactivated one-half clock cycle prior to the data and address bus information being changed. This means that the data will be held stable until after the control pulse is released. This should satisfy hold time requirements for almost all types of semiconductor memories.

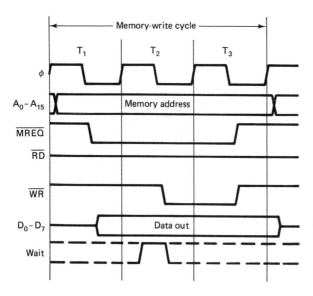

FIGURE 8-2 Z80 memory-write machine cycle. (Reproduced by permission. © 1986 Zilog, Inc. This material shall not be reproduced without the written consent of Zilog, Inc.)

8-2 READ-ONLY MEMORY

When the 8080/8085 and Z80 processors are first powered up, the reset function takes the program counter to 00 00 hex. The processor will then attempt to fetch an instruction from this location. This means that the support circuitry, in particular memory, must present a valid instruction for the processor to execute. The memory will have to be nonvolatile, which means that it can retain information when power has been removed. The most common way in which this is handled is through the use of read-only memories, known as ROMS.

ROM Types

The ROM family can be divided into two distinct areas. The first kind of ROM, the mask ROM, is programmed by the manufacturer. With this type of ROM, the customer sends a program or data table to the manufacturer, who then completes the production run by masking, a process that etches away a layer of aluminum in the IC. The remaining aluminum pattern corresponds to the data sent by the customer. This type of ROM is not field programmable. Additionally, it is not changeable, and it cannot be erased.

A programmable read-only memory, or PROM, is field programmable. In this case the customer receives a blank PROM, one with no data. Through the use of a device known as a PROM programmer, a user can enter data into the IC. A standard PROM is based on a fusible-link technology. A high current source is used to blow the fuse. When the link is open, it represents a logic 0. Fusible links that are left intact represent a logic 1. Standard PROMs are very quick to respond to data requests, have high current draw when used in a circuit, and are not erasable.

A popular type of PROM is the EPROM. This type of chip is erasable when the circuit within the IC is exposed to ultraviolet lights. To make erasure possible, these chips come with a quartz window. Erasure usually requires removal from the circuit. Many EPROMS can be erased over 100 times before the chip will fail. This makes the EPROM a valuable production tool as software is changed and modified. The 2716 and 2732 discussed in this chapter are examples of EPROMS.

EEPROMS are electrically erasable. These types of chips are sometimes referred to as "read mostly" devices. The time required by the chip to respond to read requests is much faster than the time to write new information into the memory cells of the chip. EEPROMS make in-circuit erasure possible and eliminate the quartz window required by the EPROMS.

2716 and 2732A

The 2716 is a 2K by 8 EPROM. This particular chip can store 2048 bytes of information. The pin out and the internal block diagram are shown in Figure 8-3. This chip requires a single 5 V power supply; it incorporates a standby mode to reduce power consumption when it is not in use; and it can be programmed with TTL-level pulses. The total amount of time required to program every bit position is 100 seconds.

The chip has five modes of operation. These modes are: read, standby, program, program verify, and program inhibit. The read mode requires the CE* and the OE* control inputs to be low for data to appear at the outputs of the chip. The CE* input is the power-control input. It is used for chip enable. The OE* control line is used to gate information to the output pins. Standby mode is used to reduce power consumption. This mode is selected when CE* is a logic 1. The outputs are placed in the high-impedance state. OE* will have no effect on the outputs when the 2716 is in standby.

Programming mode requires the Vpp power supply to be at 25 V. If so, the chip will accept input information when OE* is high. Data is programmed into the 2716 by applying TTL logic levels to the pins that are normally used for output. The information will be programmed into the 2716 when a 50 ms TTL-active high pulse is applied to the CE* pin. In this mode of operation this pin is labeled PGM. The program inhibit mode occurs when the PGM input is held low with Vpp at 25 V.

Program verify can be used to determine if the EPROM stored the data correctly. This mode of operation is entered with Vpp at 25 V, CE* low, and OE* low. Unless the 2716 is being programmed or is in program verify, the Vpp supply should be at 5 V.

Erasure occurs when the quartz window is left exposed. In normal room conditions with fluorescent lighting, data will be lost in approximately three years. Exposure to sunlight will erase the 2716 in about one week. In normal operation the quartz window should be covered to prevent data degradation.

Intentionally erasing the 2716 requires exposure to an ultraviolet light. When the manufacturer's guidelines are followed, complete erasure takes place in 15 to 20 minutes. This restores all cells within the 2716 to logic 1s.

The 2732A is almost pin-for-pin compatible with the 2716. The OE* and Vpp

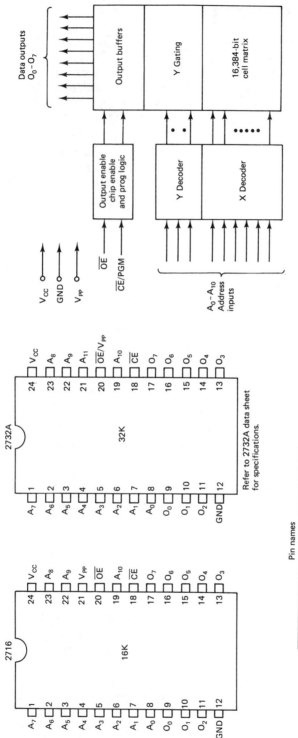

FIGURE 8-3 2716 pin out, block diagram. (Courtesy of Intel Corporation.)

268

Mode selection

Pins / Mode	$\overline{CE}$/PGM (18)	$\overline{OE}$ (20)	V_{PP} (21)	V_{CC} (24)	Outputs (9–11, 13–17)
Read	V_{IL}	V_{IL}	+5	+5	D_{OUT}
Standby	V_{IH}	Don't care	+5	+5	High Z
Program	Pulsed V_{IL} to V_{IH}	V_{IH}	+25	+5	D_{IN}
Program verify	V_{IL}	V_{IL}	+25	+5	D_{OUT}
Program inhibit	V_{IL}	V_{IH}	+25	+5	High Z

Mode selection

Pins / Mode	CE (18)	OE/V_{PP} (20)	V_{CC} (24)	Outputs (9–11, 13–17)
Read	V_{IL}	V_{IL}	+5	D_{OUT}
Standby	V_{IH}	Don't care	+5	High Z
Program	V_{IL}	V_{PP}	+5	D_{IN}
Program verify	V_{IL}	V_{IL}	+5	D_{OUT}
Program inhibit	V_{IH}	V_{PP}	+5	High Z

FIGURE 8-4   2716 and 2732 modes of operation. [(a) and (b) courtesy of Intel Corporation.]

functions have been combined at pin 20. This has freed pin 21 for an additional address line. The extra address line allows the CPU to address $4K \times 8$ locations. This EPROM, like the 2716, has five modes of operation. Figure 8-4 summarizes the modes for both the 2716 and the 2732A.

When programming the 2732A, the OE*/Vpp pin should be raised to 21 V. A warning is issued in the documentation against exceeding 22 V on this pin. Doing so will damage the 2732A. Once the address and the data are stable, an active low TTL pulse of 50 ms will program the location selected.

Although EPROM programmer circuitry is interesting, it is not an integral part of the computer. What we wish to concentrate on next is how a programmed EPROM can be wired into the computer so the CPU can access the data or program within it.

ROM Interfacing Circuitry

The first thing that should be mentioned is the internal decoding section that memory chips, ROMs included, contain within them. An examination of the internal block diagram of the 2716 in Figure 8-3 shows that the 11 address lines into the chip are decoded into x and y signals that activate the memory matrix within the chip. The actual implementation of the decoding scheme within memory chips is not our concern; however, you should be aware that memory chips come with decoding sections to activate the cell selected by the address lines connected to the IC.

This piece of information leads to the realization that memory chips, when inserted into a computer system, are already partially decoded. In the 2716, the 11 address lines used differentiate between 2K locations within the chip. It would be possible to wire the 2716 into the computer system as shown in Figure 8-5. As wired in this diagram, when the CPU attempted to fetch an instruction from 00 00 hex, the 2716 would place data onto the data bus when the chip was activated by the MEMRD* pulse connected to the CE* input of the chip. The address information into the 2716, A11 through A0, would select cell 0 with the IC. The computer system would function correctly provided no other chips were wired to the buses. Why? The diagram shown in Figure 8-5 uses partial decoding.

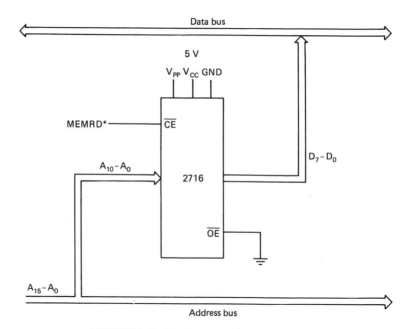

FIGURE 8-5   2716: MEMRD* to CE* interface.

When memory operations are performed, a 16-bit address is generated by the CPU. To absolutely decode this address requires a decoding scheme that uses all 16 address lines. The 2716 uses just 11 of these addresses. This means that A15, A14, A13, A12, and A11 are not part of the decoding scheme. As we learned in port decoders, this can cause ambiguities to be introduced within the system. With five unused address lines there are 32 banks of 2K possible. As wired in Figure 8-5, the 2716 will respond to every one of them.

This makes it very difficult to expand the memory system. Additionally, there are no true holes within the memory map. Any attempts to wire a memory-mapped port into a system with the 2716 wired as shown in Figure 8-5 will result in bus contentions arising.

Absolute Decoders

The preceding discussion is meant to steer you away from partial decoding of addresses used to activate memory chips. While it is possible, it introduces many problems. Furthermore, much of the address decoding work has been handled by the internal decoder inside the memory chip.

In the case of the 2716, our decoder will only have to deal with five address lines. The others are wired directly to the 2716.

Figure 8-6 shows how the lower 32K can be absolutely decoded. The unused address lines A15 through A11 are connected to a 74154. A15 is connected directly to G2. Unless it is low, the decoder chip will not activate. This is the reason the lower 32K is decoded. Address lines A14 through A11 drive the decoder chip-select inputs. These four address lines determine which bank of 2K within the lower 32K is selected. If this 2716 is responsible for the address range 00 00 hex to 07 FF, it will have the CE* input wired to the 0 line output of the decoder as shown. To provide absolute decoding for the upper 32K, the A15 input to G2 can be inverted before the connection is made to the decoder.

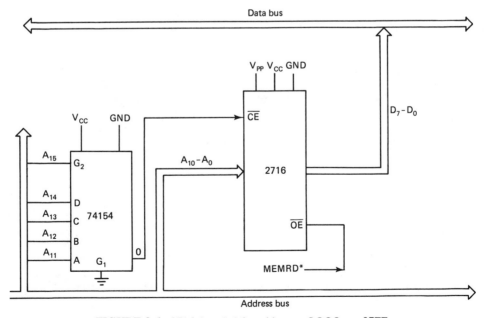

FIGURE 8-6   2716 decoded for addresses 0000_H to $07FF_H$.

The decoder as wired does not produce what we have called an address-select pulse in an earlier chapter. Address-select pulses have two components. One part is a decoded address, the other part is a control signal. The decoder in Figure 8-6 produces only a decoded address. Fortunately, the 2716 has two control inputs. The MEMRD* control line is wired to the OE* control of the 2716. The outputs of the 2716 will remain tristated until the chip is selected by the address decoder and the OE* line is pulled low by the MEMRD* pulse. With the two control inputs wired as shown, the 2716 will not turn on inadvertently.

The decoder circuit shown in Figure 8-7 uses two 74LS138 decoder chips. IC 1 provides decoding for 4K blocks of memory in the lower 32K. IC 2 decodes the upper 32K into 4K blocks. The address lines wired to these decoders drive the select lines A, B, and C, with C the most significant. The decoders will only work if G1 is high. In this case, G1 is tied to Vcc. The G2 strobe is broken into an A and B control. In Figure 8-7 the two parts of strobe G2 are tied together. When this input is low, the IC is enabled when wired as in Figure 8-7.

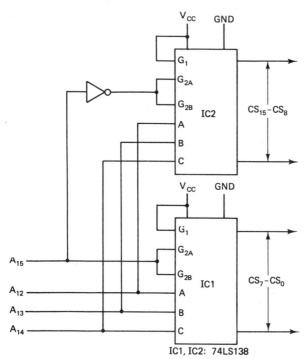

FIGURE 8-7 Address decoding: CS* signals available in 4K blocks.

The 16 chip select lines fully decode the 64K memory space into 4K blocks. This makes the decoder circuitry of Figure 8-7 useful if 2732A EPROMS will be wired into the system. Like the decoder circuit of Figure 8-6, these decoders do not produce address-select pulses. To prevent any of the 2732As from turning on inadvertently,

MEMRD* must be wired to every OE* connection on each of the EPROMS wired to the bus. The chip-select pulses will operate the CE* inputs of the 2732As.

8-3 READ/WRITE MEMORY

The memory chips just discussed have an important restriction. The CPU cannot store information in these chips. This means that the entire memory space cannot be wired to decode ROM circuitry. In this next section, we will focus on R/W memory chips and study some decoder circuits that interface these chips to the bus system.

RAM

Read/Write circuitry is often referred to as RAM. Random Access Memories allow the computer to store or read information from any cell within the IC. The other important feature of this type of memory is the ability to access any cell addressed directly. The internal decoders in these types of ICs can select any cell in the same amount of time. It does not matter if the cell specified is the first cell or the last cell in the chip. Sequential-type memories, in contrast, would cycle through all previous cells before reaching the information in the last location. Magnetic tape is an example of sequential access.

There are several other facets of R/W memory that need to be explained prior to looking at some specific ICs. First, RAM can be divided into two significantly different types. The first kind is referred to as static. Static RAM will retain information as long as power is applied. It does not require clock or timing inputs for memory refresh. This makes interfacing static RAM much easier. In general, this kind of memory chip cannot achieve the greater packing densities available with dynamic RAM.

Dynamic RAM is the second major type of R/W memory. This type of IC usually has more bits available than a comparably sized static RAM chip. The drawback to this chip is the need to provide clock or timing signals that the IC uses to replenish information stored in its cells. Without the refresh pulses, the information placed in dynamic RAM would dissipate as the voltages placed in memory cells discharged. The refresh cycles, which must occur periodically, interfere with normal memory cycles, slowing down normal memory operations. It is often necessary to provide these types of chips with a refresh controller that handles the refresh control signals and timing. It would seem that dynamic RAM, with the drawbacks listed, would not be used very often, but this is not the case. The greater storage capacities of these chips makes them an attractive alternative to static RAM.

Whichever type of RAM is chosen, it will most likely be volatile, meaning that when power is removed from the computer, memory is lost. There is considerable effort within the industry to produce cheap nonvolatile static RAM chips. The EEPROM, with fast write times as well as fast read times, would accomplish this goal. Other manufacturers are producing ICs with their own voltage-source backups. This type of IC automatically switches to the backup voltage when power is removed. At present, though,

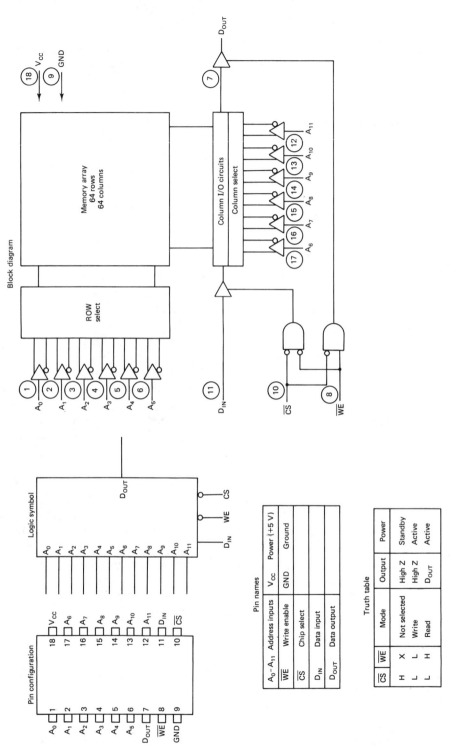

FIGURE 8-8 2147H 4096 × 1 static RAM. (Courtesy of Intel Corporation.)

you are much more likely to work with and use the volatile type of RAM that we will look at next.

   2147H 4096 × 1 static RAM.   The pin out, logic diagram, and block diagram of the 2147H static RAM IC can be studied by referring to Figure 8-8. This chip has 4096 bits of storage. The internal decoder differentiates between 4096 possibilities using address lines A0 through A11. Each chip has just a single data-pin output. To use this chip with a 8080A/8085 or Z80 system, each bank of 4K would comprise eight of these chips. One chip would be wired to D0, the next to D1, and so on until the last was wired to D7. Each bank would be wired to the same chip select, so all eight chips would turn on simultaneously, receiving or placing a byte on the data bus.

   This bank of chips would handle 4K × 8 RAM locations. This is the same size as a 2732A. The decoding circuit of Figure 8-7 produces chip selects that activate blocks of 4K. Could we wire the 2147H directly to one of these chip selects? Not quite. The 2147H has a WE* input as a control line. This line indicates the direction data should flow when the chip is selected. When the line is low, a write operation is to take place; if the line is high, a read operation should take place. If we connect MEMWR* to this input on the chip, this control signal will provide data direction information when the chip is selected.

   A problem arises when you realize that the MEMWR* and MEMRD* control signal can both be high at the same time. When does this occur? When a memory operation is not underway. Since the decoders of Figure 8-7 provide only decoded addresses, the RAM chip may turn on when the information on the address bus matches the conditions needed to activate a chip select. To see how this might happen and why it wasn't a problem with the ROM we used earlier, consider Table 8-1.

TABLE 8-1   Decoding Analysis: ROM vs. RAM

A15-A0	MEMRD*	MEMWR*	OPERATION
controlled	0	1	memory read
controlled	1	0	memory write
port #	1	1	I/O read
port #	1	1	I/O write
refresh	1	1	Z80 fetch T3, T4
unknown	1	1	T4, T5, T6, 8085
unknown	1	1	T4, T5, 8080

   The first line of the table indicates a true memory read. The address on the bus is controlled by the instruction that performs the read. This is the only line in the table in which a 2716 or 2732A EPROM will turn on as wired with the decoder circuits discussed in this chapter. The 2147H would turn on too, performing a read operation because its WE* input is high.

The second line of the table indicates a memory-write operation. This will be ignored by an EPROM with its OE* input tied to MEMRD*. Since MEMRD* is high in every location but the first, we now know why, even if a correct address is generated, the first line of the table is the only line that will activate the EPROM.

The 2147H responds to this operation provided the address driving the decoders generates a chip select. Since the address information is controlled by a legitimate memory operation, the 2147H will respond by accepting data from the bus.

The next two lines involve I/O operations. In each case, the memory-control signals are both high. If a port address corresponds to an address that activates a chip select in RAM, that RAM will respond. The 2147H would see the MEMWR* input signal high. The 2147H "thinks" a read operation is in progress and places information onto the bus. This will cause conflicts with an I/O port that is trying to use the bus at the same time. Suppose an I/O operation was underway using port 0. In the 8080A systems the address bus would contain 00 00 hex. Remember, the port number is duplicated. This decodes chip select 0. If a RAM chip is wired to this select line, it will also turn on.

The next line looks at the Z80 when it is T3 and T4 of an op code fetch. The address bus will contain refresh addresses during this time. The last two lines show the situation during op code fetches for the 8085 and the 8080. During some T states the address is not specified. This random information could easily trip a chip select and turn on a RAM accidentally.

The solution to this problem is to insure that chip selects to RAMS only turn on during true memory operations. This implies that a decoded address is insufficient to drive a RAM chip select. After we have examined several other RAM chips, examples on how to decode RAM chip selects will be discussed in RAM decoder circuitry.

81C28 2K × 8 static RAM.   The 82C128 contains 16,384 bits arranged in a 2K × 8 configuration. Each individual chip is capable of supporting byte operations over a 2048-cell memory space. The 81C28 has an OE* control that can be used to eliminate bus contentions. This means that the 82C28 could be wired into the decoders that drove the 2716s. These decoders are found in Figure 8-6. Unlike the 2716, which is a read-only device, the 82C28 can read and write information. OE* therefore cannot be controlled by MEMRD* as in the case of the 2716s. The OE* of the 81C28 will have to be connected to a control signal known as memory request (MEMRQ*), which indicates that MEMRD* or MEMWR* are low. The MEMWR* signal is then connected to WE* on the IC with the CE* input being driven by a decoded address. This RAM chip has a power-down feature plus the ability to latch address information off multiplexed data/address bus systems. The pin out, logic symbol, and block diagram are shown in Figure 8-9.

51C67 16384 × 1 static RAM.   The pin out, logic symbol, and block diagram of a 51C67 high-speed RAM chip is shown in Figure 8-10. This chip has the same bit capacity as the 81C28, but its internal configuration is wired in a 16K × 1 configuration. Each chip will have one data-bit line. To complete an entire byte, eight of these chips

Pin Configuration   **Logic Symbol**

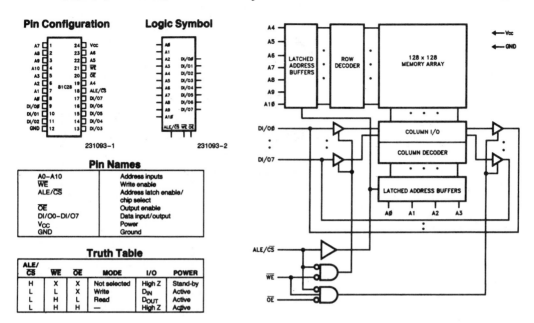

231093-1   231093-2

Pin Names

A0–A10	Address inputs
WE	Write enable
ALE/CS	Address latch enable/ chip select
OE	Output enable
DI/O0–DI/O7	Data input/output
Vcc	Power
GND	Ground

Truth Table

ALE/ CS	WE	OE	MODE	I/O	POWER
H	X	X	Not selected	High Z	Stand-by
L	L	X	Write	D$_{IN}$	Active
L	H	L	Read	D$_{OUT}$	Active
L	H	H	—	High Z	Active

FIGURE 8-9   81C28 block diagram. (Courtesy of Intel Corporation.)

must be wired. The addressing information and control signals will be wired in parallel, so that if one of these chips turns on, all eight will turn on. Then each chip will place a bit onto a data-bus line. Chip 0 will be connected to D0, chip 1 connected to D1, and so on. When a bank is properly wired, it will respond to a 16K block of memory. The decoder circuits studied so far activate 4K or 2K banks of memory. The 51C67 could not be wired into these decoders. Finally, this chip does not have an OE* control, which means that decoded addresses are insufficient to drive chip selects without the possibility of creating bus contentions.

RAM Decoder Circuitry

We know that RAM chips without an OE* control can produce bus contentions when selected by decoded addresses. This problem can be eliminated by driving chip selects from address-select pulses. The first chip we will wire this way will be the 51C67 16K × 1 RAM.

A 16K × 1 configuration must be able to distinguish between 16,384 possibilities. To do so, the chip must be able to handle 14 address lines. The decoder inside the 51C67 will accept inputs from A0 through A13. This leaves just two address lines to provide for the logical creation of a chip select.

The circuit of Figure 8-11 divides a 64K memory map into four blocks of 16K each. The decoder chip is a 74LS139 dual 2-line-to-4-line decoder with independent

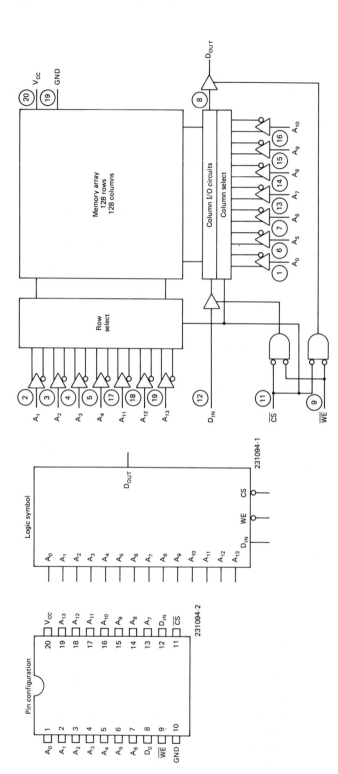

FIGURE 8-10 51C67 16K × 1 static RAM. (Courtesy of Intel Corporation.)

278

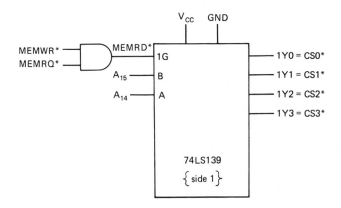

FIGURE 8-11 CS* signals available in 16K blocks.

strobe and select lines for both sections of the chip. In Figure 8-11, only section 1 is being used. The decoder will generate four different address-select pulses, each pulse controlling the following range of addresses:

CS0*—00 00 to 3F FF hex

CS1*—40 00 to 7F FF hex

CS2*—80 00 to BF FF hex

CS3*—C0 00 to FF FF hex

The decoder will only work if the strobe input is pulled low. In Figure 8-11 this strobe is controlled by the signal MEMRQ*. The MEMRQ* signal is created by gating the MEMRD* and MEMWR* signals together as shown. If either input to the AND gate is low, a valid memory operation is underway. The output of the AND gate will go low, activating the decoder. This arrangement eliminates the possibility of any bus contentions arising. In a Z80 system, MEMRQ* is available directly from the processor, eliminating the need to use an AND gate as shown in Figure 8-11.

Let's proceed to fully implement a 64K memory map. Three banks of 51C67 16K RAM chips will be wired to CS1*, CS2*, and CS3*. This means that the upper 48K of the map is now wired for RAM. The lower 16K, which uses CS0*, has not yet been wired. We will subdivide this section into 4K of ROM starting at 00 00 hex, then three sections of RAM, each bank comprising 4K.

The decoder circuit of Figure 8-12 shows how to use the second half of a 74LS139 to subdivide the lower 16K of memory. In this circuit, side 1 is wired as before. The upper 48K is activated from CS1*, CS2*, and CS3*. CS0* is connected to the strobe that activates side 2. The select lines to this part of the IC are connected to A13 and A12. If A15, A14, A13, and A12 are all low and MEMRQ* is low, the 2Y0 output will go low. This select line will activate the chip select on a 2732A. The range of addresses controlled by the new address-select pulses are:

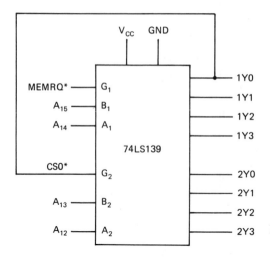

FIGURE 8-12   Subdividing the lower 16K of memory into 4K blocks.

2Y0—00 00 to 0F FF hex

2Y1—10 00 to 1F FF hex

2Y2—20 00 to 2F FF hex

2Y3—30 00 to 3F FF hex

The lower 16K has been successfully divided into blocks of 4K. As already indicated, the lowest block will be wired to a 2732A. This IC will contain the monitor and any utilities, such as delay loops, needed by the system every time the computer is powered up. Three banks of 2147H 4096 × 1 RAM chips will be wired to the remaining chip selects, completing the memory-map implementation.

8-4 DIRECT MEMORY ACCESS

Direct memory access is used when information is to be transferred into and out of memory without the CPU generating control information. During this time the CPU will relinquish control of the bus lines, placing its bus lines in the tristate condition. Another device, usually a direct memory access controller, handles the transfers and generates the correct control signals. It is possible that excessive requests to use the bus for DMA operations will interfere with normal CPU operation. If the CPU is electrically isolated from the bus during DMA operations, it cannot fetch new instructions. Handled properly, though, DMA operations can increase overall system speed. The key is to use DMA cycles when the CPU is busy performing internal operations.

The Z80 will respond to requests to release the bus through the use of BUSRQ* and BUSAK* sequences. This will cause the Z80 to enter bus request/acknowledge machine cycles. The 8080A/8085 processors handle these types of requests through the HOLD and HLDA signals. These processors enter hold states, during which time the CPU is electrically isolated from the bus by tristating the bus connections.

8080A/8085

These processors monitor the status of the hold input to decide if they should enter a hold state and tristate the bus lines. If the hold input is high and stable prior to the rising edge of the phase-two clock during T2, the processor will acknowledge the hold request at the beginning of T3 if an input or read machine cycle is underway. Otherwise, the hold is not acknowledged until the state following T3. If a machine cycle is underway that requires four or more states to complete, the CPU will complete this machine cycle internally before coming to a rest. At the end of the machine cycle, processor activity ceases. This overlap allows the overall system speed to be enhanced.

Z80 Bus Request/Acknowledge

We will focus on the Z80 bus request/acknowledge machine cycle in this section. After we have finished this discussion, we will study a DMA controller designed to interface directly to the signals generated by the Z80. The bus request/acknowledge machine cycle waveforms are depicted in Figure 8-13. The BUSRQ* control line is sampled at the rising edge of the last T state of any machine cycle. If this signal is low, the Z80 will

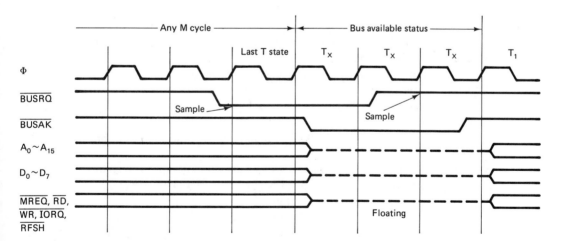

FIGURE 8-13   Z80 bus request/acknowledge cycle. (Reproduced by permission. © 1986 Zilog, Inc. This material shall not be reproduced without the written consent of Zilog, Inc.)

place the address, data, and control signals in the tristate condition at the rising edge of the next clock pulse.

The maximum delay between bus request and bus acknowledge is one machine cycle. The external controller can operate the bus for as many T states as it desires. Sampling of BUSRQ* will continue on rising edges of the master clock. One clock cycle after the request is removed, the processor will reenter normal operation. Should dynamic RAM be interfaced to the system, the DMA controller will be required to release the bus periodically so refresh cycles can occur or it must perform the refresh operations itself. One last note about the Z80 response to signals during DMA operations: The Z80 will ignore both the NMI* and INT* signals when the bus is under control of an external device such as a DMA controller.

Z8410 DMA Controller

The Z8410 manages CPU-independent data transfers. The control signals on this chip are designed to connect directly to control signals generated by the Z80 without any need to expand the bus and create additional control signals. Transfers can occur between any two ports including memory to memory, memory to I/O, and I/O to memory. Dual addresses are generated for each transfer. The addresses may be fixed or changing, depending on the programming of internal registers. This makes the Z8410 a programmable support chip. Not only can the chip perform data transfers, it can also search for information using bit-maskable bytes. This searching process can operate independently of or concurrently with data transfers.

The logic symbol for this IC and the pin out is located in Figure 8-14. A15–A0 are connected directly to the system address bus. These pins are unidirectional output pins. When not in use they are tristated to prevent interference with normal use of the address bus. The DMA controller will use these lines to provide addressing for both the source and destination ports.

BAI* signals the controller that the bus has been released for DMA operations. This pin can also be used to cascade multiple controllers by connecting it to the BAO* output of a higher-priority controller. The highest-priority controller will have BAI* connected to BUSAK* of the CPU.

BAO* is used to cascade DMA controllers, as explained in the preceding paragraph.

BUSRQ* is used by the controller to ask the CPU to relinquish control of the bus. In multiple controller systems, through the use of the BAO*–BAI* chain, this line will not be used until the higher-priority chip has finished its operation.

The line (CE/WAIT)* normally functions as a chip enable. As a chip enable, the CPU can use this line to select the DMA controller to transfer command bytes into the Z8410. The wait function can be used to slow DMA speed so the controller can interface to slower memory.

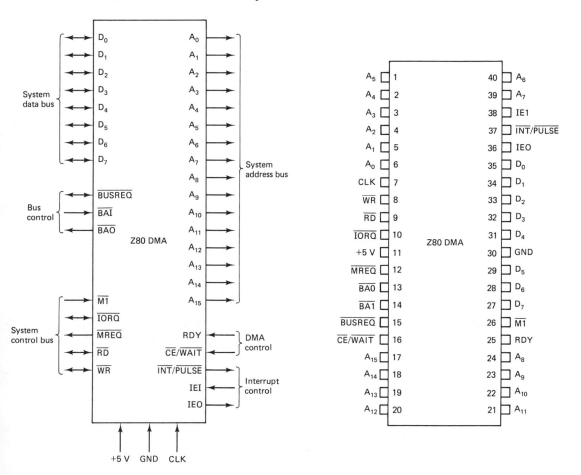

FIGURE 8-14 Z8410 pin out, logic symbol. (Reproduced by permission. © 1986 Zilog, Inc. This material shall not be reproduced without the written consent of Zilog, Inc.)

CLK is taken directly from the system clock in most cases. To clock the Z8410 at slower rates, a standard TTL output with a pull-up resistor may be adequate to provide timing pulses.

The power supply pin should be pulled up from Vcc with no more than a 10 kΩ resistor. This will insure that the controller will receive proper power when it is reset.

D7–D0 is a set of bidirectional tristate lines. These lines are used to send information into the controller from the CPU, controller status into the CPU, plus data transfers during DMA operations.

IEI is an active high daisy-chained input. It is used with IEO to establish priorities when more than one device is interrupt driven. We will not be using this function in our discussion.

The INT*/pulse line is used by the DMA to force the CPU to respond to interrupts as soon as DMA operations are completed. There are three situations in which an interrupt can be generated:

interrupt on ready (before requesting bus)

interrupt on match

interrupt on end of block

Should the DMA generate an interrupt, control would transfer to an interrupt routine when the DMA operation was completed rather than at the point in the program that was active when the BUSRQ* was acknowledged. We will not use this feature of the controller in our discussion.

The pulse feature of this pin allows the controller to generate periodic pulses to external devices when the controller is operating the bus system.

IORQ* is a bidirectional three-state active low line. When the CPU is running the bus, this line going low indicates that a valid port number is on the lower half of the data bus. The port number can be used to create a device-select pulse that will activate the Z8410. When the DMA controller is the bus master, this line acts as an output which signals devices attached to the bus that an valid 8-bit or 16-bit address can be found on the bus.

M1*, an active low input, will indicate that the CPU is performing an op code fetch. The controller uses this information to decode RETI, an op code that stands for return from interrupt.

MREQ* is an active low output used by the controller to indicate that valid ad-

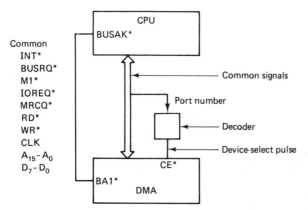

FIGURE 8-15 Z8410 system interface.

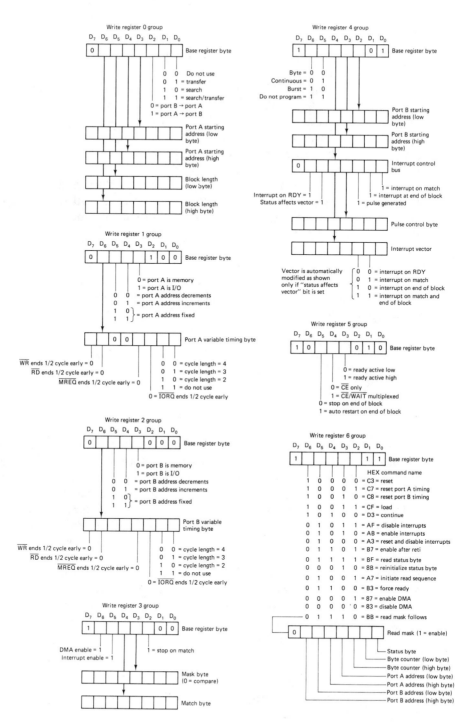

FIGURE 8-16 Z8410 command register layouts. (Reproduced by permission. © 1986 Zilog, Inc. This material shall not be reproduced without the written consent of Zilog, Inc.)

dressing information is on the address bus. The DMA will use this to indicate a transfer to or from memory.

RD* is a bidirectional active low tristate line. As an input, it indicates that the CPU wants to read status registers within the Z8410. When the DMA controller is running the bus, it indicates a DMA-controlled read from a memory or I/O port.

RDY is an input into the DMA. It can be programmed to respond as active low or active high. The controller monitors this input to determine if a port associated with a DMA operation is ready to receive or write data.

WR* is a bidirectional active low three-state line. When used as an input, it indicates that the CPU is sending information to one of the Z8410 control registers. As an output, it informs devices connected to the Z8410 that information is being written to a memory or port address specified by the controller.

Modes of operation.   Once the system interface is completed as shown in Figure 8-15, the controller is ready to accept inputs that will establish how it will function. The modes of operation are:

byte at a time
burst
continuous

In byte-at-a-time mode, the system buses are released between data transfers. Burst mode continues until the DMA input RDY goes inactive. The DMA completes the current transfer and then releases the bus. Continuous mode of operation occurs when the DMA is transferring a block of data. Transfer will continue until the end of the block is moved. If the RDY is activated in this mode, the DMA will pause until the RDY line is released.

To handle the operations necessary, the Z8410 has 21 control registers and seven status registers. The control or writable registers are organized into seven base register groups, most of which have multiple registers. Each different group will have a different impact on controller operations. Figure 8-16 shows the breakdown of the control groups. We will analyze this information when we get to a programming example.

When the Z8410 is powered up or reset, or when a control word is written to a register, the DMA controller is disabled. In this mode it will not be able to gain access to the bus. To enable the controller, a hex byte of 87 is sent to the base register or group WR6.

Programming the Z8410.   To help interpret the register layout of Figure 8-16, Example 8-1 was developed from the Z8410 documention.

The Z8410 will be initialized to:

EXAMPLE 8-1

HEX ADDRESS	HEX OP CODE	MNEMONIC	COMMENTS	OCTAL ADDRESS	OCTAL OP CODE
			Z8410 Setup		
03 00	21	LXI H	Point to command table	003 000	041
03 01		00		003 001	
03 02		04		003 002	
03 03	7E	MOV A, M	Get a command	003 003	176
03 04	D3	OUT	Transfer to Z8410	003 004	323
03 05		80		003 005	
03 06	23	INX H	Point to next command	003 006	043
03 07	7D	MOV A, L		003 007	175
03 08	FE	CPI	Check to see if finished	003 010	376
03 09		0E		003 011	
03 0A	C2	JNZ	If not continue	003 012	302
03 0B		03		003 013	
03 0C		03		003 014	
03 0D	76	HLT		003 015	166
04 00		79	Command word table		
04 01		50			
04 02		10			
04 03		00			
04 04		10			
04 05		14			
04 06		28			
04 07		C5			
04 08		05			
04 09		8A			
04 0A		CF			
04 0B		05			
04 0C		CF			
04 0D		87			

Comments	D7	D6	D5	D4	D3	D2	D1	D0	HEX
WR0 sets DMA to receive block length. Port A starting address and temporarily sets port B as source	0	1 Block length upper follows	1 Block length lower follows	1 Port A upper address follows	1 Port A lower address follows	B → A Temporary for loading B address*	0 — Transfer, no search	1	79
Port A address (lower)	0	1	0	1	0	0	0	0	50
Port A address (upper)	0	0	0	1	0	0	0	0	10
Block length (lower)	0	0	0	0	0	0	0	0	00
Block length (upper)	0	0	0	1	0	0	0	0	10
WR1 defines port A as memory with fixed incrementing address	0	0 No timing follows	0 Address changes	1 Address increments	0 Port is memory	1	0	0	14
WR2 defines port B as peripheral with fixed-address	0	0 No timing follows	1 Fixed address	0	1 Port is I/O	0	1	0	28
WR4 sets mode to burst, sets DMA to expect port B address	1	1 Burst mode	0	0 No interrupt control byte follows	0 No upper address	Port B lower address follows	0	1	C5
Port B address (lower)	0	0	0	0	0	1	0	1	05
WR sets ready active high	1	0	0 No auto restart	0 No wait states	1 RDY active high	0	1	0	8A
WR6 loads port B address and resets block counter*	1	1	0	0	1	1	1	1	CF
WR0 sets port A as source*	0	0 No address or block length bytes	0	0	0	1 A → B	0 — Transfer, no search	1	05
WR6 loads port A address and resets block counter	1	1	0	0	1	1	1	1	CF
WR6 enables DMA to start operation	1	0	0	0	0	1	1	1	87

NOTE: The actual number of bytes transferred is one more than specified by the block length.
*These entries are necessary only in the case of a fixed destination address.

FIGURE 8-17 Z8410 program sequence example. (Reproduced by permission. © 1986 Zilog, Inc. This material shall not be reproduced without the written consent of Zilog, Inc.)

1. temporarily declare port B as a source in WR0
2. load port B address in WR6
3. declare port A as a source in WR0
4. load port A address in WR6
5. enable the DMA in WR6

A command table is loaded into the computer at 04 00 hex. The program that will transfer these commands to the DMA controller starts at 03 00 hex. The first command transferred to the DMA controller is 79 hex. The program then cycles through the loop, each time passing another byte of information. This continues until all the bytes have been transferred and the DMA is enabled. The function and breakdown of each byte transferred into the DMA is shown in Figure 8-17. Notice that certain bits within a base register indicate that registers within that group will follow. If we examine 79 in binary it becomes 0111 1001. D6 through D3 are set, indicating that other registers in the group are going to be sent. The next 4 bytes in the command table of Example 8-1 must follow in the order indicated by the value loaded into the base register. The base register of any group is indicated by the bit pattern sent to the DMA. If you examine the base register for group 1, D7, D1, and D0 must be low. D2 must be set. The other bit positions indicate functions except for D6. If D6 is set, this tells the DMA that another register within the group will be programmed by a byte sent from the CPU.

The example given is meant to highlight a feature of the controller that must be recognized to insure proper operation. Fixed addresses can only be assigned to sources. To assign a fixed address to a destination, you first assign the fixed address to the port as if it were a source. Then, after setting the other port parameters, you declare the second port a source too. This forces the first port to default to a destination port, which is what the objective was in our programming example. We certainly have not used all the features of this powerful programmable support chip. What we have done is to provide an introduction to a very important concept. For further information, consult the data sheets for the Z8410.

8-5 DYNAMIC RAM

Dynamic RAM memory chips, or DRAM, are a popular choice when it comes to the selection of memory ICs for a computer system. These chips can offer greater packing densities (more bits per chip) than static memories. This reduces the cost per bit, an important consideration. Static memories are usually faster than DRAM, which can counterbalance the higher cost for bit storage when considering a static IC as opposed to a dynamic IC. The following discussion will highlight some memory concepts, provide insights into memory selection, and introduce more information about dynamic RAM.

In a dynamic memory chip, the information is stored on capacitors present inside the IC. These capacitors are so small that they are unable to hold charges for long periods of time. A quick reminder about RC time constants points this out. The time it takes a capacitor to charge or discharge depends on the RC time constant. This time constant is a function of the resistance seen by the plates of the capacitor and the capacitance of the capacitor. To achieve the great packing densities that are an advantage of dynamic RAM, the capacitors used to store information are made small. This reduces the RC time constant.

If a capacitor has a charge, it can represent one logic state. The absence of a charge can represent the other logic state. Consequently, if a charged capacitor loses the voltage across its plates, the logic state of the memory cell that the capacitor represents changes. This cannot be allowed to happen.

To prevent changes in the information stored in DRAM, memory cells undergo refresh cycles. These refresh cycles periodically read the state of the memory cells within the DRAM. Capacitors that are charged have their charge replenished during the refresh cycle. Capacitors without charges are left as is.

The need to refresh explains in part why dynamic RAM ICs are generally slower than static memories. The refresh cycles that are required to make the DRAMs work inhibit normal memory operations. This means that memory is not available to the processor when a refresh is underway.

This, however, may not be a major problem. If the refresh operations can be synchronized to processor activities so that refresh operations take place when it is unlikely the CPU will need to access memory, then the refresh cycles will not affect the throughput of the system. For example, the Z80 supports dynamic refresh during the third and fourth T state of an op code fetch. At this time, the Z80 is decoding the instruction it has just received.

Many dynamic memories require a controller. This memory controller is responsible for generating the control signals that operate the memory ICs. These control signals can include addressing functions, address multiplexing, refresh timing, and refresh counting. Address multiplexing is used by certain DRAMs to reduce pin count. In a 64K chip, 16 address lines are required to select the appropriate cell. The address bus information will be gated into the IC over eight address lines. These lines will take turns receiving the addressing information. The control signals needed by the IC to accept the two address bytes will be provided by the memory controller.

Even though a controller is required, the cost per bit stored is still usually less than an equivalent static memory system, for two reasons. First, a single controller can be used to operate an entire bank of memory. It is not necessary to have a single controller for each memory chip in the system. Second, the greater packing densities reduce the amount of PC board space taken up by the DRAM system when compared to a static system. This is true even when the controller is included in the PC board space usage.

This chapter has focused on the static memories, not because they are better or worse than DRAM systems, but because it is likely that the microprocessor trainers you will use when first introduced to microcomputer electronics will be using static RAM. Why? The static memory system is easy to interface, easier to understand (no need to learn about a memory controller), and meets the requirements of a learning environment.

8-6 CLOSING THOUGHTS

This chapter has introduced some concepts fundamental to memory and memory interfacing. It would not be practical to discuss every memory chip or technology currently available. The competition for a share of the market in memory ICs is intense. Dramatic changes in technology are the norm rather than the unusual. Nonvolatile RAM, greater packing densities, and different storage methods are being developed. Some chips using magnetic bubbles for storage of information can store up to 1 million bits per IC. Access times are becoming shorter and shorter. At one time the speed with which a memory chip could deliver data once the CPU requested the information was a vital concern in computer design. The Ready input to a processor was created so slow memories could be connected to the computer chip, which operated too fast for the memory to keep up. Today it is usually possible to find memory chips that can handle very fast processor cycles. When the cost for such ICs becomes a factor, the processor can be slowed down and most likely will still be operating in the megahertz range.

Methods have been developed that allow processors with just 16 address lines to access more than 64K. These methods usually incorporate some type of pseudo-address-line generation. A special-purpose chip known as a memory manager unit or MMU has been developed to act as an interface between the processor and memory maps larger than the 64K a 16-address-line processor can handle by itself.

An attempt to cover such a rapidly changing, diverse area within the scope of a text would have been fruitless. What we have done is to lay the foundation for you to succeed in the future when you are asked to work with memory.

SUMMARY

1. The CPU communicates with memory through the use of memory machine cycles. These cycles provide the addressing information needed to select the proper memory chip as well as the control signals that will activate the chip at the proper time.

2. ROM (ready-only memories) are used to store data that must be protected when the computer is powered down. ROM chips are nonvolatile, retaining the information stored within them even after power is off. There are different types of ROM. A mask ROM is provided by the manufacturer already preprogrammed with the desired information. PROMs are field programmable, meaning that the user can store the information required. Once programmed, these chips cannot be reprogrammed. An EPROM does have erasing capabilities, but erasure usually involves removing the chip from the socket.

3. Read/write memory is usually referred to as RAM. RAM represents random access memory. Perhaps a better name would have been *direct access*. With these chips, as well as with ROMs, it is possible for the computer to designate the location in

memory with which it wishes to interact without the need to sequence through locations.

4. Decoder circuitry for ROMs and RAMs is usually slightly different. In many applications a ROM can be activated with a decoded address and appropriate control signals. A RAM chip usually requires an address-select pulse at chip select.

5. RAM chips come in two primary types. The first type is static. Static chips retain information in internal flip-flops. Once the state of the FF is set or reset, the chip will remember the data until it is changed by the computer or the power is removed from the chip. Dynamic RAM stores information as charges across the plates of capacitors integrated into the IC. Dynamic RAM chips require refresh cycles, which replenish lost charge. In many applications this means that the DRAM system must have a refresh controller chip. The increased complexity of a DRAM system is offset by the greater packing densities available. Static chips are usually faster, but have smaller storage capabilities.

6. Direct memory access is a process in which devices can talk to memory without the need to process the requests through the CPU. In the 8080/8085 systems, DMA requests are handled through hold states. In a Z80 system, a bus idle/acknowledge cycle is used to handle DMA requests. When the CPU grants a DMA request, it tristates its bus lines and turns control of the bus over to the requesting device. In most cases, the requesting device will be a DMA controller. The DMA controller is a special programmable device that prioritizes and controls requests from different peripherals wishing to interact with memory.

QUESTIONS

1. At what clock state is the address placed on the bus during a memory-read cycle?
2. At what time does the Z80 sample the data bus during a memory-read cycle?
3. In a Z80 system performing a memory-write cycle, when does MEMRQ* go low?
4. During a memory-write cycle, why is the data maintained after the WR* pulse is deactivated?
5. Where is a mask ROM programmed?
6. The 2716 is an EPROM. How can this chip be erased?
7. What does EEPROM mean?
8. In ROM circuitry, which CPU control line is frequently wired to OE* on the ROM?
9. Explain the difference between sequential and direct access.
10. How is data retained in static memories?
11. How is data retained in dynamic memories?
12. What is meant by *volatile?*
13. What is the purpose of a refresh cycle?

14. When should a refresh cycle occur so that throughput is improved?
15. How many 16K × 1 chips are required to implement a 64K × 8 memory system?
16. What control lines are used by the 8085 to handle DMA requests?
17. What control lines are used by the Z80 to handle DMA requests?
18. What is the condition of the processor bus lines during a DMA cycle?
19. What is the function of the RDY line on the Z8410?
20. In the Z8410, how long will the continuous mode of operation last?

LAB ASSIGNMENTS

1. Using the decoding scheme of Figure 8-13, divide the 2Y3 block of memory into 1K segments. You may use any other decoder chips you have available. Have your instructor verify your schematic. Should you have 2114 memory chips, wire these to the controls you have created. Be sure that the new ICs you place into the memory map are wired where your trainer previously had a hole. Perform data transfers to and from these chips to verify circuit operation.
2. Research the 8257 DMA controller manufactured by Intel. How does it compare with the Z8410? How is it different?
3. Write a program that uses the Z8410 to transfer information from a 256-byte memory location to another 256-byte memory location. If you have access to a Z8410, wire it into your system and test the program. If you have an 8080A/8085 system you should consider using an 8257 to implement a DMA operation.

LAB QUESTIONS

1. Record your schematic for assignment 1.
2. List the support chip required by an 8257.
3. Record the control bytes used by the Z8410 in assignment 3.
4. How many 2114s are required to implement a 64K × 8 system?

9

ANALOG INTERFACING

At the end of this chapter you should be familiar with:

1. the operation of a summing amplifier
2. the operation of a binary ladder op amp circuit
3. the 1408 DAC
4. DAC applications
5. ADC techniques
    a. dual slope
    b. direct
    c. pulse width
    d. binary counter
    e. successive approximation
6. sample-and-hold concepts
7. an overview of control loops

INTRODUCTION

As electronic technicians, we are interested in more than just the data-processing uses of a computer. It is important to understand how the computer can be used to interact with and control other circuitry. The chapter on digital interfacing went a long way in satisfying this goal, but it left unexplained the techniques used to interface analog circuitry to the computer.

This chapter will examine the "heart" of interfacing analog devices to the computer. The focus will consist of an examination of digital-to-analog conversions and their complement, analog-to-digital conversions. After examining the interfacing techniques and supporting software of these devices, we will take a look at how to use the 555 timer in a computer application. The chapter concludes with an examination of a basic control loop.

9-1 DIGITAL-TO-ANALOG CONVERSION PRINCIPLES

The Summing Amplifier

The first circuit we will examine in this chapter is a summing amplifier. The summing amplifier uses an op amp to convert input voltages into current that affects the final output voltage. A four-input summing amplifier is shown in Figure 9-1. This circuit uses an operational amplifier to produce the voltage at the output. The characteristics of an op amp are such that, wired as shown in Figure 9-1, the connections to the inverting input terminal are at ground potential. Since this point is not actually wired to ground, but is at ground potential, the inverting input terminal is said to be a *virtual ground*. This is very important. A voltage wired to an input will drop its entire potential across the input resistor. If, for example, 5 V was applied to the R branch, the entire 5 V will be dropped

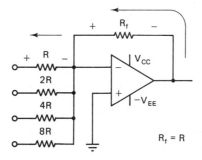

Arrows indicate electron flow
with positive voltage inputs.

FIGURE 9-1   Summing amplifier.

across R. For the sake of discussion, let's assume an R value of 1 kΩ. Under these conditions, 5 ma will be flowing through R. The next important point involves the direction of that current flow.

The input to the op amp is to the first approximation an infinite resistance. Practically, it is over 1 million Ω, and often in the hundreds of millions. Additionally, the input terminals of the op amp provide a path for bias current to flow. This bias current is necessary to the function of the first stage of the op amp; it is usually in the nanoamp range. At this stage in the analysis, it is inconsequential. The 5 ma input swamps out the bias current.

Since the bias current is not enough to satisfy the current requirements set up in the R branch, the output of the op amp will provide the current through the feedback resistor Rf. Since Rf is equal to R, 5 V must be dropped across Rf when the output of the op amp provides 5 ma of current.

With the inverting terminal at ground potential, the right-hand side of Rf must be at a −5 V. This means that the output of the op amp had to drop 5 V below ground to provide the current required by the R branch when 5 V was applied to the input resistor. The arrows in Figure 9-1 indicate electron flow with positive voltages at the input of the circuit.

If a 5 V input were applied to the 2R branch, given that R = 1 kΩ, the current flowing in this branch would equal 2.5 ma. If a 5 V source were applied to the 4R branch, the current flowing through the 4K branch would equal 1.25 ma. Finally, the last branch in Figure 9-1 would produce .625 ma of current when 5 V was applied to the inputs.

Where does all this current come from? From the output of the op amp, as it did when we discussed the 5 ma branch. Since each branch is connected to the output of the op amp through Rf, all the current for all the branches must flow through Rf. This means that if all the inputs are powered by 5 V, the total current through Rf must equal 5 + 2.5 + 1.25 + .625 ma, which is 9.375 ma. Since Rf is set to 1K in this circuit, the output of the op amp must drop 9.375 V below ground potential. As you should be able to see, the currents through Rf are the sum of all the branches activated by 5 V inputs. Thus the name *summing amplifier*.

If the input to the input resistors is restricted to two voltage levels, such as 0 V and 5 V, the inputs can then be driven by a digital source such as a TTL gate. The final output of the summing network is an analog representation of the binary pattern that is connected to the inputs of the circuit.

A truth table indicating all the possible patterns for the inputs can be seen in Table 9-1.

The R input is the most significant since it produces the most current. Each branch is set to produce half again as much current by doubling the resistor size. Fractionally, R is equivalent to ½, 2R equivalent to ¼, 4R equals ⅛, and 8R equals 1/16. Ideally, the output when all the inputs are high should equal −10 V when the R branch produces 5 V. As can be seen from the truth table, the maximum output of the circuit is −9.375 V. The difference between the actual and the theoretical output is the *quantitization* error of the circuit.

TABLE 9-1   Binary to Voltage Correspondence

R	2R	4R	8R	$-V_{OUT}$
0	0	0	0	0
0	0	0	1	0.625
0	0	1	0	1.25
0	0	1	1	1.875
0	1	0	0	2.5
0	1	0	1	3.125
0	1	1	0	3.75
0	1	1	1	4.375
1	0	0	0	5
1	0	0	1	5.625
1	0	1	0	6.25
1	0	1	1	6.875
1	1	0	0	7.5
1	1	0	1	8.125
1	1	1	0	8.75
1	1	1	1	9.375

The *resolution* of the system is the smallest difference the output can produce. It is equivalent to the output of the circuit when a binary 1 is applied to the inputs. In our example, that resolution is .625 V. To improve the resolution, more branches would have to be added to the circuit. If a 16R branch were added, this branch would produce .3125 ma of current when powered by 5 V. The inputs would be able to differentiate 32 different states rather than the 16 available in Figure 9-1. A 32-state converter would drop by .3125 V at the output each time the digital input was incremented. If we take the $-.3125$, which is now the unit value times the maximum count of 31, we obtain -9.6875 V. Not only was the resolution improved, the quantitization error has been reduced. If we were able to add inputs forever, the final output of the circuit would equal the full 10 V out that the system should produce.

Practically, continuing to add branches has drawbacks. Each time a branch is added, a larger resistor value must be chosen. Eventually the value selected is so large that the input currents become very small. This makes the branches using very large R values susceptible to electric noise, which affects the accuracy of the converter. Additionally, the bias currents that were ignored earlier in our analysis become important. If the current through an input branch becomes too small, it will no longer swamp out bias currents. If this happens, the summing amplifier will not work correctly.

If we try to eliminate this problem by selecting reasonable R values for the smallest-weight branches, then as we move toward the branch that represents the ½ fractional value, the resistances decrease. The current draw can become excessive.

The Binary Ladder

The binary ladder is a resistive network used to convert digital inputs into analog equivalents. It eliminates the problem of the weighted resistor network by using just two values of resistance.

A 4-bit binary ladder converter is shown in Figure 9-2. Node 1 is attached to the inverting input of the op amp. This node, as we already know, is at ground potential. This means that a 5 V input applied to the branch labeled ½ will force the output to respond by changing to 5 V. The polarity of the output is actually negative, as it was in the weighted resistor network, due to the op amp inverting the input. This, however, is not a concern here, as we are interested in the voltage level.

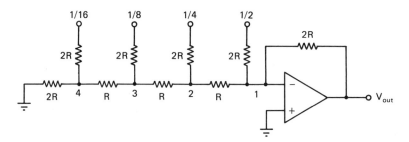

FIGURE 9-2   Binary ladder converter.

A 5 V input at the ¼ branch will force the output to respond by changing 2.5 V, the ⅛ at 5 V will change the output by 1.25 volts, and so on. The R/2R network continues in this manner until a terminating resistor of 2R takes the network to ground. This resistor is found to the left of node 4. If the network had to be extended to improve the resolution, the 2R terminating resistor to the left of node 4 would be replaced with an R value, another branch would be added, and then the terminating resistor would be connected back into the network.

In both converters discussed so far, we have pointed out that resolution can be improved by adding more branches. Remember that resolution is a measure of the number of states by which the output of the converter can be divided. It is equal in weight to the weight of the least significant bit of the converter. This is being pointed out again because resolution is often confused with accuracy. *Accuracy* is a measure of how close a converter's output comes to the predicted or expected output. In a good converter the accuracy should be less than ($\pm$) one half the value of the least significant bit. In discrete circuits, such as we have just discussed, it is difficult to achieve good accuracy due to the tolerances of the components. Precision resistors with tolerances of one percent can be purchased, but this makes the converter expensive. Fortunately, digital-to-analog converters are now available in a wide variety of integrated circuits. This is the focus of the next section.

The 1408 Digital-to-Analog Converter (DAC)

The 1408 converter uses an R/2R internal ladder network which will accept up to eight inputs. These inputs are TTL- and CMOS-compatible. The output current of the chip depends on the binary value placed on the inputs and a reference voltage. The current can reach a maximum of 255/256 of the reference amplifier current due to internal characteristics of the chip. With a reference amplifier current of 2 ma, the output will reach 1.992 ma maximum. The pin out for the IC is shown in Figure 9-3. Take careful note that the order of the inputs is opposite to the way in which computer inputs would be labeled. A8 is the LSB of the input and A1 is the MSB of the input. The chip requires two power supplies, Vcc is normally set to 5 V and Vee is normally set to −15 V. The output current is available at pin 4. This current is a function of the voltage applied to the reference at pin 14. If a 5 V supply was connected to pin 14 through a 2.5 kΩ resistor, the reference current would be 2 ma, with full-scale output at 1.992 ma, as indicated earlier.

To see this clearly, look at Figure 9-4. This is a typical setup using the 1408. The circuit connections at pin 14 set up the 2 ma reference current just discussed. The resistor connected to pin 15 is selected so it matches R14. This helps to prevent imbalances from

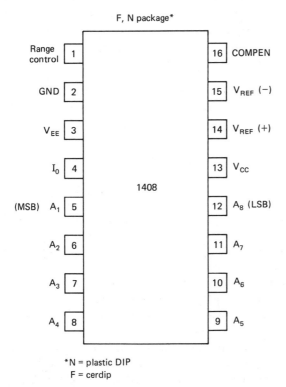

F, N package*

Range control	1		16	COMPEN
GND	2		15	V_{REF} (−)
V_{EE}	3		14	V_{REF} (+)
I_0	4	1408	13	V_{CC}
(MSB) A_1	5		12	A_8 (LSB)
A_2	6		11	A_7
A_3	7		10	A_6
A_4	8		9	A_5

*N = plastic DIP
F = cerdip

FIGURE 9-3   1408 pin out.

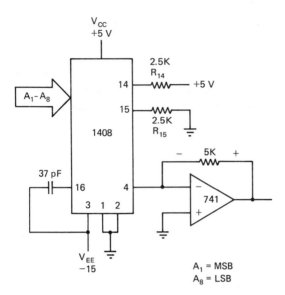

FIGURE 9-4   Typical DAC circuitry.

developing in the 1408's internal circuitry. Pins 1 and 2 are grounded. The negative supply connected to pin 3 is decoupled through a compensating capacitor between pins 3 and 16. The value of the compensating capacitor is listed in the 1408 specification sheet. With a 1K R14 value the compensating capacitor must be at least 15 pF; with a 2.5K R14 value, C must be at least 37 pF; and with an R14 value of 5K, C must be at least 75 pF. The 741 op amp will convert the output current to a voltage. In this configuration the op amp is wired as a current-to-voltage transducer. With a 2 ma reference, this voltage will be a maximum of 10 V in the circuit of Figure 9-4.

Although the inputs to the 1408 are TTL- and CMOS compatible, they are not capable of latching information. To interface the DAC to a computer bus, an 8-bit latch can be used. Figure 9-5 shows how the 8212 can be wired to accomplish this function. The MD input is tied high. This constantly enables the 8212 outputs, so the inputs to the DAC will not have to interpret the tristate output condition of the 8212. The strobe is grounded and has no function as wired in Figure 9-5. The two important controls are the device-select inputs. DSI* is wired to an OUT* signal generated by the CPU. DS2 is wired to the output of a port address decoder—in this case, port 10 hex. If you wish to wire this circuit into your system, this port number can be any convenient active high port signal. When the computer performs an OUT to port 10, the device select AND gate within the 8212 will be enabled. This will gate information on the data bus into the 8212 latches, where it is immediately presented to the inputs of the DAC. When the OUT machine cycle is over, the 8212 will hold the inputs of the DAC steady, allowing it to complete the digital-to-analog conversion.

Example 9-1 shows how to drive the DAC through the 8212 to produce a triangular waveform. The program starts by setting up a stack. After this, the A register is cleared by subtracting A from itself. This information is then output to the DAC. With the DAC

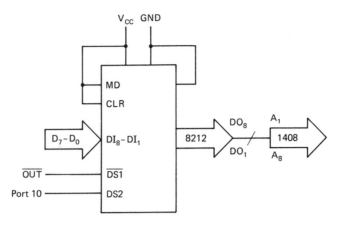

FIGURE 9-5 8212 latch interface to 1408 DAC.

set up as shown in Figure 9-4, the output should be at 0 V. A time delay is then called. This serves two purposes: The delay will allow the DAC to complete the conversion if the processor is running too fast; second, by adjusting the delay bytes within the delay, the slope of the ramp can be altered. After the delay, the program creates a rising ramp by counting up to 80 hex from 00. Once 80 is reached, the logic causes execution to fall through to line 03 0F, where the program produces a negative-going ramp by counting down to 00 hex. Finally, the program will repeat the entire process by branching back to line 03 04, where the positive-going ramp is produced again. The overall result is an output at the op amp that looks like a triangular waveform. Filtering may be necessary at the final output to reduce the bumpy appearance caused by the DAC.

This brings up an interesting point. The output of a properly functioning DAC driven by a counting circuit looks like the staircase waveform shown in Figure 9-6. To allow you to see this, replace the 8212 computer interface driving the DAC inputs with a 7490 decade counter. The four MSBs are connected to the outputs of the 7490. The DAC's four LSBs are grounded. The interface is diagrammed in Figure 9-6(a). Operated in this manner, the circuit of Figure 9-5, with a 1 ma reference current (change R14, R15 to 5K and C to 75 pF), will produce a waveform where the steps are easily discernible (see Fig. 9-6(b)).

As the resolution is improved, the step increases get smaller and smaller. When all eight inputs of the DAC are used, the output change per step in the circuit in Figure 9-4 would be about 40 mV. Each increase in the binary input changes the output of the DAC about 8 μA. Multiply the 8 μA by the 5K feedback resistor connected between the output and input of the op amp to arrive at the 40 mV value. Admittedly, this is a very small change in voltage, but it is still a step increase. This means the output of the DAC is not a true analog voltage; it is an analog equivalent of a binary value. Filtering smooths the output, making it closer to a true analog output.

Under the conditions set up by using the 7490, it is very easy to see what effect an open or grounded input has on the DAC. Once again, if you try this, do not ground

EXAMPLE 9-1

HEX ADDRESS	HEX OP CODE	MNEMONIC	COMMENTS	OCTAL ADDRESS	OCTAL OP CODE
03 00	31	LXI SP	Set up a stack	003 000	061
03 01		00		003 001	
03 02		20		003 002	
03 03	97	SUB A	Clear the accumulator	003 003	227
03 04	D3	OUT	Send binary input to DAC	003 004	323
03 05		10		003 005	
03 06	CD	CALL	Time delay	003 006	315
03 07		LO		003 007	
03 08		HI		003 010	
03 09	3C	INR A	Rising ramp	003 011	074
03 0A	FE	CPI	Ramp at max?	003 012	376
03 0B		80		003 013	
03 0C	C2	JNZ	If not, continue rising	003 014	302
03 0D		04		003 015	
03 0E		03		003 016	
03 0F	CD	CALL	Time delay	003 017	315
03 10		LO		003 020	
03 11		HI		003 021	
03 12	D3	OUT	Transfer byte to DAC	003 022	323
03 13		10		003 023	
03 14	3D	DCRA	Falling ramp	003 024	075
03 15	C2	JNZ	If not at zero, continue	003 025	302
03 16		0F	falling	003 026	
03 17		03		003 027	
03 18	C3	JMP	Continue with wave form	003 030	303
03 19		04		003 031	
03 1A		03		003 032	

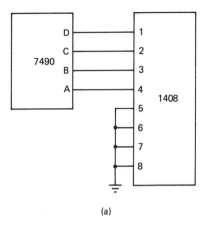

(a)

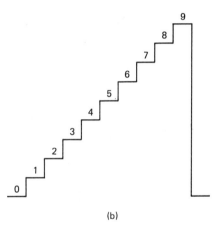

(b)

FIGURE 9-6 (a) 7490 driving high-order nibble of DAC; (b) staircase waveform developed from (a).

the inputs of the DAC with the 7490 still connected to that input. Figure 9-7 shows the output of the circuit from Figure 9-4 with the 7490 QB output disconnected and A6 of the DAC grounded. This waveform indicates that a 2 is missing from the 7490 count at the input of the DAC. When the 7490 reaches 2, QB is set and all other lines are low. The DAC sees QB as low and the other inputs properly low. The DAC interprets this situation as a zero and the output returns to ground. States 2, 3, 6, and 7 all use a 2. Therefore, the amplitudes at these steps are two steps lower than normal. States 0, 1, 4, 5, 8, and 9 do not use 2 and are at their proper voltage level.

The circuit setup used with the 1408 so far results in output voltage swings above ground at the output of the op amp in Figure 9-4. Electron current flows out of the 1408, producing a positive polarity on the right of the 5K resistor connected across the op amp. When operated in this fashion, the converter is said to produce unipolar outputs.

Figure 9-8 shows how the converter circuit can be reconfigured to provide bipolar operation. In this circuit the output will swing from -5 V to $+5$ V. Resistor Rb is

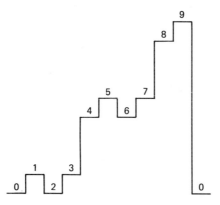

Q_B disconnectial
A_6 grounded

FIGURE 9-7 Faulty DAC circuit: 2'
bit held at 0.

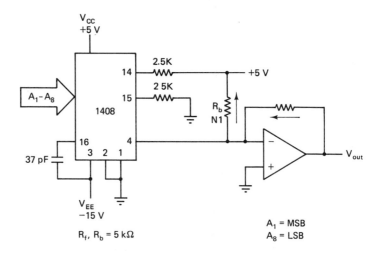

FIGURE 9-8 Bipolar DAC circuit.

connected between the reference voltage and the inverting input of the op amp. Since the inverting input of the op amp is at ground potential, there will be 5 V dropped across Rb. The value of Rb is selected so the current that flows through it will be half of the current produced by the reference voltage at pin 14. In the circuit in Figure 9-8 the reference current is 2 mA, so Rb is chosen as a 5K resistor with 1 mA of current flow.

When the input to the DAC is at 00 hex, there is no current flow out of pin 4, which means that the DAC does not send any current into node N1. According to Kirchhoff's current law, the sum of currents entering a node must be equal to the sum of currents leaving a node. We already know that there is 1 mA of current leaving node N1, flowing up through Rb as indicated by the arrow next to Rb. That current must come from somewhere. At 00 hex the DAC is ruled out. The input of the op amp may contribute some current, but it will be in the nanoamps and is negligible. The only possible source of current is the output of the op amp. Current will flow through Rf, when the DAC inputs are at zero, as indicated by the arrow next to Rf. This current must be 1 mA. Consequently, 5 V will be developed across Rf, and the polarity will be negative at the op amp output with respect to ground.

As the binary input is increased, the DAC will begin to supply current to node N1. Only 1 mA is leaving the node through Rf, therefore, only 1 mA can enter. This implies that as the DAC output current rises, the current taken from the output of the op amp will be reduced. The voltage across Rf decreases and the circuit output starts to rise toward 0 V.

When the DAC has reached a count of 80 hex, it will be at midrange. The current out of the DAC will then be 1 mA. At this time the current through Rf has been reduced to 0 A. The output will then be 0 V. Further increases in the binary input to the DAC will force more than 1 mA out of pin 4. With a fixed 1 mA through Rb, this extra current must leave node N1 flowing through Rf. This will change the polarity across Rf, producing positive output voltages at the output of the op amp.

When the DAC input is at maximum, FF hex, the output of the DAC will be at +5 V.

DAC Applications

Digital-to-analog conversions have a wide range of applications. DACs can be used to track A-to-D converters, for waveform synthesis, for peak detectors, for programmable power supplies, for stepping motor drives, and for speech compression and expansion. DACs often are incorporated into DVMs, find uses in sample and hold circuitry and audio digitizing and decoding. This list of examples is just the beginning.

To truly understand just how much can be done with a DAC, especially under computer control, consider what you have available at the output. In the case of the 1408, there is an output current that can be programmed by the computer to provide different current levels. If a voltage is needed, an op amp wired as shown in Figure 9-4 can convert the current output to a voltage. The output can be scaled (amplified or attenuated) to meet the requirements of the device that will be controlled by the computer/DAC interface.

The bias voltage in a transistor amp can be adjusted under computer control, which can then be used to alter gain. The binary input to the DAC can be changed, altering the current out of the DAC, then amplified to a level required by a DC motor. As the binary input to the DAC changes, the speed of the DC motor will change. We have studied how a waveform can be produced and how the DAC converter circuit of Figure 9-8 produces voltages from −5 to +5 V. When the DAC inputs are connected to a computer, we have a programmable power supply. We could use the computer/DAC interface to control lighting and heating. We could go on, but the list is really limited only by the imagination.

9-2 ANALOG-TO-DIGITAL CONVERSION PRINCIPLES

In the preceding discussion, we saw how the computer through a DAC interface could connect to and control analog processes and devices. These examples illustrated what is often called *open loop control.* In an open loop situation, there is no feedback to the controlling element, in this case the computer. The computer could change the inputs of the DAC, the DAC would convert this information into an analog equivalent, and some circuit, process, or device would respond. Due to the open-loop nature of the circuitry presented, the computer had no way in which to measure the response to the value it sent to the DAC. A closed-loop situation allows the controlling device a method of obtaining information about circuit or device operation. This information can then be used to adjust the control inputs, allowing the controller to fine tune operation or correct for variables such as excessive heating, incorrect motor speed, and so on.

In the chapter on digital interfacing we saw that the computer could obtain information about events external to its circuitry through the use of input ports. This was possible only if the information was already in a digital form with logic levels that matched the levels the computer could handle. In this section we will investigate how analog signals can be converted into digital information for input through a port.

ADC Conversion Methods

We will begin the discussion of ADC methods assuming that an unknown analog voltage to be converted into a digital representation is fixed and unchanging. This will let us concentrate on conversion techniques. After we have discussed some basic analog-to-digital conversion methods, we will concentrate on one that can be partially implemented in software. Then we will take a look at the control signals for a typical ADC converter chip. Finally, we will examine what must be done if the analog voltage is changing.

Dual-slope integration.   The first A-to-D conversion method we will discuss is based on integration. The waveform in Figure 9-9 shows how a dual-slope integrator

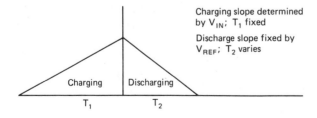

Charging slope determined by V_{IN}; T_1 fixed

Discharge slope fixed by V_{REF}; T_2 varies

Charging   Discharging

T_1 T_2

FIGURE 9-9 Dual slope integration.

converts an unknown voltage into a digital representation. An unknown voltage is applied to an integrator that produces a positive-going ramp. The greater the unknown voltage, the steeper the ramp. The capacitor in the integrator is allowed to charge for a fixed time. This time is a function of the input clock and a counter that tracks the number of clock pulses. When the fixed time is reached, the input is disconnected and switched to a known reference. The capacitor is then allowed to discharge, with the clock and the counter tracking how long it takes. When the negative-going ramp reaches zero, the conversion process is complete. The unknown voltage can now be calculated by comparing the time it took to discharge back to zero to the fixed charging time. This relationship can be expressed as:

$$Vin = \frac{(T2 \times Vref)}{T1} \qquad or \qquad \frac{Vin}{Vref} = \frac{T2}{T1}$$

T1—fixed charging time

T2—discharge time

Vref—fixed reference voltage

Vin—unknown analog voltage

Dual-slope integrators are very useful in converting fixed or slowly changing voltages. They can be very precise if the clock input is precise and the ramp is kept linear. Dual-slope integrators are widely used in digital voltmeters.

Direct conversion.   The second A-to-D conversion method is the parallel or direct converter. One possible way in which this conversion process can be implemented is shown in Figure 9-10. This converter relies on the input voltage being sampled simultaneously by multiple comparators, each of which is set to a different level within the range to be sampled. The reference voltage V1, input to the comparator at the bottom of the array in Figure 9-10, is set to the level of the LSB; V2 is set to a level equal to the weight of twice the LSB; V3 is set to a weight of three times the LSE; and so on. For purposes of discussion, assume that the analog input is equal to 4.2 times the weight of the LSB. The output of the comparators with inputs less than this level will be lows. Focusing on the LSB comparator, the analog input to the inverting terminal of the op amp is the larger of the two inputs. Consequently, the output of the comparator is forced low. The same situation holds for the 2LSB, 3LSB, and 4LSB comparators. Reference voltages V5, V6, and V7 are larger than the input, so the comparators with those inputs will have a high out. This means that the priority encoder, the 74148, sees a binary input of 111 0000 0. The strange partitioning of the binary number indicates that the three most significant inputs to the encoder are high, the next four inputs are low, and the least significant input is grounded, so it is always low.

The inputs to the 74148 are active lows. This means that the most significant input with a low level in will determine the output of the encoder. In our example, that input is input I4. The outputs of the 74148 are also active low, therefore, the outputs were

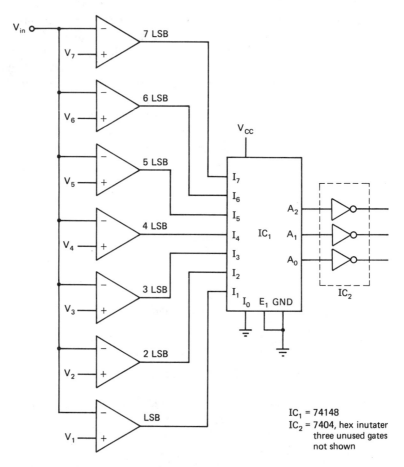

FIGURE 9-10 Direct analog-to-digital converter.

inverted to make the final answer from the circuit use positive logic. This output will be equal to 100.

The circuit of Figure 9-10 produced an output that had just 3-bit resolution. It used seven comparators and a priority encoder. The disadvantage of this conversion method lies in the extensive amount of circuitry required for implementation. The number of comparators needed is equal to $2^n - 1$, where n is the number of bits used in the answer. A 4-bit system would need 15 comparators and an 8-bit system would use 255 comparators. With the larger number of comparators, a larger number of priority encoders would have to be used. The 74148 has a provision for cascading, but even so, the circuit will have a large number of components.

Pulse-width conversion.   The next conversion method uses an analog-to-pulse-width conversion method. Figure 9-11 depicts a 555 timer wired as a oneshot. The

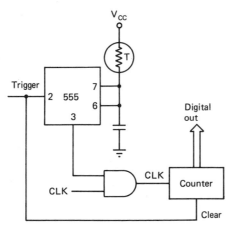

FIGURE 9-11 Pulse width converter.

analog information to be sensed in this circuit is temperature. A thermistor is inserted in the RC circuit that determines the pulse width when the 555 is triggered. As the temperature changes, the output pulse width will change. The circuit will begin a conversion when a trigger is applied to the timer chip. This trigger is also used to clear a counter. The 555 responds to the trigger by entering the quasi-stable state. This means that the output from pin 3 will go high. The output is sent to the input of the AND gate. As long as the 555 oneshot remains in the quasi-stable state, clock pulses will get through the AND gate and pulse the counter. When the pulse width elapses, the oneshot returns to the quiescent state. When this happens, the output from pin 3 will go back low. This will then prevent the clock pulses from reaching the counter. The end result is that the counter will hold a digital value representing the width of the pulse, which was determined by the thermistor's resistance.

The advantage to the method depicted in Figure 9-11 is the ability to sense analog conditions not directly represented by voltages and currents. The disadvantage lies in the type of sensor used. Thermistors and other transducers that convert some condition to a resistance are often nonlinear. This makes it difficult to calibrate a converter using such a sensing device. The easiest way around this problem is to restrict the device to a portion of its operating range that is linear or nearly so. Of course, this restricts the sensitivity of the converter.

One final thought about Figure 9-11 before we investigate the next method of A-to-D conversion. As shown, the thermistor must have a positive temperature coefficient. This means that as temperature rises, its resistance goes up. If the resistance goes up, the output pulse will be longer, which means a higher value in the counter at the end of the conversion.

Binary counting conversion.   The block diagram of Figure 9-12 can be used with two different conversion methods. The first of these is the binary counting method. In this method the computer will take the place of a counting circuit that will drive the

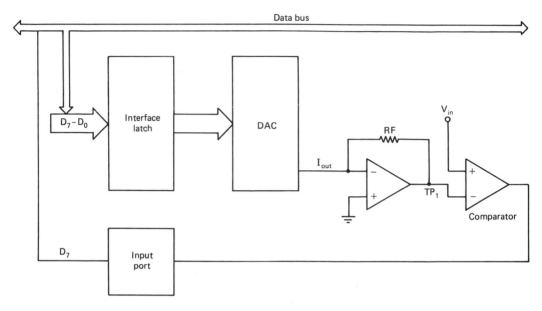

FIGURE 9-12   Computer-driven ADC circuit.

inputs of a DAC. Starting from 00 hex, the computer outputs increasing binary values, each time incrementing by 1. The DAC accepts this information and converts the numbers to analog equivalents. This will cause the voltage at TP1 to rise in a staircase fashion. At some point, the staircase voltage will be higher than the analog input. When this happens, the output of the comparator will go to logic 0. The computer, which has been monitoring the comparator's output through an input port, recognizes this change and ceases counting. The value reached by the counting is the digital representation of the analog input.

The counting method is not difficult to understand. Unfortunately, there is a drawback. The time required for conversions is not a constant. If the counting process goes through 234 base 10 counts, the conversion process will be much slower than if the count value had to reach just 5, for example. On average, the counting process will complete conversions 128 base 10 counts into the conversion. In many instances this might be too slow. Luckily, there is another way to drive the circuitry of Figure 9-12.

Successive approximation.   Successive approximation is very similar to the binary search method presented earlier in the section on software debugging. It uses the same concept of dividing the range of values in half each time a test is made.

This process starts by setting the MSB. The DAC converts this into an analog voltage. The comparator output is monitored by the computer to determine if the voltage created by the DAC is larger than the analog input into the converter. If the DAC voltage is larger, the bit is cleared; if the DAC voltage is smaller, the bit remains set. Then the next bit, D6, is set. The results from the first test, in D7 and the set bit D6, are sent to the DAC. Once again, the comparator is monitored. If the DAC voltage is too high, the bit is cleared. If the voltage is too low, the bit remains set. This process continues until all 8 bits are tested. The advantage to successive approximation is a constant known conversion time. It is also, on the average, much faster than the counting conversion method.

A flowchart for a program that will operate the converter of Figure 9-12 is shown in Figure 9-13. The associated code is found in Example 9-2. Turning our attention to the example, we see another way in which the A register can be cleared. The XRA A instruction EXCLUSIVE OR the A register with itself. This forces all bit positions to zero. This cleared value is then copied into the C register, which will be used to hold the digital representation of the analog voltage. Register B is the loop counter and bit tracker. At line 03 02 it is set to 80 hex, which sets D7 and clears all the other bits. This value will be rotated to the right each pass through the loop, moving from D7 to D6 to D5 and so on. Line 03 04 begins the start of the loop. The current value in the C register is moved to the accumulator. This information is then XORed with the bit tracker. The first time this happens C is 00 and B is 80. Bit D7 is set and then output to the latch.

The results of the current bit under test is then input into A, overwriting the bit pattern sent to the output port. This explains why the bit pattern in A was saved in C prior to the input. The only bit that has any meaning is D7. The other input bits are ''don't cares.'' D7 is rotated into the carry flag with the RLC instruction at 03 0B.

If the comparator output remained high, the carry flag will be set, and setting D7 did not produce enough output voltage from the DAC. This indicates that the bit under test should remain set. The JC instruction jumps around the bit clearing code.

If the comparator output went low, the RLC instruction rotates a logic 0 into the carry flag. This means that the DAC voltage was too high. The bit under test should be cleared. If this happens, the JC instruction is ignored and the bit clearing code is performed.

Lines 03 OF through 03 11 clear the bit under test. Assume that the bit under test was D5. If so, the D5 bit within the B register is set, while all other bits in B are zero. At no time in this program will there be more than one bit set in B. The XRA B instruction clears D5, leaving all other bit positions alone. The pass through the loop after this would affect D4 and so on.

The block of code starting at 03 12 rotates the bit tracker and updates the loop-counting feature of B, all in the same operation.

If B has rotated through all eight bit positions, the single high bit will be moved into the carry flag and the program will be terminated when the JNC instruction is ignored. At this time, the value in the C register will be the digital equivalent of the analog input.

ADC Chip Interface

The control signals required by a typical ADC computer interface are shown in Figure 9-14. Chip select can be connected to a device-select or address-select pulse circuit. When the chip is selected, it momentarily pulls WR* low. This starts the conversion

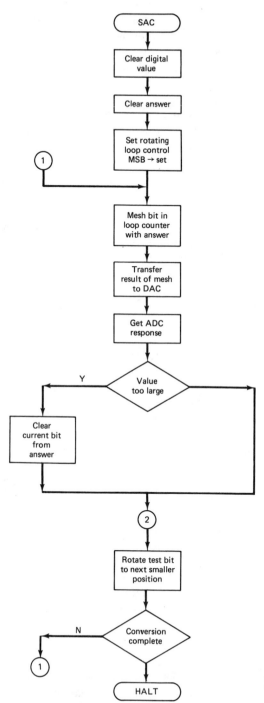

FIGURE 9-13 SAC flowchart sheet 1.
SAC flowchart sheet 2.

EXAMPLE 9-2

HEX ADDRESS	HEX OP CODE	MNEMONIC	COMMENTS	OCTAL ADDRESS	OCTAL OP CODE
03 00	AF	XRA A	Clear A	003 000	257
03 01	4F	MOV C, A	Clear Answer	003 001	117
03 02	06	MVI B	Set loop counter with MSB	003 002	006
03 03		80	set	003 003	
03 04	79	MOV A, C	Set bit for current conversion	003 004	171
03 05	A8	XRA B		003 005	250
03 06	4F	MOV C, A		003 006	117
03 07	D3	OUT	Performance conversion	003 007	323
03 08		10		003 010	
03 09	DB	IN	Get Result	003 011	333
03 0A		10		003 012	
03 0B	07	RLC	Is value too large	003 013	007
03 0C	DA	JC	If not, leave bit set	003 014	332
03 0D		12		003 015	
03 0F		03		003 016	
03 0F	79	MOV A, C	If so, clear bit	003 017	171
03 10	A8	XRA B		003 020	250
03 11	4F	MOV C, A		003 021	117
03 12	78	MOV A, B	Update bit tracker and loop	003 022	170
03 13	0F	RRC	counter	003 023	017
03 14	47	MOV B, A		003 024	107
03 15	D2	JNC	Continue until all 8 bits	003 025	322
03 16		04	tested	003 026	
03 17		03		003 027	
03 18	76	HLT		003 030	166

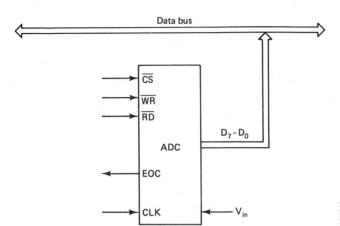

FIGURE 9-14 Typical ADC with up interface.

process. When the chip completes the conversion process, it signals this by activating EOC, which stands for End Of Conversion. The computer responds to this signal by activating RD*, enabling the ADC chip outputs, which then transfer the conversion answer onto the data bus.

It is possible to operate this type of chip independently of the microcomputer. The CS* signal must be tied to ground. The WR* line is then relabeled SC, for Start Conversion. The output enable function is then implemented through the RD* input.

Another interesting feature of such a setup is the ability to produce continuous conversions. In this situation the CS* input is grounded and the WR* input is connected to EOC. Every time a conversion is completed, the SC function will be activated. To insure start-up at power on the WR*, the EOC node should be temporarily forced low.

Unfortunately for the student, ADC chips are hard to use in lab situations. ADC chip data sheets caution the user about the difficulties that can be encountered. In some cases, wire wrapping the chip into a circuit is insufficient to make the chip function correctly. This can be frustrating. Consequently, you have been exposed to alternate ADC techniques, which should provide you with background in this important area.

9-3 SAMPLE AND HOLD

As indicated in the preliminary part of the A-to-D discussion, we were going to pretend that the analog voltage to be converted was stable and unchanging. This assumption was made so we could focus on conversion techniques. Realistically, it is not possible to always have these types of conditions. Our converting circuitry must be able to handle situations in which the analog input is not constant. The solution is to use a sample-and-hold circuit.

Every time a conversion takes place, we can say that the digital circuitry is sampling the analog input. If a voltage is changing, the converter must be preceded by a sample-and-hold circuit. A simplified sample-and-hold circuit is shown in Figure 9-15.

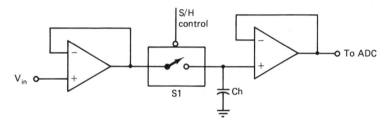

FIGURE 9-15 Sample-and-hold circuit.

In this circuit the op amps are wired as voltage followers. This means the op amps have unity gain and the output will "track" the input. When the switch is closed, the holding capacitor is exposed to the input voltage. This capacitor has very low leakage. This is to insure that it does not discharge during the sample interval. The second op amp must have very high input impedance. This, too, is designed to prevent the holding capacitor from discharging. Together, the op amps isolate the holding capacitor from potential discharge paths. Once a sample has been taken, the switch—which, by the way, is electronic (i.e., a transistor switch)—opens and the sample is held constant during the conversion. This allows the ADC circuitry to proceed with the conversion as if it were dealing with a fixed, unchanging voltage.

Through the hold feature of the circuit shown in Figure 9-15, potential errors caused by the analog input changing during the conversion process can be eliminated. This, however, does not mean that the digital circuitry has a true picture of how the analog voltage is changing.

To obtain this picture, many sample points must be taken. The greater the number of sampling points, the more exact will be the digital representation of the analog voltage. The question arises, just how many sampling points must be taken? In many applications, sampling is performed at a frequency 10 times the frequency of the voltage or signal being sampled. This indicates that the sampling gate is turned on 10 times for every cycle or repetition of the waveform being tested. It also implies that the ADC circuitry can complete at least 10 conversions within the time of a single cycle or repetition.

9-4 CONTROL LOOPS

Figure 9-16 is a block diagram of the position of the computer within a control loop. The first section of the control loop handles the information gathering for the computer. Devices in this part of the loop are likely to be *transducers*. Within the context of our discussion, a transducer will convert some nonelectrical quantity into a current or voltage that an electrical circuit can measure. Thermistors, thermocouples, light-sensitive resistors, hall effect sensors, and pressure transducers are just a few examples of sensing devices that can be used to create a current or voltage. Many of these devices produce very small current or voltage changes in the circuitry to which they are attached. The

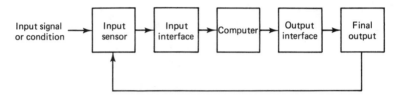

FIGURE 9-16   Control loop block diagram.

input interface section of the control loop usually contains amplifiers and signal conditioners that make the information from the sensors usable by digital input ports or the ADC input ports to the computer. In some cases, the condition being monitored produces a voltage or current too large for the input devices to handle. In this case, the signal must be attenuated. Once the information is scaled and conditioned, it is passed on to the computers by the digital and analog-to-digital circuits just mentioned.

The computer accepts the information, makes a decision based on the information it has received, and generates control signals or data which are sent to the output interface.

The output interface section of the control loop is very similar to the input interface. Signals may be scaled, conditioned, or changed. The DAC is part of this section of the loop. In situations where the computer will control devices that use large amounts of voltage or current, the computer and its ports must be protected from voltages feeding back into the low-power section of the loop. One popular method is to use a solid-state relay that accepts control information in the form of TTL or CMOS logic levels. The output of the relay can then be used to switch AC or DC voltages too large to be connected directly to the digital circuitry.

The solid-state relay comes in two general types. The first is *instant on,* the second is *zero crossing.* An instant-on relay activates its output terminals the moment the logic into the relay is activated. Zero-crossing relays do not energize loads until the AC line is sensed at 0 V, crossing from one alternation to the other. In each case, the load-controlling element of the relay is likely to be an SCR or TRIAC. Additionally, the low-power side of the relay is isolated from the high-power side. One method of isolation employed in many relays is the opto-isolator. A light source such as an LED is turned on by the low-powered logic. This light then strikes a light-sensitive region of an SCR or TRIAC, triggering the solid-state latch. In this way, electrical isolation is maintained and the low-power computer circuitry is protected from feedback from the output devices.

The output section of the loop can contain motors, heating elements, lighting, actuating cylinders, presses, conveyor belt drives, and cooling elements. This, of course, is just a small example of the types of final output devices available.

If the loop is closed, some condition associated with the final output will be fed back into the input side of the loop. This information can then be used to adjust or fine tune the process that is being controlled.

9-5 CLOSING THOUGHTS

This chapter has focused on the process of converting digital-to-analog and analog-to-digital signals and information. Various techniques, concepts, and applications related to this area of electronics were discussed. The role of the computer in this process was also examined. Two software examples were presented—one where the program controlled a DAC and the other where the program replaced part of the ADC circuitry.

The chapter finished with a discussion of the computer's function in a control loop. Certain devices such as transducers were not covered in detail, but the relationship of these devices to a computer control loop was explained. A study of such devices is an important part of electronics, however, the focus of this text has been the computer and its associated circuitry. It is hoped that when you study devices such as transducers you will be able to work with the input and output blocks of the control loop as well as the computer circuitry you are learning about here.

SUMMARY

1. A summing amplifier uses an op amp to add together input currents. The total current input is then converted to an output voltage by a feedback resistor. The greater the number of input branches, the greater the number of states the summing amplifier can represent. Each branch will have a resistance that is half the preceding branch. This arrangement creates binary weights for each input, making it possible to convert digital inputs to an analog output.

2. The binary ladder converter uses just two different resistor values. This eliminates the problems associated with having to use many different-sized resistors. It works by halving the voltage levels at each node in the circuit. Thus, each node has an equivalent binary weight.

3. The 1408 is an 8-bit DAC chip. Internally, it is configured as a binary ladder. The output is a current that is a function of the binary input and a reference current established at a pin other than the ones used for the binary input. In most circuits this current is converted to a voltage by an op amp wired as a current-to-voltage transducer.

4. There are many different ADC techniques. The ones covered in this chapter are typical of those in use today. Pulse-width conversions, binary counters, and successive-approximation conversions are often interfaced to a computer with a software routine performing many of the steps needed for the conversion.

5. Sample-and-hold gates are used when the analog voltage to be converted to digital is not a constant. It is suggested that the rate at which the changing analog voltage is sampled be at least 10 times the frequency of the analog input to the sample-and-hold gate.

6. A control loop consists of inputs, input interface circuits, decision-making circuits (typically a computer), output interface circuits, and a final output. Additionally, there is some type of feedback that allows the decision-making circuit to determine how the final output reacts to commands. This feedback can then be used to make adjustments or fine tune the operation.

QUESTIONS

1. How many states can a seven-branch summing amp represent?
2. What is the input impedance of an op amp?
    Ideally_____   Typically_____
3. What is meant by *resolution?*
4. What is meant by *quantitization error?*
5. How does accuracy differ from resolution in a DAC?
6. What advantages are gained by using a binary ladder converter when compared to an R, 2R, 4R, etc., converter?
7. What is the pin mnemonic of the MSB input to a 1408? How does this relate to the data-bus mnemonic used by the computer?
8. What logic families are compatible with the 1408 inputs?
9. Is the output of a 1408 a true analog signal?
10. Draw a staircase waveform for a DAC driven from a 7490 as shown in Figure 9-6 (b). Assume the 4's input to the DAC is floating high.
11. What is the disadvantage of using a direct ADC circuit?
12. What is a disadvantage of using a pulse-width ADC technique? List an advantage of this technique.
13. On average, how many counts must an 8-bit ADC binary circuit count to complete a conversion?
14. How many times must an 8-bit SAC ADC circuit step to complete a conversion?
15. List the control signals required by a typical ADC chip.
16. What is the function of a sample-and-hold circuit?
17. In what section of a control loop might a DAC circuit be found?
18. In what section of a control loop might an ADC circuit be found?
19. List two general types of solid-state relays.
20. What is the function of an opto-isolator?
21. What is the function of a filter in a DAC circuit?
22. When sampling a changing analog voltage, what is the required sampling frequency if the analog signal has a 1 Hz frequency?

LAB ASSIGNMENTS

1. Write a program to control a DAC so that the final output is a negative-going ramp.
2. Write a program to control a DAC so that the final output is a 30 percent duty cycle pulse waveform.
3. Wire the circuitry to implement the programs above.
4. Write a binary counter program to convert an analog voltage-to-digital equivalent.
5. Wire a 555 as a oneshot with a thermistor in the RC network. Replace the counter with a computer program. Generate a device-select pulse to trigger the 555 timer. If you have a thermistor with a negative temperature coefficient, it is recommended that the count sequence count down. Insert delay loops to calibrate your temperature readings.

LAB QUESTIONS

1. What happens to ramp amplitude if your program loops 128 times for each ramp rather than 256?
2. What happens to ramp frequency as you change the value of the loop counter controlling the number of the steps per ramp?
3. What is the fastest ramp frequency you can obtain with your trainer when the steps per ramp are set at 128? Why?
4. With a fixed number of steps per ramp, how could you obtain slower ramp frequencies?
5. If an unknown analog voltage can be a maximum of 5 V, what resolution is possible when a conversion process is controlled by the Z80 or 8085 using a binary counter method and the 1408?

10

SYSTEM OPERATION

At the end of this chapter you should be familiar with:

1. loading considerations
    a. current
    b. capacitive
2. characteristics of buffer drivers
3. propagation delays
4. how to perform a timing analysis
5. the characteristics of the STD bus
6. how a software-encoded keyboard can be implemented
7. how simple display ports can be wired
8. how a simple monitor program performs the four basic functions needed to operate a computer

INTRODUCTION

In Chapter 1 we presented an overview of a typical microprocessor system. Since then, various blocks of that typical system have been explained in greater detail. Our tour through the microcomputer system has stressed the logical connections necessary to implement the various blocks within a microcomputer. In Chapter 4 we took a detailed look at the timing functions of the computer chip, then used this information to learn when certain data or addresses would be present on the bus. Software-delay loops were built using ideas in this chapter. Chapter 5 developed the skills we would need to connect digital ports to the CPU. When we reached Chapter 8, we focused on the ways in which memory could be added to the computer. Chapter 9 was a discussion on how analog ports could be interfaced to the computer. Along the way, as our hardware knowledge was increasing, other chapters were developing our software skills.

The assumption that was made in those chapters was that if we could logically combine the right signals, then attach the circuitry to the bus, the circuit would work. We left out considerations such as current and voltage levels. We did not discuss fan out or loading. Furthermore, although we examined software related to a particular section of the computer, we did not look at the overall software necessary to operate the CPU and a minimum port configuration, a keyboard for data entry, and some type of display.

This chapter will focus on what has been assumed so far. Fan-out considerations, loading, buffering, propagation delays, memory speed, and system software will be discussed. We will look at a keyboard and some simple display ports. This chapter will also include an examination of a standard bus, with an explanation of the signals used in the bus. This information, tied in with the logical analysis of the computer, should give you a good fundamental knowledge of a typical microcomputer. With the exception of interrupts and interrupt architecture, to be covered in the next chapter, the basic architectural features of a microcomputer will have been explained.

10-1 LOADING CONSIDERATIONS

The three processors we are examining in this text cannot operate an infinite number of chips connected to their pins. In fact, the ability of the processors is quite limited. In most cases it will be necessary to provide buffer/drivers to help operate the bus system.

Fan out is a measure of how many loads can be connected to an output. Fan out differs from logic family to logic family. In standard TTL, fan-out limitations are set at 10. Low-level output current for standard TTL is listed as 16 mA. A TTL input, when low, will use 1.6 mA; when a standard TTL output is high, it can handle 400 μA. A high-level input will use 40 μA. In either case, the input current for an input, divided into the output current, yields 10.

When a device or chip states that it is TTL compatible, this statement refers to the voltage levels that mark logic 0s and logic 1s. It is important that the current capabilities of the devices be considered. The three processors we have chosen for examination are based on variations of MOS technologies. Yet it is possible to hook standard TTL chips to the buses of these CPUs. What we must be able to determine is just how many ICs there are and of what logic families.

The 8080A voltage levels are tested at 1.9 mA for logic 0 and 150 μA for logic 1. If you exceed these currents, the voltage specifications are not guaranteed. The 8085A is tested at 2 mA for logic 0 and 400 μA for logic 1. The Z80 is tested at 1.8 mA for logic 0 and 250 μA for logic 1. This means that connecting more than one standard TTL load to these processors will exceed their limits when the logic level is low.

If LSTTL, low-power schottky gates are used, each gate will require 20 μA for high-level inputs and 400 μA for low-level inputs. Five times 400 μA results in 2 mA of current. Consequently, the 8080A and Z80 could handle four inputs without exceeding their limitations, and the 8085A could handle five LSTTL gates without exceeding its limitation when the output voltage is low level.

A MOS input typically uses 10 μA for low-level and high-level voltage inputs. The limiting factor in all three processors will be the high-level situation.

The 8080A could handle 15 MOS inputs, the 8085A 40 MOS inputs, and the Z80 25 MOS inputs. It begins to seem that we at last have a situation where a decent number of loads can be attached to the processor without the need for buffering. Unfortunately, capacitive loading has yet to be considered.

Capacitive loading affects the dynamic characteristics of the processors. If the capacitance becomes excessive, system timing starts to degrade. Additionally, electrical noise becomes a problem. Capacitive loading is a function of the components attached to a line, wire, or trace capacitance and parasitic capacitance.

The 8080A address and data lines were tested under dynamic conditions of 100 pF. The control lines WR*, HLDA, and DBIN were tested at 50 pF. The timing specifications for the 8085A are guaranteed as long as 150 pF is not exceeded. The Z80 timing was tested at 50 pF of capacitance. The Z80 documentation stipulates that 10 ns delays are added for each 50 pF capacitance increase up to a maximum of 100 pF for address and control lines and 200 pF for the data bus.

This concern about capacitance helps to explain the large number of decoupling capacitors that are placed around a microprocessor board. Decoupling capacitors help to smooth out current spikes that occur when devices turn on and off. These capacitors should have a low inductance, be about .01 to .1 μF of capacitance and should be used for every four ICs on the board. This ratio of one capacitor to four ICs varies with the logic family in use. Consulting a manufacturer's application manuals may be necessary to determine the decoupling capacitor spread required.

The large-bulk capacitors found on many processor boards are not used for decoupling; rather, they are meant to prevent power supply droop. Large current demands when a multiple number of devices turn on, can cause the power-supply voltage to decrease temporarily. The bulk capacitors, usually located across the power supply inputs to a card, can provide the extra current needed for short periods of time, thus enabling the power supply to maintain its normal voltage levels during high current demands.

With an understanding of the preceding discussion, it becomes clear that loading is often a problem. To prevent loading problems, plus allow for larger systems, buffer/driver chips are often added to the CPU subsystem.

Buffer/Drivers

There are a large number of chips available with tristate outputs, control lines, and the ability to sink and source large amounts of currents. Any of the chips with these characteristics could serve as buffer/drivers for the I/O bus. Most of the chips are unidirectional. This means that a unidirectional chip would have to be wired back to back to operate as a data-bus buffer/driver. We will see how to do this in just a moment. Transceiver chips, chips that are bidirectional, are also available. These chips make an ideal choice for the data bus. A special-purpose I/O chip such as a peripheral interface adapter or a programmable peripheral interface chip could be used to buffer/drive part of the bus system. Finally, in the case of the 8080A, there is a special-purpose bus controller buffer/driver available.

Figure 10-1 shows two 8212 chips wired back to back as a data-bus buffer/driver controller. The top 8212 in the diagram will activate when the WR* line is low. This implies that a write operation is underway. Data will flow through this chip from the CPU to the chips and peripherals attached to the data-bus lines. The bottom 8212 will be activated when the RD* line is low. This will allow information from the devices, ports, and memory to pass through the bus buffer into the CPU. When the CPU enters a hold state or bus idle cycle, the WR* and RD* lines will be tristated and both 8212s will have their outputs placed in the tristate condition.

Figure 10-2 shows how 74367s can be wired to buffer/drive the address lines. Each 74367 is a hex noninverting driver. The top 74367 handles A0 through A5, the middle driver handles lines A6 through A11, and the bottom driver handles A12 through A15. Each chip has two enables, G1 and G2. Each enable handles three of the buffers within the IC. In this case, the enables are wired together and controlled by HLDA. When the 8080/8085A CPU enters a tristate condition, probably in response to a DMA request, the address drivers must be disabled. When HLDA goes high, the 74367s will enter a tristate condition. If this configuration were wired to a Z80, HLDA would have to be replaced with BUSAK*. Since BUSAK* is active low, it would have to be inverted prior to connection to G1 and G2.

The 8228 is a special-purpose bus driver/controller for use in 8080A systems. See Figure 10-3. This IC is capable of latching the status bits that are placed on the data bus during T1 by the 8080A. From these status bits and other control signals, the 8228 generates control signals that are not directly available at the 8080A pins. The 8228 also includes a bidirectional bus driver that can be used to isolate the data-bus pins of the processor from system components. It will handle 2 mA at low-level logic and 10 μA when the data-bus line is at high-level logic. The control line outputs are able to handle 10 mA at low-level logic and 1 mA at high-level logic.

The 74LS245 is an octal bus transceiver with three state outputs. The pin-out and function table are shown in Figure 10-4. As a transceiver, this chip can gate information

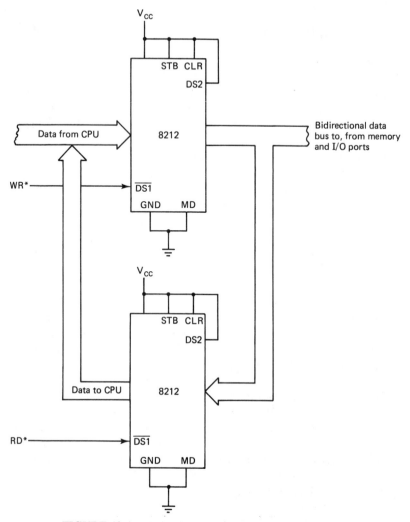

FIGURE 10-1   8212: bidirectional data bus driver circuit.

in two directions. The direction control, when low, will allow information to pass from the B inputs to the A bus. When the direction control is high, information flows from the A inputs to the B bus. Careful inspection of the pin out of the chip indicates that each group of data pins—that is, group A and group B—can serve as inputs or outputs. The function depends on the direction control, as we have just explained.

The CPU could control data flow by driving the direction control from the RD* line. The chip can be placed in an isolation state. This is done by taking the enable line

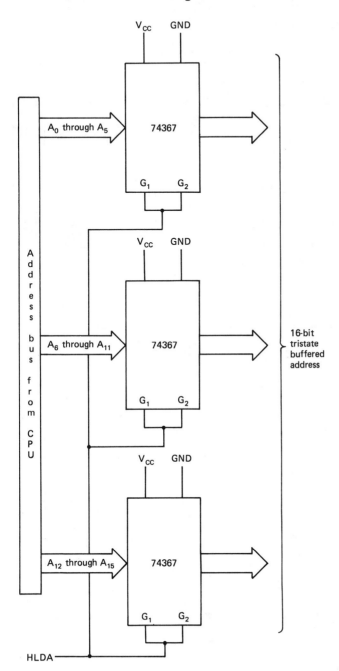

FIGURE 10-2 74367s wired as tristate address bus driver circuit.

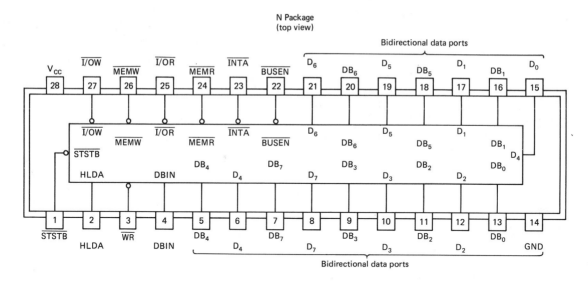

N Package
(top view)

Bidirectional data ports

| 28 | 27 | 26 | 25 | 24 | 23 | 22 | 21 | 20 | 19 | 18 | 17 | 16 | 15 |

Bidirectional data ports

Table A — Status words

Status word	8080A status output								Type of machine cycle	'S428/'S438 command generated
	D_0	D_1	D_2	D_3	D_4	D_5	D_6	D_7		
1	L	H	L	L	L	H	L	H	Instruction fetch	$\overline{MEMR}$
2	L	H	L	L	L	L	L	H	Memory read	$\overline{MEMR}$
3	L	L	L	L	L	L	L	L	Memory write	$\overline{MEMW}$
4	L	H	H	L	L	L	L	H	Stack read	$\overline{MEMR}$
5	L	L	H	L	L	L	L	L	Stack write	$\overline{MEMW}$
6	L	H	L	L	L	L	H	L	Input read	$\overline{I/OR}$
7	I	L	L	L	H	L	L	L	Output write	$\overline{I/OW}$
8	H	H	L	L	L	H	L	L	Interrupt acknowledge	$\overline{INTA}$
9	L	H	L	H	L	L	L	H	Halt acknowledge	NONE
10	H	H	L	H	L	H	L	L	Interrupt acknowledge at halt	$\overline{INTA}$
	INTA	$\overline{WO}$	STACK	HLTA	OUT	M1	INP	MEMR		
				Status information						

74S428, 8228 equivalent.

FIGURE 10-3   74S428, 8228 equivalent. (Courtesy of Texas Instruments Incorporated.)

Functional block diagram

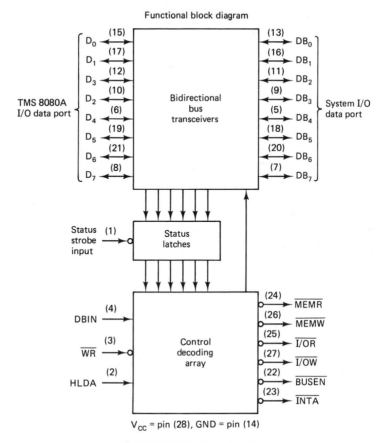

V_{CC} = pin (28), GND = pin (14)

FIGURE 10-3 (*continued*)

high. This input could be used by a CPU to deactivate the driver during a DMA operation.

The current capability of this driver when activated is excellent. The low-level output current is rated at 24 mA. The high-level output current is rated at 15 mA.

Parts Replacement/Add-ons

A technician, unless working as part of a design team, usually will not be involved in the selection of a buffer/driver for the original computer circuitry. The abilities of the buffer/driver will be important in two other phases of the technician's job, parts replacement and add-ons.

SN54LS245 . . . J package
SN74LS245 . . . J or N package
(top view)

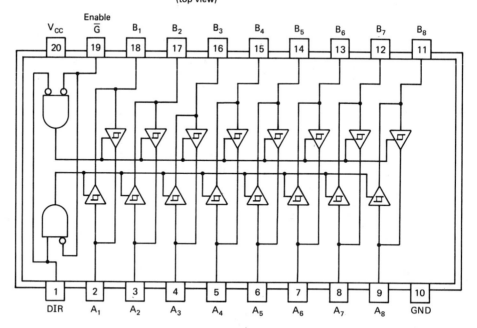

Positive logic: see function table

Function table

Enable $\overline{G}$	Direction control DIR	Operation
L	L	B data to A bus
L	H	A data to B bus
H	X	Isolation

H = high level, L = low level, X = irrelevant

FIGURE 10-4 74LS245 buffer/drivers, pin out and function table. (Courtesy of Texas Instruments Incorporated.)

A good design should not push a component to its limits. This is true for buffer/ drivers as well. It is customary to leave some room for expansion, at the same time letting the buffer/driver run at less than maximum. The buffer/driver should run cooler and have a longer useful life. As a technician, when replacing parts or adding circuits to a computer, it is important that you consider the capabilities of a buffer/driver when adding on or replacing parts.

Consider the situation of Figure 10-5. Gate 2 has burned out. This gate and gate 3 are in the same IC package. Replacing gate 2 involves replacing gate 3. The technician goes to the parts bin to get a replacement. The only NAND gate available is a standard TTL 7400. Could this be placed into the circuit without exceeding the abilities of the driver, gate 1?

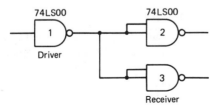

FIGURE 10-5 Parts replacement considerations: Gate 2 has burned out.

To answer this question, refer to Table 10-1. This table highlights the current and voltage characteristics of the 74LS00 and the 7400. The LS NAND gate will produce a minimum of 2.5 V when the output is a logic 1. The 7400 will interpret any voltage above 2 V as a logic 1. This is workable, proving a noise margin of .5 V. When the driver output is at logic 0, the maximum output voltage will be .5 V. The proposed replacement receiver will accept anything up to .8 V as a logic 0. Again, the situation is workable with a noise margin of .3 V.

TABLE 10-1   Mixed Family Logic—Loading Considerations

Voltage Driver	Receiver	
Output	Input	
74LS00	7400	
2.5 V min	2 V min	high-level logic
.5 V max	.8 V max	low-level logic
Current		
−400 μA max	40 μA max	high-level logic
8 mA max	−1.6 mA max	low-level logic

The current situation is more critical. A high-level output at the driver will handle a maximum of 400 μA. The receivers each use 40 μA with a high-level input. Since there are two receivers, the total draw will be 80 μA. This is well below the 400 μA maximum. When the driver produces a low-level output, the maximum current available is 8 mA. Each receiver will use 1.6 mA. Consequently, the 7400 can be used in this situation to replace the 74LS00.

Suppose, however, that the driver was already at or near its maximum fan out. For the sake of argument, assume the low-level current to be at 7 mA prior to the replacement of gates 2 and 3. Changing the receivers to standard TTL would increase the total current required of the output to more than 8 mA, exceeding the fan out of the driver.

A 7400 IC has four NAND gates available. It is likely that the two gates not discussed so far are used in another part of the computer circuitry. If so, the fan out of the drivers affected by placing standard TTL loads into the circuit would have to be calculated.

Add-ons occur when the computer circuitry is to be expanded. Some new part or chip will be attached to the I/O bus. The first thing that should be done is to calculate the currents available from the drivers presently used in the computer and how much of these currents is used. Find out if the designer allowed for expansion. If so, it might be possible to add on without wiring additional drivers. If the add-on takes the buffer/driver to its maximum rating, it is probably wise to add an additional driver anyway.

When calculating the current draws already in use, do not forget off-state leakage currents. Many chips can deactivate their data lines, both in the receive mode and the output mode. These tristate currents are minimal when considering just one chip, but can become significant in large systems.

When selecting chips for add-ons, try to use chips that can place the data lines in the tristate condition for both input as well as output, when not in use. This will reduce the amount of current used. If you cannot obtain a chip that can tristate the inputs, pay careful attention to the input current specifications.

A very simple effective demonstration of just how important this can be involves testing two different types of latches. The 7475 is a quad D latch with a control function that determines when the latch will accept information. It does not place the D input into a tristate condition. Consequently, even when the latch is not in use, it is drawing a significant amount of current. The 8212 octal latch accepts TTL-level inputs, but uses much less current at its inputs. The maximum current usage at the data inputs occurs with the input logic level low. The specification for IIL is 250 μA maximum. Measurement with a microammeter usually results in a value far less than this maximum. The 7475, by comparison, even when the D input is not in use, can draw a maximum of 3.2 mA. Typical values are likely to be near 1 mA. If you decide to make this comparison in lab for yourself, remember that when the input logic levels change, the direction of current flow changes. If you use an analog meter, reverse the leads before changing logic levels or you can peg the needle when it moves backwards. Refer to a TTL data book for current directions.

The discussion in this section focused mostly on the data lines. They often present more problems than other bus lines, for several reasons. First, many data lines are in the tristate condition when not in use—a good feature, but, as mentioned above, the off-state leakage currents must be determined. Second, drivers used for an I/O bus often provide less current for the data lines than for other lines. The 8228 bus controller is a case in point. As we found out, the data lines can handle 2 mA, while all other outputs can handle 10 mA. It is possible to overlook this difference in drive capabilities on different lines of the I/O bus. Be thorough; investigate all pertinent specifications.

Finally, this discussion indicates one area in which a computer can fail, but still be logically correct. As we saw, replacing parts with logic similar to that removed leads to problems. It is a good idea to avoid changing logic families or even changing to a different subfamily if it can be avoided. When add-ons were discussed, two points of concern arose. How much current can the circuitry already in use provide and how much current will the new circuitry use?

10-2 CIRCUIT SPEED

Another area of system operation that must be considered is the rate at which signals transfer from point to point in the computer. A circuit can be logically correct, provide the correct amounts of current, and still fail. If a signal that activates a latch arrives after the data is no longer present on the data bus, the correct information will not be gated into that latch.

Propagation delay is a measure of how long it takes a signal generated at one point in the circuit to arrive at another point in the circuit. A good data book will not only indicate pin outs and logic functions, but will include electrical specification for the parts in question. One of those specifications is the propagation delay introduced by the switching elements of the logic functions. A gate will usually have two delays indicated. These delays are frequently refered to as tplh and tphl, representing propation time when the output switches from a low to a high (tplh) and propagation time when the output switches from a high to a low (tphl).

For a standard TTL 7400 AND gate, tphl is listed as a maximum of 15 ns and tplh is listed at a maximum of 22 ns. In a beginning digital class, these billionths of seconds are hardly ever noticed. In a computer system, operating in the millions of hertz, long strings of logic may cause significant problems to arise.

A system's critical path is defined to be the signal path with the longest propagation delay needed to provide correct system operation. To determine this path requires that every signal path in a computer or proposed computer be analyzed. For a technician to do this by paper, schematic, and calculator involves a lot of time. The design engineer will probably have the help of a computer program written to calculate such things. What is the technician to do if a question arises about such things as chip speed? In the chapter on hardware troubleshooting, we will examine how to find such problems. At this time we will look at how to determine if a chip will operate quickly enough in a given situation.

The areas of a computer that present the most problems in timing center around RAMs and ROMs. Arithmetic units and multilevel logic paths are also prime candidates for timing problems. One- or two-level gating networks can almost always be eliminated from consideration as timing source problems.

To help you get started in timing analysis, we will investigate the timing functions of a 2716 EPROM in a Z80 system operating at 2 MHz. At this speed, the basic clock cycle will be 500 ns. The question we will consider is, Can the 2716 provide data to the Z80 at the proper time during an op code fetch?

2716 Timing Analysis

The block diagram of Figure 10-6 shows the situation we are going to consider. The address buffers will be 74367s, the decoder will be a 74154, the buffer for the read line will be a 7407, and the bidirectional data bus will be two 8212s wired back to back. The logical operation of each block within Figure 10-6 has already been explored. At this time, we will concentrate on speed of operation and propagation delays. To simplify calculations, the delays introduced by the transmission lines, traces, or wires will be considered nil.

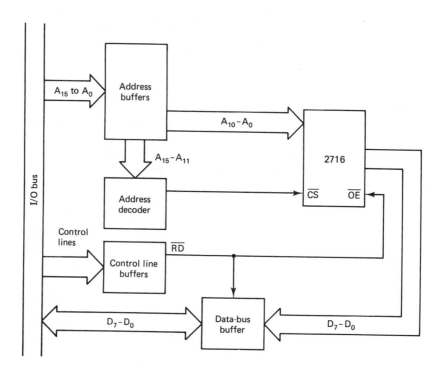

FIGURE 10-6   Critical path analysis for a Z716 interface.

The Z80 op code fetch waveforms are shown in Figure 10-7. We investigated this machine cycle earlier; now we will take a closer look at the timing. As we learned before, the data is sampled on the rising edge of T_3. The information must be on the data bus when the RD* pulse is low. Two complete cycles will elapse before T_3 is reached. This means that 1000 ns will elapse before the sampling begins. The setup time

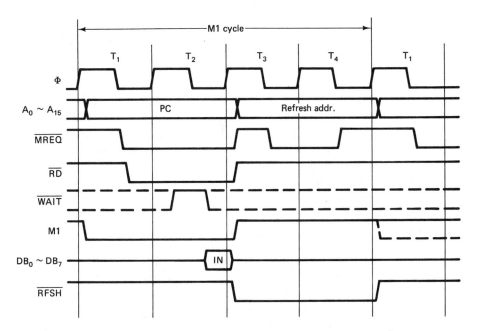

FIGURE 10-7 Z80 op code fetch. (Reproduced by permission. © 1986 Zilog, Inc. This material shall not be reproduced without the written consent of Zilog, Inc.)

for data during op code fetch cycles is 50 ns to the rising edge of the master clock. The maximum time to get data onto the data pins of the CPU in time to stabilize is therefore 950 ns.

The 2716 requires three sets of signals to work. Addressing information must be present on the address pins, chip select must be low, and OE* must be low. All three signal paths must be investigated to insure that timing will not be a problem.

At the start of the cycle, the addressing information does not appear instantly on the Z80 address lines. A maximum delay of 145 ns can occur. This means that the address information may not get to the address buffers until 145 ns into the cycle. The address buffers are 74367s. The tplh for these chips' worst case is 16 ns and for tphl 22 ns. Since we do not know whether the address information will be rising or falling, we will use the 22 ns as our worst-case delay. So it is possible that the 2716 does not see A10 through A0 until 167 ns into the cycle. Once it receives the address, assuming all other control functions are correct, 450 ns will elapse before the data appears on the output pins. This information must then be transferred to the Z80 through the data-bus buffer. Passing through the buffer will add another 30 ns in worst-case conditions. The total delay for this path becomes 145 + 22 + 450 + 30 = 647 ns. This means that the delays in this part of the circuit are not so long as to prevent the data from arriving back at the CPU in time.

Chip select is developed from an address that comes from the CPU, then through the address buffer, and finally through the decoder. We start with the maximum delay of 145 ns out of the CPU, account for the 22 ns of the address buffers, add in the 36 ns delay introduced by the 74154, and include the 450 ns delay from CS* in the 2716. Finally, with the data buffers, the entire delay for this path becomes 145 + 22 + 36 + 450 + 30 = 683 ns. This is well within the 950 ns limit.

The last control line of the 2716 that must be activated is the OE* control line. As you can tell from Figure 10-7, the RD* signal does not go low until after the falling edge of T_1. If a complete cycle is 500 ns, when operating at 2 MHz, we must determine the pulse-width time and the falling edge of T_1. Rising and falling edges are listed as a maximum of 30 ns. Subtracting the edge time from the cycle time leaves 460 ns. Dividing this by 2—the time is shared equally by the pulse width and the space when the duty cycle is 50 percent—we get a pulse-width time of 230 ns. The pulse-width time plus the falling edge of T_1 is 260 ns. Z80 specifications indicate that RD* will go low no later than a maximum of 130 ns after this. Therefore, we know that RD* will be available no later than 260 + 130 = 390 ns into the cycle. The 7407 buffer can add a maximum of 30 ns delay. The output will have been high and we know it is going low, therefore, tphl specification for the 7407 is being used. The circuit cannot be guaranteed to deliver a pulse to OE* prior to 420 ns into the cycle. The 2716 will respond, assuming other control functions are correct 120 ns after this line goes low. The total delay is now at 420 + 120 = 540 ns. Another 30 ns for the data buffer finalizes the total at 570 ns. This result meets the 950 ns criterion.

The path involving the CS* function totaled 683 ns. This was more than the total of the address path and more than the total of the OE* path. This makes the CS* path the critical path in the circuitry we have just analyzed.

What could be done if the circuit did not respond quickly enough? Perhaps a faster version of the 2716, such as the 2716-2, could be used. Another solution is to add circuitry that places wait states into the cycle timing. A third solution involves slowing down the processor. The choice will depend on cost, desired operating speed, and if you need to predict CPU timing accurately. Adding wait states for some circuitry, while not using it for others, complicates such things as developing software delay loops.

10-3 STANDARDIZED BUS SYSTEMS

The preceding topics show that interfacing and expansion are more than just assuring that the logic is correct. Current, timing, and logic family type need to be considered. Additionally, the control signals available from the processor or the I/O bus have to be considered. As we have discovered, despite the similarities of the 8080, 8085, and Z80, there are differences. Processors such as the 6800, 6809, and 6502 have a different design philosophy, with a different set of control lines available. As a technician, if your job involves updating equipment, interfacing new control ports, and adding memory, a lot of time can be devoted to this part of the job.

Standardized bus systems are an attempt to reduce this problem and make system expansion easier. Each standardized bus will provide signal definitions, pin numbers where the signals can be found, and frequently mechanical information such as card size. There are many standard bus systems available. The popularity of a bus system is often determined by the number of manufacturers that make interface cards for the bus. The greater the industry support for a bus, the better chance you have of finding a card that meets your needs. When you cannot find a card to meet your needs, it becomes necessary to design a special interface card. This process will include the considerations of the previous sections on current, loading, and timing. It will also include working with the bus system that operates the computer. As a technician, you should know the bus system of the computers you will work on, the signals available, and their characteristics.

It would take up a lot of the text if we described the signals and characteristics of every popular bus available. Furthermore, after several buses were described, a lot of the information would become repetitious. Our goal will be to examine the characteristics that can be found in a bus standard by examining one bus. From this examination, we hope that you will obtain an understanding of how bus standards are developed and used by the industry.

The STD Bus

When the STD bus was first developed, the goal was to make a bus system that was processor-independent. The idea was that any processor could connect to and operate the STD bus. To accomplish this, the signals were defined for a general-purpose CPU.

Advances in CPU design, design philosophy differences between manufacturers, and the advent of 16-bit processors has made this goal of a processor-independent bus difficult to achieve. Despite this, the 8080, 8085, Z80, 6800, 6809, NSC800, 8088, and 6502 microprocessors are available for STD bus applications. If a computer system is to be built around an STD bus configuration, it should be possible to obtain most of the functions required on STD cards. Only in a few cases, such as driving a nonstandard peripheral, will it be necessary to build a custom interface.

The STD bus is a 56-signal bus divided into four functional groups. These groups are:

> dual power buses
> data bus
> address bus
> control bus

The signals used on this bus are meant to interface to TTL circuitry. Logic levels found on the bus will be compatible with the levels used in the TTL family. The layout of the signals on the STD is summarized in Table 10-2.

The dual power buses are found on lines 1 through 6 and 53 through 56. Pins 1 and 2 are 5 V logic power source. Pins 3 and 4 are used for logic ground. Pins 5 and 6 are low-level current—5 V supplies used for logic bias. Pins 53 and 54 are used as

TABLE 10-2 STD Bus Pin Assignments Signal Flow Referenced to Processor Card

	COMPONENT SIDE			CIRCUIT SIDE	
Pin	Name	Flow	Pin	Name	Flow
Logic Power Bus					
1	+5 vdc	in	2	+5 vdc	in
3	gnd	in	4	gnd	in
5	Vbb#1	in	6	Vbb#2	in
Data Bus					
7	D3	I/O	8	D7	I/O
9	D2	I/O	10	D6	I/O
11	D1	I/O	12	D5	I/O
13	DO	I/O	14	D4	I/O
Address Bus					
15	A7	out	16	A15	out
17	A6	out	18	A14	out
19	A5	out	20	A13	out
21	A4	out	22	A12	out
23	A3	out	24	A11	out
25	A2	out	26	A10	out
27	A1	out	28	A9	out
29	A0	out	30	A8	out
Control Bus					
31	WR*	out	32	RD*	out
33	IORQ*	out	34	MEMRQ*	out
35	IOEXP	I/O	36	MEMEX	I/O
37	REFRESH*	out	38	MCSYNC*	out
39	STATUS 1*	out	40	STATUS 0*	out
41	BUSAK*	out	42	BUSRQ*	in
43	INTAK*	out	44	INTRQ*	in
45	WAITRQ*	in	46	NMIRO*	in
47	SYSRESET*	out	48	PBRESET*	in
49	CLOCK*	out	50	CNTRL*	in
51	PCO	out	52	PCI	in
Auxiliary Power Bus					
53	Aux Gnd	in	54	Aux Gnd	in
55	+ 12 v	in	56	−12 v	in

auxiliary ground for the power supply voltages found on 55 and 56. Pin 55 is $+$ 12 V and pin 56 is $-$12 V.

The data bus lines are located on pins 7 through 14. These pins are bidirectional tristate lines using active-high logic. All cards are required to release these lines to a high impedance state when the card is not in use. The processor card will release the bus in response to requests on the BUSRQ* control line.

The address lines are located on pins 15 through 30. It is a 16-bit, three-state, active-high logic bus. The addresses are normally generated at the processor card. The information on these lines provides information for memory operations and for I/O transfers. The 6800, 6809, and 6502 do not support isolated I/O directly.

The control-bus pins start at 31 and continue through 52.

Wr, pin 31.*   This is an active-low three-state signal indicating that the bus holds information to be written to memory or I/O.

RD, pin 32.*   This is an active-low three-state signal indicating that the processor or other controller will accept information from the bus.

IORQ, pin 33.*   This is an active-low three-state signal indicating an I/O operation. The address lines will hold a valid I/O address when this signal is low.

MEMRQ, pin 34.*   This is an active-low three-state signal indicating a memory operation. The address lines will hold a valid 16-bit address when this signal is active.

IOEXP, pin 35.   This active low indicates a primary I/O operation is underway. When high, this signal can be used to allow common address decoding in memory-mapped operations. In simple systems this line is grounded.

MEMEX, pin 36.   This active low indicates that the primary memory is in use. A high on this line can be used to switch to alternate memories. It can be used to toggle between banks of 64K. Simple systems will ground this line.

REFRESH, pin 37.*   This is an active-low three-state signal used to refresh dynamic RAM. Not all processors operating STD buses will use this signal. See Table 10-3.

MCSYNC, pin 38.*   This is an active-low three-state signal indicating the beginning of a machine cycle. The function of this line is processor dependent (see Table 10-3).

STATUS 1, pin 39.*   This active-low three-state signal indicates an instruction fetch. Not all processors using STD cards will generate this signal (see Table 10-3).

STATUS 0, pin 40.*   This is an active-low three-state signal. This line is processor dependent (see Table 10-3).

BUSAK, pin 41.*   This is an active-low three-state signal indicating that the processor will release the bus to another bus-controlling device. It is primarily used in DMA operations.

TABLE 10-3   Processor-Specific Signals on the STD Bus

CPU	REFRESH* Pin 37	MCSYNC* Pin 38	STATUS1* Pin 39	STATUS0* Pin 40
8080	—	SYNC*	M1*	—
8085	—	ALE*	S1*	SO*
Z80	REFRESH*	(RD*+WR* +INTACK*)	M1*	—
NSC800	REFRESH*	ALE*	S1*	SO*
6809E	—	EOUT*(02*)	—	R/W*
6502	—	EOUT*(02*)	SYNC*	R/W*

— not used   * active low

BUSRQ*, pin 42.   This is an active-low three-state signal indicating that a device external to the processor wishes to gain control of the bus.

INTAK*, pin 43.   This is an active-low signal indicating that the processor has responded to a request to interrupt the execution of a program and interact with the device requesting the interrupt. See Chapter 11, Interrupts, for further details.

INTRQ*, pin 44.   This is an active-low open collector signal used by peripherals to request an interrupt. The signal is maskable and can be ignored by the processor. See Chapter 11, Interrupts, for further details.

WAITRQ*, pin 45.   This is an active-low open collector signal. As long as this signal is low, the processor will suspend activity. Normally, the processor will maintain a valid address when in the wait state. The signal can be used to interface slow memories or for single stepping. The single-stepping feature will be examined in Chapter 12, Hardware Troubleshooting.

NMIRQ*, pin 46.   This is an active-low open collector signal. Interrupt requests on this line cannot be ignored. Critical functions such as imminent power failure are often connected to this line.

SYSRESET*, pin 47.   This is an active-low signal generated by the processor. It can be triggered from power up or push button reset. It should be gated into all cards with components that require initialization.

PBRESET*, pin 48.   This is an active-low signal into the processor that can be used to perform warm resets.

CLOCK*, pin 49.   This signal is a buffered processor-clock signal that can be used for system synchronization and general timing functions.

CNTRL*, pin 50.   This signal is an auxiliary timing waveform. It may be a multiple of the master clock, a real time clock signal, or an external input to the processor.

PCO, pin 51. This signal is sent to the next lower card in the priority chain. A card requesting priority should hold PCO low. See the information on interrupt chaining in Chapter 11, Interrupts, to see how this signal might be used.

PCI, pin 52. This signal is taken from PCO of the next higher card in the priority chain. A high level on PCI gives priority to the card sensing the PCI input high.

An STD card should be 6.5 in. long and 4.5 in. in height, the plated board thickness should be .062 in. and card spacing should be a minimum of .5 in. The printed circuit edge connector finger—that is, the part of the card that inserts into an edge connector slot (the female part of the connection)—will be on one of the 4.5 in. sides. The component side of the card will have the odd-numbered pins; the circuit side will have the even-numbered pins. The spacing between pins and the length of the finger are also specified. If a card varies from the physical standards, it will most likely be that the card will be longer than the 6.5 in. parameter. Cards that cannot meet the minimum card spacing due to component size may require multiple slots, where adjacent slots are left unused.

Table 10-3 indicates those signals that are not standard. The primary reason for these differences is processor design. This can be an important point. STD cards designed to operate with a 6502 processor may not work with an STD bus driven by an 8085. Manufacturers will often sell STD cards as STD 6502 or STD 8085, for example. So remember, not all STD cards are completely compatible.

The memory locations reserved by processors when interfaced to an STD bus are listed in Table 10-4. User functions should not use these locations other than as indicated. If a user function interferes with these locations, interfacing problems can arise.

TABLE 10-4   STD Memory-Map Locations

CPU	RESET	INTERRUPTS	STACK
8080	0000*	0000-0038	anywhere
8085	0000*	0000-003C	anywhere
Z80	0000*	0000-0038, anywhere	anywhere
NSC800	0000*	0000-0038, anywhere	anywhere
6089E	FFFE[†]	FFFO-FFFD	anywhere
6502	FFFC[†]	FFFE, FFFA	0100-01FF

*contains first instruction to be executed
[†]contains address of first instruction to be executed

There are processors other than those listed in Tables 10-3 and 10-4 available for use with an STD bus, but those listed are the processors you are most likely to use in an introduction to microprocessor electronics. The three processors we are focusing on are listed in the first three locations of each table.

Table 10-5 indicates how STD signals can be combined to create additional control

TABLE 10-5   Combinations of STD Signals

RD*	WR*	IORQ*	MEMRQ*	Operation
0	1	0	1	I/O read
1	0	0	1	I/O write
0	1	1	0	mem read
1	0	1	0	mem write
1	1	1	1	internal

*active low

signals. These signals are not part of the STD standard and will not be bused from card to card. Each interface card that needs the additional control signals will create the signal for its own use by logically combining the STD signals as shown.

Before we leave the discussion on bus standards, a few remaining points are to be made. The 8080, 8085, and Z80 are available for use with other standard buses. If you wish to pursue an investigation into other buses, it is recommended that you consider the S-100 bus, Multibus™,* and the IEEE 488 bus.

Finally, the voltages used by the bus are specified to meet TTL logic levels, as indicated earlier. Current capability was not discussed. It is a function of the power supply driving the bus. As in the loading discussion, you as a technician must insure that adding extra cards onto a bus system does not load down the supply by drawing currents the power supply cannot handle.

10-4 KEYBOARD AND DISPLAY PORTS

A computer, to be of any use, must have some way in which a program can be entered and the results monitored. A very basic setup might involve a front panel where codes are entered in binary through switches and outputs are monitored through the use of LEDs. A step or two above this level, we might find the computer using hex-pad keyboards for data entry and monitoring the results through output ports wired to a hex display or seven-segment display. These are the first type of input/output ports that you will probably use. The information garnered from a study of these two types of ports can provide the starting point for an understanding of more complex peripherals, as well as provide the information necessary to help use and fix such ports.

Keypads

Keypads provide a way for the computer user to enter information through switch closures. Keypads come in various sizes, from full-size keyboards found on typewriters and display terminals, to keypads for data entry with only decimal numbers, to touch-tone

*Multibus™ is a registered trademark of Intel Corporation.

dialing pads, to calculator keypads, and to hexpads frequently found on small computer systems.

Keypads can be debounced through hardware or software; they can also be encoded or not encoded. An encoded keypad or keyboard would generate a code that represents the key closure being made. A very common type of encoded keyboard generates ASCII codes. When a keyboard is not encoded, the software must generate a code or value that depends on which key was sensed. These types of keypads can be reconfigured simply by changing the software that monitors the key closures.

The first example we will study will be a hex pad with the switches debounced through hardware, the key codes determined through software, and the keyboard wired in a matrix fashion.

Figure 10-8 shows a hex pad and some of the hardware associated with its operation. The debouncing hardware has not been drawn in the schematic. The 16 keys have been assigned the values 0 through 15. If data entry were to be in hex, the keys from

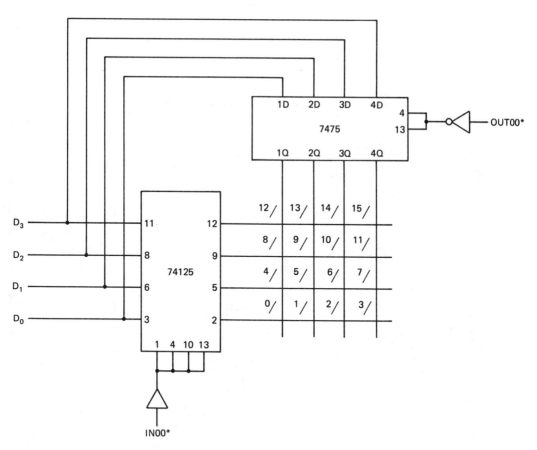

FIGURE 10-8 4 × 4 matrix keyboard.

10 through 15 would be renamed A through F. As we will see, the correct binary pattern will wind up in the computer for these six keys whether we call them 10 through 15 or A through F.

The pad is wired as a matrix. Keys 0 through 3 share a common line into the 74125. The input to the 74125 at pin 2 is pulled up to Vcc through a pull-up resistor (not shown). The keys are normally open. This means that without a key closure pin 2 will be at a logic 1 level. The path to ground for a closed key is provided by the 7475 quad latch. If the latch is cleared to all zeroes, then any key can be used. If the latch is filled with 0111, then the only column of keys that can be used is the 0, 4, 8, and 12 column. If a key is pressed in this column, the corresponding input to the 74125 will be lowered to ground. If key 0 were pressed while this column was active, the input to the 74125 would be logic 0. The computer will control the latch by outputting information to port zero. When the computer is ready to sense a key closure, it will activate the 74125 by generating an input from port zero. If this input reads all highs, then no key closures have been made. The software can then rescan the keyboard or go on to another function. A software routine that scans the keypad of Figure 10-8 is found in Example 10-1.

This matrix scan routine of Example 10-1 is packaged as a subroutine. When called, it will scan the keypad for a key closure. The logic will repeat scanning until a

EXAMPLE 10-1

HEX ADDRESS	HEX OP CODE	MNEMONIC	COMMENTS	OCTAL ADDRESS	OCTAL OP CODE
01 00	F5	PUSH PSW		001 000	365
01 01	C5	PUSH B		001 001	305
01 02	E5	PUSH H		001 002	345
01 03	AF	XRA A	Clear key code	001 003	257
01 04	4F	MOV C, A		001 004	117
01 05	06	MVI B	Set column control	001 005	006
01 06		376		001 006	
01 07	78	MOV A, B	Activate a column	001 007	170
01 08	D3	OUT		001 010	323
01 09		00		001 011	
01 0A	DB	IN	Get keyboard response	001 012	333
01 0B		00		001 013	

EXAMPLE 10-1 (*continued*)

HEX ADDRESS	HEX OP CODE	MNEMONIC	COMMENTS	OCTAL ADDRESS	OCTAL OP CODE
01 0C	E6	ANI	Mask out D_7–D_4 not used	001 014	346
01 0D		0F		001 015	
01 0E	FE	CPI	Key pressed in active	001 016	376
01 0F		0F	column?	001 017	
01 10	C4	CNZ	If so, call row scan	001 020	304
01 11		50		001 021	
01 12		01		001 022	
01 13	C2	JNZ	And then return to calling	001 023	302
01 14		23	routine	001 024	
01 15		01		001 025	
01 16	78	MOV A, B	Update column driver	001 026	170
01 17	07	RLC		001 027	007
01 18	47	MOV B, A		001 030	107
01 19	0C	INRC	Increment key code to next	001 031	014
			column base code		
01 1A	79	MOV A, C	Check for complete scan	001 032	171
01 1B	FE	CPI		001 033	376
01 1C		04		001 034	
01 1D	CA	JZ	Start a new scan	001 035	312
01 1E		03		001 036	
01 1F		01		001 037	
01 20	C3	JMP	Continue present scan	001 040	303
01 21		07		001 041	
01 22		01		001 042	
01 23	E1	POP H	Exit sequence	001 043	341
01 24	C1	POP B		001 044	301
01 25	F1	POP PSW		001 045	361

EXAMPLE 10-1 (*continued*)

HEX ADDRESS	HEX OP CODE	MNEMONIC	COMMENTS	OCTAL ADDRESS	OCTAL OP CODE
01 26	C9	RET		001 046	311
			Row Scan		
01 50	F5	PUSH PSW	Save A, flags	001 120	365
01 51	0F	RRC		001 121	017
01 52	D2	JNC		001 122	322
01 53		62		001 123	
01 54		01		001 124	
01 55	32	STA	Save key closure position	001 125	062
01 56		00		001 126	
01 57		19		001 127	
01 58	79	MOV A, C	Update key code	001 130	171
01 59	C6	ADI		001 131	306
01 5A		04		001 132	
01 5B	4F	MOV C, A		001 133	117
01 5C	3A	LDA	Restore key closure position	001 134	072
01 5D		00		001 135	
01 5E		19		001 136	
01 5F	C3	JMP		001 137	303
01 60		51			
01 61		01			
01 62	21	LXI H	Key code storage location	001 140	041
01 63		01		001 141	
01 64		19		001 142	
01 65	71	MOV M, C	Store key code	001 143	161
01 66	F1	PUSH PSW	Exit	001 144	361
01 67	C9	RET	Sequence	001 145	311

key closure has been detected. When this occurs, the software will produce a code that represents the key closed, store this code in memory, and return to the calling routine.

The program starts at line 01 00. The first three instructions save the calling routine's register values. These will be restored just before this subroutine returns through the use of the three POPS at starting at 01 23 hex.

The next block of code clears the A register and the C register. The C register will be used to hold the key code prior to storage in memory.

The B register is loaded with 1111 1110. The contents of this register will be used to drive the columns of the matrix keypads. Since only one bit position is low in this register, only one column will be active at a time. The column attached to DO is activated when the B value is transferred to port O the first time through the loop. This means that the only keys with a potential ground are 0, 4, 8, and 12. All other keys will have logic 1 potentials on both sides of the contacts.

The IN instruction at 01 0A obtains the status of the keyboard. If no key was pressed, then the low-order nibble of the data bus will be all highs. The ANI instruction that follows the IN eliminates the information in the high-order nibble by masking it out. This information is not vital since it is not wired to the keyboard. The block of code starting at 01 0E checks to see if a key has been pressed. If so, the result of the CPI OF will clear the zero flag. This will force the subroutine to call another subroutine that calculates the value of the key pressed.

If no key has been pressed, there will be a match with OF and the zero flag will be set. In this case, the CNZ and JNZ instructions just after the CPI will be ignored.

When program flow proceeds to 01 16, the B value is rotated once to the left. This will allow the next column to be activated when the scanning loop is repeated. The value in the C register is then incremented. This will change C from a 0, which it contained the first time through, to a 1. This value reflects the lowest key value in the next column to be activated.

At 01 1A, a CPI 04 determines if the entire keypad has been scanned. If it has, control is returned to line 01 03, so C and B can be reinitialized and the whole process repeated. If the entire keyboard has not been scanned, control passes to 01 07, which allows the next column to be scanned.

With this background information, let's determine what will happen if key 7 is pressed. The first time through the main loop keys 0, 4, 8, and 12 have grounds. None of these keys are pressed. Key 7 has 5 V applied to both its contacts. This means that when the computer inputs from port 00, it receives 1111. This information tells the program that none of the keys in the first column has been pressed. C is incremented to 1, the B value is rotated, and the column with keys 1, 5, 9, and 13 now have the potential to pull a line low. Since none of these keys are pressed, the IN instruction obtains 1111 the second pass through the loop. C is incremented to 2, the B value is rotated, and the column with 2, 6, 10, and 14 is scanned. Once again, the IN obtains 1111. No key closure has been detected in this column. C is incremented to 3, B is rotated once more, and the next column is scanned. Remember, scanning will continue until C reaches 4. This column contains the keys 3, 7, 11, and 15. Since 7 now has a ground, the closure will produce 1101 in the low-order nibble. This does not match 1111, so the CNZ instruction at line 01 10 will be carried out.

The subroutine begins at 01 50. It saves the PSW so when control returns to the JNZ after the CNZ, the flags will be valid for use with this instruction.

After the PUSH, the information obtained from the keyboard is rotated right into the carry flag. DO was a high, so the JNC at 01 52 will be ignored. This means that key 3 was not pressed. The key closure position is stored temporarily at 19 00.

The C register value is then transferred into the A register. In our example, C had a 3 before the subroutine at 01 50 was called. This value is then added with an immediate 04 at 01 56. The new value of 7 is returned to the C register at 01 5B. The key-closure position is restored to A by the LDA instruction and control passes back to 01 50 when the JMP instruction is executed.

The next time, RRC rotates a zero into the carry flag. Therefore, the JNC instruction will be performed. Control transfers to 01 62, where a sequence of instructions stores the key code in 19 01. An exit sequence is performed which returns control back to the scanning subroutine.

Once back to the scanning subroutine, the first instruction to be performed is the JNZ at line 01 13. The zero flag was cleared prior to calling the key-code computation subroutine; this flag was restored by the PUSH PSW at the end of the computation subroutine; therefore, the JNZ will be performed. Control transfers to 01 23, which restores all the register values of the calling routine and returns with the key-code value located at 19 01.

Display Ports

Figure 10-9 shows how to wire displays to the bus. In (a), an 8212 acts as a latch/buffer for two hexadecimal displays. The displays are assumed to include decoder/drivers in-

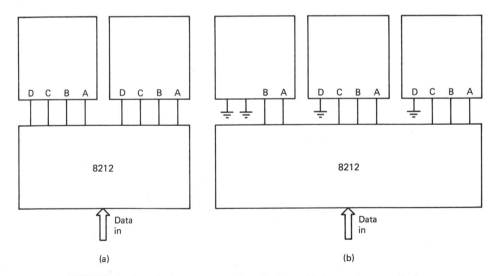

FIGURE 10-9   Display ports. (a) Hex displays; (b) Seven-segment displays, octal presentation.

ternally that will activate the correct display based on the inputs from the 8212. If the hex displays include a latch, and many do, the 8212 might not be necessary. The current used by the display inputs must be considered. If it will cause fan outs to be exceeded, a buffer will have to be used even when the displays contain a latch.

Seven-segment displays can be used to handle hex numbers, but certain problems must be overcome. First, standard decoders for seven-segment displays will not recognize A through F as valid information. This means that individual segments must be controlled through hardware, software, or a combination of both. Even when this is done, the representations of A through F use a mixture of upper and lower cases: A b C d E F. A capital B would look like an 8 on seven-segment displays; a capital D would look like 0. The hex display avoids this problem by using dots, which allow rounding.

Attempts to use seven-segment displays for other alphabetics results in strange-looking characters. X is a particular problem, with different representations often used; Q is also a problem.

Figure 10-9(b) shows how 3 seven-segment displays can be wired to an 8212 to provide octal representation of the information to be displayed. Since the largest number allowed in octal is 7, the displays will not have to handle any alphabetics. The most significant display has the D and C inputs grounded. This results in a maximum of three that can be displayed. The other two displays have D grounded. This will allow up to seven to be displayed. Together, the maximum value is 377 base 8, equivalent to FF hex. The circuits in Figure 10-9 can be operated with simple output or I/O write logic. Figures (a) and (b) also show one reason why hexadecimal is more popular than octal. Representing a byte of information took one less display when hex is used.

10-5 SYSTEM MONITORS

We are now at the point where we can consider the software needed to operate a simple computer. We have discussed the various sections of the computer both from a logical and an electrical perspective. This discussion also included a study of the signals used by the computer to transfer information from one section to another. In several cases, software directly related to a hardware function was discussed.

A *monitor* program is responsible for system-wide operation. It must be available each time the computer is powered up. In some cases, a short program known as a *bootstrap* is stored in ROM. The bootstrap will then load the rest of the system monitor when the computer is powered up. In small systems, particularly small one-board systems, the entire monitor can be stored in ROM.

The monitor will be responsible for basic functions that allow the operator to interact with the computer chip. At a minimum, these functions should include the ability to:

1. Specify any 16-bit address.
2. Examine the contents of any memory location.

3. Change the contents of any read/write location.
4. Start program execution from any memory location.

Another function that is not absolutely necessary but is very convenient is the ability to scroll through memory by allowing the operator to increment or decrement the memory pointer by one location each time a key is pressed. In this way, blocks of contiguous code can be checked or entered without having to specify a full 16-bit address each time a different cell is accessed.

Once the basic features of a monitor are in place, expanding the monitor to add additional features can take place. The features most likely to be added after the basics are:

1. The ability to set breakpoints for software debugging.
2. A register mode, where the contents of the registers can be inspected and changed. Changing register values allows a programmer to force certain decisions, which is another software debugging technique.
3. An interface routine that offloads R/W information into permanent backup storage. In a small trainer, this is likely to be a cassette interface. The routine should also have the ability to reload the data when needed by the operator.

As the monitor becomes more complex, it develops into an *operating system.* An operating system will control the central computer and peripherals more sophisticated than simple keyboards and displays. The next step above a simple computer trainer is probably a home computer. At this level, the operating system will probably be responsible for these additional devices:

1. one or two disk drives
2. a CRT display
3. a printer
4. game paddles
5. RS-232 C port, most likely used for modem interfacing
6. an audio output port

As the computer system grows in complexity, the monitor or operating system must grow. To handle the additional instructions that need to be included in an operating system, the central computer will need access to larger amounts of memory.

Eventually, the system may be large enough to handle multiple users and support time sharing. The details of a control program for such a situation are well beyond the introductory level of this text. What we will attempt to provide, however, is a step in this direction by looking at the code and logic of a simple monitor.

Examination of a Simple Monitor

The monitor program we are going to study was written to operate a simple computer centered around a Z80 microprocessor. This computer was built using parts that are easily obtainable from most electronic parts dealers. The construction technique used wire wrapping to wire the circuitry onto prototype boards. To meet the minimum standards for a monitor, a simple port structure was interfaced to the Z80 computer chip. The System Monitor Layout Sheet details the logical specifications for this project (see Layout Sheet 10-1).

Layout Sheet 10-1

SYSTEM MONITOR LAYOUT SHEET

OBJECTIVE:

To write a system monitor for a simple Z80 computer.

HARDWARE ENVIRONMENT:

Z80-based CPU
Isolated I/O

Memory Map:

000 000 — 007 377 Rom
010 000 — 017 377 R/W

Support Chips:

1. 8255 single-line decoded from A7
   Port A — high address byte, octal display
   Port B — low address byte, octal display
   Port C — display for data value at address displayed
2. 8255 single-line decoded from A6
   Port A — numeric input from keypad
   Port B — alphabetic input from keypad
   Port C — user available octal display port

SOFTWARE ENVIRONMENT:

8080A instruction subset of Z80 instruction set

Layout Sheet 10-1 (*continued*)

Memory Allocations:

000 000 through 003 377 — monitor
004 000 through 007 377 — utilities
010 000 through 010 377 — system stack
011 000 through 011 377 — not assigned R/W
012 000 through 015 377 — user R/W
016 000 through 017 333 — restart vectors, service routines

Register Allocations:

A — general-purpose
B — number/letter flag
C — primary keyboard/secondary keyboard function flag
D — temporary data storage
E — key read register
H — high address byte
L — low address byte

PORT ALLOCATIONS:

200 — 8255/1 port A, high address display
201 — 8255/1 port B, low address display
202 — 8255/1 port C, data display
203 — 8255/1 control register
100 — 8255/2 port A, numeric input
101 — 8255/2 port B, alphabetic input
102 — 8255/2 port C, user available display
103 — 8255/2 control register

Special Codes:

200 — control word for 8255/1, mode 0, all ports — output
222 — control word 8255/2 mode 0, ports A, B — input, C — output
123 — power-up signature
100 — number entry — see B register
101 — letter entry — see B register
000 — primary keypad function — see C register
001 — secondary keypad function — see C register

HARDWARE/SOFTWARE INTERFACE:

Numeric entry
D0 — 0, D1 — 1, D2 — 2, etc.
Port A 8255/2

Alphabetic entry
D0 — H, D1 — L, D2 — G, D3 — S, D4 — not used, D5 — A, D6 — B,
  D7 — C
Port B 8255/2

A Z80 will be used to operate a single-board computer using isolated I/O. Two memory chips will be interfaced to the I/O bus. The first is a 2716 EPROM, which occupies 000 000 through 007 377 (addresses throughout this project are in octal). The ROM will contain the system monitor and any software utilities that might be needed by the system. A 2K block of R/W will reside from 010 000 through 017 377. In this case a 2K × 8 RAM chip was used. Other configurations are possible, of course. Refer back to Chapter 8, Memory, for more details.

Two 8255 programmable peripheral interface chips will handle the I/O ports. The first 8255, designated 8255/1 in this project, is single-line decoded from A7. This chip responds to ports 200 through 203. It will handle three sets of displays wired to ports A, B, and C for octal presentation. Refer back to Figure 10-9(b). These ports will display the high address byte, the low address byte, and the contents of the memory location pointed to by the address displayed.

A second 8255, designated 8255/2 for this project, will handle data entry from a hex pad. Figure 10-10 shows the keyboard interface. The keyboard selected used normally open, nonencoded, nondebounced keys. Debouncing and encoding will be handled through software. Additionally, the keypad was not wired in a matrix—rather, each individual key had a separate line to Vcc or logic 1. All the keys shared a common line to ground. This wiring scheme required the full use of two ports and used 16 lines. This means that the monitor will have to read the keyboard twice to determine if a key closure has been made. Port A of 8255/2 handles the numeric inputs from the keypad. Port B of the 8255/2 handles alphabetic inputs from the keypad. These alphabetics will represent commands.

The software environment is restricted to the 8080A subset of Z80 instructions. This corresponds to the practice established in this text of making all programs written executable on the three processors we are examining. The op codes in the monitor are listed in octal to match the data display format. Hex displays were not available when the computer was built, therefore, seven-segment displays were used. To reduce hardware, it was decided not to drive each individual segment.

The memory allocations for the project are set for six regions of the 4K available. The lower 2K will hold the monitor and any utilities that might be added to enhance system operation. The upper 2K will handle the system stack, an unassigned section of RAM, a section of user RAM, and a section of RAM devoted to interrupt functions. The address boundaries of each of these sections is shown in the layout sheet.

The register allocations for the main routine of the monitor are listed in the project layout sheet. The B register will be used by the monitor as a flag to determine if the information from the keypad is numeric or alphabetic. The C register was to be used to alternate between primary key functions and backup key functions. This feature of the monitor was not developed and was left stubbed out. The other register functions are self-explanatory.

The port allocations used by the computer are listed next in the layout sheet. These port numbers activate the 8255s. Due to single-line decoding, there are ambiguities. Using a port number of 300 would activate port A in both the 8255s, as A7 and A6

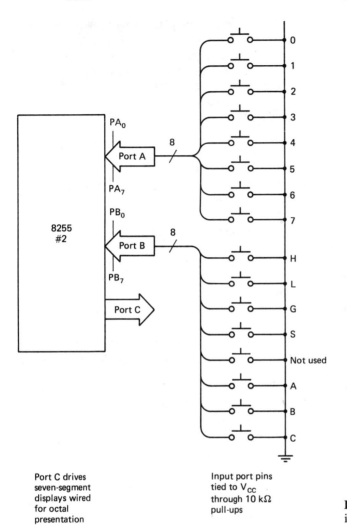

Port C drives
seven-segment
displays wired
for octal
presentation

Input port pins
tied to V_{CC}
through 10 kΩ
pull-ups

FIGURE 10-10 Nonmatrix keypad interface.

would both be high. The system can easily be expanded by insuring that new ports are selected with a port number of 077 or below.

The special codes used by the monitor are listed next in the layout sheet. This section includes the control words for the 8255s, the flag values for the B register, and the flag values for the C register. Finally, 123 is a code that will be output to a port every time the computer is powered up or reset. This code is the monitor signature used to tell the operator that the monitor has started to function.

The last section of the layout sheet indicates the bit positions affected by key closures from the keypad. This information is used by the monitor to establish codes for the keys that are pressed.

The monitor listing.   The monitor can be found in Example 10-2. The bulk of the first page involves unconditional jumps to page 016. These jumps redirect restart vectors used for interrupt servicing. This will be explained in detail in Chapter 11. The first unconditional jump at 000 000 directs program flow to 000 070. Thus, when the system is reset, control will immediately transfer to 000 070. This location is really the start of the monitor.

EXAMPLE 10-2

HEX ADDRESS	HEX OP CODE	MNEMONIC	COMMENTS	OCTAL ADDRESS	OCTAL OP CODE
00 00	C3	JMP	Restart 0 system boot	000 000	303
00 01		070		000 001	
00 02		000		000 002	
00 08	C3	JMP	Restart 1 jump vector	000 010	303
00 09		010		000 011	
00 0A		016		000 012	
00 10	C3	JMP	Restart 2 jump vector	000 020	303
00 11		020		000 021	
00 12		016		000 022	
00 18	C3	JMP	Restart 3 jump vector	000 030	303
00 19		030		000 031	
00 1A		016		000 032	
00 20	C3	JMP	Restart 4 jump vector	000 040	303
00 21		040		000 041	
00 22		016		000 042	
00 28	C3	JMP	Restart 5 jump vector	000 050	303
00 29		050		000 051	
00 2A		016		000 052	
00 30	C3	JMP	Restart 6 jump vector	000 060	303
00 31		060		000 061	
00 32		016		000 062	

EXAMPLE 10-2 (*continued*)

HEX ADDRESS	HEX OP CODE	MNEMONIC	COMMENTS	OCTAL ADDRESS	OCTAL OP CODE
00 38	31	LXI SP	Monitor start	000 070	061
00 39		000		000 071	
00 3A		011	System stack	000 072	
00 3B	CD	CALL	8255 initialization	000 073	315
00 3C		000	subroutine	000 074	
00 3D		001		000 075	
00 3E	CD	CALL	Power up display	000 076	315
00 3F		050	subroutine	000 077	
00 40		001		000 100	
00 41	0E	MVI C	Set keyboard to primary	000 101	016
00 42		000	function	000 102	
00 43	CD	CALL	Key board scan routine	000 103	315
00 '44		100		000 104	
00 45		001		000 105	
00 46	78	MOV A, B	Get #/letter flag	000 106	170
00 47	FE	CPI	# pressed?	000 107	376
00 48		100		000 110	
00 49	CC	CZ	Data port update	000 111	314
00 4A		200		000 112	
00 4B		002		000 113	
00 4C	C4	CNZ	Command decoder	000 114	304
00 4D		377		000 115	
00 4E		002		000 116	
00 4F	C3	JMP	Go back to key scan routine	000 117	303
00 50		103		000 120	
00 51		000		000 121	

EXAMPLE 10-2 (*continued*)

HEX ADDRESS	HEX OP CODE	MNEMONIC	COMMENTS	OCTAL ADDRESS	OCTAL OP CODE
			8255 Start-up		
01 00	3E	MVI A		001 000	076
01 01		200	8255-1 mode 0 output	001 001	
01 02	D3	OUT		001 002	323
01 03		203		001 003	
01 04	3E	MVI A	8255-2 mode 0	001 004	076
01 05		222	A, B Inputs C-output	001 005	
01 06	D3	OUT		001 006	323
01 07		103		001 007	
01 08	C9	RET		001 010	311
			Power-up routine		
01 28	21	LXI H	Point to start of user	001 050	041
01 29		000	routines	001 051	
01 2A		012		001 052	
01 2B	7C	MOV A, H	Display high-order address	001 053	174
01 2C	D3	OUT	byte	001 054	323
01 2D		200		001 055	
01 2E	7D	MOV A, L	Display low-order address	001 056	175
01 2F	D3	OUT	byte	001 057	323
01 30		201		001 060	
01 31	56	MOV D, M	Get current data	001 061	126
01 32	7A	MOV A, D	Display data	001 062	172
01 33	D3	OUT		001 063	323
01 34		202		001 064	
01 35	3E	MVI A	Display power-up	001 065	076
01 36		123	signature	001 066	
01 37	D3	OUT		001 067	323
01 38		102		001 070	
01 39	C9	RET		001 071	311

EXAMPLE 10-2 *(continued)*

HEX ADDRESS	HEX OP CODE	MNEMONIC	COMMENTS	OCTAL ADDRESS	OCTAL OP CODE
			Key Scan		
01 40	06	MVI B	Set # flag	001 100	006
01 41		100		001 101	
01 42	DB	IN	Check for number	001 102	333
01 43		100	entry	001 103	
01 44	2F	CMA		001 104	057
01 45	B7	ORA A		001 105	267
01 46	CA	JZ	No # pressed, check for	001 106	312
01 47		132	letters	001 107	
01 48		001		001 110	
01 49	CD	CALL	Time delay key	001 111	315
01 4A		000	debouncing	001 112	
01 4B		002		001 113	
01 4C	DB	IN	Recheck keyboard	001 114	333
01 4D		100		001 115	
01 4E	2F	CMA		001 116	057
01 4F	B7	ORA A		001 117	267
01 50	CA	JZ		001 120	312
01 51		100	False trigger rescan	001 121	
01 52		001		001 122	
01 53	5F	MOV E, A	Save key code	001 123	137
01 54	CD	CALL	Release subroutine	001 124	315
01 55		100		001 125	
01 56		002		001 126	
01 57	C3	JMP	Go to return	001 127	303
01 58		161		001 130	
01 59		001		001 131	
01 5A	06	MVI B	Set up letter flag	001 132	006
01 5B		101		001 133	

EXAMPLE 10-2 (*continued*)

HEX ADDRESS	HEX OP CODE	MNEMONIC	COMMENTS	OCTAL ADDRESS	OCTAL OP CODE
01 5C	DB	IN	Check for letter entry	001 134	333
01 5D		101		001 135	
01 5E	2F	CMA		001 136	057
01 5F	B7	ORA A		001 137	267
01 60	CA	JZ	No keys pressed, continue	001 140	312
01 61		100	scan	001 141	
01 62		001		001 142	
01 63	CD	CALL	Time delay	001 143	315
01 64		000		001 144	
01 65		002		001 145	
01 66	DB	IN	Check letters again	001 146	333
01 67		101		001 147	
01 68	2F	CMA		001 150	057
01 69	B7	ORA A		001 151	267
01 6A	CA	JZ	False trigger?	001 152	312
01 6B		100	Resume scan	001 153	
01 6C		001		001 154	
01 6D	5F	MOV E, A	Save key code	001 155	137
01 6E	CD	CALL	Release subroutine	001 156	315
01 6F		100		001 157	
01 70		002		001 160	
01 71	C9	RET		001 161	311
			Release subroutine		
02 40	DB	IN	Check # keys	002 100	333
02 41		100		002 101	
02 42	FE	CPI	No keys pressed for	002 102	376
02 43		377	port 100?	002 103	
02 44	C2	JNZ		002 104	302

EXAMPLE 10-2 (*continued*)

HEX ADDRESS	HEX OP CODE	MNEMONIC	COMMENTS	OCTAL ADDRESS	OCTAL OP CODE
02 45		100		002 105	
02 46		002		002 106	
02 47	DB	IN	Check letter keys	002 107	333
02 48		101		002 110	
02 49	FE	CPI	No letter keys pressed?	002 111	376
02 4A		377		002 112	
02 4B	C2	JNZ		002 113	302
02 4C		107		002 114	
02 4D		002		002 115	
02 4E	CD	CALL	Time delay	002 116	315
02 4F		000		002 117	
02 50		002		002 120	
02 51	C9	RET		002 121	311
			Data port update		
02 80	F5	PUSH PSW		002 200	365
02 81	CD	CALL	Key code converter	002 201	315
02 82		300		002 202	
02 83		002		002 203	
02 84	5F	MOV E, A	SAVE # in E	002 204	137
02 85	7A	MOV A, D	Old data in A	002 205	172
02 86	07	RLC	Move octal digits to make	002 206	007
02 87	07	RLC	room for LS digit	002 207	007
02 88	07	RLC		002 210	007
02 89	E6	ANI	Eliminate garbage in LSD	002 211	346
02 8A		370		002 212	

EXAMPLE 10-2 (*continued*)

HEX ADDRESS	HEX OP CODE	MNEMONIC	COMMENTS	OCTAL ADDRESS	OCTAL OP CODE
02 8B	83	ADD E	Insert new LSD	002 213	203
02 8C	D3	OUT	Display new data	002 214	323
02 8D		202		002 215	
02 8E	57	MOV D, A	Save new data	002 216	127
02 8F	F1	POP PSW		002 217	361
02 90	C9	RET		002 220	311
			Key code converter		
02 C0	E5	PUSH H	Free a reg. pair	002 300	345
02 C1	7B	MOV A, E	Get key code	002 301	173
02 C2	2E	MVI L	Rotation counter	002 302	056
02 C3		000		002 303	
02 C4	0F	RRC	Convert code	002 304	017
02 C5	DA	JC		002 305	332
02 C6		314		002 306	
02 C7		002		002 307	
02 C8	2C	INRL	Update rotation counter	002 310	054
02 C9	C3	JMP		002 311	303
02 CA		304	Continue conversion	002 312	
02 CB		002		002 313	
02 CC	7D	MOV A, L	Place # m A	002 314	175
02 CD	E1	POP H		002 315	341
02 CE	C9	RET		002 316	311

EXAMPLE 10-2 (*continued*)

HEX ADDRESS	HEX OP CODE	MNEMONIC	COMMENTS	OCTAL ADDRESS	OCTAL OP CODE
			Command decoder		
02 FF	7B	MOV A, E	Get letter code	002 377	173
03 00	0F	RRC	Check for H	003 000	017
03 01	D2	JNC		003 001	322
03 02		015		003 002	
03 03		003		003 003	
03 04	62	MOV H, D	Update high address	003 004	142
03 05	7C	MOV A, H	Display new high address	003 005	174
03 06	D3	OUT		003 006	323
03 07		200		003 007	
03 08	56	MOV D, M	Display new data at new	003 010	126
03 09	7A	MOV A, D	address	003 011	172
03 0A	D3	OUT		003 012	323
03 0B		202		003 013	
03 0C	C9	RET		003 014	311
03 0D	0F	RRC	Check for L	003 015	017
03 0E	D2	JNC		003 016	322
03 0F		032		003 017	
03 10		003		003 020	
03 11	6A	MOV L, D	Update low address	003 021	152
03 12	7D	MOV A, L		003 022	175
03 13	D3	OUT		003 023	323
03 14		201		003 024	
03 15	56	MOV D, M	Display new data at	003 025	126
03 16	7A	MOV A, D	new address	003 026	172
03 17	D3	OUT		003 027	323
03 18		202		003 030	
03 19	C9	RET		003 031	311

EXAMPLE 10-2 (*continued*)

HEX ADDRESS	HEX OP CODE	MNEMONIC	COMMENTS	OCTAL ADDRESS	OCTAL OP CODE
03 1A	0F	RRC	Check for G	003 032	017
03 1B	D2	JNC		003 033	322
03 1C		037		003 034	
03 1D		003		003 035	
03 1E	E9	PCHL	Activate "Go"	003 036	351
03 1F	0F	RRC	Check for S	003 037	017
03 20	D2	JNC		003 040	322
03 21		051		003 041	
03 22		003		003 042	
03 23	72	MOV M, D	Store and stop	003 043	162
03 24	23	INX H		003 044	043
03 25	CD	CALL	Update displays	003 045	315
03 26		053		003 046	
03 27		001		003 047	
03 28	C9	RET		003 050	311
03 29	0F	RRC	Check for A	003 051	017
03 2A	0F	RRC	.	003 052	017
03 2B	D2	JNC		003 053	322
03 2C		063		003 054	
03 2D		003		003 055	
03 2E	23	INX H	Advance	003 056	043
03 2F	CD	CALL	Update displays	003 057	315
03 30		053		003 060	
03 31		001		003 061	
03 32	C9	RET		003 062	311

EXAMPLE 10-2 (*continued*)

HEX ADDRESS	HEX OP CODE	MNEMONIC	COMMENTS	OCTAL ADDRESS	OCTAL OP CODE
03 33	0F	RRC	Check for B	003 063	017
03 34	D2	JNC		003 064	322
03 35		073		003 065	
03 36		003		003 066	
03 37	2B	DCX H	Decrement pointer	003 067	053
03 38	CD	CALL	Update displays	003 070	315
03 39		053		003 071	
03 3A		001		003 072	
03 3B	C9	RET		003 073	311
			Time delay		
02 00	E5	PUSH H		002 000	345
02 01	F5	PUSH PSW		002 001	365
02 02	21	LXI H		002 002	041
02 03		000		002 003	
02 04		010		002 004	
02 05	2B	DCX H		002 005	053
02 06	7C	MOV A, H		002 006	174
02 07	B5	ORA L		002 007	265
02 08	C2	JNZ		002 010	302
02 09		005		002 011	
02 0A		002		002 012	
02 0B	F1	POP PSW		002 013	361
02 0C	E1	POP H		002 014	341
02 0D	C9	RET		002 015	311

The monitor starts with an LXI SP that sets up a system stack. It then proceeds to call a subroutine that initializes the two 8255s connected to the I/O bus. This and other subroutines will be explained after the main section of the driver has been explained.

The second call accesses a subroutine that sets up the beginning conditions for the displays. The address will be set to 012 000, the start of user RAM. Of course, as we will see, the user can alter this address if desired.

After the displays are set up, the C register is loaded with 000, indicating that the primary key functions are active. These functions are:

1. data entry from keys 0 through 7
2. commands from the letter keys:
   A—advance the memory pointer one location
   B—decrease the memory pointer one location
   C—toggle between primary and backup key usage; this is not implemented
   H—transfer the data-port value to the high address byte
   L—transfer the data-port value to the low address byte
   G—start a program from the address specified by the address displayed
   S—store data-port value at memory location specified by address displayed and advance to the next memory location
   R—not used, reset feature already wired elsewhere

Once the key functions are set to standard, the key scan subroutine is called. The monitor will stay in this subroutine until a key closure is detected. When control is returned to the main program, the monitor examines the value in the B register. If B contains 100, a number has been pressed. If a number was entered, a data-port update subroutine is called. If B contains a 101, the CZ instruction at line 000 107 will be ignored and the CNZ call will be performed. When the CNZ is performed, control passes to a subroutine known as a command decoder that implements the key function as detailed above.

The only function that will not return control to the monitor when it is implemented is the GO function, which transfers control to a user routine. All other commands will return to line 000 017, where a JMP loops back to the key scan CALL instruction. The monitor will continue this flow until an interrupt occurs, a reset is performed, or the GO key is pressed.

The subroutines used by the main section of the monitor begin at line 001 000 in the listing. The first subroutine is a short sequence of code that establishes control words for the 8255s in the A register and then transfers this information to the 8255s via the control-register ports.

The second subroutine was loaded at 001 050. It initializes register pair H as the memory pointer. This value starts at 012 000, the start of user RAM. This information is then moved to the high and low address display ports. The monitor then obtains whatever value is currently stored in this location by performing a MOV D, M. D will be used to hold data as the port is updated. Right after power up, this information will be random, but this monitor does not distinguish between a cold and warm reset. Any reset of the system will cause execution of the monitor to begin at 000 070, so the data value at the default location 012 000 is immediately displayed by the block of code beginning at 001 065. Once the port displays have been initialized, control returns to the main section of the monitor.

The third subroutine used by the monitor is the key-scan subroutine. This section of code begins at 001 100. The first instruction sets the letter/number flag to the number condition. The block of code following this operation checks for key closures from port 100. The keyboard inputs active low signals that are changed back into active high logic by the CMA instruction at line 001 104. The A register is then ORed with itself. If a key had been pressed, a bit position within the A register would have been high.

The JZ instruction at 001 106 will be ignored if a number key has been pressed. Execution will fall through to a time delay subroutine that waits until key closure debouncing has expired. The keyboard is rechecked to see if the key is still pressed. If so, a valid key entry has occurred. If the second check of the keyboard indicates that a key is not pressed, then a false signal was generated, perhaps by electrical noise. If this is the case, control will pass back to the top of the subroutine, where the scanning process begins anew.

When the monitor is satisfied that a valid key has been pressed, the byte obtained from the keyboard is saved in the E register. This information will be used later to determine which key was pressed. See the hardware/software interface section of the layout sheet that specifies which bit represents which key.

Once a key code has been saved, the monitor calls a subroutine, which waits until the key has been released. This helps prevent bouncing from the opening of the key closure from falsely triggering the monitor the next pass through the key-scan logic.

Should the flow of logic reach 001 127, a valid key code representing a number has been stored. The JMP at this location will jump to the return at the end of the subroutine, which will return control back to the main section of the monitor.

Line 001 132 marks the start of the section that checks for alphabetic entry. This line is reached if the JZ instruction at 001 106 is performed. That JZ will occur only if no number key closure has been detected. If a number key closure has been detected, the monitor will perform the logic that obtains the key code for the number key, as already explained.

The first task performed by the section of code that checks for a letter entry toggles the number/letter flag to the letter representation. Register B is set to 101 by the MVI B instruction at 001 132.

The monitor then checks port 101 for letter key closures. The logic proceeds as it did when a number closure was detected. A software delay is called to check for accidental or false triggering. If, after the delay, a key closure is still detected, the monitor accepts this closure as legitimate. A false trigger transfers control back to the start of the key-scan subroutine. A true key closure will cause the monitor to store the key code in register E. This occurs at line 001 155. A release subroutine is called to debounce the key when it is released. After the release subroutine delay is performed, control passes back to the main program by performing the RET at 001 161.

The release subroutine is listed at 002 100. This routine checks to see if both the number keys and the letter keys are open. This is done by inputting the key status from ports 100 and 101. The keyboard will be polled because the subroutine will loop repeatedly until it receives a 377. This pattern represents a binary value of 11111111. Since the key closures are active low, the keys attached to this port must have been released. The time delay call at the end of the release routine takes care of release bounce.

The data port update subroutine will be called when the key-scan routine returns to the main section of the monitor with 100 in the B register. The data-port update listing starts at line 002 200. This subroutine first saves the PSW, which contains the A register and the flags of the main routine. It then calls a section of code that converts the binary pattern stored in E, which came from the keyboard, into a number. The number value calculated by the converter subroutine is stored in E temporarily when control returns to 002 204. The old data value is stored in A, then rotated three times to the left. This places the least significant octal digit in the middle of the byte. The middle octal digit is moved to the most significant digit position. The most significant digit is transferred into the least significant position. An example follows:

134 stored prior to the update

341 after the three rotates

The ANI instruction at line 002 211 masks out the least significant digit. This leaves:

340 after the mask operation

The new number, which was placed in the E register, is added to this value. Say the 7 key had been pressed. The result of the ADD E creates:

347 after the ADD E

This result is then transferred to the data port by the OUT instruction at 002 214. The new data value is then placed into the D register.

If, after the 7 key was pressed, a 5 was entered, the sequence of numbers would be:

347 stored prior to the update

473 after three rotates

470 after the mask operation

475 after the ADD E

Suppose a 2 was entered next. The sequence would be:

475 stored prior to the update

354 after three rotates

This last result indicates what happens if a number larger than 3 is rotated into the most significant digit position within the byte when using octal. The 4's position is lost. Thus,

7 becomes 3, 6 becomes 2, 5 becomes 1, and 4 becomes 0. This presents no problem as long as the operator remembers that the maximum value in a byte is 377 octal. Proceeding:

350 after the mask

352 after the ADD E

From the foregoing, it can be seen that to completely change the data port requires three key closures. Therefore, to completely enter an octal number requires three number key closures.

Please pay close attention to this point: *Although the data port has been changed, the new number is not yet stored in the memory location pointed to by the memory pointer.* Storage will occur only at the direction of a command key.

The section of the monitor that converts the number in the E register into an octal digit starts at 002 300. The first instruction in this section of code is PUSH H. Since all registers were assigned functions in the main program, a register must be freed to perform a second task. The L register contents are destroyed by this routine, so a copy is placed on the stack.

The L register is cleared at line 002 302 by the MVI L instruction. The key code that was placed in the A register at 002 301 is rotated into the carry flag. If the carry flag was set, the bit rotated into the carry flag marked the key that was pressed. If so, the JC instruction will be performed and the INR L will not be performed. Each pass through the loop indicates that the high bit representing the key closure has not been detected. Consequently, L increments to track the value of the key pressed. The hardware/software interface set indicated in Layout Sheet 10-1 was implemented so this logic could be used to determine the value of the key pressed. This explains why D0 = 0, D1 = 1, D2 = 2, etc. This correspondence was not an arbitrary choice. When the looping is completed by performing the JC instruction at 002 305, the value in L will equal the value of the key pressed. This value is moved back into A so it can be passed to the data port update subroutine that called the converter. The POP H instruction restores L to its original value just before the RET transfers control back to the data port update subroutine.

The command decoder, which carries out the commands associated with the letter keys, begins at 002 377. The original starting location was 003 000, but an oversight required that a patch (a section of code correcting a problem) be added prior to 003 000. The CALL address to the command decoder was changed to reflect this change.

The MOV A, E instruction at 002 377 is vital to the operation of the command decoder. It places the key-code value from the key-scan subroutine in the A register where it can be rotated.

The logic structure of the command decoder follows that of a skip chain, discussed earlier in the text. Each time an RRC instruction is performed the key code is rotated into the carry flag. When the carry flag is set, the key pressed has been detected. This means that a JNC, located throughout the command decoder code underneath the RRC, will be ignored. When this happens, the code underneath the JNC performs a task associated with the key pressed.

The hardware/software interface section of the layout sheet indicates that H will cause DO to be cleared. The CMA instruction in the key scan will set this bit and clear all the other bits. We discussed the CMA earlier, but are reminding you so it will be possible to follow the logic of the command decoder. The order of the skip chain follows the order specified by the layout sheet. The first section of code below a JNC responds to the H key, the second block of code below a JNC responds to an L key closure, and so on.

Suppose the L key had been pressed. The first RRC at line 003 000 would rotate a logic 0 into the carry flag. DO is cleared because H was not pressed. The JNC at line 003 001 skips to 003 015, where the second RRC takes place. This RRC rotates a logic 1 into the carry flag because L was pressed. The JNC instruction at 003 016 is ignored, with control passing to 003 021, where the data value stored in the data register is moved to the L register. The L register's new value is then transferred to the low address byte display. This is why the data-port update routine did not store information. The contents of the data port can be transferred into the H register, the L register, or a memory cell. The command keys determine the destination.

After the function required by the L key closure has been performed, control returns to the main program and then the key-scan routine. If the G key had been pressed, the skip chain would have arrived at line 003 032. The JNC at 003 033 would be ignored, with the logic falling through to line 003 036, where the H register pair is transferred into the program counter. After this instruction is performed, the code beginning at the address pointed to by H and L will have control of the computer. This code is probably a user routine.

If the S button is pressed, the skip-chain logic will end up at line 003 037. After falling through the JNC, the data-port value is stored in M, the H pair is incremented, and the information at the new address is displayed by calling the display routine.

The A feature is almost identical to the S, but the important MOV M, D instruction, which transfers the data port into memory, is not performed. This allows the operator to scan memory without changing the contents of a location.

The DCX H instruction at line 003 067 decrements the H register pair, then calls the display routine. This function is associated with the B button.

The double RRCs at lines 003 051–052 bypass the unused R key, which is wired to Vcc. Finally, the skip chain terminates at the L key decision. If L was not pressed, the chain simply jumps to the RET at 003 073. Since this location in the chain represents the section of code for C, pressing the C key results in nothing being done. If C was used to toggle between primary and secondary key functions, the flag value assigned in the layout sheet would be updated here. Doing this would make it necessary to alter the logic of the monitor by providing a command decoder for the additional commands.

The last section of code in the monitor starts at 002 000. It is a transparent time-delay subroutine used to debounce the keys. The logic structure of this section of code follows the software delay loop structure explained in the chapter on timing.

10-6 CLOSING THOUGHTS

The information in this chapter will often explain why a computer system is not functioning even when the logical connections are correct. Study the information on loading, fan out, and propagation delay problems carefully. In some cases it can make the difference between fixing a computer and being stumped.

With the exception of interrupts, small system operation was examined in an overall fashion. It is hoped that the discussion included enough information to make you realize how a larger computer system could be built using the hardware and software techniques included here and in earlier chapters.

A bus standard was examined. You were encouraged afterward and are being encouraged again to research other bus standards that you might expect to see when you go to work. If you have a company in mind for which you wish to work, find out if they support or use a particular bus standard. Learning about that bus standard should increase your chances of working for that company.

The last section of the chapter dealt with a simple system monitor. Understanding control programs such as this can help you differentiate between software errors and hardware errors when troubleshooting. Control programs for small systems should not be a mystery to a computer technician.

SUMMARY

1. Fan out is a measure of how many unit loads can be driven from a single output.

2. The 8080A, 8085, and Z80 processors have limited current capabilities. Expanding a computer system beyond a few chips requires the addition of buffer/driver circuits. Buffer/driver ICs are special ICs designed to handle high current requirements.

3. Decoupling capacitors are placed in computer circuitry to smooth out current spikes as devices turn on and off. The standard ratio is one decoupling capacitor per four ICs.

4. Noise margin is the difference between an output voltage and what is accepted by an input as the same logic level. For example, a TTL output will produce no less than 2.4 V when a logic 1, yet a TTL input will accept anything above 2 V as a logic 1. Consequently, the noise margin is .4 V.

5. Off-state leakage currents are those used by circuitry in the tristate condition.

6. A critical path is defined as the signal path with the longest propagation delay needed to provide correct system operation.

7. The areas of a computer most sensitive to timing problems center around ROMS and RAMS.

8. Standard bus systems have been designed to make system expansion and interfacing easier.

9. A system monitor is a program responsible for system-wide operation. At a minimum, a system monitor must be able to:

   a. Specify any 16-bit address.

   b. Examine the contents of any memory location.

   c. Change the contents of any R/W memory location.

   d. Start program execution from any memory location.

QUESTIONS

1. What is meant by *fan out?*
2. What is the fan out for standard TTL family gates?
3. What are the test currents for logic 1 and logic 0 for the 8080, 8085, and Z80? What happens if these test currents are exceeded?
4. What happens to bus operations if capacitive loading becomes excessive?
5. What is the "standard" ratio of decoupling capacitors to ICs in a computer system?
6. What is the function of the large bulk capacitor(s) found in many computer systems?
7. Why is the HLDA signal connected to the strobes of buffer/driver chips in 8080/8085 systems?
8. What is meant by *noise margin?*
9. What is *off-state leakage current?*
10. What is meant by *tphl?*
11. What is the maximum tplh for a standard TTL 7400?
12. What is the definition of *critical path?*
13. List those areas of the computer that are the most sensitive to timing problems.
14. What is the maximum allowable time for external circuits to present data to the Z80 during an op code fetch?
15. List three ways in which a timing problem could be corrected.
16. In a simple system, how is the STD bus signal MEMEX handled?
17. What are the characteristics of the STD bus signal RD*?
18. What are the mechanical specifications of an STD card?
19. What STD signals are combined to form a MEMRD* control signal?
20. Explain what is meant by a *software-encoded keyboard?*
21. What is the function of the 7475 in Figure 10-8?
22. Can a seven-segment display driven by standard decoder drivers display hex digits?

23. What difference is there between a bootstrap and monitor program?

24. What are the four basic functions a monitor program must perform?

25. Which additional features are most likely to be added to a monitor after the four basic functions have been implemented?

LAB ASSIGNMENTS

1. Without looking at the system monitor that operates the trainer you are using, determine the port structure of the trainer from the schematic. Use this information to write a program that will accept information from the trainer's keyboard and store the information in memory.

2. Repeat assignment 1, but this time transfer the entered data to the displays.

11

INTERRUPTS

At the end of this chapter you should be familiar with:

1. 8080A interrupt architecture
2. restart instructions
3. jump tables
4. how a single-line interrupt system is implemented
5. the uses of polling routines
6. the structure of service routines
7. how restarts can be used as vectors
8. how hardware can be used to implement interrupt priorities
   a. through priority chains
   b. through priority interrupt controllers
9. the function of masking in an interrupt system
10. the 8259A interrupt controller
11. 8085 interrupt architecture
12. Z80 interrupt architecture

INTRODUCTION

In a small system environment such as the one controlled by the system monitor studied in the last chapter, the CPU can spend much of its time monitoring the keypad and running the displays without seriously affecting overall system operation.

The types of peripherals connected to the computer in the small system were relatively simple, few in number, and most likely controlled by a user program when the monitor program was not running the computer.

As the number of peripherals grow, and the peripheral complexity increases, the CPU must spend more time running software to operate the I/O bus. As this situation builds, the CPU is able to spend less and less time running user programs.

Certain peripherals such as keyboards consume a lot of computer time when handled as in the system monitor example. In that situation the software forced the CPU to constantly monitor the status of the keyboard, waiting for a key entry to occur. Until this happened, the CPU was not free to do anything else. Even if the world's fastest typist were inputting information through a keyboard, the CPU would still spend an inordinate amount of its time waiting for inputs.

After a while, we tend to overlook just how fast the electronics in the computer circuitry is operating. One of the first things we as technicians learn is scientific notation. We quickly adjust to small units in the milli and micro range as well as large units in the kilo and mega ranges. After a time this shorthand obscures the true nature of the quantities with which we work. The CPUs with which we are dealing in this text are capable of operating in the millions of hertz. A clock cycle will be a microsecond or less. Instruction cycles will be just a little longer. When discussing timing, as we did earlier, this information is at the front of our minds. Once timing concepts are mastered, they fade into the background.

The quickness of the electronic circuitry is being reemphasized to make a point: that it is very inefficient for a computer to wait for a human while that person is pressing a key or activating some other type of control. In the time it takes to make a key closure the CPU can perform thousands of instructions or more. If the CPU is freed to compute while waiting for input, the overall system throughput will be improved.

This situation is not quite as bad as when the computer is waiting for some type of machine. If the machine involves some mechanical operation, the computer can be put to other uses while waiting for the machine to respond. Only in those cases where the input from a person or a machine is necessary before the computer can proceed to another task would we consider forcing the computer to wait. The waiting process can be handled either through a section of code that constantly checks the status of a peripheral or peripherals (polling) or through a software delay loop.

If the computer is freed from a task—say, checking a keyboard—to do something else, perhaps run a user program, a way should be provided to alert the computer that the keyboard has entered information. Computer chips handle this situation by responding to an *interrupt request signal.*

The interrupt request can, when allowed, momentarily stop the program currently running. When the computer responds to the interrupt request, it transfers control to a software routine commonly called an *interrupt service routine* or just *service routine*. The service routine handles the situation that caused the interrupt. In our example, it would accept the data from the keyboard, then perhaps act upon this information. After the service routine had finished its task, in most cases, control would be returned to the program being run prior to the interrupt. If the CPU did not have this interrupt capability, the peripherals not used by a section of code would be inactive. To illustrate this point for yourself, insert an unconditional jump into the trainer you are using. Have the jump address force control back to the jump op code location. When you press the "go" button, the computer will be locked into an infinite loop. The keyboard, displays, and other I/O ports on the computer will not be active. Pressing data keys would have no effect, output ports would not update information, cassette loading and dumping could not take place. In short, the computer would seem dead to the world.

The infinite loop and, of course, any legitimate program could be stopped in two ways: One, reset the system. This returns control to the monitor. The second way involves generating an interrupt. If the interrupt architecture of the CPU has been enabled, the CPU will respond to the interrupt request, allowing control of the system to pass from the program that was running.

This chapter will examine the ways in which each of the three processors this text has covered implements an interrupt system, how interrupt-support circuitry can be added to the computer circuitry, and how interrupt software handles interrupt situations.

11-1 8080A INTERRUPT ARCHITECTURE

The 8080A has a single input labeled INT through which external devices can signal the processor that they require attention. To enable the interrupt system, a special instruction, EI, must be performed. When the computer is powered up or reset, the interrupt system is disabled. Requests on the interrupt pin will be ignored until EI is executed.

EI is the mnemonic for enable interrupt. This op code sets the interrupt enable flip-flop within the 8080A. The status of this flip-flop can be monitored on the INTE output from the processor.

Once the interrupt request flip-flop is set, the CPU will respond to interrupt requests on the INT pin. The signal into this pin must be logic high and maintained until the CPU responds to the request.

Since an interrupt can occur at any time, it is considered an asynchronous event as far as the CPU is concerned. To synchronize the request to CPU timing, the 8080A does not set its internal interrupt latch until the last clock state of an instruction cycle. This guarantees that the instruction underway when the interrupt request occurs is completed.

When the CPU does acknowledge the interrupt request, it begins an interrupt acknowledge machine cycle. This machine cycle is very similar to an op code fetch. The M1 status bit is transmitted during the SYNC interval marking the start of a new machine cycle. At the same time, the INTA status bit is placed on DO. This does not happen during a normal op code fetch. External circuitry is responsible for using this status bit to create an INTA control signal. The INTA control signal is used by the CPU to inform an external device to place an instruction onto the data bus. The 8080A will automatically disable the interrupt system when it responds to an interrupt. This means that each time an interrupt request is acknowledged, further interrupts are impossible until another EI instruction is performed.

Restart Instructions

While it is possible to place any instruction onto the bus in response to an INTA signal, the restart instructions are used most often. These instructions act like single-byte calls with predefined addresses. There are a total of eight restarts, listed in Table 11-1. The op codes are listed in octal to show the correspondance between the restart instruction and the address associated with the instruction. First notice that all restart instructions vector into page zero. This modified page-zero addressing was discussed earlier when addressing modes were detailed. *The low-order byte of the address is determined by the middle octal digit of the op code.* An RST 5, for example, forces the CPU to transfer control to 000 050.

TABLE 11-1   Restart Op Codes and Addresses

MNEMONIC	OCTAL	ADDRESS
RST 0	307	000 000
RST 1	317	000 010
RST 2	327	000 020
RST 3	337	000 030
RST 4	347	000 040
RST 5	357	000 050
RST 6	367	000 060
RST 7	377	000 070

The sequence performed by the CPU when it receives a restart is shown in Table 11-2. With the exception of the predefined address determined by the op code, the CPU handles the restarts like CALL instructions. In effect, a restart is a single-byte call to a special location.

TABLE 11-2   CPU Response to an RST

1. Place the 16-bit address of the next instruction to be performed onto the stack.
2. The stack pointer is then automatically decremented by 2.
3. A predefined address determined by the restart used is placed into the program counter.
4. Control passes to the instruction at the address placed into the program counter.

Jump Tables

In many systems, page zero happens to be ROM. Frequently this page is used to store the start of the monitor. This is done to facilitate cold resets. When power is applied, location 000 000 must contain the first instruction the CPU will fetch. It is easy to accomplish this by starting the monitor from this location. When this is done, the addresses associated with the restarts are already in use. Many monitors, therefore, begin with a jump table that redirects the CPU to another section of memory, where the service routine(s) is stored. In the monitor listed in Chapter 10, the jump table redirected the restarts to page 016. Six of the restarts were still available for interrupts, while restarts 0 and 7 were associated with the reset function.

An examination of the structure of the jump table used in Example 10-2 shows how a false interrupt request can cause control to pass back to the monitor. Suppose you are running a program when an interrupt is acknowledged by the CPU, perhaps due to electrical noise. The CPU generates an INTA. Since no circuit asked to be serviced, no restart is placed onto the data bus. The data bus is floating at a time when an op code should be present. If the data bus has pull-up resistors to minimize electrical noise, the CPU will "see" 377. This happens to be the op code for RST 7 that is in page zero where the monitor is stored.

11-2 IMPLEMENTING A SINGLE-LINE SYSTEM

Since the 8080A has just one INT line, it has to be shared when more than one device will be requesting interrupt service. Figure 11-1 is a block diagram that depicts how this can be done. In this diagram, three interface cards (often called controllers), have the ability to request an interrupt. The interrupt request line from each controller is gated into an OR gate, which has its output connected to the INT pin. The normal status of the interrupt request lines from the controllers is logic 0. This means that the output of the OR gate is normally logic 0, allowing the CPU to perform tasks not associated with these controllers. When any interface card takes its interrupt request line high, the output of the OR gate goes high.

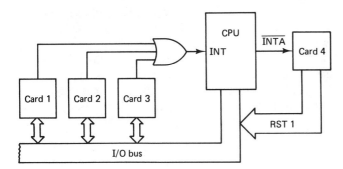

FIGURE 11-1 Block diagram of a single line interrupt system.

If the interrupt system is on, an EI was performed, and the 8080A enters an interrupt machine cycle. As we know, this causes an INTA to be generated, while internally the CPU locks out all further requests by clearing INTE.

Card 4 is a special-purpose card that generates an RST in response to the INTA. In this example, restart 1 was chosen. The op code for RST 1 is placed onto the data bus, then transferred into the instruction register. This step in the process is known as *jamming* an instruction into the CPU.

The CPU will decode this RST 1 and respond as indicated in Table 11-2. To complete the example, let us assume that this is happening in the computer controlled by the monitor listed in Chapter 10. The monitor contains a jump table that directs the processor to 016 010.

Polling Routine

The code stored at 016 010 is shown in Example 11-1. This block of code is referred to as a *polling routine*. It is the responsibility of the code to determine which card has requested the interrupt, then direct the CPU to the correct service routine.

The polling routine will interact with an interrupt request flip-flop by performing an IN instruction. The first instruction in the polling inputs the status of the INTR FF from card 1. To see how this affects the interface electronics, see Figure 11-2. The port number is transferred to an on-card decoder. If the port number matches a port number wired into the card, the output of the decoder (block 5 in Fig. 11-2) goes high. The decoder can easily be implemented by using comparator chips or by having the inverter positions to an AND gate circuit like the one shown in Figure 5-8 selectable by on-card jumpers.

If the card is selected, the RD* pulse can pass through the NAND gate 4. The other cards wired to respond to other port numbers ignore the RD* pulse.

The RD* goes low, activating the tristate buffer wired to the Q output of the INTR FF. This status bit is then transferred into the CPU over DO.

The polling routine then rotates DO into the carry flag. If the carry flag is set, the card just polled is requesting an interrupt. If this is the case, control is transferred to the starting address of the service routine for that card. If DO was low, the polling routine ignores the JC at 016 013 and polls the next card.

Should all the cards be polled, with none responding with DO high, an erroneous interrupt request was somehow generated. The OUT instruction at 016 022 generates a device-select pulse that turns on a light informing the computer operator that this has happened. Control is then returned to the program that was interrupted.

This is accomplished through the use of the RET instruction at line 016 024. As we will see in a moment, the service routines will also terminate in RETs. The RET gets the address placed on the stack by the RST, places that address into the program counter, and increments the stack pointer two locations. The CPU then proceeds from the address in the program counter.

EXAMPLE 11-1

HEX ADDRESS	HEX OP CODE	MNEMONIC	COMMENTS	OCTAL ADDRESS	OCTAL OP CODE
0E 00	DB	IN	Check card 1	016 000	333
0E 01		001		016 001	
0E 02	0F	RRC	Card 1 interrupt?	016 002	017
0E 03	DA	JC		016 003	332
0E 04		000	Go to service 1 routine	016 004	
0E 05		017		016 005	
0E 06	DB	IN	Check card 2	016 006	333
0E 07		002		016 007	
0E 08	0F	RRC	Card 2 interrupt?	016 010	017
0E 09	DA	JC		016 011	332
0E 0A		LO	Go to service 2 routine	016 012	
0E 0B		HI		016 013	
0E 0C	DB	IN	Check card 3	016 014	333
0E 0D		003		016 015	
0E 0E	0F	RRC	Card 3 interrupt?	016 016	017
0E 0F	DA	JC		016 017	332
0E 10		LO	Go to service 3 routine	016 020	
0E 11		HI		016 021	
0E 12	D3	OUT	Set invalid	016 022	323
0E 13		xxx	Interrupt light	016 023	
0E 14	C9	RET		016 024	311

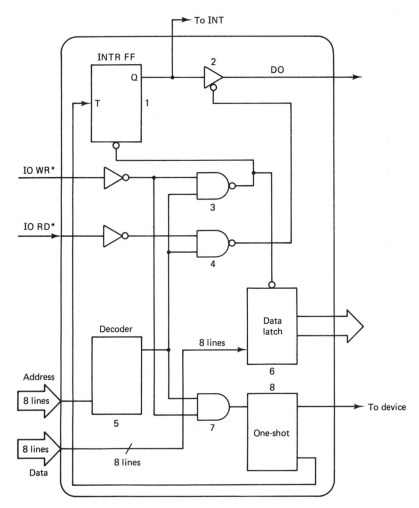

FIGURE 11-2 Typical polling circuitry (using SSI) found on a controller card.

There are several points yet to be answered about this part of the process before proceeding to the service routine. First, the order in which the devices are polled determines the priority of the request. In Example 11-1, card 1 is polled first. If card 3 requests an interrupt during the same instruction cycle as card 1, the polling routine will cause card 1 to be serviced first. This leads to the next point. The interrupt requests should be latched by the controller cards. If the cards produced pulses, the pulse from 3 could elapse before the service routine for card 1 was finished. If that happened, the pulse from card 3 would never generate an interrupt request. If, however, it is latched, that request would still be pending when the task associated with card 1 was finished.

When using a polling routine such as the one in Example 11-1, it is an easy matter to change the priorities. All you need to do is change the order in which the cards are polled.

Service Routine

A service routine is a section of code packaged as a subroutine that handles tasks associated with a particular peripheral or piece of hardware. These routines are frequently used in response to interrupts.

The block diagram of Figure 11-3 shows how an interrupt service routine should be organized. *The first task of the service routine is to save all the registers.* This is necessary. Why? This routine is being performed in response to an interrupt. The interrupt request can occur at any time. This makes it difficult for the programmer of the service routine to know what registers were in use when the interrupt happened. Therefore, all the registers are saved. The software that actually handles the task is performed next. When the task has been completed, all the registers are restored by POPing them off the stack. Then EI is performed to reenable the interrupt system. *Should an interrupt already be pending, it will be ignored until the RET instruction is performed.* This prevents the new interrupt from placing a return address onto the stack before the old return address is removed. If interrupts were acknowledged before the RET was completed, addresses could stack up so deep that the stack might overwrite a program.

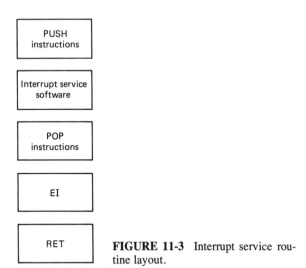

FIGURE 11-3 Interrupt service routine layout.

In our example, a polling routine was performed before the computer reached the service routine. Reexamine Example 11-1. What do you think happened to the values in the A and flag registers? The values from the program that was interrupted were destroyed by the polling process. PUSHing the PSW at the start of the service routine in this case is too late. This is often forgotten. When using a polling routine, PUSH the registers onto the stack at the start of the polling, not at the start of the service routine.

The service routine that interacts with the card shown in Figure 11-2 is coded in Example 11-2. This routine assumes that the polling routine has already saved the registers. It therefore enters the service software immediately. The LHLD instruction loads H and L with an address that points to a data table that is being transferred to port 1. This address is then used to retrieve the next byte. The MOV A,M instruction obtains this information; the OUT instruction performs the transfer. The card is wired in such a way that several things happen at this time. First, the decoder turns on, responding to the port number. This allows the card to accept the IOWR* pulse. NAND gate 3 output

EXAMPLE 11-2

HEX ADDRESS	HEX OP CODE	MNEMONIC	COMMENTS	OCTAL ADDRESS	OCTAL OP CODE
0F 00	2A	LHLD	Get service routine	017 000	052
0F 01		xxx	memory pointer	017 001	
0F 02		xxx		017 002	
0F 03	7E	MOV A, M	Get a new byte	017 003	176
0F 04	D3	OUT	Transfer byte to card 1	017 004	323
0F 05		001		017 005	
0F 06	23	INX H	Point to next byte	017 006	043
0F 07	22	SHLD	Save updated pointer	017 007	042
0F 08		xxx		017 010	
0F 09		xxx		017 011	
0F 0A	E1	POP H	Restore registers	017 012	341
0F 0B	D1	POP D		017 013	321
0F 0C	C1	POP B		017 014	301
0F 0D	F1	POP PSW		017 015	361
0F 0E	FB	EI	Enable interrupt	017 016	373
0F 0F	C9	RET		017 017	311

will go low. This clears the latched interrupt request on the card. This is necessary. If the request were to remain latched, the computer would lock into an infinite loop servicing only this card. How? Well, as soon as the service routine is completed, the CPU acknowledges the latched request from card 1. Back we go to the service routine. Another byte is transferred, even if the card is not ready. The service routine is then completed, the EI, RET is performed, and the CPU acknowledges card 1. Around and around we go.

Clearing the latch prevents this. The output of gate 3 also activates the data latch on the controller card. The latch can then capture the information present on the data bus. At the same time the AND gate (7) output goes high, triggering the oneshot. This oneshot is set to time out when the device attached to the controller has processed the data in the latch. The oneshot output could even be used to activate the device when valid data was in the latch. When the oneshot times out, the device could be turned off. The Q* output of the oneshot goes high when time has elapsed. This output is sent to the INTR FF, which is a JK wired to toggle on every clock. Since the computer cleared the FF, the clock will set the JK, requesting an interrupt. The service routine would then respond by sending another byte to be processed.

This entire process and the circuitry that supports it have one purpose: to free the processor to perform other tasks while the device attached to card 1 is acting on the data. During the time the oneshot is timing out, the CPU can handle other cards, run user programs, and accept input from other users.

Through the use of interrupts, the 8080A/8085A and Z80, which are single-tasking processors, can be made to handle multiple tasks and users. Each interface and user would gain the use of the CPU when it acknowledges the interrupt from the interface or user.

11-3 RESTARTS AS VECTORS

It is possible to use the restart instructions to go directly to a service routine without having to poll the cards attached to the I/O bus. In the block diagram of Figure 11-1, card 4, which issued a RST 1 in response to the INTA* signal from the computer, is replaced with different hardware.

The first way this can be done is to let each individual card generate a restart itself. This restart would be unique to the card, identifying the peripheral that required the attention of the CPU. Card 3 in Figure 11-1 could generate a restart 3 when it received the interrupt acknowledge from the CPU. This restart would then vector the computer to the address for the service routine associated with card 3.

Several things have to happen to make this new situation workable. First, each individual service routine should now PUSH registers when it is entered. This will be necessary because the polling routine will no longer be used. Second, there must be some way to prevent all the cards from placing their vectors onto the data bus in response to the interrupt acknowledge. If this were to happen, the restart information would become garbled.

Remember, we are still working with a CPU that has just one interrupt pin. The input to this pin would still be wired as it was in Figure 11-1. The computer would respond to this input by going high as before. The INTA* must give each card an opportunity to place its restart onto the data bus, but only at the correct time. Since the polling routine is no longer in use, another method must be established to create priorities. There are several ways in which this can be done.

11-4 PRIORITY CHAINS

The circuit shown in Figure 11-4 shows how a priority chain could be implemented using the INTA* signal. If a card wired like the one in Figure 11-4 receives the INTA* signal, it can use this signal to place its restart vector onto the data bus. In our example circuit, the INTA* signal is inverted and gated through an AND gate to the DS2 input of an 8212. If the card had requested an interrupt, the Q output of the interrupt flip-flop would be high. This would allow the positive-going INTA to reach DS2. When this happens, the tristate outputs of the 8212 are enabled, passing the information wired to the 8212's inputs to the data bus. This information would be a binary pattern that represents one of the restarts. Perhaps the restart pattern is hardwired to the inputs of the 8212. It is more likely that the pattern can be changed by on-card jumpers.

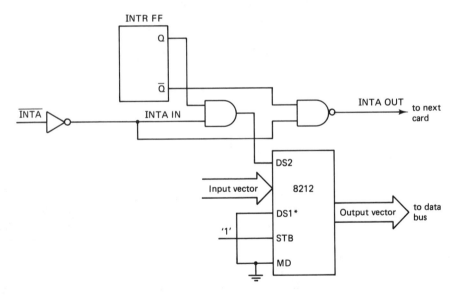

FIGURE 11-4 Implementing an interrupt priority chain.

Since this card has just placed the restart that identifies it onto the bus, any other card requesting an interrupt must be prevented from doing the same. This is handled by the AND gate wired to the Q* output of the interrupt request flip-flop. When the card has requested an interrupt, the Q* output will be low. This blocks the positive INTA from reaching the output of the AND gate. In effect, the chain is broken and the INTA signal never reaches the other cards.

When we were discussing the STD bus, the PCI (priority chain in) and PCO (priority chain out) pins were reserved for use in priority chains. In our example, we are developing a priority chain driven by the INTA signal. The priority in such a system is actually determined by the physical proximity of the card to the processor board. Only the highest priority card in the system will receive the INTA* signal from the CPU. It will then be up to this card's electronics to break the chain and respond with a restart or to ignore the INTA* signal and pass it on to the next card in the chain. Turning power off, removing and inserting cards into the edge connectors in a different order will change the priorities.

11-5 PRIORITY-INTERRUPT CONTROLLERS

The second way in which restarts can be used to vector directly to a service routine without having to use a polling routine is to replace card 4 in Figure 11-1 with a priority-interrupt controller card. This card can be implemented with small- and medium-scale integration or it can have a special-purpose priority-interrupt controller chip. We will examine both approaches.

Figure 11-5 shows a relatively simple priority-interrupt controller circuit using three ICs. The 74148 is a chip we have discussed before. It is an 8-input-to-3-output priority encoder. The highest level input will be at input 7. If this line goes low, the other inputs enter "don't care" status. The outputs are active low, thus the inverters. With an input low at input 7, the output of the inverters will be 111. If line 6 were to go low, when 7 was not in use, the output of the inverters would be 110, and so on. This chip will handle the priority function for the interrupt controller. The system user would establish priorities by wiring or jumpering the highest priority card to input 7, the next to 6, then to 5 until finally reaching input 0, which has the lowest priority.

The output from the inverters is gated to the inputs of an 8212. Five of the inputs to the 8212 are hardwired to Vcc. This is done in such a way that the octal input to the 8212 becomes 3X7, where X is the middle octal digit controlled by the priority encoder circuit and the inverters. If input 4 to the 74148 goes low, with no higher inputs being low, the input to the 8212 would become 347, which happens to be the op code for RST 4. At the same time the 74148 generates the middle octal digit of one of the RST instructions, the output pin EO on the priority encoder goes high. This will signal the CPU that an interrupt is being requested. If EI has enabled the interrupt system, the CPU will respond with an INTA*. The INTA* signal activates the tristate outputs of the 8212, gating the restart instruction onto the data bus. The INTA* signal is used at the same time to control the D input of a 4-line-to-10-line decoder.

When the D input to the 7442 is high, it will not be possible for the outputs shown to go low. The 7442 will either have output 8 or 9 low or it will be in an invalid state. This chip will only accept 0000 through 1001. When the INTA* signal on D goes low,

C through A can determine which of the eight output lines 7 through 0 will go low. The C through A inputs to the 7442 are controlled by the output from the inverters. The inverter outputs in turn are controlled by the interrupt request that has been activated. Thus, if input 3 to the priority encoder goes low, the inputs to the 7442 on C through A will be 011. This means that as soon as the INTA* signal goes low on D, the output of the 7442 will go low on output 3. This pulse can then be gated back to card 3, clearing its request latch.

Masking

Another feature that might be added to the interrupt controller in Figure 11-5 is the ability to mask out or prevent certain devices from being able to generate an interrupt request.

As the circuit in Figure 11-5 is currently wired, the only way to prevent interrupts once EI has been performed without resetting the system is to have a program perform DI, the mnemonic for disable interrupt. When this instruction is performed, the 8080A/ 8085A and Z80 will all ignore requests on the interrupt pin. (Yes, all three processors have such a pin, but the 8085A and Z80 have additional interrupt features. More about those extra features later.)

This means that the entire interrupt system is disabled and none of the restarts can be jammed into the instruction register since an interrupt machine cycle will never take place. This is a drastic measure to take, especially if the CPU has to handle many devices that interact with the processor via the interrupt system. Yet there are times when a DI is used to protect a section of code that is time critical. Such a section of code must be allowed to complete a task within a given time frame. Failure to allow this type of code to complete its job because an interrupt came along is prevented by bracketing the section of code with a DI–EI sequence. This would look something like this:

```
            DI

            |time critical code|

            |time critical code|

            |time critical code|

            EI
```

This type of situation can occur when the code is involved in some control application. Such an example might be the positioning of an X–Y table before a drill or punch was to take place. If an interrupt prevented the positioning from being completed, the drill or punch would not take place at the correct location.

There are other times when it might be useful to shut down just part of the interrupt system. To do this, additional circuitry would have to be added to our controller.

The circuit of Figure 11-6 shows a modification to 11-5 that would allow the CPU to selectively mask out interrupts from controllers. Two 7475 latches are wired to respond to an active high signal generated when the CPU does an OUT to port 50. This

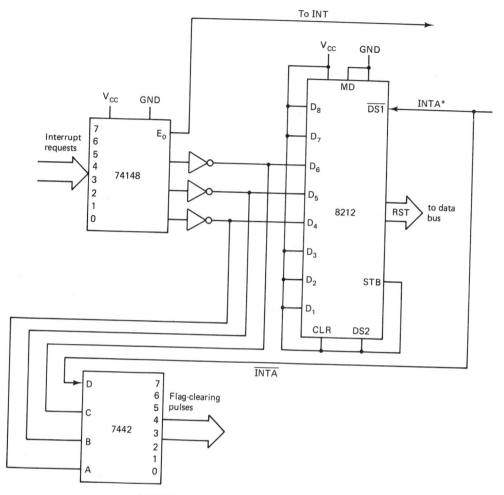

FIGURE 11-5 Priority interrupt controller circuitry.

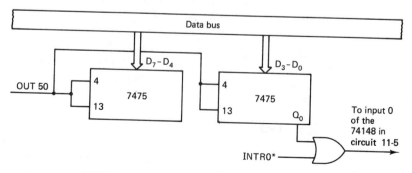

FIGURE 11-6 Priority interrupt masking circuitry.

out instruction will transfer the interrupt mask byte to the latches. All eight outputs from the latches would be wired as shown for QO. If QO were set high, this would prevent active low signals from getting through the OR gate. Since the inputs to the priority encoder of Figure 11-5 are active low, this interrupt line would be masked out.

Example 11-3 shows how the additional circuitry of Figure 11-6 can be used to mask out selected interrupts. In this listing the mask byte is 0110 1111. The byte is transferred to the latch, where six OR gate outputs go high. Only D7 and D4 can pass an active low signal through to the priority encoder. After the mask byte has been set to the latch, the interrupt system is enabled with an EI.

EXAMPLE 11-3

HEX ADDRESS	HEX OP CODE	MNEMONIC	COMMENTS	OCTAL ADDRESS	OCTAL OP CODE
03 00	3E	MVI A	Interrupt mask 011 0 1111	003 000	076
03 01		6F		003 001	
03 02	D3	OUT		003 002	323
03 03		50		003 003	
03 04	FB	EI		003 004	373
		·	Main task		
		·			
		·			

The code preceding the EI instruction in Example 11-3 is called an initialization sequence. In this case, the only task that was performed was establishing the interrupt mask. In many instances, the initialization sequence will have a lot more to do than is shown in Example 11-3. Consider the interrupt request flip-flops on each controller card. When powered up, these flip-flops can come up in the interrupt request mode. If EI is performed before the interrupt request flip-flops are cleared, an erroneous interrupt request will occur. To prevent this from happening, an initialization sequence should force every controller that can cause an interrupt to the state required for correct power up before the EI is issued.

Low-Priority Lockout

When establishing priorities in an interrupt system, the high-speed devices are given the highest priorities. Peripherals such as printers. teletypes, and paper tape readers/punches are assigned lower priorities. In general, devices in which operation will not suffer if the CPU ignores them for short periods of time will be assigned lower priorities.

Now suppose we decide to hook a high-speed disk drive to input 6 of the priority encoder in Figure 11-5 through the mask interface shown in Figure 11-6, then a high-speed tape drive to input 5. Finally, a printer is connected to input 0. For the moment, assume that the other interrupt lines are masked out.

We start our analysis of this situation with the disk drive requesting an interrupt. Since it has the highest priority of those interrupts allowed, the encoder generates a 110 and signals the CPU that an interrupt request has occurred. The CPU responds and the interrupt controller gates a RST 6 onto the data bus.

While the service routine for the disk drive is being performed, both the tape drive and the printer generate interrupt requests. The encoder outputs 101 for the tape drive and generates an interrupt request. This request is ignored until the level 6 service routine is completed and EI is performed. Right after the RET in the disk drive service routine is executed, the CPU acknowledges the RST 5. Control is passed to the tape drive service routine with the printer request still pending.

While this routine is being performed, the disk drive requests another interrupt. The level 6 request overrides the level 0 request from the printer and changes the encoder's outputs to 110. When the level 5 routine is finally completed, the CPU responds to the encoder, which jams an RST 6 into the instruction register. The level 0 request is still pending.

It is possible for high-level requests to toggle back and forth like this, locking out lower-level devices. This must be prevented because at some point the printer or other low-level device must be allowed to function.

One way we can prevent low-priority lockout with our controller is to attach a clock to the level 7 input. Whenever the clock times out, it receives the highest priority and is assured that it will be serviced no later than when the current service routine transfers control back to the main task.

The service routine for the clock can output a mask byte that temporarily disables the high-level priority inputs, thus allowing the low-level inputs to place their restart instruction on the data bus. The next time the clock timed out, it could switch the mask back to the pattern that allowed the high-level interrupts. The clock waveform need not be a 50 percent duty cycle waveform. In fact, the high-level priorities should be allowed the majority of the time. After all, they are high-level for a reason. Perhaps a duty cycle of 80 percent might be chosen. Thus, 20 percent of the time the low-level priorities would not have to worry about being locked out of the system.

High-Priority Lockout

The problem of high-priority lockout is easier to solve than the situation involving low-level lockout. You might think that a low-level priority could not possibly prevent a higher level from gaining control. After all, the priority encoder will see to it that the high-level priority gains control if it requests service at the same time as the low-level request comes in. Suppose, though, that the low-level request occurred first. The encoder would generate the low-level restart and signal the CPU that an interrupt is pending. The CPU, upon completing the current instruction cycle, acknowledges the interrupt. Control is transferred to the low-level service routine. If the low-level service routine is structured as indicated in Figure 11-3, the high-level request must wait until the EI-RET sequence at the end of the routine is completed.

This wait may not be acceptable. To prevent this from happening, place the EI instruction near the beginning of the service routine. If the task that is being performed by the low-level routine can take place in segments, there is no reason why it cannot be interrupted.

If the EI is at the start of a service routine, then the interrupt system is enabled. This means that other interrupts can occur. If we were in the middle of the level 0 routine when RST 5 was generated, control would pass to the level 5 routine. The return address placed on the stack would be the location of an instruction in the level 0 routine. When the level 5 routine finished, assuming no further interrupts, control would pass back to the level 0 routine before going back to the main task. The stack will handle this situation very nicely.

Is it possible to get partway into a routine, then get stuck there as higher-level requests control the system? Of course, but the clock at level 7 would eventually mask out the higher-level requests, allowing the low-level request to be completed.

Priority-Interrupt Controllers

As the preceding discussion should make clear, the handling of interrupts can become a complex problem within a computer system. When a problem is complex and important, it is nice when a special-purpose IC can be purchased to handle most of the tasks needed to solve that problem. This section will introduce you to the 8259A, a programmable interrupt controller.

The 8259A

This chip can be programmed to handle up to eight vectored priority interrupts. It can be cascaded in a master/slave configuration to handle up to 64 levels of priority interrupts. The block diagram and pin out for this chip are depicted in Figure 11-7.

Block diagram/pin-out summary. The interrupt inputs to the 8259 are handled by the interrupt request register, IRR, and the in-service register, ISR. The IRR is used to store all pending interrupt requests, while the ISR is used to store all the interrupt levels currently being serviced.

The priority-resolver section of the 8259A determines the highest priority of the bits set within the IRR. When the 8259A receives an INTA*, the priority resolver strobes the highest priority request into the ISR. The resolver takes the place of the 74148 encoder we used in Figure 11-5.

The interrupt mask register, IMR, is programmable. It can be used to mask out

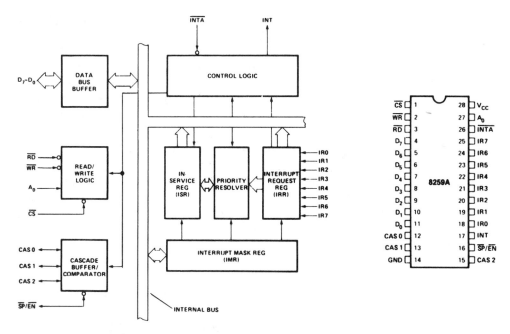

FIGURE 11-7   8259A internal logic and pin out. (Courtesy of Intel Corporation.)

unwanted interrupt requests. The outputs of this register will affect the IRR, preventing the masked bits from transferring to the ISR when the 8259A receives an INTA*.

The INT output will be wired directly to the CPU interrupt input. The output voltage is fully compatible with the 8080A/8085A processors as well as the 8086.

Interrupt acknowledge signals will be gated into the 8259A INTA*. Pulsing this line will cause the 8259A to release vector information. The format of this information will depend on the 8259A programming.

The *tristate bidirectional data-bus buffer* is the standard functional block that we have seen in other programmable support chips. This block allows control words generated by the CPU into the 8259A. The CPU can also read the status of certain registers within the controller by reading their contents through this buffer.

The *read/write control block* accepts initialization command words and operational command words when outputted from the CPU. The ICW and OCW formats determine the operational mode of the chip. We will investigate these control words in the section on programming the 8259A.

Chip select is used to activate the 8259A. Reading or writing to the controller will be inhibited unless CS* is pulled low. This input should be driven by a device-select pulse.

The WR* and RD* lines determine the direction of data flow. These lines will have no effect unless CS* is low at the same time one of these lines is activated. To send command words to the controller, the WR* line must be active low. To read status information from the controller, the RD* line must be low.

The A0 input is used in conjunction with the WR* and RD* lines to determine which of the command registers or status registers within the controller will be accessed. It is usually tied to A0 on the address bus, but can be attached to any of the address lines. As we will see when we get to the programming section on the 8259A, A0 by itself is not sufficient to fully direct the command words to the correct destination. The sequence in which the command words are sent as well as certain bit positions within the command words will determine, along with A0, the register to be accessed.

A typical interrupt sequence using the 8259A.   The 8259A will place a CALL instruction onto the data bus in response to the INTA* signal. In 8080A/8085A systems the processor subsystem will generate two additional INTA* to receive the second and third bytes of the CALL. This address is stored within the 8259A and can designate any area within the 64K memory map. What follows is a typical sequence when using the 8259A with an 8080A or 8085A.

1. One or more of the interrupt inputs will go high. This sets the corresponding bit position(s) within the interrupt request register (IRR).
2. The 8259A evaluates the requests. If the requests have not been masked out, an INT signal is generated informing the CPU that an interrupt is pending.
3. If the interrupt system is enabled, the CPU responds by generating an INTA*.
4. When the 8259A receives the INTA* from the CPU or its support chips (remember, the 8080 does not directly generate the INTA*), the 8259A transfers the highest-priority bit that is not masked in the IRR into the ISR. The corresponding bit in the IRR will be reset. At the same time, the controller will generate a CALL. The CALL will be jammed into the CPU's instruction register.
5. The CALL will initiate two more INTA* signals.
6. The additional INTA* signals will be used to make the 8259A release the preprogrammed subroutine address onto the data bus. The low-order address byte will be transferred first. The high-order address byte will be transferred second.
7. If the automatic end of interrupt (AEOI) feature is set, the ISR bit set will be cleared at the end of the third INTA*. If this feature is not used, the ISR bit will remain set until the 8259A receives the appropriate end of interrupt command (EOI).

Programming the 8259A.   The 8259A can be programmed through a sequence of simple, isolated I/O operations. The system interface for an 8259A is shown in Figure 11-8. Chip select will be driven by a device-select pulse taken from some type of decoder circuit. The CAS0, CAS1, CAS2, and SP*/EN* control lines will only be used if more than one 8259A is to be wired into the system. We will not examine this feature of the 8259A. For information on how to expand the controller connections to operate more than eight levels of interrupts, see the specification sheets on the 8259A.

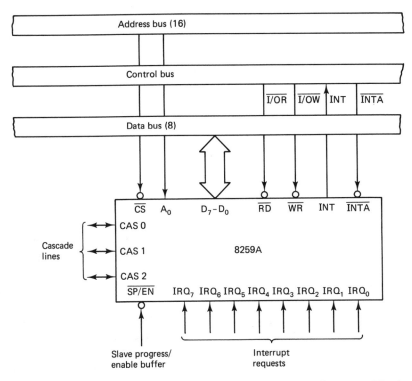

FIGURE 11-8 8259A interface to standard system bus. (Courtesy of Intel Corporation.)

The 8259A accepts two types of command words. The first type is known as an *initialization command word*. The ICWs are used to start the 8259A before normal operations can begin. Two to four ICWs must be sent to the 8259A after power up before it will process interrupt requests. The second type of command word is referred to as an *operational command word*. The OCWs determine which of the interrupt modes will be used by the 8259A. These interrupt modes are:

1. fully nested mode
2. rotating priority mode
3. special mask mode
4. polled mode

The operational command words can be written to the controller any time after initialization.

   To start the initialization process, ICW1 must first be written to the 8259A. When A0 is logic 0 and D4 of the command word is a logic 1, the controller interprets this as command word 1. Once the controller accepts ICW1, the following events automatically occur:

1. The edge sensitive circuit is reset. This means that after initialization an interrupt request must make a low-to-high transition to trigger a request.
2. The interrupt mask is cleared. This enables all eight levels of interrupts.
3. Input 7 is assigned to priority 7.
4. The slave mode address is set to 7.
5. Special mask mode is cleared. The status read is set to IRR.
6. If IC4 of ICW1 is a logic 0, then all functions associated with ICW4 are cleared. This sets the controller to the nonbuffered mode, with no automatic EOI, and to the 8085 system.

The breakdown of the ICW1 command word is shown in Figure 11-9(a). Bit DO determines if the initialization sequence will include ICW4. If the bit is cleared, no ICW4 will be issued and the default parameters listed in point 6 above will be set. The buffered mode will allow the controller to enable buffers when the system uses more than just one 8259A. Since we are not going to investigate cascading, the nonbuffered default will be used. We wish to use the 8259A in an 8080A/8085 system, so defaulting to that mode is no problem either. Finally, the AEOI function can be ignored if the software sends an EOI message at the end of a service routine.

D1 in ICW1 determines if cascading will be used. Setting this bit high tells the controller that a single 8259A will be used in the system. Furthermore, with the bit high, the controller will not need an ICW3. Initialization will be complete after two initialization command words have been sent to the 8259A.

D2 in the ICW1 determines the spacing or interval between the jump instructions used by the CPU to redirect flow to the service routines. The controller does not directly address the service routine associated with an interrupt request. Rather, the CALL instruction addresses a location within a jump table. Then the processor executes the jump that takes the program flow to the first instruction of the service routine. We have previously seen jump tables when the monitor program was studied in Chapter 10. The jump table can be anywhere in memory, as we will see in a moment. The length of this jump table will be either 64 bytes or 32 bytes depending on the interval set by D2. If D2 is logic 0, the intervals between jumps in the table will be 8 bytes. This corresponds to the intervals between the restart instructions in page zero. If the user wishes to implement a compact jump table, the interval is set to 4 by setting D2. In either case, the low-order byte of the address to the jump table is not fully programmable. If the user elects to have an interval of 8 bytes between jumps, then A7, A6, A5 can be programmed by the user. This is done by setting or clearing the corresponding bits within ICW1. See the breakdown of the command word in Figure 11-9(a). If the user elects to use a compact jump table 32 bytes in length, then only A7 and A6 can be programmed by the user. The 8259A will generate the remaining bits of the low-order address. See the interval tables in Figure 11-10.

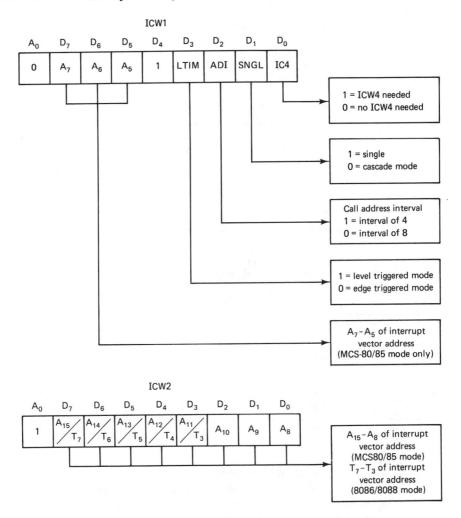

FIGURE 11-9   8259A ICW1, ICW2. (Courtesy of Intel Corporation.)

D3 of ICW1 determines if the input requests to the controller will be edge sensitive or level sensitive. If the bit is set, the inputs must be level sensitive; if D3 is cleared, the input requests are edge sensitive. In either case, the request must be maintained at a high level until the first falling edge of INTA*. If this does not happen the controller will treat the request as if it were false. This helps to reject spurious requests that might be caused by electrical noise and transients. Should an input request not maintain a high level until the first falling edge of INTA*, the 8259A responds to this situation by issuing a default IR7. The service routine for IR7 would simply be a return. Thus, all glitches into the interrupt request lines would be ignored. If the system requires the use of IR7,

Content of second interrupt vector byte

IR	Interval = 4							
	D_7	D_6	D_5	D_4	D_3	D_2	D_1	D_0
7	A_7	A_6	A_5	1	1	1	0	0
6	A_7	A_6	A_5	1	1	0	0	0
5	A_7	A_6	A_5	1	0	1	0	0
4	A_7	A_6	A_5	1	0	0	0	0
3	A_7	A_6	A_5	0	1	1	0	0
2	A_7	A_6	A_5	0	1	0	0	0
1	A_7	A_6	A_5	0	0	1	0	0
0	A_7	A_6	A_5	0	0	0	0	0

IR	Interval = 8							
	D_7	D_6	D_5	D_4	D_3	D_2	D_1	D_0
7	A_7	A_6	1	1	1	0	0	0
6	A_7	A_6	1	1	0	0	0	0
5	A_7	A_6	1	0	1	0	0	0
4	A_7	A_6	1	0	0	0	0	0
3	A_7	A_6	0	1	1	0	0	0
2	A_7	A_6	0	1	0	0	0	0
1	A_7	A_6	0	0	1	0	0	0
0	A_7	A_6	0	0	0	0	0	0

FIGURE 11-10   8259A low-order address byte format. (Courtesy of Intel Corporation.)

the service routine for IR7 must read the ISR register. A normal interrupt request on IR7 will set bit 7 in the in service register. If a default IR7 has occurred, ISR7 will be cleared.

D4 marks the control word as ICW1 when A0 into the controller is low.

The address bits have already been explained in conjunction with the interval tables.

ICW2 is much simpler. This byte is the high-order address to the jump table. It can be set to any page in memory. It is detected by the 8259A as the second byte in the initialization sequence. The A0 input to the controller must be high when writing ICW2.

With A0 being used by the controller to help direct the flow of command words into the 8259A, the controller will respond to two port addresses. The easiest way to implement this is to not use A0 as part of the address that activates the device-select decoder driving chip select. This can be seen by referring once again to the system interface diagram of Figure 11-8.

When ICW1 indicates that ICW3 and ICW4 will not be used, the initialization sequence is complete. The controller is ready to accept interrupt requests. The default mode of operation is the fully nested mode.

In the fully nested mode of operation, the priorities of the interrupt requests are set so request zero has the highest priority and level seven has the lowest priority. When the controller issues an interrupt request, it sets the bit in the interrupt service register. This bit will prevent all interrupts of the same or lower level. The bit in the ISR will remain set until an EOI instruction is sent to the controller at the end of the service routine. If AOEI is set, then the ISR bit is reset at the end of the third INTA* pulse.

To send EOI instructions, to mask out interrupts, to change priorities, and to alter the mode of operation of the controller, operational command words must be sent. The breakdown of the operational command words is shown in Figure 11-11.

The first of these words is the mask control word. If A0 goes high during an I/O write after the initialization sequence is completed, the 8259A interprets the incoming byte as an OCW1. To mask out a channel, simply take the corresponding bit high. To leave a channel enabled, clear the corresponding bit.

OCW2, operational command word 2, determines the rotate and end of interrupt modes. These functions are determined by the bit pattern in the first three bits. The controller will accept an output from the computer as OCW2 if the initialization sequence has been completed, A0 is low, and D4 and D3 of the command word are low.

The first two entries in the chart detailing the use of OCW2 are used upon end of interrupt. A nonspecific end of interrupt command directs the controller to reset a bit in the in service register. In the fully nested mode, this will be the highest in service level, since the last request to be serviced must have been the highest request. A nonspecific EOI does not need to use the lower 3 bits of OCW2. When a mode of operation is used that disturbs the fully nested mode of operation, the 8259A may not be able to tell which interrupt was just acknowledged. In this case, a specific end of interrupt command must be sent to the controller via OCW2. When a specific end of interrupt command is sent, the last 3 bits of OCW2 tell the controller which bit in the ISR to clear.

The next four bit patterns for D7, D6, and D5, as detailed in the breakdown of OCW2, involve rotating priorities.

In some cases, the devices attached to the controller will have equal priorities. In such a case, the rotating priority mode of operation can be used to implement a system where the interrupt just serviced is moved to the bottom of the priority list. This means that the device just serviced is moved to the bottom of the list. In the worst case, it would have to wait until seven other interrupts were serviced once. Of course, if no other interrupts are pending, being moved to the bottom of the list does not cause an interrupt request to wait.

To see how this is implemented, see Figure 11-12. Figure (a) shows the in service register as it would be set up in the fully nested mode just after initialization. IS0 has the highest priority, with IS7 having the lowest priority. As indicated by our example, level two is currently being serviced. When the level-two service routine is finished, it can issue a rotate on nonspecific EOI command. This would change the priorities as indicated by Figure 11-12(b). Not only does the EOI command clear the IS2 bit, it places IS2 at the bottom of the priority list. IS3 now has the highest priority. Of course, with no further interrupts pending, IS2 could request an interrupt and gain access to the CPU. However, if every device on the bus was requesting servicing, IS2 would have to wait

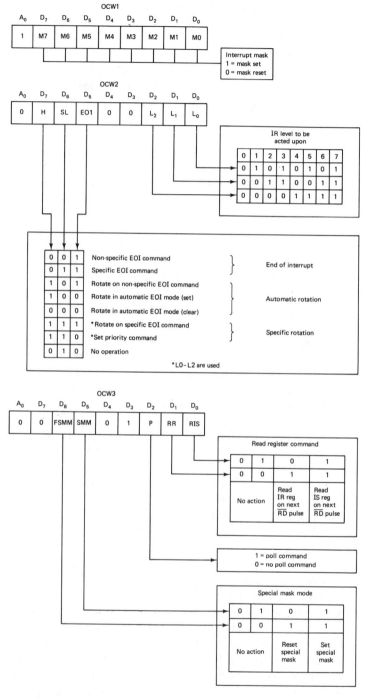

FIGURE 11-11 8259A operational command word formats. (Courtesy of Intel Corporation.)

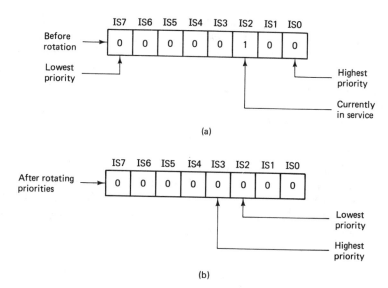

FIGURE 11-12   8259A: Effect of rotating priorities.

until all other interrupts had been serviced before its turn came up again. In automatic EOI mode, rotation can be enabled by sending a OCW2 command with D7, D6, and D4 being 1, 0, 0 respectively.

To clear stop rotation when using the AEOI mode, choose the rotate on AEOI clear command format for OCW2.

The last rotate format allows the programmer to specify which ISR bit to reset on EOI. The three L bits within OCW2 then clear the bit specified and rotate the priorities.

If, for some reason, the programmer does not want to wait until an end of interrupt, the priorities can be changed by issuing a set priority command. The set priority command specifies which bit to place at the bottom of the priority list. This bit will be determined by the binary value in the L bits of OCW2. If the set priority command sets IR3 as the lowest priority, then IR4 is set as the highest-level priority.

Operational control word 3 is recognized by the controller after the initialization sequence is completed, when the CPU outputs a byte to the controller with A0 a logic 0, D7 and D4 a logic 0, and D3 a logic 1.

D6 and D5 are used to establish the special mask mode where a service routine can change the priority structure while the service code is being performed. For further details on this special mode of operation, refer to the 8259A specifications.

The bits that are of interest here in OCW3 are D2, D1, and D0. If D2 is set, the controller will be placed in the polling mode of operation. In this mode, the INT output is not used or the CPU's interrupt system is not enabled. The first RD* after the polling mode is set will be treated by the controller as an interrupt acknowledge. The 8259A will set the appropriate bit in the ISR and transfer to the CPU a binary code in D2, D1, and D0 that indicates the priority of the level requesting an interrupt. The interrupt status is frozen from the WR*, establishing the polling mode, until the RD* obtaining the binary pattern indicates the level requesting service.

D1 and D0 of OCW3 are used to read the IR register and the IS register. A read register command is issued, then upon receiving the next RD*, the controller places the called-for register onto the data bus. The IMR, mask register, can be read directly whenever RD* is low and A0 is 1.

To complete the discussion on the 8259A we will look at an initialization sequence, how a jump table is set up, and the block structure of a service routine that is selected by the 8259A.

Example 11-4 is an initialization routine for the 8259A. The first section of code sets up ICW1. In this example, ICW1 calls for no ICW4, specifies that the controller is the only 8259A in the system, and sets the interval in the jump table to 8. High logic levels will activate the interrupt request inputs to the controller. The low-order byte pointing to the jump table will start with A7 and A6 low. Since the interval specified was 8, we cannot program A5.

EXAMPLE 11-4

HEX ADDRESS	HEX OP CODE	MNEMONIC	COMMENTS	OCTAL ADDRESS	OCTAL OP CODE
03 00	3E	MV1 A	8259A ICW1	003 000	076
03 01		1A	0001 1010	003 001	
03 02	D3	OUT	Initialize ICW1	003 002	323
03 03		50		003 003	
03 04	3E	MV1 A	ICW2, jump table high byte	003 004	076
03 05		20		003 005	
03 06	D3	OUT	Initialize ICW2	003 006	323
03 07		51		003 007	
03 08	FB	E1		003 010	373
		.	Main task		
		.			
		.			
		.			

The MVI A 20 at line 03 04 is ICW2. The 20 is the high-order byte of the address where the jump table is located. Since OCW1 is not issued, all levels of interrupts are enabled. The section of code ends by enabling the CPU INT function by executing EI just before entering the main task.

Example 11-5 shows the first three entries in the jump table. Each jump instruction will be 8 bytes apart. Consult the interval tables found in Figure 11-10 to determine the remaining low-order addresses.

EXAMPLE 11-5

HEX ADDRESS	HEX OP CODE	MNEMONIC	COMMENTS	OCTAL ADDRESS	OCTAL OP CODE
20 00	C3	JMP	Transfer to service routine 0	040 000	303
20 01		XX		040 001	
20 02		XX		040 002	
.					
.					
.					
.					
.					
20 08	C3	JMP	Transfer to service routine 1	040 010	303
.		XX		040 011	
.		XX		040 012	
.					
.					
.					
20 10	C3	JMP	Transfer to service routine 2	040 020	303
20 11		XX		040 021	
20 12		XX		040 022	
.					
.					

Example 11-6 is more a block diagram than a listing. Since the service routine shown was not accessed through a polling routine, all the registers are saved on the stack. The service code for the device is the next section in the listing. This service code must clear the interrupt request latch of the requesting peripheral. This is not handled by the interrupt controller.

EXAMPLE 11-6

HEX ADDRESS	HEX OP CODE	MNEMONIC	COMMENTS	OCTAL ADDRESS	OCTAL OP CODE
.					
.					
.					
			PUSH all registers		
			Service code		
		MV1 A	Nonspecific E01 command		
		20			
		OUT			
		50			
			POP all registers		
		E1			
		RET			

After the service code is performed and before the registers are POPed, the service routine issues a nonspecific EOI command that is sent to the 8259A. This clears the service bit set in the ISR register. Doing this before POPing insures that the A register is returned correctly. The section of code finishes by restoring registers, reenabling the interrupt system of the CPU, and returning to the main task.

11-6 8085 INTERRUPT ARCHITECTURE

The 8085 has the ability to support the interrupt system used in the 8080. This is handled through the INTR pin on the 8085. Like the 8080, this pin must be taken high to generate an interrupt request. If the interrupt system is enabled through the EI instruction, the 8085 will respond with an INTA*. This signal is available directly from the CPU, unlike the 8080, where an external device had to create INTA* from the interrupt status bit.

In response to the INTA* signal, the interrupting device is expected to place an instruction onto the data bus during the INT machine cycle. In most cases, the instruction jammed into the instruction register will be one of the restarts. If a monitor occupies page zero, a jump table must redirect the restart vectors to another area of memory.

The 8085 will generate one, two, or three INTA* signals, depending on which instruction is jammed into the instruction register during the first INT cycle. This means that the 8259A priority-interrupt controller will work with the 8085 as well as the 8080.

In addition to supporting the 8080 interrupt system, the 8085 has additional interrupt features.

Multiline System

A multiline system has the capability of supporting more than one interrupt request pin. Additionally, some of the lines, if not all, have special vectors associated with the request on the special interrupt pins. The 8085 interrupt system is shown in Figure 11-13. Figure (a) indicates the new interrupt pins. These pins are TRAP, RST 7.5, RST 6.5, and RST 5.5. The addresses associated with each of these interrupts is given in Figure 11-13(b). The vectors do not have to be supplied by an external circuitry, as taking any of these lines high will cause circuitry within the 8085 to generate the vector itself and place the address in the program counter. The 8085 instruction set does not contain instructions equivalent to TRAP, RST 7.5, RST 6.5, and RST 5.5. These functions are implemented through hardware circuitry as described.

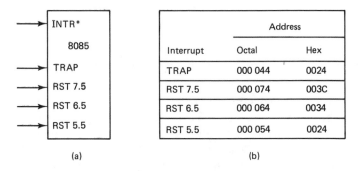

Interrupt	Address	
	Octal	Hex
TRAP	000 044	0024
RST 7.5	000 074	003C
RST 6.5	000 064	0034
RST 5.5	000 054	0024

(a)   (b)

FIGURE 11-13   The 8085 multiline interrupt system.

The five pins available for interrupt requests on the 8085 have an established priority of TRAP, RST 7.5, RST 6.5, RST 5.5, and INTR. The TRAP input is a nonmaskable interrupt. It cannot be shut off by issuing a DI. It does not require an EI to enable it. When the 8085 is powered up, this interrupt request is available for use. Since the TRAP cannot be shut off and is the highest-priority interrupt in the 8085 system, it is used for situations that are absolutely critical to processor function. The TRAP can be used for early warning of impending power loss or other emergency situations.

The other half restarts, so called because their vector addresses lie halfway between the regular restarts, are not enabled until an EI has been performed. They can be masked off as a group by performing DI. They can also be masked off individually by an instruction unique to the 8085. This instruction is SIM, the mnemonic for set interrupt mask.

The interrupt mask patterns used when performing SIM are indicated in Table 11-3. Bit position D3 is the switch that will activate the mask process when an SIM is performed. If D3 is high, the 3 lowests bits in the byte determine the status of the half restarts. D2 controls 7.5, D1 controls 6.5, and D0 controls 5.5. If a bit is cleared in this group, the corresponding half restart is enabled. If the bit is set, then that particular half restart is masked off. Note that it is possible to disable all the half restarts by using line 8 of the function table, then issuing an EI, which will activate the INTR pin but leave the half restarts masked off.

TABLE 11-3   Interrupt Mask Bits for the 8085

D3	D2	D1	D0	RESULTS
1	0	0	0	7.5, 6.5, 5.5 enabled
1	0	0	1	5.5 disabled, others active
1	0	1	0	6.5 disabled, others active
1	0	1	1	only 7.5 active
1	1	0	0	7.5 disabled, others active
1	1	0	1	only 6.5 active
1	1	1	0	only 5.5 active
1	1	1	1	all disabled
0	X	X	X	no effect on interrupts

To set up an interrupt mask, the bit pattern representing the desired masking should be placed in the A register. Immediately after this has been done, perform a SIM. This transfers the masking information into the interrupt mask register.

Make sure that when setting up a mask for the half restarts that D6 is low. If D6 is high, the 8085 will transfer the contents of D7 out of the CPU on the serial output data pin (SOD).

If it becomes necessary to verify or check the status of the mask register controlling the half restarts, a copy of the current pattern will be transferred into the A register when the instruction RIM is performed. RIM is the mnemonic for read interrupt mask. Once a copy has been moved into A, it can be checked or output for inspection.

Triggering Characteristics of the Interrupts

The TRAP input will not be recognized until the trigger goes high and stays high until sampled. Thus, it is both edge sensitive and level sensitive. This double requirement reduces the chance of spurious noise causing an interrupt on TRAP. This feature is incorporated into the TRAP input because it can not be masked out; in many instances TRAP is used to indicate catastrophic problems.

RST 7.5 is edge sensitive. A rising edge on RST 7.5 will cause an internal request latch to be set. This latch will remain set until 7.5 is serviced.

The remaining interrupts, RST 6.5, 5.5, and INTR are level sensitive. These inputs must remain high until the CPU samples their status. Like the 8080, the CPU will not check the status of an interrupt line until the last clock state of an instruction cycle, insuring that the current instruction is completed.

Whenever any interrupt is serviced, the 8085 automatically disables all further interrupts, excluding TRAP, until the EI instruction is performed. In most cases, this will be done in the service routine.

11-7   Z80 INTERRUPT ARCHITECTURE

The Z80 has two interrupt pins. One of these is a non-maskable interrupt that cannot be disabled by the programmer. This input is labeled NMI*. The EI instruction does not need to be performed prior to the NMI's functioning. The Z80 will generate an internal vector of 00 66 hex when it accepts an NMI input. This value is placed in the program counter and execution will transfer to the vector location.

The other pin supporting interrupt functions is labeled INT*. It is possible to operate this pin in three different modes.

Mode 0

Mode 0 is similar to the 8080/8085 INT function. The logic level into the Z80 is active low, while the logic level into the 8080/8085 is active high. Another important difference is the number of INTA* signals the Z80 will issue in response to an interrupt request. Unlike the 8080/8085, which can generate up to three INTA* signals in an interrupt sequence, the Z80 responds with just one INTA* signal. If a CALL instruction is placed on the data bus in response to an INTA* signal, the Z80 will perform two memory reads after receiving the CALL. This means that the 8259A is not usable as a priority interrupt controller in a Z80 system.

The normal way to respond to the Z80 INTA* signal is to place one of the restarts on the data bus. Like the 8080/8085 system, the restarts will vector the CPU to a location in page zero. As in the other systems, if a monitor occupies page zero, a jump table must redirect the processor to another location in memory.

In order to establish priorities, a choice must be made between a priority interrupt controller circuit that uses restarts, a software polling routine, or the priority chain. The design philosophy of the Z80 family supports the priority-chain method of establishing priorities in the interrupt system. First, the interrupt machine cycle deliberately introduces two wait states that allow the INTA* signal to pass down the chain. Second, all the currently available interface chips made by Zilog for the Z80 family have a priority in and priority out feature. Thus, the capability to implement a priority chain is inherent in the Z80 family support chips.

Finally, mode 0 is the default mode. When the Z80 is reset, this mode is enabled. To transfer back to mode 0 without resetting the system can be done by performing IM0. This instruction is not found in the 8080/8085 systems. IM0 sets the CPU to mode 0 operation.

Mode 1

When this mode is selected by the programmer, the Z80 responds to interrupt requests on the INT* pin by generating an internal vector that transfers the CPU to 00 38 hex. To implement this mode, the programmer must use IM1, which sets interrupt mode 1. Remember, this mode is accessed by pulling the INT* pin low. If the Z80 is in mode 1, it will not recognize the mode 0 restarts.

Mode 2

This mode of operation allows the programmer to vector to any location in memory. When the CPU responds with an INTA* signal, external circuitry must place a low-order address byte onto the bus. This byte is combined with the high-order byte stored in the interrupt vector register to form a complete 16-bit address. The 16-bit address does not point to the start of a service routine; rather, it points to a location in an address table where the address of the first instruction of a service routine is located.

Example 11-7 begins with an initialization sequence. First, the A register is loaded with 0A hex. This is the page where the address table will be stored. Then 0A is transferred into the interrupt vector register with the LD I, A instruction. Mode 2 is activated by performing IM2. Finally, the INT* input is turned on through the use of the EI instruction. Program flow then enters the main task.

When the Z80 responds to a request on the INT* pin, it generates an INTA*. If more than one device could have caused the interrupt, a method of establishing priorities must be used to prevent multiple devices from responding. In a Z80 system, that method is most likely the priority chain. When the device causing the interrupt receives the INTA* signal, it responds by placing the low-order address byte on the data bus. This must be done in such a way that the D0 input is logic 0.

In our example, assume that the byte inputted from the external circuitry was 00 hex. This combines to form the address 0A 00. The CPU then vectors to this address, where it finds the address of the service routine to be performed. The address table in our listing has 00 0B in the first two locations. The first byte is the low-order byte of the address. The second byte is the high-order byte of the address. When the Z80 has obtained this address, it places it in the program counter, then fetches an instruction from this location.

As you can see, each entry in the address table is a 16-bit address. This means every time the address table is accessed, 2 bytes are read. Internal Z80 architecture

EXAMPLE 11-7

HEX ADDRESS	HEX OP CODE	MNEMONIC	COMMENTS	OCTAL ADDRESS	OCTAL OP CODE
			Z80 Mode 2		
03 00		LD A			
03 01		0A			
03 02		LDI A			
03 03		IM 2			
03 04		EI			
03 05			Main task		
0A 00		00			
0A 01		0B			
0A 02		xx			
0A 03		xx			
0A 04		xx			
0A 05		.			
.		.			
.		.			
.					
0B 00			PUSH reg start service code		

requires the addresses to be stored at even-byte boundaries. This is why the external circuit that provides the low-order address byte must input D0 at a logic 0.

The RETN Instruction

When a non-maskable interrupt is serviced, a copy of IFF1, interrupt flip-flop 1, is transferred to IFF2, interrupt flip-flop 2. These flip-flops indicate the status of the mask-

able interrupt pin. Issuing EI sets both flip-flops, allowing interrupts from INT*. DI will
clear both flip-flops. As with the 8080/8085 system, the acceptance of any interrupt
disables the interrupt function until another EI is issued. So when the NMI* is accepted,
the maskable interrupts are disabled. It is possible that the maskable interrupts were not
enabled when the Z80 accepted NMI*. This means that it would be incorrect to end a
service routine for NMI* with an EI–RET sequence. Rather, the copied value in IFF2
can be transferred back to IFF1 at the end of the service routine by ending the routine
with RETN. This instruction restores the maskable condition of the INT* pin to the
status it had prior to the acceptance of the NMI* interrupt.

Triggering Characteristics of the Inputs

The INT* input is an active low-level sensitive input. The NMI* input is a negative-
going edge-sensitive input. Neither is acknowledged until the current instruction cycle
is completed. The BUSRQ* signal, when active low, will override either of these signals. This means the BUSRQ* signal has a higher priority than either of the interrupt
functions.

11-8 SECURITY DOOR PROJECT

This project is a good example of how to use interrupts to free the CPU from a task that
might need occasional attention. In this situation, the computer will monitor two security
doors. Upon receipt of the correct code, the CPU will generate an output that will activate a solenoid latch to open a door. Door 2 will have an additional security feature.
If this door is left open for more than a minute, an alarm will sound.

The two interface chips used in this project are an 8255, programmable peripheral
interface, and an 8253, programmable interval timer. The 8255 will be used in a mode
that has not yet been discussed. Therefore, before investigating the project in detail, we
will look at this mode of operation.

8255 Mode 1, Status-Driven I/O

When the 8255 is placed in mode 1 through the use of a mode control word, certain pins
from port C take on predefined hardware tasks associated with the operational requirements of the mode. Figure 11-14 shows the logical functions when the 8255 is placed
into mode 1.

When a group is placed into mode 1 input, the functional layout is indicated by
11-14   (a) and (b). As can be seen, an input port in this mode has two status lines that
interface to the device the 8255 is controlling. These lines are STB* and IBF. The STB*
line is an input to the 8255 used by the device to gate information into the 8255 input
port. IBF represents input buffer full. This signal should be monitored by the device
attached to the 8255. When high, the device should refrain from strobing information

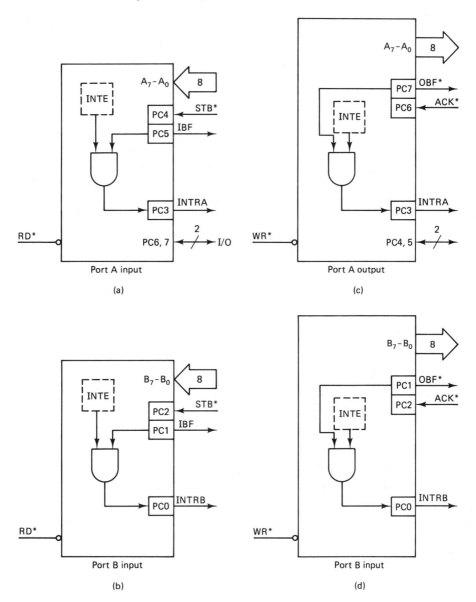

FIGURE 11-14 8255 mode 1.

into the 8255. If the IBF signal is ignored, the old information will be overwritten by the new information.

The third status line is an INTR output that interfaces to the CPU. Upon receipt of data into a port, the 8255 can generate an interrupt request if the INTE mask bit is set high. If this mask bit is set low, the INTR output line is prevented from going high.

Typical input sequence.   Mode 1 is referred to as status-driven, because data transfers will not take place unless the logic levels of the status lines are correct. This means that data transfers are conditional. In contrast, mode 0 used unconditional data transfers. In conditional data transfers, the status lines provide "handshaking" signals that allow the 8255 to talk to the device it is controlling and allow the 8255 to talk to the CPU.

A typical input data transfer begins with the device checking the status of the IBF line. If this line is high, the device will refrain from inputting new information. Once this line is sensed at a low logic level, the device connected to the 8255 will strobe information into the port by pulling the STB* line low. At this time, the information is gated into the port, where it is latched. Once this happens, the IBF signal goes high, preventing further data transfers. If the INTE mask bit is set, the output of the internal AND gate will go high, causing an INTR signal to be generated.

When the CPU accepts the INTR signal at its INT pin, a service routine is called to read the data. When the RD* function of the 8255 is accessed, the data is transferred into the CPU, IBF goes low, and the INTR request from the 8255 is cleared. The device senses IBF going low, which will allow it to transfer another byte of information.

When the INTE mask bit is set, the process of inputting data causes an interrupt. If the mask bit is reset, the input port can not cause an interrupt. In this case, the 8255 must wait to be polled. To set the mask bit, a set/reset control word is sent to the 8255 via the control port. The pin location accessed is PC4 for group A and PC2 for group B. These mask bits occupy the logical positions indicated, and are electrically isolated from the STB* function. This means that it is not possible to determine the status of the mask bit by sensing the logic level on the STB* input pins. To determine the status of these bits, a status read operation must be performed. We will look at this right after we discuss a typical output sequence.

Typical output sequence.   Figures 11-14 (c) and (d) show the functional layout of the ports when they are configured as output ports. Two new status lines are now in use. These are OBF*, output buffer full, and ACK*, acknowledge. In a typical polled output sequence, the CPU monitors the status of OBF*. If OBF* is low, the output port contains valid information that has not yet been gated to the device. So when OBF* is low, the CPU will refrain from sending additional information.

When the device is ready to accept information, it checks OBF*. If it is low, the device generates a low-level ACK* pulse. This pulse gates information into the device and sets OBF high. The next time the CPU polls the OBF* status bit, it detects a high and transfers the next byte.

In an output situation using interrupts, the CPU must enable INTR by setting the mask bit. These bits are PC6 for group A and PC2 for group B. As before, they are electrically isolated from the pins, which this time are used for the ACK* function.

Once the mask is set, the CPU must transfer the first byte to start the cycle. When this first byte is transferred, the OBF* output goes low. This is sensed by the device, which, when ready, generates an ACK*. The ACK* going low transfers the information to the device and sends OBF* back high. When OBF* goes high, the output of the internal AND gate goes high, signaling an interrupt. This request causes the CPU to execute a service routine that sends another byte of information, repeating the process.

The status register.   The status register layout is shown in Figure 11-15. Please note that the status flags change position and function for different formats. It is possible to mix modes and input/output configurations. Port A can be mode 1 input while port B is mode 1 output or even mode 0 input or output. In the example that follows, both group A and group B are configured to mode 1 input. This means that the status-word format we will be using is depicted in Figure 11-15 (a). To obtain this status information, the CPU must perform an RD* from port C. Finally, two port C pins are available for I/O. These two pins are either PC6 and PC7 or PC5 and PC4, depending on the configuration programmed. When used as outputs, these lines are set or cleared using the set/reset control word. When used as inputs, the logic levels can be monitored from the status register.

Input configuration

I/O	I/O	IBF_A	$INTE_A$	INTRA	$INTE_B$	IBF	$INTR_B$

(a)

Output configuration

$\overline{OBF}_A$	$INTE_A$	I/O	I/O	INTRA	$INTE_B$	OBF_B^*	$INTR_B$

(b)

FIGURE 11-15 8255 status-word format.

Project Implementation

Refer to Layout Sheet 11-1. The objective indicates that a computer system will monitor two security doors. Access codes will be checked by the program logic. If correct, the door will be opened; if incorrect, a security guard station will be informed that an invalid code was tried. In addition to this security, door 2 has a timing function associated with it. Should this door be open more than one minute at a time, an alarm will sound. The only way to deactivate this alarm will be to reset the system.

The computer controlling the project will be based on an 8085. Signals will be transferred into and out of the computer via isolated I/O. Two support chips, an 8255 programmable peripheral interface and an 8253 programmable interval timer, will be used to help implement the security system. This system will be interrupt driven, with the CPU spending most of its time performing other tasks. In our documentation we will refer to these other functions as the *main task*.

The logical connections to the support chips are diagrammed in Figure 11-16. The 8255 will be configured in mode 1 operation with both port A and port B designated as inputs. As we know, most of port C handles the handshaking signals necessary to im-

Layout Sheet 11-1

SECURITY DOOR PROJECT

OBJECTIVE:

To monitor the access code for two security doors. If improper access codes are entered, inform a security guard through an output. Additionally, if door 2 is open for more than a minute, sound an alarm.

HARDWARE ENVIRONMENT:

8085-based CPU
Isolated I/O

Support Chips:

1. 8255, PPI, single-line decoded from A7, mode 1 status-driven I/O with interrupt capability

   Port A input for access code from door 1
   Port B input for access code from door 2
   Port C predefined hardware functions used in mode 1,
       PC6, PC7, outputs—gate control 8253 counter 0, counter 1, respectively
2. 8253, timer, single-line decoded from A6

   Counter 0, oneshot mode, door 1 solenoid control
   Counter 1, oneshot mode, door 2 solenoid control
   Counter 2, interrupt mode, door 2 alarm trigger

SOFTWARE ENVIRONMENT

Memory Map:

03 00 — initialization routine
03 2B — main task
05 08 — polling routine
07 00 — open door 2 routine
08 00 — open door 1 routine

Register Usage:

A — general-purpose, I/O

Layout Sheet 11-1 (*continued*)

Port Allocations:

04 — door 1 security panel
05 — door 2 security panel
06 — door 2 alarm
80 — 8255 port A, door 1 access code input
81 — 8255 port B, door 2 access code input
83 — 8255 control register, bit set/reset register
40 — counter 0, door 1 solenoid control
41 — counter 1, door 2 solenoid control
42 — counter 2, door 2 monitor
43 — 8253 control register

Special Codes:

10110110, mode 1 port A, B; PC6, PC7 outputs
00001001, activate 8255 group A interrupt function
00000101, activate 8255 group B interrupt function
00001100, resets PC6
00001110, resets PC7
00001101, sets PC6
00001111, sets PC7
00010010, counter 0 to mode 1, use lower byte only
01010010, counter 1 to mode 1, use lower byte only
10010000, counter 2 to mode 0, use lower byte only

HARDWARE/SOFTWARE INTERFACE:

Standard data bus interface connections

plement this mode. A key encoder circuit will read a magnetic key code, strobe this information into the CPU, and wait for a computer response. The CPU will recognize an entry attempt when it receives an interrupt. After polling to determine which interrupt port signaled, the CPU will read the key code. If the code is correct, a pulse will be sent to the 8253 gate controls via PC6 or PC7. This pulse will activate a counter on the 8253 that is configured for oneshot operation. The oneshot pulse activates a solenoid that unlocks the door. This is similar to a buzzer system in an apartment building. When the door is shut it will automatically relock when the oneshot pulse elapses.

Door 2 is timed when it is open. Counter 2 of the 8253 is set to 60 seconds. The

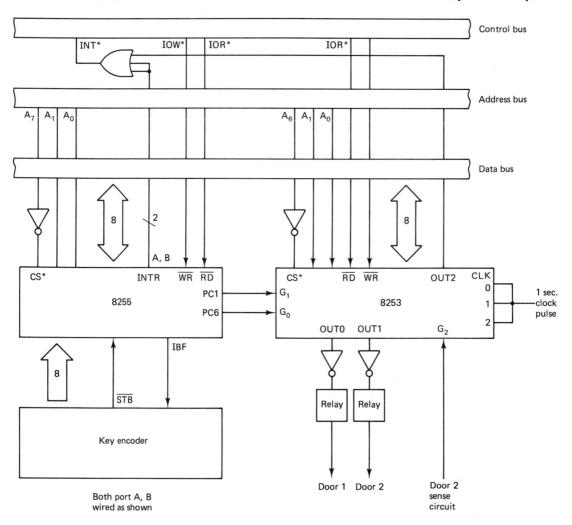

FIGURE 11-16 Security door circuit.

gate control of this counter is operated by a switch attached to door 2. When the door is closed, the logic level from the switch, applied to the gate, prevents counter 2 from timing down. When the door is open, counter 2 can time down. If the counter reaches terminal count, it will generate an interrupt from OUT 2.

The port allocations and special codes used in this project are found in Layout Sheet 11-1. Ports 04, 05, and 06 were wired into the CPU system prior to this project being implemented. The ports for the additional interface chips are determined by single-line decoding A7 for the 8255 and A6 for the 8253.

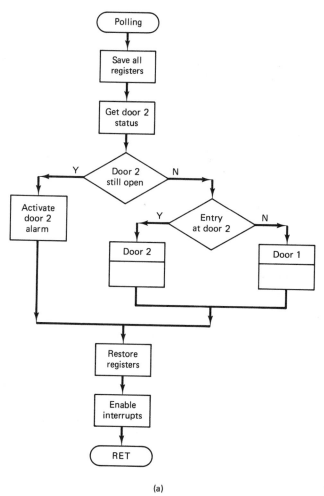

(a)

FIGURE 11-17

The flowcharts for the project are provided in Figure 11-17. The initialization routine is a straight-line routine with no branching. Therefore, the flowchart has not been provided. The polling routine and the service routines for doors 2 and 1 are flowcharted.

The initialization sequence starts at line 03 00 in Example 11-8. It is a series of outputs to the programmable chips. Mode words and control words are sent to the 8255 and 8253. Each is listed in binary, so you can check them against the chip documentation. Pay particular attention to the blocks of code that set PC4 and PC2. These blocks enable the group A and B interrupt functions. You will find them starting at lines 03 04 and 03 08.

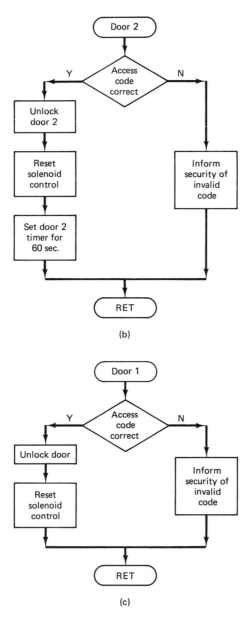

(b)

(c)

FIGURE 11-17 (*continued*)

The 10-second timing for the oneshots is established starting at line 03 20. Note that loading an 8253 counter in this mode does not start the timing process. The gate must receive a rising edge. Since PC6 and PC7 were cleared earlier in the initialization sequence, the oneshot counter will not activate until instructed to do so in a service routine.

EXAMPLE 11-8

HEX ADDRESS	HEX OP CODE	MNEMONIC	COMMENTS	OCTAL ADDRESS	OCTAL OP CODE
03 00	3E	MVI A	Mode 1 input	003 000	076
03 01		B6	1011 0110	003 001	
03 02	D3	OUT		003 002	323
03 03		83		003 003	
03 04	3E	MVI A	Enable INTRA	003 004	076
03 05		09	0000 1001	003 005	
03 06	D3	OUT		003 006	323
03 07		83		003 007	
03 08	3E	MVI A	Enable INTRB	003 010	076
03 09		05	0000 0101	003 011	
03 0A	D3	OUT		003 012	323
03 0B		83		003 013	
03 0C	3E	MVI A	Clear PC6	003 014	076
03 0D		0C	0000 1100	003 015	
03 0E	D3	OUT		003 016	323
03 0F		83		003 017	
03 10	3E	MVI A	Clear PC7	003 020	076
03 11		0E	0000 1110	003 021	
03 12	D3	OUT		003 022	323
03 13		83		003 023	
03 14	3E	MVI A	Counter 0, mode 1	003 024	076
03 15		12	0001 0010	003 025	
03 16	D3	OUT		003 026	323
03 17		43		003 027	
03 18	3E	MVI A	Counter 1, mode 1	003 030	076
03 19		52	0101 0010	003 031	
03 1A	DE	OUT		003 032	323
03 1B		43		003 033	

EXAMPLE 11-8 (*continued*)

HEX ADDRESS	HEX OP CODE	MNEMONIC	COMMENTS	OCTAL ADDRESS	OCTAL OP CODE
03 1C	3E	MVI A			076
03 1D		90	1001 0000		
03 1E	D3	OUT	8253 counter 2 mode 0		323
03 1F		43			
03 20	3E	MVI A	Counter 0, counter 1		076
03 21		0A	Set for 10-second pulses		
03 22	D3	OUT			323
03 23		40			
03 24	D3	OUT			323
03 25		41			
03 26	0E	MVI C	Set counter 2 for 1-minute		016
03 27		3C	interval		
03 28	D3	OUT			323
03 29		42			
03 2A	FB	EI			373
		.	Main task		
		.			
		.			
		.			
		.			
05 08	F5	PUSH PSW		005 010	365
05 09	C5	PUSH B		005 011	305
05 0A	D5	PUSH D		005 012	325
05 0B	E5	PUSH H		005 013	345
05 0C	3E	MVI A	Latch and read counter 2	005 014	076
05 0D		80		005 015	
05 0E	D3	OUT		005 016	323
05 0F		43		005 017	
05 10	DB	IN		005 020	333
05 11		42		005 021	

416

EXAMPLE 11-8 (*continued*)

Hex Address	Hex Op Code	Mnemonic	Comments	Octal Address	Octal Op Code
05 12	FE	CPI	Door 2 open?	005 022	376
05 13		00		005 023	
05 14	C2	JNZ	No, go check on door 2	005 024	302
05 15		1C	entry	005 025	
05 16		05		005 026	
05 17	D3	OUT	If open, activate the alarm	005 027	323
05 18		06		005 030	
05 19	C3	JMP	Go to exit sequence	005 031	303
05 1A		2C		005 032	
05 1B		05		005 033	
05 1C	DB	IN	Entry attempted at door 2?	005 034	333
05 1D		82		005 035	
05 1E	E6	ANI		005 036	346
05 1F		01		005 037	
05 20	C2	JNZ	If not, go to door 1 service	005 040	302
05 21		29		005 041	
05 22		05		005 042	
05 23	CD	CALL	If so, service door 2	005 043	315
05 24		00		005 044	
05 25		07		005 045	
05 26	C3	JMP		005 046	303
05 27		2C		005 047	
05 28		05		005 050	
05 29	CD	CALL	Service door 1	005 051	315
05 2A		00		005 052	
05 2B		08		005 053	
05 2C	E1	POP H	Restore main routine	005 054	341
05 2D	D1	POP D	registers	005 055	321
05 2E	C1	POP B		005 056	301
05 2F	F1	POP PSW		005 057	361

EXAMPLE 11-8 (*continued*)

HEX ADDRESS	HEX OP CODE	MNEMONIC	COMMENTS	OCTAL ADDRESS	OCTAL OP CODE
				005 060	373
05 30	FB	EI			
05 31	C9	RET		005 061	311
			Door 2 routine		
07 00	DB	IN	Check door 2 access code	007 000	333
07 01		81		007 001	
07 02	FE	CPI		007 002	376
07 03		51		007 003	
07 04	C2	JNZ	If wrong, go activate	007 004	302
07 05		15	security panel	007 005	
07 06		07		007 006	
07 07	3E	MVI A	OK? Open door 2	007 007	076
07 08		OF		007 010	
07 09	D3	OUT	Pulse PC7	007 011	323
07 0A		83		007 012	
07 0B	3D	DCRA	Reset PC7 for next use	007 013	075
07 0C	D3	OUT		007 014	323
07 0D		83		007 015	
07 0E	3E	MVI A	Allow door 2 to be opened	007 016	076
07 0F		3C	for 1 minute	007 017	
07 10	D3	OUT		007 020	323
07 11		42		007 021	
07 12	C3	JMP		007 022	303
07 13		19		007 023	
07 14		07		007 024	
07 15	3E	MVI A	Indicate bad access code	007 025	076
07 16		02		007 026	
07 17	D3	OUT		007 027	323
07 18		05		007 030	

EXAMPLE 11-8 (*continued*)

HEX ADDRESS	HEX OP CODE	MNEMONIC	COMMENTS	OCTAL ADDRESS	OCTAL OP CODE
07 19	C9	RET		007 031	311
			Door 1 routine		
08 00	DB	IN	Check door 1 access code	010 000	333
08 01		80		010 001	
08 02	FE	CPI		010 002	376
08 03		27		010 003	
08 04	C2	JNZ	If code is wrong, go to	010 004	302
08 05		11	panel output	010 005	
08 06		08		010 006	
08 07	3E	MVI A	If code is right, open door	010 007	076
08 08		0D	pulse PC6	010 010	
08 09	D3	OUT		010 011	323
08 0A		83		010 012	
08 0B	3D	DCR A	Reset PC6 for next use	010 013	075
08 0C	D3	OUT		010 014	323
08 0D		83		010 015	
08 0E	C3	JMP		010 016	303
08 0F		15		010 017	
08 10		08		010 020	
08 11	3E	MVI A	Indicate incorrect code	010 021	076
08 12		01	at door 1	010 022	
08 13	D3	OUT		010 023	323
08 14		04		010 024	
08 15	C9	RET		010 025	311

The polling routine begins at line 05 08. It is accessed via a jump table. The vector that caused this particular polling routine to be called was restart 1.

The first task performed by the polling routine is to save all the register values from the main task. The logic then determines the cause of the interrupt. The order in which the devices are polled establishes the situation of door 2 being open more than one minute as the highest priority. Attempted entry at door 2 is the second highest priority. Attempted entry at door 1 is the lowest priority in this system.

The polling routine will pass control to the proper service routine. Note that line 05 17 generates a device-select pulse that activates an alarm. Since this control pulse was needed to turn something on, the data in the A register was immaterial. In addition, because this was such a simple function to implement, the polling routine logic performed the operation rather than CALL another section of code.

The polling routine finishes by restoring all registers, then reenabling the interrupt system with EI. Since all service routines reenter the polling routine when finished, the exit sequence at the end of the polling routine takes the place of the exit sequences normally found at the end of a service routine. This method of restoring and reenabling saves some bytes, especially if there are a lot of service routines.

The door 2 service routine begins at 07 00. It starts by reading the key code stored in port B of the 8255. If the code matches 51 hex, the door will be unlocked. This process is carried out by setting PC7. Doing so provides a rising edge at gate 1 of the 8253. The oneshot will then activate, turning on the solenoid controlling the door lock. The section of code at line 07 0B takes PC7 low. This prepares the 8255 so that it can provide a rising edge the next time door 2 must be opened. Taking the gate low has no effect on the oneshot action. Right after unlocking the door, the door 2 counter is reset to 60 seconds. If the door is not closed prior to this time, an alarm will sound. Note that when the door is closed, the counter will pause. The remaining value can be used to generate an interrupt should someone force door 2 open. Only valid entries will reset this counter. This means that the maximum elapsed time prior to an alarm sounding is one minute after the door has been opened.

If an incorrect code was entered, the service routine jumps to 07 15, where an output informs security that an invalid code has been entered.

The structure of the door 1 service routine is identical to the door 2 routine structure, with the exception of resetting counter 2 in the 8253. Functionally, it checks for access code 27 and opens door 1 by pulsing PC6.

11-9 CLOSING THOUGHTS

The proper use of interrupts greatly enhances the power of the system being used. It also increases the complexity of the control functions. This makes it harder to troubleshoot than the system that polls until it receives the information for which it is waiting. In this chapter we saw how to set up service routines with and without polling and looked at the interrupt architecture of the 8080, 8085, and Z80. Additionally, we learned about two different ways to set up priorities using hardware. One method relied on the use of an interrupt controller; the second relied on the use of the priority chain.

Jump tables, restart instructions, masking interrupts, and interrupt problems such as low-priority lockout were discussed. The chapter finished with an interrupt project that operated two security doors. In this project we learned about 8255 mode 1 operation.

One parting comment. We saw that it is necessary to save the main task registers either before polling or before the service routine began. These registers were saved on the stack. In some cases, it will be necessary to save register values associated with service routines. A typical instance involves a counter that increments each time the service routine is called. Trying to save this information on the stack will not work. Interrupts, being asynchronous, can occur at any time. This means that the stack pointer could be pointing to the correct location to retrieve our data or a moment later be pointing to some other data. Information that must be remembered between interrupts should be stored in memory, then retrieved when needed. In Z80 systems, if enough registers are available, interrupt data could be stored in the alternate register set. This set could then be activated when the interrupt occurred.

SUMMARY

1. Interrupts are used to signal the processor that a task not associated with the main program needs attention. If an interrupt system has been turned on, it will respond to the request at the end of the current instruction cycle.

2. In a single-line system with multiple devices sharing a common interrupt request line, the processor should enter a polling routine upon acknowledging the interrupt request. It is the function of the polling routine to determine which device requested service via the interrupt line.

3. In systems with interrupt controllers or interrupt chains, it is possible to use the RST instructions as vectors. When this is the case, it is possible to bypass the polling process. Control will then pass to a service routine.

4. A service routine is a block of code designed to handle the situation involving the interrupt. Service routines are usually written to interact with specific peripherals.

5. Jump tables are used when it is necessary to place service routines at addresses other than those associated with the restarts. One common use of jump tables involves directing interrupt requests out of page zero because the system monitor is resident in this page.

6. Interrupt control circuitry can become complex. Preventing certain interrupt requests from reaching the processor's attention is referred to as *masking*. In addition to masking, interrupt controllers can establish priorities. In some cases, the priority of interrupts can change dynamically, meaning that priorities change as the interrupt system is used. Fortunately, interrupt controllers are now available to handle

the interrupt system of a computer. The 8259A is an example of such a chip. This controller works well with the 8080/8085 processors. The Z80 interrupt architecture is distributed throughout the system, with each support chip having interrupt control lines. This concept is usually referred to as an *interrupt chain*.

7. The 8085 and Z80 have multiline interrupt capabilities. In addition, each has a non-maskable interrupt that can be used in cases where catastrophic events need immediate attention from the processor. Informing the processor of impending power failure is a typical use for a non-maskable interrupt.

QUESTIONS

1. List two ways in which a processor locked into an infinite loop can be freed from continuing to perform the loop.
2. How many INT request pins are there on the 8080? 8085? Z80?
3. What instruction is used to turn on the 8080 interrupt system?
4. In an 8080-based system, how long must an interrupt request be maintained?
5. How does the 8080 synchronize its operations with interrupt requests?
6. How does an 8080 interrupt machine cycle differ from an op code fetch?
7. What is the function of the INTA control signal?
8. List the hex and octal addresses associated with the restart instructions.
9. Explain how a RST instruction is performed.
10. What is the purpose of a jump table?
11. Explain how the CPU can inadvertently transfer control back to the monitor when it receives a false interrupt signal.
12. What is an alternate name for an interface card?
13. When implementing a single-line system, what logic function is used to gate interrupt requests onto an 8080?
14. When the CPU responds to an interrupt request, what happens to INTE? With this in mind, how are further interrupt requests treated?
15. What does *jamming* mean?
16. How do you change interrupt priorities when using a polling routine?
17. When a service routine is called directly by a restart, what is the first task it should perform?
18. Where is EI usually placed within a service routine?
19. Explain how a priority chain functions.
20. What function does masking have in an interrupt system?
21. Explain how time-critical code can be protected from interrupt requests.
22. What can be done to prevent low-priority lockout?

23. How can high-priority lockout be prevented?
24. What instruction does the 8259 generate in response to an INTA signal?
25. What are the four modes of operation used by an 8259?
26. Which command word is sent to an 8259 first during an initialization sequence?
27. Which mode of operation is the default mode in an 8259?
28. What are the addresses associated with the half restarts in an 8085? List these addresses in hex and octal.
29. Which 8085 interrupt is non-maskable?
30. Which 8085 instruction is used to control the half restarts?
31. Which Z80 interrupt mode is similar to the 8080 interrupt system?
32. What is the hex address used by the Z80 when operating in interrupt mode 1?

LAB ASSIGNMENTS

1. Wire an 8255 to your trainer using the standard system interface used throughout this text. Single-line decode the chip from A7. Configure port A as a mode 1 output port. Initiate the first output as detailed in the section on a typical output sequence. Control the ACK* input from a debounced switch. Perform five data transfers, each time checking to see that the 8255 got the correct data. (Transfer a table with the values 1, 2, 3, 4, and 5.) Have a main task running, perhaps a simple counting program that displays the count as it changes. Verify circuit operation with your instructor.

2. Design an interrupt controller using small- and medium-scale integration. Interface this circuit to your trainer. Have your instructor check the system interface prior to applying power. Write several service routines that output different signatures to a port already wired to the trainer. When the interrupt controller is activated, it should call a service routine. Check to see that the code output corresponds to the controller requests. If the controller is functional, you should be able to interrupt repeatedly without failure. If the logic is set up correctly, low-level interrupts should be interruptible by higher-level interrupts. To see this feature, a time delay will have to be written for the low-level routines, giving you time to manually interrupt the low-level routines.

LAB QUESTIONS

1. In assignment 1, did you notice any effect on the main task when you generated an interrupt request through the 8255?
2. Discuss with your instructor at what point interrupts can begin to interfere with the

main task. Is it possible to lock out the main task by continuously servicing interrupts?

3. Turn in your schematic for assignment 2 with an explanation of circuit operation.

4. What must occur in your low-level service routines so higher-level requests from your controller can interrupt the computer as soon as the current instruction cycle is completed?

5. What do you think would happen to the interrupt system if the stack were accidentally located in a hole in the memory map?

12

HARDWARE TROUBLESHOOTING

At the end of this chapter you should be familiar with:

1. standard troubleshooting techniques as they apply to microprocessors
2. the importance of knowing loading effects of test equipment when inserted into a computer
3. the technique of building a test program that allows you to monitor computer information on an oscilloscope
4. how to interpret computer signals as they appear on an oscilloscope
5. some of the functions of advanced test equipment designed specifically to test computer circuitry

INTRODUCTION

This chapter deals with the equipment and techniques used when troubleshooting the hardware of a computer system. We will start with a section on what not to do, followed by a section on commonly available test equipment that can be used to troubleshoot computer circuitry. The strengths, weaknesses, and limitations of this equipment when used for computer troubleshooting will be explained.

The heart of the chapter will detail techniques that can be used to isolate faults in computer circuitry. The order in which the techniques will be employed can be determined by the type of problem or suspected type of problem. For beginning computer technicians, however, a structured troubleshooting task list is recommended. Such a list can follow the order in which the tasks are performed here or follow an outline of steps developed by the manufacturer of the equipment you are fixing. In either case, following standard procedures improves thoroughness. It is true that, on occasion, intuitive reasoning leads to quicker solutions, but as a rule the technician who is thorough will spend less time over many projects than the technician who relies on intuition.

The chapter concludes with a look at some advanced test equipment specifically designed to test computer circuitry. If you are lucky enough to have access to such equipment, spend the time to become familiar with all the features available. The equipment, which we will discuss generally rather than specifically, has many functions that are hard to understand at first. Once mastered, these complex functions can greatly reduce the amount of time spent finding a problem. Typically, the equipment discussed in this last section of the chapter is expensive. If you do not understand how to use all the features, the money spent for such equipment will be wasted.

12-1 WHAT NOT TO DO

As in regular troubleshooting, there are certain things that should not be done when working on computer systems. Some of what follows is a carry-over from regular troubleshooting rules; other points are specific to computer troubleshooting:

1. Do not remove or insert components or PC cards with power applied. It is a good idea to wait 10 to 15 seconds so charges built up on the bypass and decoupling capacitors have a chance to dissipate.

2. Do not push on ICs or components. Many beginning technicians seem to think that perhaps a part is loose or not making good contact, and push the suspected part. Such pushing can stress the PC board, creating tiny cracks in the traces. These cracks are frequently hard to find, often requiring a magnifying glass to locate.

3. Do not measure voltages with the meter set to measure current. Resistors, capacitors, and the components that you worked with in your first electronics class are better able to handle such mistakes on your part. ICs are more sensitive. What is really being stressed here is, Do not forget your fundamentals now that you are working on advanced equipment.

4. Do not use probes with bulky tips. Pin spacing in ICs is tight. Standard TTL mechanical specifications have pins spaced a tenth of an inch apart. A fat probe tip may short two pins together, damaging an IC.

5. Do not remove ICs or PC cards from a system *unless you suspect the card or part is bad.* There are several reasons why you should follow this guideline. First, many ICs are static sensitive. Removal may damage a good IC. If you do decide an IC is bad, remember, you could be wrong. Follow antistatic procedures as outlined by the chip manufacturer. This usually involves grounding yourself, having antistatic mats on the floor, and placing the chip in antistatic conductive foam when removed. The second reason this guideline should be followed involves the socket reliability. Some technicians, upon seeing sockets, think ''Good, I can remove the part, stick a new one in, and see what happens.'' As already mentioned, this could damage the chip; it can also damage the socket. Unless a socket is designed as a zero force insertion socket, frequent removal and insertion will spread the socket contacts. This could lead to a bad connection between the IC and the socket. Remember, most sockets are not designed for frequent removals and insertions, so try to keep these to a minimum. Edge connector cards are usually plated with a fine layer of gold. This layer is placed on the contacts to inhibit corrosion. Removal and insertion of edge connector cards wears away this plating. Consequently, contacts can degrade, corrosion can build up, and a card that worked stops working because the technician could not resist the ''let's remove this and see what happens'' technique of troubleshooting.

6. Do not use a probe or piece of test equipment without knowing how it will affect the loading of the circuit under test. Pay close attention to both input impedance and capacitive characteristics of the probe or test equipment. It is possible to exceed the capacitive load limit of drivers by inserting a probe into a circuit. A good oscilloscope usually has 35 pF or less at its inputs. In some cases this may be too high. Probes with input capacitance of 2 to 5 pF may be required. Fortunately, such probes have been designed specifically for computer work.

12-2 STANDARD EQUIPMENT

Logic Probes

Logic probes are great for troubleshooting steady-state problems. A logic probe's usefulness decreases when it is necessary to work with a system under dynamic conditions. The probe will tell you if a line is pulsing. It does not tell you anything about the timing of the line, nor does it tell you anything about the shape of the waveform. This information can be vital when looking for problems under dynamic conditions. Does the foregoing indicate that a probe is limited in microcomputer troubleshooting? Yes and no. If it is possible to place the system in single-step mode, where conditions can be held static, then the probe becomes very useful. Later, in the section on techniques, we will investigate a way in which the computer can be single stepped, allowing the use of a probe.

Do not use a probe to check power supply voltages. The probe detects logic levels, not voltages. A standard TTL chip requires a Vcc between 4.75 and 5.25 V. If a probe is touched to the Vcc pin, it will indicate a logic 1 when the power supply voltage is correct. It will also indicate a logic 1 as low as 2 V. Obviously 2 V is not enough to handle the Vcc requirements of the chip. Use a DVM to measure voltages.

Digital Multimeter

A good digital multimeter will be required to measure voltages and check for opens and shorts. This meter should have a high input impedance and low capacitance at the inputs. When using the voltage function, measure the voltages at the pins of the ICs that you suspect are bad. Measurements taken from the circuit side of the board may indicate a correct voltage, while a measurement taken from the component side of the board may show that voltage to be missing. This is usually caused by a bad socket-to-chip connection. The ohmmeter will be used to detect shorts between signal lines, shorts between Vcc and signal lines, and shorts between signal lines and ground. In other situations, when signals are present at one part of the circuit and not another, the ohmmeter can be used to check for opens. Later, when discussing troubleshooting techniques, we will look at some ways that can be used to reduce the number of lines that are checked.

Oscilloscope

The oscilloscope is a great tool for investigating repetitive waveforms. Asynchronous events, glitches that occur infrequently and randomly, and waveforms that change as program logic changes are difficult to monitor with an oscilloscope. If possible, try to use a storage oscilloscope. An oscilloscope is most useful in situations where most of the computer circuitry is functioning. Short looping test programs can then be written to produce repetitive waveforms that the scope can monitor. Timing problems can often be found using the scope to track a looping program as it pulses the control, address, and data-bus lines. At a minimum, you should have a dual-trace scope with a bandwidth well in excess of the frequency at which the master clock drives the computer. Learn the characteristics of the triggering system of the scope. Pay close attention to the alternate method of triggering. In some scopes, timing relationships between different signals can be obscured if the triggering is not used correctly. Be familiar with the use of the external triggering circuitry of the scope you are using. It will be necessary in many cases to trigger from a waveform generated by the computer. As with any piece of equipment, know the loading factors involved when the test equipment is attached to the circuit under test.

Signal Generator

There will be times when it will be convenient to input a signal into the system, then trace that signal to the point in the system where the signal disappears. To do this, you will require a signal generator that outputs TTL-compatible waveforms.

Current Probe

A current probe detects the presence of current in a wire by sensing the changing magnetic field around the wire. In cases of a line shorted to ground, the logic probe is little help—there will be no voltage for it to measure. Current will flow, though, allowing the current probe to detect the signal, perhaps the one generated by our signal generator. When the current is no longer detected, the point in the circuit that is causing the problem has been found. More about this procedure later.

12-3 TROUBLESHOOTING TECHNIQUES

The most important thing that can be done when starting to troubleshoot a piece of equipment is to learn how it operates when it is working correctly. If you have a working piece of equipment, study its normal operation. Do not wait to do this until a broken model enters the shop. Learn about the equipment you will fix beforehand, if possible. Some of the information that you should determine is:

1. What does the system do when first powered up? Is a signature displayed that indicates if the system is working? If so, what is it and where will it be displayed? What is it likely to mean if the signature does not appear?

2. If you have a copy of the system monitor, study how it operates the system. At a minimum, you should be familiar with any initialization sequences that must occur when the system is powered up.

3. Study the schematics for the equipment you will fix. Make sure you know how to read them. Locate the physical placement of the parts shown in the schematic. Once the parts are located, record information about the parts that might be important. For instance, does the part normally run hot?

4. Try to obtain information from the manufacturer on how often a part fails. Associated with this, find out what symptoms are connected with such a failure. If you have difficulty getting this information, start your own log to record this information as broken equipment comes into the shop.

5. Learn the bus structure of the computers you will fix.

6. Learn the port structure used by the computer. What port numbers are in use? How are they decoded? Is there the possibility of ambiguities being created if new ports are added to the computer?

7. Determine the memory map for the system. Either get this information from the manufacturer or develop it yourself by analyzing the memory-decoder circuitry. Determine if memory addresses are absolutely decoded. This will let you know how hard it will be to expand memory.

8. In a multicard system, does the position of the cards affect system operation? If so, find out how.

9. Know the power supply characteristics. Determine how much current it can provide. Measure the current draw from the supply when a system is working. Record this information. Then when a malfunctioning unit arrives at the shop, check the current draw. Currents well in excess of the normal indicate a short somewhere in the system.

After you have learned about the systems that you will be asked to fix, develop a procedure for thoroughly checking for faults. Either follow the guidelines established by the manufacturer or use your own. If you are new to microcomputer work, the methods used in this chapter will help you get started.

A Troubleshooting Approach

Physical inspection.   When a computer system comes into the shop for repair, the first thing you should do is inspect it for broken, burnt, or missing parts. A quick visual inspection can usually locate these types of problems. Parts that are inserted backward or incorrect replacement parts are not as easy to spot.

Testing the power supply.   If you do not spot anything obvious, power up the computer. Check the power supply output. If it is not within specifications, turn power off and disconnect the power supply from the system. With a dummy load attached, turn the power supply back on. If the supply is still not within specifications, focus on the power supply before proceeding to the computer itself. It may be that the only problem is the power supply. It is also possible that the voltage went wild; perhaps the regulator malfunctioned. If this is the case, many sections of the computer might have been damaged when this occurred. In either case, fix or replace the power supply first.

If the power supply works correctly with the dummy load, then something in the computer itself is causing the problem. Reconnect the power supply and power up the system. Smell can often lead you to the part that is loading down the supply. Excessive current draw causes power supply loading. The part that is causing the short usually smells or is very hot or both. If you are careful, touch can lead to the bad component. If you are not careful, you can burn your fingers as you probe around the circuit. Try to rely on smell, if possible.

Once the power supply has been checked, you can proceed to the computer itself. *Remember, some systems require multiple voltages.* Check each voltage level delivered by a power supply for correct operation.

Testing the computer.   It is finally time to check the circuit operation of the computer itself. After learning about the computer chip, the bus drivers, the decoder circuitry, the memory chips, the bus system, and the peripheral interface chips, you might wonder where to start checking. This is a very reasonable question. To answer it, we will first list those things a computer must be able to do if it is to work.

1. The computer chip must be able to read from memory.
2. The computer chip must be able to write to memory.
3. The computer chip must be able to read from an I/O port.
4. The computer chip must be able to write to an I/O port.
5. The computer chip must be able to perform internal operations.

To insure that the system is operational, we must find ways to check each of the above operations.

The starting point is to identify the problem. Perhaps we will be fortunate in that the user knows enough to correctly identify the problem. This is not likely, though. In most cases, a system will enter the shop with symptoms listed. These symptoms can often be caused by different malfunctions. It will be up to us to isolate and fix the fault.

When a computer system has been in use for some time, it is likely that the problems encountered will be with the hardware rather than the software. We will start with this assumption, then prove it false if necessary.

Step 1.   The first things that should be checked are the signal inputs into the CPU chip. If the voltage levels into the CPU are incorrect, the CPU may be kept from operating. In an 8080 system, check the following inputs:

1. The power supply level(s) at the CPU pins. Make sure chip ground is at the same potential as the bus ground.
2. The free-running clock inputs to the CPU. Verify that the voltage levels and timing are correct. Use the oscilloscope for this test.
3. The reset pin. If the CPU is constantly held in a reset condition, it will not be able to function. If the level is correct, check to see that the reset circuitry can deliver a reset pulse to the CPU.
4. The ready input. If this is logic 0, the CPU will be placed in a wait state.
5. The hold input. If this input is logic 1, the CPU will enter hold states with the bus lines placed in the tristate condition.
6. The INT line. If the CPU is functioning, it should ignore interrupt requests just after power up. Remember, EI must be performed. If this line is high, determine the device generating the request. If this is a random power up condition, try clearing the request using a logic pulser to generate a clear. If you suspect the CPU is responding to INT requests, monitor the INTA line. If it is pulsing just after power up, something is probably wrong with the CPU chip.

In an 8085 system we should check the following inputs:

1. voltage, including proper grounding
2. clock in (the X1 and X2 inputs)
3. READY

4. reset in

5. HOLD

6. INT

7. TRAP

The only significant addition here is the TRAP input. This is a non-maskable interrupt. If it is asserted incorrectly, the 8085 may be prevented from working.

A system driven by a Z80 should have these processor inputs checked:

1. power supply connections

2. INT*

3. NMI*

4. RESET*

5. BUSRQ*

6. CLOCK

7. WAIT*

As with TRAP, NMI* is non-maskable. If NMI* is low, the processor will not be allowed to perform its power up sequence. It will attempt to respond to the NMI* request. If this is accomplished correctly, the CPU should return to the power up sequence when finished with the service routine.

Step 2. If the inputs to the CPU are correct, the CPU should be working. The system might seem dead, but there could be a lot of processor activity happening. Suppose that the CPU cannot talk to memory. This means that the CPU will receive RST 7s (FF) when accessing memory. The CPU tries to fetch an instruction, gets a RST 7, vectors to 00 38, tries to fetch an instruction, gets another RST 7, then repeats this sequence over and over. In another instance the processor might receive code that is meaningless. Perhaps it is wandering around RAM, trying to execute whatever it fetches. In any case, if the CPU is functional, most of the bus lines should be pulsing. Quickly scan through the outputs from the CPU with a logic probe. Do this at the output of the CPU and the bus drivers. If all the CPU outputs are dead, replace the CPU, assuming you are following the sequence laid down here. If so, you have already checked the CPU inputs.

If you find the bus driver outputs dead, proceed to step 4. Do not replace the buffer/ driver chip yet.

When scanning the bus lines with the logic probe, record those lines that are not changing. There may be some. This can even be the case when the processor is working. The logic being performed might not require a MEMWR*, for example.

Step 3. Turn off power. Check the lines that were not changing for shorts to Vcc or ground. Do not forget that to a changing voltage, DC power supplies look like ground.

Those lines that do not indicate shorts to ground or Vcc can probably be crossed off the list of the lines to check next.

Electrically isolate the CPU from the system. Do this by asserting the BUSRQ* (Z80) or HOLD lines (8080/8085). This will force the CPU to tristate its outputs. Make sure that the lines are indeed tristated. The logic probe should indicate open/bad. If the CPU does not respond to the request to release the bus, verify that the logic level at the pins mentioned above is correct. If so, replace the processor. If the processor does respond by tristating its outputs, you are now ready to check the lines that indicated a short to ground or Vcc. *If something prevents you from using the BUSRQ* or HOLD functions it may be necessary to remove the CPU to perform the next check.*

Inject a TTL-compatible waveform into the computer on the lines that had shorts or appeared stuck at a particular logic level. *Protect your generator by placing a current-limiting resistor in series with the injected signal.* Inject the signal at the output of the CPU to check the CPU-to-bus-driver connection. Follow the injected signal with the current probe. A line shorted to ground may not be able to develop a voltage, but current will certainly flow. When the current probe no longer detects a changing magnetic field, the area of the computer responsible for the problem has been pinpointed. See Figure 12-1 to visualize how this technique can be utilized. Test each suspected line separately. If nothing is found, repeat the process from the output of the buffer. Remember, if the CPU is off, the control signal operating the drivers will be off. Use the schematic and the current probe to follow the signal as it travels down the line under test. The schematic will indicate all the connections to the driver output.

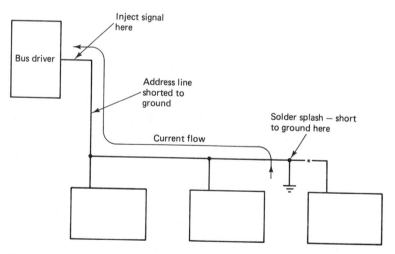

*Probe no longer sensor current.

FIGURE 12-1 Locating bus faults.

Step 4. Turn power off and connect a machine cycle stepper to the CPU. The stepper circuitry will allow you to step the processor by machine cycles. After T2 of each machine cycle, the stepper will force the CPU into a wait state. During this time the address lines, control lines, and data lines will be held in a static state. There is no need to be concerned about the contents of dynamic RAM. If the computer is not functioning, the information will not be usable.

A single-stepper circuit for an 8080-based computer is shown in Figure 12-2. The 8080 signals external devices that it is in a wait state by taking the WAIT output high. When the CPU is running, this line is low. To understand this stepper, assume that the CPU is running. This means that the WAIT line is low. This output is connected to the CLR of the D latch. This forces Q low. The output from the latch is gated through the 8224 to the READY line of the CPU. At the next falling edge of T2, the processor senses that the READY input is low and enters a wait state. When it does this, the WAIT output goes high, freeing the CLR input. The latch will now respond to pulses applied to the clock input. When you have finished inspecting the static conditions on the bus, pulse the latch. This causes Q to go high, allowing the 8080 to complete the machine cycle. Of course, once it proceeds, the WAIT line goes low. This will stop the 8080 at the next subsequent falling edge of T2, when it again enters a wait state.

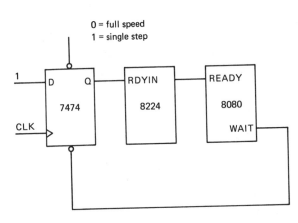

FIGURE 12-2 8080 machine cycle stepper.

A machine cycle stepper for the Z80 and 8085 is shown in Figure 12-3. With the exception of the information gated into test point 1, the stepper circuitry is the same.

When the system is reset, the latch on the right of the diagram has its Q output go high. This allows the CPU to proceed with the machine cycle. The control signals will remain high for a short period of time prior to activating. This small amount of time causes a CLR pulse to be delivered to latch 2, forcing Q2 to go low. At the falling edge of T2, the processor senses the low condition and enters a wait state. During this time, the data lines, address lines, and control signals will be static.

When you have inspected the bus, the machine cycle can be completed by activating the CLR function on latch 1. The push button will force the latch to clear when

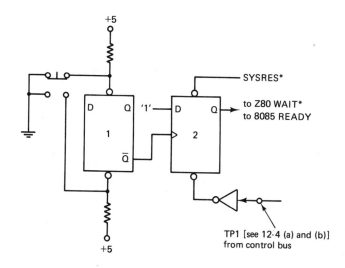

FIGURE 12-3   8085, Z80 machine cycle stepper.

it touches the bottom set of contacts. This will make Q* go high, clocking a 1 into latch 2. When the processor senses the high level coming from Q2, it proceeds with the machine cycle. At the end of the machine cycle, the control lines going high force the CLR on latch 2 to activate. This means that the processor will enter a wait state automatically at the next falling edge of T2.

The timing for the Z80 and 8085 machine cycles is not identical. The circuitry driving TP1 for each processor is shown in Figure 12-4. In (a), we see the signals used in a Z80 system. MEMRQ* covers the memory read and memory write machine cycles. It is prevented from double pulsing during op code fetches by the OR gate with the inverted RFRSH* signal. IOREQ* covers the input and output machine cycles. M1 handles the op code fetch and the interrupt acknowledge machine cycles.

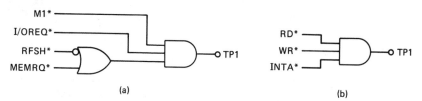

FIGURE 12-4   (a) Z80 machine cycle stepper driver. (b) 8085 machine cycle stepper driver.

The 8085 driver for TP1 is shown in Figure 12-4 (b). The RD* signal takes care of the memory read and IO read cycles, the WR* pulse handles the memory write and the IO write machine cycles, and the INTA* controls the interrupt cycle stepping.

The requirement for TP1 in the circuit in Figure 12-3 is that it go low prior to T2 and stay low during the time the CPU decides if it should enter a wait state. This allows the CLR function of latch 2 to be high while the CPU is in a wait state. Consequently, latch 2 can be clocked by pulsing latch 1 to proceed with the machine cycle. At the end of a machine cycle, TP1 is required to go high, clearing latch 2.

Once the single stepper is connected to the computer, power up the system. The power-up circuitry should force the processor to vector to 00 00 hex. Since the CPU will enter a wait state, this can be verified statically with a logic probe. The control lines for the processor should indicate an op code fetch. Check this pattern with the logic probe too.

The address and control signals are used by the CPU to activate the ROM containing the first instruction to be executed. Locate this ROM on the computer with which you are working. It will either be the monitor ROM or the bootstrap ROM. Since the bus will be held in a static condition as long as the CPU is in a wait state, the control lines and address lines into the ROM can be checked with a logic probe. If they are correct, probe the data output from the ROM. Record the byte presented by the ROM and compare it to the first byte in the monitor listing. If it matches, the CPU has accessed the monitor correctly at power up. Finally, make sure this information reaches the data pins of the CPU. If not, trace the signal path looking for shorts or opens. Another possibility is a bus contention.

If the data out of the ROM is garbled or garbled before it reaches the CPU, it is possible another device or chip turned on at the same time. The most likely candidates are circuits wired to respond to port 00 hex. Turn power off and remove the ROM. Reboot the system. If the data lines still contain information, another device must be on. We are assuming, of course, that shorts and opens were already removed from the bus earlier in the troubleshooting sequence. If the data lines now appear open/bad to the logic probe, the ROM was either faulty or contained the wrong information.

The other possibility that might occur is that the data out of the ROM is correct but never reaches the CPU. If, after checking all the lines for opens or shorts, everything seems to be in order, check the control signals to the data-bus buffer/driver. If these signals are correct, with correct data into the buffer, then the buffer/driver should be replaced. Faulty buffer/drivers for the other signals should be detected easily during this time. After correcting any problems with the buffer/drivers, return to step 2 and verify that there are no stuck lines.

Step 5.   At this point in the troubleshooting process, short-test programs will be written and executed to test for various malfunctions in the system. These programs will be stored in a ROM that will be inserted into the system. This ROM, which we will call an AUTOmatic TEST ROM, will reside in the same memory location as the bootstrap or monitor ROM. This means that the monitor ROM must be removed and replaced with the AUTO TEST ROM. In systems that have the monitor ROM soldered in place, carefully desolder a control line such as CS* or OE*. Then, with a test clip, jumper the desoldered control to Vcc. This will electrically remove the bootstrap or monitor ROM from the system. In systems where the monitor is in a socket, carefully remove the monitor and replace it with the AUTO TEST ROM.

The test programs in the AUTO TEST ROM will help us troubleshoot the system by performing self-diagnostic routines. These routines are stored in ROM because, at this stage of the troubleshooting, RAM has not been tested, nor has the keyboard. Placing the programs in ROM bypasses the RAM and keyboard until they have been checked.

Each test program should be a short repetitive loop that has a narrow goal. That goal should be to test a particular function or section of the computer.

To start the AUTO TEST ROM, place the computer in the single-step mode and reboot the system. Since we already know that the CPU can communicate with the first location in the ROM, this will get the first test program underway.

The start of an AUTO TEST ROM is shown in Example 12-1. The first instruction, EI, enables the interrupt system. We will use this function after we have completed the first test program.

At this point, the only thing we know about the ROM is that there is no problem with location 00 00 hex. It is possible that bus contentions exist at other locations within the ROM. The locations of the short test programs will be checked by single stepping through one pass of the loop. Pressing the step button takes us to the OUT instruction at 00 01 hex. As we progress through the loop, check to see that the information is arriving correctly at the CPU inputs. If it is, no bus contentions exist at the address. Check to see that the CPU is performing the instructions correctly by monitoring the control lines. If the CPU does not increment the address bus correctly or generate the correct control information for the machine cycle in progress, replace the CPU if it is still receiving the correct inputs.

After you have verified a single pass of the test program, remove the single-step control and allow the CPU to free run through the test program. A mechanical switch inserted in the line to the CPU from Q2 in the circuit in Figure 12-3 with a pole connected to Vcc will allow you to toggle between full speed and single step.

Once the short program is running at full speed, the functions being tested can now be analyzed dynamically. The first program in our sample AUTO TEST ROM is pulsing the control lines. In particular, we are interested in the four primary control functions. In a Z80 system such as we are testing in this example, those lines are MEMRQ*, IOREQ*, RD*, and WR*. In an 8080 system they would be MEMRD*, MEMWR*, IN*, and OUT*. In an 8085 system we would check for MEMRD*, MEMWR*, IOWR*, and IORD*. Depending on the bus system in use with the processor, other names may be applicable.

The collected data from our first test run is shown in Figures 12-5 and 12-6. Photograph (a) in 12-5 is taken from IOREQ* and STAT 1*. Analysis of the test program shows five op code fetches. Since STAT 1* indicates an op code fetch, this control line is working correctly. The two STAT 1* pulses just to the right of the center line are the EI and OUT fetches. The two IORQ*s to the right of the screen are the IOWR* machine cycle and the IORD* machine cycle. The IORQ* pulse at the left of the screen is the IORD* machine cycle from the previous pass through the loop.

Photograph (b) from 12-5 compares IOREQ* to MEMRQ*. These control signals should never be active low at the same time. Photograph (c) compares IORQ* with RD*. First note that there are far fewer reads than memory requests. This is due to MEMRQ* pulsing during a dynamic refresh. You should note that the RD* signal can

EXAMPLE 12-1

HEX ADDRESS	HEX OP CODE	MNEMONIC	COMMENTS	OCTAL ADDRESS	OCTAL OP CODE
			Auto test layout		
00 00	FB	EI		000 000	373
00 01	D3	OUT	Simple display	000 001	323
00 02		xx		000 002	
00 03	DB	IN	Simple keyboard	000 003	333
00 04		xx		000 004	
00 05	32	STA		000 005	062
00 06		xx		000 006	
00 07		xx		000 007	
00 08	C3	JMP		000 010	303
00 09		00		000 011	
00 0A		00		000 012	
00 10	C3	JMP	First ROM	000 020	303
00 11		xx	test	000 021	
00 12		xx		000 022	
00 18	C3	JMP	RAM test 1 R/W	000 030	303
00 19		xx	AA = 1010 1010	000 031	
00 1A		xx		000 032	
00 20	C3	JMP	RAM Test 2 R/W	000 040	303
00 21		xx	55 = 0101 0101	000 041	
00 22		xx		000 042	
00 28	C3	JMP	Complex keyboard test	000 050	303
00 29		xx		000 051	
00 2A		xx		000 052	

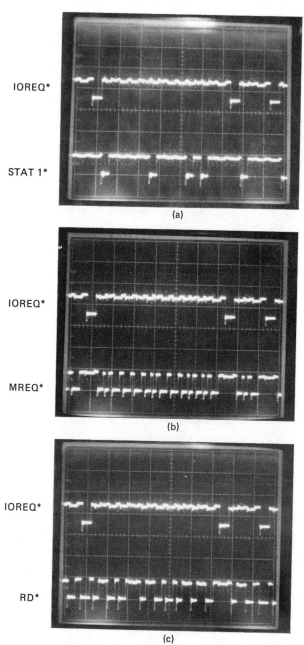

(a)

(b)

(c)

FIGURE 12-5 Control signals developed by Auto Test Program 1 found in Example 12-1.

be low when IORQ* is low. There are two locations on the screen where this happens. These occurrences mark the machine cycle as an IORD*. The IORQ* pulse that does not occur when the RD* is low must mark the IOWR* machine cycle.

The photograph (a) of Figure 12-6 shows the IOWR* cycle clearly. In addition, there is another WR* pulse on the screen. This is the MEMWR* caused by the STA instruction. The fourth division on the screen in photograph (b) of Figure 12-5 shows MEMRQ* low. Coupled with the WR* pulse, this marks the MEMWR* cycle.

The photograph of Figure 12-6 (b) compares the RD* pulses to the WR* pulses. These pulses should never be low at the same time.

The last photograph in the sequence is 12-6 (c). This shows the MCSYNC* pulse available at the STD bus this computer uses. From the falling edge of the IOREQ at the left of the screen to the falling edge of the IORQ* pulse at the far right side of the screen, there are 14 of these pulses. This is the correct number. One pass through the loop should produce the following machine cycles:

EI	op code fetch
OUT	op code fetch
	memory read
	IOWR
IN	op code fetch
	memory read
	IORD
STA	op code fetch
	memory read
	memory read
	memory write
JMP	op code fetch
	memory read
	memory read

Use this information to check your understanding of the control signals presented in the photographs shown in Figures 12-5 and 12-6. The interpretation of information presented on an oscilloscope when testing a CPU is an important skill.

To access the second test program within the ROM, there must be a way for us to get to the start of that routine. Our test programs will be continuous never-ending loops. This is necessary to facilitate scope display. Consequently, logic causing branches to other routines is not usually included. In addition to this, the test programs should be as short as possible to ease single stepping through the routine the first time it is used.

To gain access to the other test programs within the AUTO TEST ROM, we will wire an 8212 as an interrupting port. The logic connections for this circuit are shown in Figure 12-7. Only the inputs wired to the middle octal digit need to be wired to switches; the other five inputs are wired to Vcc. See Chapter 11, Interrupts, for further details.

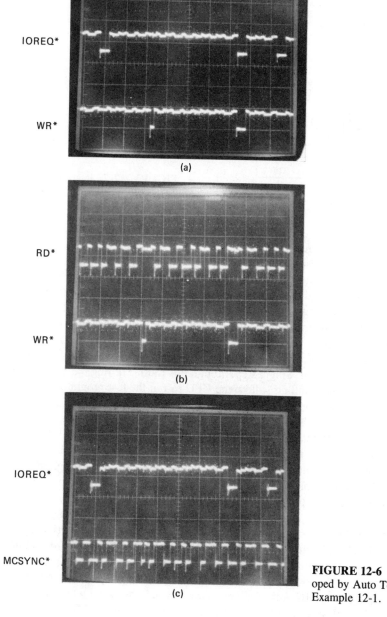

(a)

(b)

(c)

FIGURE 12-6 Control signals developed by Auto Test Program 1 found in Example 12-1.

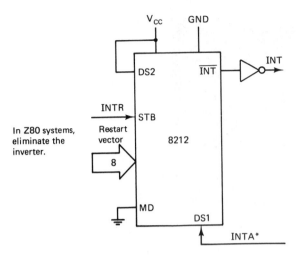

FIGURE 12-7 Interrupt vector circuit.

When the circuit is wired, reboot the system with the computer in the single-step mode. This vectors us to the EI instruction at 00 00 hex. Step through this instruction, enabling the interrupt system. Generate an interrupt request by strobing the restart vector into the 8212. The 8212 will signal an interrupt. Our stepper circuitry will allow us to single step through an interrupt machine cycle, so we can check this feature of the computer at this time. Once the interrupt machine cycle is completed, the CPU should transfer control to the test program specified by the RST we gated into the CPU. In Example 12-1, this would be RST 1, which gets us to the 00 10 hex. A JMP redirects us to the start of the next test program. Single step through this routine during the first pass. Once you have insured no bus conflicts, allow the CPU to run the test program at full speed.

In our case, that program would automatically test the rest of the AUTO TEST ROM for bus contentions. This would be done by checking the locations not in use by test programs for FF. Blank locations not programmed will be FF. The logic structure for such a program is flowcharted in Figure 12-8. Checking just for FF does not insure that there are no bus contentions at any of the addresses tested in the program. Another AUTO TEST ROM with unused locations programmed to 00 hex will have to be inserted into the system. Then the ROM test routine will be run, checking for 00.

Other suggested test programs to use in an AUTO TEST ROM are a RAM test and a complex keyboard test routine. If you have a simple keyboard interface, it might be possible to IN directly from the keyboard port. Otherwise, the keyboard routine will have to be written to initialize the ICs that operate the keyboard. Do not put the initialization sequence into the loop section of the test program. Key closures can be checked by single stepping to the IN from the keyboard and pressing keys while this machine cycle is static. Key closures can then be detected on the data bus.

Other test programs will depend on the system being tested. Possibilities include port drivers, display test routines, and advanced RAM tests. The flowcharts for the RAM

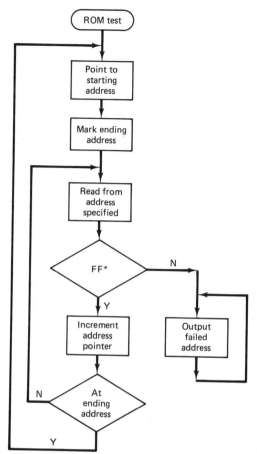

FIGURE 12-8 ROM test flowchart with oscilloscope as an output port.

tests suggested in Figure 12-9 can determine gross RAM failures. Subtle RAM failures such as pattern failures require extensive testing. A gross RAM failure is usually related to a cell not storing or returning the correct value. Pattern failures occur when activity in one cell affects the contents of another cell.

Reading the Oscilloscope

The information displayed in the photographs so far has not been hard to decipher. The control pulses are relatively noise free, are unidirectional signals, and look much as we would expect from seeing idealized waveform drawings in technical literature. As we will see in a moment, it is not always so easy.

Suppose we are running the ROM test routine from the AUTO TEST ROM and a ROM location fails to return the expected FF. The flowchart logic indicates that the

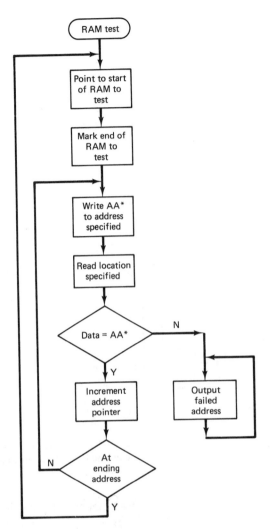

FIGURE 12-9 RAM test flowchart with oscilloscope as an output port.

failed output address should be displayed. This address is repeatedly output by the logic, making it possible for us to read the information from the oscilloscope. This is done because, at this point, the computer may be unable to send the information to an output port correctly. Rather than rely on the computer circuitry, which is suspect at this time, the test equipment must be used to determine the contents of the address bus and data bus.

Example 12-2 is a short test program that outputs information to port 01 hex. It is used in this application to test an output port. It could easily be modified to output a

EXAMPLE 12-2

HEX ADDRESS	HEX OP CODE	MNEMONIC	COMMENTS	OCTAL ADDRESS	OCTAL OP CODE
03 00	3E	MVI A	2 machine cycles	003 000	076
03 01		AF		003 001	
03 02	D3	OUT	3 machine cycles	003 002	323
03 03		01		003 003	
03 04	00	NOP	1 machine cycle	003 004	000
03 05	00	NOP	1 machine cycle	003 005	000
03 06	C3	JMP	3 machine cycles	003 006	303
03 07		00		003 007	
03 08		03		003 010	

failed address. An important part of this example is the number of machine cycles. The program comprises 10 machine cycles. This is the same as the number of divisions across the face of the oscilloscope screen. Additionally, the program has been written to generate a single unique event. In this case, the OUT machine cycle or IOWR cycle will occur once each pass through the loop. This single unique event will be used to trigger the oscilloscope.

The IOWR* pulse is coupled to channel 1 of the scope, with the external trigger also receiving the IOWR* pulse. This waveform is spread so it occupies the entire screen area (see Fig. 12-10 (a)). This can be done by adjusting the time base until two or three pulses are on the screen. Then activate the variable sweep function. This will decalibrate the time base, but in this application that is not important. Adjust the variable sweep control until the trigger pulse is at the left of the screen, with the next pulse just off the right edge of the scope's screen. In Figure 12-10 (a), the pulses are just about placed correctly. In some scopes it may be necessary to activate the times-10 function in addition to the above to spread the trigger pulse as shown in Figure 12-10 (a).

Once the trigger pulse has been spread, it can be coupled into the external trigger or left on the screen for a reference point. In any case, since there are 10 divisions and 10 machine cycles, each division on the scope face will represent one machine cycle. The remaining photographs in Figure 12-10 show control line information generated by

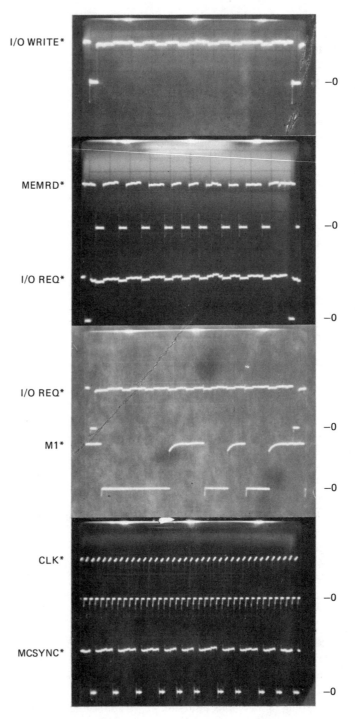

FIGURE 12-10 Interpreting control waveforms using air oscilloscope.

the test program in Example 12-2. There are nine memory reads between the IOWR*
pulses. This agrees with an analysis of the program:

MVI A	op code fetch
	memory read
OUT	op code fetch
	memory read
	IOWR
NOP	op code fetch
NOP	op code fetch
JMP	op code fetch
	memory read
	memory read

The op code fetches and memory read cycles will pulse the memory read control line.
The other control information can be verified as an exercise.

The data bus information generated by this program can be found in Figure 12-11.
These photographs were taken from the scope two lines at a time. The photographs were
then connected together so that all eight lines could be examined at the same time. The
first area of interest is at the far left side of the screen. The first division on the screen
face is used to roughly locate the outputted information. From top to bottom, we see a
10101111 for D7 through D0 respectively. This represents AF hex, which is the data
byte that is placed on the computer's data lines at this time.

You must develop the knack of ignoring the extra noise and invalid information
on the data bus. The contents of this bus are not always specified by the processor. There
will be times when the data is floating, pulled up to Vcc, or just random noise. The
easiest way to determine if data is valid is to leave the control signal that activates the
data transfer on the scope screen. Then superimpose the control information onto the
data bus one line at a time. Record the data as you move the second channel input from
one data line to the next. It also helps if you can quickly scan a trace and recognize
when the bus is in use.

Analyzing data-bus signals.   Figure 12-12 (a) is a tracing taken from D7, shown
in Figure 12-11. It indicates how to tell when the data-bus waveform is indicating a valid
datum. First look at figure (b). This indicates an exponential rise in voltage. Valid data-
bus information is characterized by step changes in voltage. Consequently, this is a
period of invalid data. After the exponential rise is terminated, there is a sharp step
down to logic 0. That part of the waveform is valid data. Figures (c) and (d) indicate
what to look for if a logic 1 follows an exponential rise. A spike or step indicates a
switching point in the waveform. This, coupled with amplitude and timing considerations, determines a valid logic 1. Figure (e) indicates a point in the waveform where the
data bus does not have time to rise between valid intervals. Here we have two successive
logic 0 levels separated by a high-frequency spike, which indicates switching action.

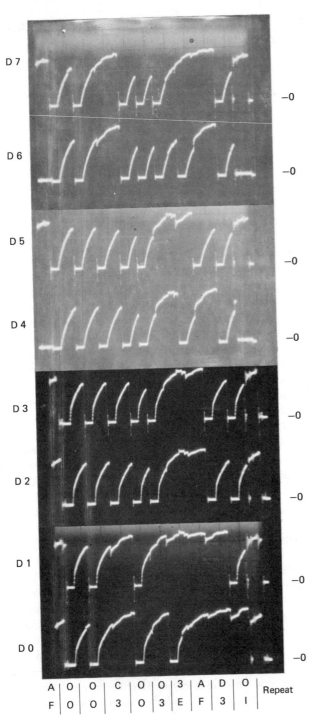

FIGURE 12-11 Interpreting data bus waveforms using an oscilloscope.

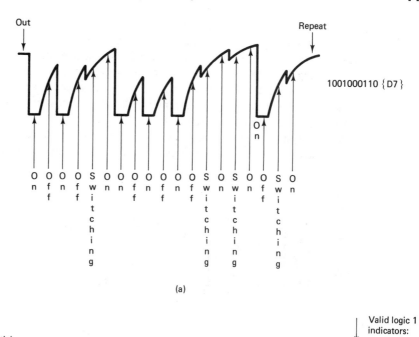

1001000110 {D7}

(a)

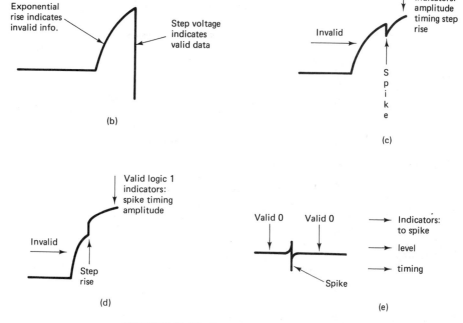

FIGURE 12-12   Data bus waveform analysis.

This information, coupled with a legitimate logic level and the expected timing interval, indicate a valid datum on the bus line. Two such occurrences can be found on D6 and D4 just after the output operation on the left side of the screen.

A tracing from D5 is evaluated using the techniques illustrated in Figure 12-13. You can find this evaluation in Figure 12-13. When the screen image has been evaluated, the projected image is computed by examining the program that generated the waveform. The other data lines are left as exercises.

This analysis technique, coupled with the use of control signals to mark valid times in a data waveform, should make it possible for you to read accurately the data-bus

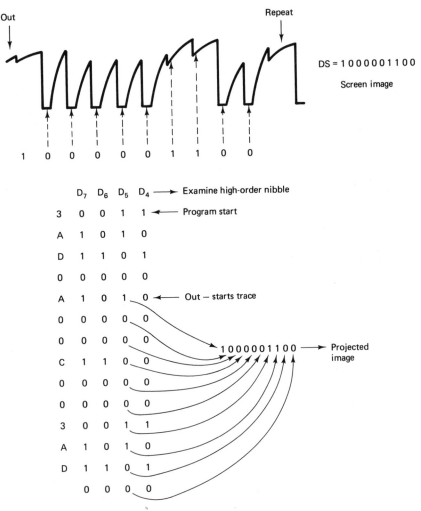

FIGURE 12-13 Using data bus analysis techniques to read D5 taken from Example 12-2.

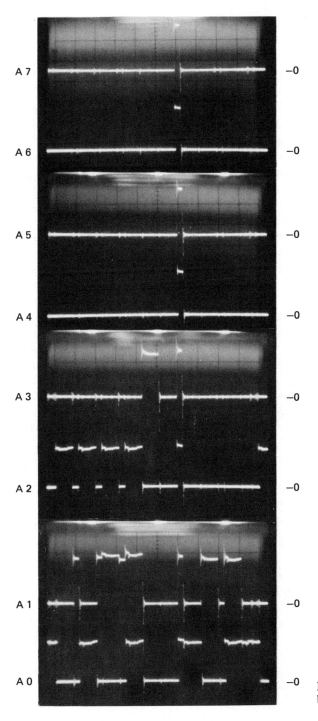

FIGURE 12-14 Interpreting address bus waveforms using an oscilloscope.

information presented on an oscilloscope. It takes time, patience, and above all a stable trigger source into the scope.

Analyzing the address lines.   The address information generated by the test program of Example 12-2 can be found in Figure 12-14. As you should be able to tell, the information is much clearer. The address lines, like the control lines, are unidirectional. This accounts for much of the improvement in the signal quality. Reading the address information is not quite as easy as it seems, however. There are times when the address lines, like the data lines, are not specified. In a Z80 system, these lines are also used for dynamic refresh. This means that there will be times in a Z80 system when valid addresses having nothing to do with the logic of your program will be on the address bus.

In our example, the high-order address is fixed throughout the program, so it was not photographed. The low-order address lines are shown from A7 through A0. These photographs were taken with two traces on the scope face, then assembled for easy reading. At the far left side of the screen, we know that an OUT is taking place. Therefore, the port number should be readable at this location. Scanning the waveforms, a 01 hex can be read from top to bottom. This corresponds with the port number used in the program. In our short test program, this will be the only address placed on the bus that does not occur when memory read is low. Using the MEMRD* signal from Figure 12-10, it is possible to partition the scope face into areas containing addresses that are used by our program. If you look carefully at the grid line just to the right of center, you will notice that all the addresses are high. Yet the MEMRD* pulse in Figure 12-10 is high at this time. The address FF is therefore not of concern in the analysis of our program. Without knowing the contents of the refresh register prior to starting the program, it is not possible to say with certainty that this is a refresh address. The M1* waveform in Figure 12-10 indicates that an op code fetch is ongoing at the grid line just to the right of center. Since dynamic refresh occurs during op code fetches, FF is most likely a refresh address.

If you wish to track refresh addresses, the refresh control signal could be placed on the screen. When this signal is active low, the addressing information would be refresh addresses. Incidentally, the Z80 computer used to obtain these waveforms used static RAM chips. The refresh operation is carried out by the Z80 regardless.

12-4 ADVANCED TEST EQUIPMENT

The following sections present a general overview of concepts used in advanced test equipment. Such equipment is frequently very expensive due to its many advanced features. It is not our intention to analyze a single piece of equipment, but to provide a background that will help you understand why such equipment exists and perhaps encourage you to learn the operation of such equipment if it is available for your use.

Signature Analysis

Signature analysis is based on the idea that a bit stream can be represented by a unique signature that represents the pattern of ones and zeros flowing at a particular point in the circuit. Usually the point under test is the output or input to a particular IO.

   Figure 12-15 depicts a simple block diagram that shows how signature analysis can be applied to a digital circuit. The shift register incorporates feedback paths that affect the values that are shifted from stage to stage. Previous bits stored in the shift register combine logically with new bits at nodes that affect the value to be shifted into a stage. In our example, the logic at the nodes is exclusive OR. At any instant in time, the value in the shift register is a representation of the past inputs and the present inputs. This feedback arrangement allows the shift register to remember what has been sampled. The placement of feedback paths, the number of nodes, and the type of logic used at the node are determined by advanced calculations. If these calculations are done correctly, it is unlikely that different bit streams into a shift register wired in similar fashion to the one shown in Figure 12-15 would produce identical patterns. A typical length for such a shift register is 16 bits.

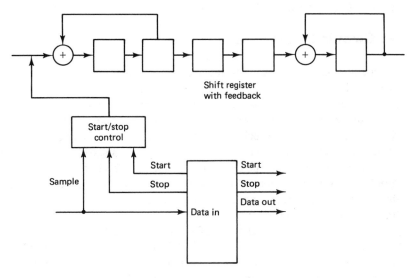

FIGURE 12-15   Signature analysis.

   The start/stop logic tells the shift register when to start sampling data from the point under test. When the stop signal is applied to the shift register logic, the register will contain a pattern that should be unique to the data stream just sampled. This pattern represents the signature of the information just sampled. The number of bits sampled can be far in excess of the storage capacity of the shift register. A data stream from start to stop might be 256 bytes in length, for example. The value in the shift register at the end of the sampling interval has been compressed to the storage capability of the shift register.

This compressed representation, which is the signature for the data stream, can then be compared to a signature that was recorded on a known working piece of equipment. If the signatures do not match, the information at the test point was invalid.

To use signature analysis in a computer system, the circuitry necessary to provide the start and stop signals must be built into the system. This increases the cost of the computer. If the control signals for signature analysis are not built into the system, technicians must provide for this by building it themselves. Furthermore, known good signatures must be collected prior to the actual troubleshooting of the bad circuitry. The technician must also insure that the system is operating in the mode that produces the signatures to be checked. Consider Figure 12-15. If the block under test is an I/O port, the data into this port can change dependent on the application in use. The correct application for the signature to be tested must be loaded into the processor system prior to the troubleshooting process.

If everything is set up for signature analysis, the technician can move from test point to test point in a data path until a bad signature has been detected. The fault will then be located between the last good signature and the bad signature just detected.

In-Circuit Emulators

In-circuit emulators are used to replace the microprocessor chip in a system under test. The emulator takes the place of the processor in the system to be tested. This processor is often called the *target processor*. As far as the remaining circuitry is concerned, the emulator responds as if it were the computer chip. The software features incorporated in the emulator allow the technician or engineer to monitor internal processor operations, usually through a display on a CRT. Register values can be changed, the program counter can be altered, and machine cycles can deliberately be implemented to test certain control lines, ports, or sections of the computer circuitry. The more complex emulators will have powerful programs that allow the operator to control many, if not all, facets of microprocessor operation.

There are two general types of emulators available. Processor-specific emulators will act as a single type of processor. This type of emulator will be less costly. The other type of emulator is one that can replace many different types of processors. Of course, this greater flexibility adds to the cost of the emulator.

Logic Analyzers

Logic analyzers are sometimes referred to as *digital domain analyzers*. This kind of test equipment is specifically designed for troubleshooting computer-based systems.

Analyzers are expensive, complex pieces of equipment. Some analyzers include the ability to perform signature analysis. Data transmissions can be monitored in some analyzers, with the analyzer converting the serial data into parallel format and displaying the information in ASCII code. Despite the complexity and the expense, logic analyzers can be a very important tool in digital troubleshooting. Serious computer technicians will make the effort to learn to use logic analyzers. Seminars, training sessions, and product demonstrations are an excellent way to obtain information about them.

What follows is a brief rundown on some of the features included in most logic analyzers.

1. Multiline displays. An analyzer will display 8- or 16-bit streams or waveforms at a time.

2. Extended trigger capabilities. A typical analyzer can be set to trigger upon recognizing a particular pattern at its inputs. The trigger can be anywhere from 1 bit up to 25 bits in length. In an 8-bit data-bus system, this means the trigger can be set for a particular byte at a particular address with a qualifier bit such as a control line monitored before the analyzer will trigger. Sixteen-bit data-bus systems could be used with analyzers that have more than 25-bit triggers.

3. Storage facilities. An analyzer, once triggered, can store the information leading up to the trigger, following the trigger, or before and after the trigger. This is usually operator selectable. The data can then be analyzed by scrolling through the collected information. Storage capabilities are usually small compared to memory in a computer system.

4. The data can be displayed in waveform or number representation. The number bases chosen for display are usually hexadecimal, octal, binary, and decimal. Not all of these bases will be available on every analyzer.

5. Many analyzers will have the ability to continue to collect data as long as the processor repeats a particular activity. Then, when something different happens, such as an intermittent failure, the analyzer will collect the events before or after the failure and store that sequence for evaluation by the technician.

6. Analyzers have the ability to react to and record asynchronous events such as interrupts. The computer does not have to be placed into a repeating loop so the waveforms can be displayed on a scope.

7. Most analyzers have the ability to highlight information that has changed. A failed bit, one that does not stay constant when it should, can be highlighted, focusing the technician's attention on this particular problem. In a similar fashion, a bit that never changes would not be highlighted, indicating the possibility of a stuck line.

12-5 CLOSING THOUGHTS

This chapter has outlined a troubleshooting method that should provide you with insights into how to approach microcomputer troubleshooting. Various techniques, test circuitry, and test programs were examined. It is not the intention of the chapter that you should troubleshoot exactly as outlined here; the intention was to provide enough information and examples to help you develop a system to fit your skills and aptitudes.

Whatever method you decide to use, remember, organization and thoroughness are important. Allow time to run the computer in a test mode after you have fixed a problem. This allows burn-in time for new parts and helps to insure that there are no other problems in the system.

Intermittents are often very difficult to detect. Continuous never-ending test programs that repeatedly exercise a particular part of the system are useful here. This is why the ROM and RAM test logic repeated until the operator stopped the test process. In cases where temperature is a problem, a heat gun and a can of freeze spray can be used to find the component that is failing because of heat. If you use a heat gun, be careful that the temperature is not so high as to damage the components being tested or desolder the circuitry under test.

If you like the approach used in this chapter, the support circuitry and AUTO TEST ROM should be developed for the systems you will be asked to test. Do this once for each system. Wire wrap the circuitry on a prototype board with an edge connector that fits into the bus connector used by the computer. Check to insure that your test circuitry does not load down the bus causing additional problems. Once you are satisfied with how your test board operates, you might consider transferring it to a PC board. Whatever you do, do not build the test circuitry each time it is needed. This is inefficient, time-consuming, and may lead to troubleshooting the test circuitry rather than the computer if you wire the test circuitry incorrectly. As you gain experience, it will not be as necessary to be a slave to a troubleshooting outline. If you have seen a problem hundreds of times, go ahead and try a quick fix. For the sake of the socket, solder connections, etc., at least make some preliminary tests. If the quick fix does not work, return to the thoroughness of an outline.

SUMMARY

1. It is a good idea to learn as much as possible about how a computer works when operating properly. This information will be invaluable when the time comes to make repairs.

2. Try to avoid the ''let's remove this and see what happens'' type of troubleshooting. If you remove a part or PC board, *have a reason*. Frequent removal and insertion of good parts can make a good system go bad.

3. Perform a visual inspection of the system. This often leads to quick solutions when burnt or broken parts are noticed.

4. Check the power supply. If it is not working, fix it first, then proceed to the computer circuitry.

5. In order for a computer to function, the CPU on which it is based must be working. Whenever a problem seems system-wide or the computer appears dead, start your

troubleshooting at the CPU. When it is obvious that the problem is local to a particular section of the computer, you can troubleshoot from the section that is bad and go toward the CPU.

6. Until you have gained a great deal of experience troubleshooting computer systems, it is a good idea to be as complete as possible. Follow a suggested outline from the manufacturer or develop one of your own.

7. If most of the computer is functional, have it help you fix the problem. Learn to write short diagnostic programs that can test the various subsystems. Incorporate the ones you will use often into an AUTO TEST ROM. Plug this ROM into the computer as soon as you believe the CPU can talk to the ROM and begin automatic testing.

8. The logic analyzer is designed specifically to be used in troubleshooting computer circuitry. As a rule, logic analyzers are expensive. If you have access to such a piece of equipment, learn about every feature available. The more you understand about an analyzer, the easier it will be for you to solve complex troubleshooting problems.

QUESTIONS

1. What considerations are important when inserting a test probe into a computer circuit?

2. List two reasons why the "Good, I can remove this and stick a new one in" method of troubleshooting is a bad technique.

3. Why shouldn't a logic probe be used to test Vcc?

4. What is the first step you should perform when troubleshooting?

5. What five tasks must a CPU be able to perform to operate correctly?

6. After a computer has been in service for some time, is it more likely that the hardware or system software will be responsible for malfunctions?

7. After the power supply has been tested, what is the next step in the troubleshooting approach discussed in this chapter?

8. Where should CPU power supply levels be checked?

9. Which CPU inputs should be checked in an 8080-based system? In an 8085 system? In a Z80-based system?

10. How can the processor be electrically isolated from the system?

11. When injecting a signal into the computer circuitry, what should you do to protect the signal generator?

12. When a machine cycle stepper is controlling the CPU, at what clock state will the CPU enter a wait state?

13. Why is EI the first instruction in the AUTO TEST ROM used in this chapter?

14. What are the four primary control signals that should always be checked when troubleshooting an 8080-based system? An 8085-based system? A Z80-based system?

15. List three programs that should be included in an AUTO test ROM.
16. What is pattern failure?
17. When troubleshooting, how many machine cycles should be in a test program that will be monitored by an oscilloscope?
18. What oscilloscope controls are used to spread the trigger signal so a pulse is on each side of the screen?
19. What method makes it easier for a technician to analyze data bus signals when using an oscilloscope?
20. How can valid data-bus information be recognized on an oscilloscope?

ASSIGNMENTS

1. Code a RAM test. Insert the routine in a section of RAM known to be good. Try to obtain a faulty RAM to insert into the system. If none is available, carefully bend a data pin so it is not connected to the circuit when the chip is inserted into the socket. Have the program output the failed location so you can read the address off of the oscilloscope.

2. Build a machine cycle stepper for the computer you are using. Verify circuit operation by single stepping through a simple program loop stored in RAM. Run the program with the computer operating at full speed. When placed in single-step mode, the computer must be somewhere within the loop. You can quickly determine where by checking the address lines with a logic probe.

3. Test key closures on your system by single stepping through a routine that inputs from the keyboard. It might be possible to single step through the section of the monitor that handles the keyboard until the IN from the keyboard occurs. If the monitor debounces key closures through software, single stepping through the delays is tiresome. If so, write yourself a short test routine that activates the keyboard circuitry, then quickly inputs from the keyboard. Do not worry about bouncing, since you will hold the IN cycle static once it is reached with the single stepper. With the IN cycle active, you should be able to test key closures by pressing a key and checking the data-bus lines for changing data.

4. Have your instructor place faults into the system that you are learning. Troubleshoot those faults, recording what you tested and why. Get into the habit of keeping a log of the faults and symptoms that you encounter. Troubleshoot as many problems as possible. The more experience you gain now, the better.

Appendix A

TWO'S-COMPLEMENT NUMBERS

As you already know, an 8-bit register can represent 256 possibilities in binary. The range of the register is determined by the way in which the program interprets the 8 bits. If you elect to ignore the sign flag, then all 8 bits are available for data representation. In this case, the range of a register would be from 0 to 255 in decimal or 00 to FF hex. If the program logic can deal with negatives as well as positives, the sign flag must be used to differentiate between them. In the processors you have studied, the most significant bit of an answer is transferred into the sign flag. This corresponds to two's-complement numbers and arithmetic.

In two's-complement arithmetic, a leading bit of 0 indicates a positive number. If the MS bit is logic 1, then the result is negative. Once you assign the MS bit as a sign bit, you leave only 7 bits to handle the data. This makes the positive limit of a register +127. Since 00 hex has an MS bit equal to logic 0, it is considered a positive number in this form of arithmetic. The positives, including 00 hex, account for 128 of the 256 possibilities available in an 8-bit register. The negative limit of an 8-bit register using two's-complement arithmetic is −128 base 10. Starting from −1, the negatives account for the other 128 possibilities. Thus, the range of an 8-bit register, using two's-complement arithmetic, is +127 to −128.

To interpret results using this arithmetic, all positive results can be read as if they were regular binary. Consider 0010 0010. This is +34 in decimal. Whether we say this is in binary or two's-complement form makes no difference. The negatives are a different matter, though. If you look at 1000 0000, the first reaction is to call this +128. This is incorrect, if negatives are recognized by program logic. The leading 1 indicates a negative result. Nor is it a negative zero. In two's-complement arithmetic, there is a single zero and it is positive. To determine the value of the negative result, invert every binary position within the register to form the one's complement. In our example this would be

$$0111\ 1111\ -\ \text{one's complement}$$

then add 1 to this result to form the two's complement:

$$0111\ 1111$$
$$\underline{\hspace{4em}1}$$
$$1000\ 0000$$

This is not a trick nor is it meant to be confusing. It just happens that the number is -128. The only negative that resembles its positive form is the negative limit of the register.

Suppose we look at the other end of the negative numbers. A negative 1 in any register, regardless of the register length, will be represented by every bit position being high. Examine the following:

$$1111\ 1111$$

Inverting to get the one's complement, we obtain

$$0000\ 0000$$

Adding 1 to reach the two's-complement form, we see

$$0000\ 0000$$
$$\underline{\hspace{4em}1}$$
$$0000\ 0001$$

The result of the conversion yielded a 1, therefore $1111\ 1111$ is -1.

This is important. When dealing with answers that appear in hex, remember the hex is just a shorthand representation of the binary within the register. This means that we need to know this form of arithmetic, because the processor will perform it, when the logic of a program creates a situation where a negative result will occur. Suppose that you wish to subtract 5 from 3. In binary this would look like:

$$0000\ 0011$$
$$\underline{-0000\ 0101}$$
$$1111\ 1110$$

To interpret the answer as a $+254$ is obviously incorrect. The computer chip, however, does not care what this binary pattern represents. It is up to you as a programmer to find out. Analyzing the answer, you see that the sign bit is set. So the result is negative. Performing the conversion:

1111 1110 becomes

0000 0001

Then adding 1

$$
\begin{array}{r}
0000\ 0001 \\
1 \\
\hline
0000\ 0010
\end{array}
$$

Is it necessary to perform these calculations on paper? No. The instruction CMA forms the one's-complement of the A register contents. Then do an ADI 01 to obtain the two's-complement representation of the negative. If your program outputs the results, remember to send an indication that the number was negative.

Appendix B

TIME-DELAY SUBROUTINES

EXAMPLE A-1
1-Second Delay with 1mHz Master Clock

HEX ADDRESS	HEX OP CODE	MNEMONIC	COMMENTS	OCTAL ADDRESS	OCTAL OP CODE
Any 00		PUSH PSW	Approximate 1 sec. delay		
			with 1		
Any 01		PUSH H	MHz Master		
			clock		
Any 02		LXI H			
Any 03		C2	302 octal		
Any 04		A2	242 octal		
Any 05		DCX H			
Any 06		MOV A, L			
Any 07		ORA H			
Any 08		JNZ			
Any 09		05			
Any 0A		Any			

EXAMPLE A-1 *(continued)*

HEX ADDRESS	HEX OP CODE	MNEMONIC	COMMENTS	OCTAL ADDRESS	OCTAL OP CODE
Any 0B		POP H			
Any 0C		POP PSW			
Any 0D		RET			

EXAMPLE A-2
1-Second Delay with 2 MHz Master Clock

HEX ADDRESS	HEX OP CODE	MNEMONIC	COMMENTS	OCTAL ADDRESS	OCTAL OP CODE
Any 00		PUSH PSW	Approximate 1 sec. delay		
Any 01		PUSH H	with a 2 MHz master clock		
Any 02		PUSH D			
Any 03		MVI D			
Any 04		02			
Any 05		LXI H			
Any 06		CO	300 octal		
Any 07		A2	242 octal		
Any 08		DCX H			
Any 09		MOV A, L			
Any 0A		ORA H			
Any 0B		JNZ			
Any 0C		08			
Any 0D		Any			
Any 0E		DCRD			
Any 0F		JNZ			
Any 10		05			
Any 11		Any			

EXAMPLE A-2 (*continued*)

HEX ADDRESS	HEX OP CODE	MNEMONIC	COMMENTS	OCTAL ADDRESS	OCTAL OP CODE
Any 12		POP D			
Any 13		POP H			
Any 14		POP PSW			
Any 15		RET			

Appendix C

8080 INSTRUCTION SET*

*Courtesy of Intel Corporation

INSTRUCTION SET

The accumulator group instructions include arithmetic and logical operators with direct, indirect, and immediate addressing modes.

Move, load, and store instruction groups provide the ability to move either 8 or 16 bits of data between memory, the six working registers and the accumulator using direct, indirect, and immediate addressing modes.

The ability to branch to different portions of the program is provided with jump, jump conditional, and computed jumps. Also the ability to call to and return from subroutines is provided both conditionally and unconditionally. The RESTART (or single byte call instruction) is useful for interrupt vector operation.

Double precision operators such as stack manipulation and double add instructions extend both the arithmetic and interrupt handling capability of the 8080A. The ability to increment and decrement memory, the six general registers and the accumulator is provided as well as extended increment and decrement instructions to operate on the register pairs and stack pointer. Further capability is provided by the ability to rotate the accumulator left or right through or around the carry bit.

Input and output may be accomplished using memory addresses as I/O ports or the directly addressed I/O provided for in the 8080A instruction set.

The following special instruction group completes the 8080A instruction set: the NOP instruction, HALT to stop processor execution and the DAA instructions provide decimal arithmetic capability. STC allows the carry flag to be directly set, and the CMC instruction allows it to be complemented. CMA complements the contents of the accumulator and XCHG exchanges the contents of two 16-bit register pairs directly.

Data and Instruction Formats

Data in the 8080A is stored in the form of 8-bit binary integers. All data transfers to the system data bus will be in the same format.

$$D_7 \; D_6 \; D_5 \; D_4 \; D_3 \; D_2 \; D_1 \; D_0$$
DATA WORD

The program instructions may be one, two, or three bytes in length. Multiple byte instructions must be stored in successive words in program memory. The instruction formats then depend on the particular operation executed.

One Byte Instructions

$$D_7 \; D_6 \; D_5 \; D_4 \; D_3 \; D_2 \; D_1 \; D_0$$ OP CODE

TYPICAL INSTRUCTIONS

Register to register, memory reference, arithmetic or logical, rotate, return, push, pop, enable or disable Interrupt instructions

Two Byte Instructions

$$D_7 \; D_6 \; D_5 \; D_4 \; D_3 \; D_2 \; D_1 \; D_0$$ OP CODE
$$D_7 \; D_6 \; D_5 \; D_4 \; D_3 \; D_2 \; D_1 \; D_0$$ OPERAND

Immediate mode or I/O instructions

Three Byte Instructions

$$D_7 \; D_6 \; D_5 \; D_4 \; D_3 \; D_2 \; D_1 \; D_0$$ OP CODE
$$D_7 \; D_6 \; D_5 \; D_4 \; D_3 \; D_2 \; D_1 \; D_0$$ LOW ADDRESS OR OPERAND 1
$$D_7 \; D_6 \; D_5 \; D_4 \; D_3 \; D_2 \; D_1 \; D_0$$ HIGH ADDRESS OR OPERAND 2

Jump, call or direct load and store instructions

For the 8080A a logic "1" is defined as a high level and a logic "0" is defined as a low level.

Table 2. Instruction Set Summary

Mnemonic	Instruction Code [1] D7	D6	D5	D4	D3	D2	D1	D0	Operations Description	Clock Cycles [2]
MOVE, LOAD, AND STORE										
MOV r1,r2	0	1	D	D	D	S	S	S	Move register to register	5
MOV M,r	0	1	1	1	0	S	S	S	Move register to memory	7
MOV r,M	0	1	D	D	D	1	1	0	Move memory to register	7
MVI r	0	0	D	D	D	1	1	0	Move immediate register	7
MVI M	0	0	1	1	0	1	1	0	Move immediate memory	10
LXI B	0	0	0	0	0	0	0	1	Load immediate register Pair B & C	10
LXI D	0	0	0	1	0	0	0	1	Load immediate register Pair D & E	10
LXI H	0	0	1	0	0	0	0	1	Load immediate register Pair H & L	10
STAX B	0	0	0	0	0	0	1	0	Store A indirect	7
STAX D	0	0	0	1	0	0	1	0	Store A indirect	7
LDAX B	0	0	0	0	1	0	1	0	Load A indirect	7
LDAX D	0	0	0	1	1	0	1	0	Load A indirect	7
STA	0	0	1	1	0	0	1	0	Store A direct	13
LDA	0	0	1	1	1	0	1	0	Load A direct	13
SHLD	0	0	1	0	0	0	1	0	Store H & L direct	16
LHLD	0	0	1	0	1	0	1	0	Load H & L direct	16
XCHG	1	1	1	0	1	0	1	1	Exchange D & E, H & L Registers	4
STACK OPS										
PUSH B	1	1	0	0	0	1	0	1	Push register Pair B & C on stack	11
PUSH D	1	1	0	1	0	1	0	1	Push register Pair D & E on stack	11
PUSH H	1	1	1	0	0	1	0	1	Push register Pair H & L on stack	11
PUSH PSW	1	1	1	1	0	1	0	1	Push A and Flags on stack	11
POP B	1	1	0	0	0	0	0	1	Pop register Pair B & C off stack	10
POP D	1	1	0	1	0	0	0	1	Pop register Pair D & E off stack	10
POP H	1	1	1	0	0	0	0	1	Pop register Pair H & L off stack	10
POP PSW	1	1	1	1	0	0	0	1	Pop A and Flags off stack	10
XTHL	1	1	1	0	0	0	1	1	Exchange top of stack, H & L	18
SPHL	1	1	1	1	1	0	0	1	H & L to stack pointer	5
LXI SP	0	0	1	1	0	0	0	1	Load immediate stack pointer	10
INX SP	0	0	1	1	0	0	1	1	Increment stack pointer	5
DCX SP	0	0	1	1	1	0	1	1	Decrement stack pointer	5
JUMP										
JMP	1	1	0	0	0	0	1	1	Jump unconditional	10
JC	1	1	0	1	1	0	1	0	Jump on carry	10
JNC	1	1	0	1	0	0	1	0	Jump on no carry	10
JZ	1	1	0	0	1	0	1	0	Jump on zero	10
JNZ	1	1	0	0	0	0	1	0	Jump on no zero	10
JP	1	1	1	1	0	0	1	0	Jump on positive	10
JM	1	1	1	1	1	0	1	0	Jump on minus	10
JPE	1	1	1	0	1	0	1	0	Jump on parity even	10

Mnemonic	Instruction Code [1] D7	D6	D5	D4	D3	D2	D1	D0	Operations Description	Clock Cycles [2]
JPO	1	1	1	0	0	0	1	0	Jump on parity odd	10
PCHL	1	1	1	0	1	0	0	1	H & L to program counter	5
CALL										
CALL	1	1	0	0	1	1	0	1	Call unconditional	17
CC	1	1	0	1	1	1	0	0	Call on carry	11/17
CNC	1	1	0	1	0	1	0	0	Call on no carry	11/17
CZ	1	1	0	0	1	1	0	0	Call on zero	11/17
CNZ	1	1	0	0	0	1	0	0	Call on no zero	11/17
CP	1	1	1	1	0	1	0	0	Call on positive	11/17
CM	1	1	1	1	1	1	0	0	Call on minus	11/17
CPE	1	1	1	0	1	1	0	0	Call on parity even	11/17
CPO	1	1	1	0	0	1	0	0	Call on parity odd	11/17
RETURN										
RET	1	1	0	0	1	0	0	1	Return	10
RC	1	1	0	1	1	0	0	0	Return on carry	5/11
RNC	1	1	0	1	0	0	0	0	Return on no carry	5/11
RZ	1	1	0	0	1	0	0	0	Return on zero	5/11
RNZ	1	1	0	0	0	0	0	0	Return on no zero	5/11
RP	1	1	1	1	0	0	0	0	Return on positive	5/11
RM	1	1	1	1	1	0	0	0	Return on minus	5/11
RPE	1	1	1	0	1	0	0	0	Return on parity even	5/11
RPO	1	1	1	0	0	0	0	0	Return on parity odd	5/11
RESTART										
RST	1	1	A	A	A	1	1	1	Restart	11
INCREMENT AND DECREMENT										
INR r	0	0	D	D	D	1	0	0	Increment register	5
DCR r	0	0	D	D	D	1	0	1	Decrement register	5
INR M	0	0	1	1	0	1	0	0	Increment memory	10
DCR M	0	0	1	1	0	1	0	1	Decrement memory	10
INX B	0	0	0	0	0	0	1	1	Increment B & C registers	5
INX D	0	0	0	1	0	0	1	1	Increment D & E registers	5
INX H	0	0	1	0	0	0	1	1	Increment H & L registers	5
DCX B	0	0	0	0	1	0	1	1	Decrement B & C	5
DCX D	0	0	0	1	1	0	1	1	Decrement D & E	5
DCX H	0	0	1	0	1	0	1	1	Decrement H & L	5
ADD										
ADD r	1	0	0	0	0	S	S	S	Add register to A	4
ADC r	1	0	0	0	1	S	S	S	Add register to A with carry	4
ADD M	1	0	0	0	0	1	1	0	Add memory to A	7
ADC M	1	0	0	0	1	1	1	0	Add memory to A with carry	7
ADI	1	1	0	0	0	1	1	0	Add immediate to A	7
ACI	1	1	0	0	1	1	1	0	Add immediate to A with carry	7
DAD B	0	0	0	0	1	0	0	1	Add B & C to H & L	10
DAD D	0	0	0	1	1	0	0	1	Add D & E to H & L	10
DAD H	0	0	1	0	1	0	0	1	Add H & L to H & L	10
DAD SP	0	0	1	1	1	0	0	1	Add stack pointer to H & L	10

Summary of Processor Instructions (Cont.)

Mnemonic	D_7	D_6	D_5	D_4	D_3	D_2	D_1	D_0	Operations Description	Clock Cycles [2]
SUBTRACT										
SUB r	1	0	0	1	0	S	S	S	Subtract register from A	4
SBB r	1	0	0	1	1	S	S	S	Subtract register from A with borrow	4
SUB M	1	0	0	1	0	1	1	0	Subtract memory from A	7
SBB M	1	0	0	1	1	1	1	0	Subtract memory from A with borrow	7
SUI	1	1	0	1	0	1	1	0	Subtract immediate from A	7
SBI	1	1	0	1	1	1	1	0	Subtract immediate from A with borrow	7
LOGICAL										
ANA r	1	0	1	0	0	S	S	S	And register with A	4
XRA r	1	0	1	0	1	S	S	S	Exclusive Or register with A	4
ORA r	1	0	1	1	0	S	S	S	Or register with A	4
CMP r	1	0	1	1	1	S	S	S	Compare register with A	4
ANA M	1	0	1	0	0	1	1	0	And memory with A	7
XRA M	1	0	1	0	1	1	1	0	Exclusive Or memory with A	7
ORA M	1	0	1	1	0	1	1	0	Or memory with A	7
CMP M	1	0	1	1	1	1	1	0	Compare memory with A	7
ANI	1	1	1	0	0	1	1	0	And immediate with A	7
XRI	1	1	1	0	1	1	1	0	Exclusive Or immediate with A	7
ORI	1	1	1	1	0	1	1	0	Or immediate with A	7
CPI	1	1	1	1	1	1	1	0	Compare immediate with A	7

Mnemonic	D_7	D_6	D_5	D_4	D_3	D_2	D_1	D_0	Operations Description	Clock Cycles [2]
ROTATE										
RLC	0	0	0	0	0	1	1	1	Rotate A left	4
RRC	0	0	0	0	1	1	1	1	Rotate A right	4
RAL	0	0	0	1	0	1	1	1	Rotate A left through carry	4
RAR	0	0	0	1	1	1	1	1	Rotate A right through carry	4
SPECIALS										
CMA	0	0	1	0	1	1	1	1	Complement A	4
STC	0	0	1	1	0	1	1	1	Set carry	4
CMC	0	0	1	1	1	1	1	1	Complement carry	4
DAA	0	0	1	0	0	1	1	1	Decimal adjust A	4
INPUT/OUTPUT										
IN	1	1	0	1	1	0	1	1	Input	10
OUT	1	1	0	1	0	0	1	1	Output	10
CONTROL										
EI	1	1	1	1	1	0	1	1	Enable Interrupts	4
DI	1	1	1	1	0	0	1	1	Disable Interrupt	4
NOP	0	0	0	0	0	0	0	0	No-operation	4
HLT	0	1	1	1	0	1	1	0	Halt	7

NOTES:

1. DDD or SSS: B=000, C=001, D=010, E=011, H=100, L=101, Memory=110, A=111.

2. Two possible cycle times (6/12) indicate instruction cycles dependent on condition flags.

*All mnemonics copyright ©Intel Corporation 1977

Appendix D

Z80 SPECIFICATION SHEETS*

*Courtesy of Zilog

Absolute Maximum Ratings

Temperature Under Bias	Specified operating range.
Storage Temperature	-65°C to +150°C
Voltage On Any Pin	-0.3V to +7V
with Respect to Ground	
Power Dissipation	1.5W

*Comment

Stresses above those listed under "Absolute Maximum Rating" may cause permanent damage to the device. This is a stress rating only and functional operation of the device at these or any other condition above those indicated in the operational sections of this specification is not implied. Exposure to absolute maximum rating conditions for extended periods may affect device reliability.

Note: For Z80-CPU all AC and DC characteristics remain the same for the military grade parts except I_{cc}.

$$I_{cc} = 200\ mA$$

Z80-CPU D.C. Characteristics

$T_A = 0°C$ to $70°C$, $V_{cc} = 5V \pm 5\%$ unless otherwise specified

Symbol	Parameter	Min.	Typ.	Max.	Unit	Test Condition
V_{ILC}	Clock Input Low Voltage	-0.3		0.45	V	
V_{IHC}	Clock Input High Voltage	V_{cc} –.6		V_{cc}+.3	V	
V_{IL}	Input Low Voltage	-0.3		0.8	V	
V_{IH}	Input High Voltage	2.0		V_{cc}	V	
V_{OL}	Output Low Voltage			0.4	V	I_{OL}=1.8mA
V_{OH}	Output High Voltage	2.4			V	I_{OH} = –250μA
I_{CC}	Power Supply Current			150	mA	
I_{LI}	Input Leakage Current			10	μA	V_{IN}=0 to V_{cc}
I_{LOH}	Tri-State Output Leakage Current in Float			10	μA	V_{OUT}=2.4 to V_{cc}
I_{LOL}	Tri-State Output Leakage Current in Float			-10	μA	V_{OUT}=0.4V
I_{LD}	Data Bus Leakage Current in Input Mode			±10	μA	$0 \le V_{IN} \le V_{cc}$

Capacitance

$T_A = 25°C$, f = 1 MHz, unmeasured pins returned to ground

Symbol	Parameter	Max.	Unit
C_Φ	Clock Capacitance	35	pF
C_{IN}	Input Capacitance	5	pF
C_{OUT}	Output Capacitance	10	pF

Z80-CPU Ordering Information

C – Ceramic
P – Plastic
S – Standard 5V ±5% 0° to 70°C
E – Extended 5V ±5% –40° to 85°C
M – Military 5V ±10% –55° to 125°C

Z80A-CPU D.C. Characteristics

$T_A = 0°C$ to $70°C$, $V_{cc} = 5V \pm 5\%$ unless otherwise specified

Symbol	Parameter	Min.	Typ.	Max.	Unit	Test Condition
V_{ILC}	Clock Input Low Voltage	-0.3		0.45	V	
V_{IHC}	Clock Input High Voltage	V_{cc} –.6		V_{cc}+.3	V	
V_{IL}	Input Low Voltage	-0.3		0.8	V	
V_{IH}	Input High Voltage	2.0		V_{cc}	V	
V_{OL}	Output Low Voltage			0.4	V	I_{OL}=1.8mA
V_{OH}	Output High Voltage	2.4			V	I_{OH} = –250μA
I_{CC}	Power Supply Current		90	200	mA	
I_{LI}	Input Leakage Current			10	μA	V_{IN}=0 to V_{cc}
I_{LOH}	Tri-State Output Leakage Current in Float			10	μA	V_{OUT}=2.4 to V_{cc}
I_{LOL}	Tri-State Output Leakage Current in Float			-10	μA	V_{OUT}=0.4V
I_{LD}	Data Bus Leakage Current in Input Mode			±10	μA	$0 \le V_{IN} \le V_{cc}$

Capacitance

$T_A = 25°C$, f = 1 MHz, unmeasured pins returned to ground

Symbol	Parameter	Max.	Unit
C_Φ	Clock Capacitance	35	pF
C_{IN}	Input Capacitance	5	pF
C_{OUT}	Output Capacitance	10	pF

Z80A-CPU Ordering Information

C – Ceramic
P – Plastic
S – Standard 5V ±5% 0° to 70°C

$T_A = 0°C$ to $70°C$, $V_{CC} = +5V \pm 5\%$, Unless Otherwise Noted.

Signal	Symbol	Parameter	Min	Max	Unit	Test Condition
φ	t_c	Clock Period	.4	[12]	μsec	
	$t_w(\Phi H)$	Clock Pulse Width, Clock High	180	[E]	nsec	
	$t_w(\Phi L)$	Clock Pulse Width, Clock Low	180	2000	nsec	
	$t_{r, f}$	Clock Rise and Fall Time		30	nsec	
A_{0-15}	$t_D(AD)$	Address Output Delay		145	nsec	
	$t_F(AD)$	Delay to Float		110	nsec	
	t_{acm}	Address Stable Prior to MREQ (Memory Cycle)	[1]		nsec	$C_L = 50pF$
	t_{aci}	Address Stable Prior to IORQ, RD or WR (I/O Cycle)	[2]		nsec	
	t_{ca}	Address Stable from RD, WR, IORQ or MREQ	[3]		nsec	
	t_{caf}	Address Stable From RD or WR During Float	[4]		nsec	
D_{0-7}	$t_D(D)$	Data Output Delay		230	nsec	
	$t_F(D)$	Delay to Float During Write Cycle		90	nsec	
	$t_{S\Phi}(D)$	Data Setup Time to Rising Edge of Clock During M1 Cycle	50		nsec	
	$t_{S\Phi}(D)$	Data Setup Time to Falling Edge of Clock During M2 to M5	60		nsec	$C_L = 50pF$
	t_{dcm}	Data Stable Prior to WR (Memory Cycle)	[5]		nsec	
	t_{dci}	Data Stable Prior to WR (I/O Cycle)	[6]		nsec	
	t_{cdf}	Data Stable From WR	[7]			
	t_H	Any Hold Time for Setup Time	0		nsec	
MREQ	$t_{DL\Phi}(MR)$	MREQ Delay From Falling Edge of Clock, MREQ Low		100	nsec	
	$t_{DH\Phi}(MR)$	MREQ Delay From Rising Edge of Clock, MREQ High		100	nsec	
	$t_{DH\Phi}(MR)$	MREQ Delay From Falling Edge of Clock, MREQ High		100	nsec	$C_L = 50pF$
	$t_w(MRL)$	Pulse Width, MREQ Low	[8]		nsec	
	$t_w(MRH)$	Pulse Width, MREQ High	[9]		nsec	
IORQ	$t_{DL\Phi}(IR)$	IORQ Delay From Rising Edge of Clock, IORQ Low		90	nsec	
	$t_{DL\Phi}(IR)$	IORQ Delay From Falling Edge of Clock, IORQ Low		110	nsec	
	$t_{DH\Phi}(IR)$	IORQ Delay From Rising Edge of Clock, IORQ High		100	nsec	$C_L = 50pF$
	$t_{DH\Phi}(IR)$	IORQ Delay From Falling Edge of Clock, IORQ High		110	nsec	
RD	$t_{DL\Phi}(RD)$	RD Delay From Rising Edge of Clock, RD Low		100	nsec	
	$t_{DL\Phi}(RD)$	RD Delay From Falling Edge of Clock, RD Low		130	nsec	
	$t_{DH\Phi}(RD)$	RD Delay From Rising Edge of Clock, RD High		100	nsec	$C_L = 50pF$
	$t_{DH\Phi}(RD)$	RD Delay From Falling Edge of Clock, RD High		110	nsec	
WR	$t_{DL\Phi}(WR)$	WR Delay From Rising Edge of Clock, WR Low		80	nsec	
	$t_{DL\Phi}(WR)$	WR Delay From Falling Edge of Clock, WR Low		90	nsec	
	$t_{DH\Phi}(WR)$	WR Delay From Falling Edge of Clock, WR High		100	nsec	$C_L = 50pF$
	$t_w(WRL)$	Pulse Width, WR Low	[10]		nsec	
M1	$t_{DL}(M1)$	M1 Delay From Rising Edge of Clock, M1 Low		130	nsec	$C_L = 50pF$
	$t_{DH}(M1)$	M1 Delay From Rising Edge of Clock, M1 High		130	nsec	
RFSH	$t_{DL}(RF)$	RFSH Delay From Rising Edge of Clock, RFSH Low		180	nsec	$C_L = 50pF$
	$t_{DH}(RF)$	RFSH Delay From Rising Edge of Clock, RFSH High		150	nsec	
WAIT	$t_s(WT)$	WAIT Setup Time to Falling Edge of Clock	70		nsec	
HALT	$t_D(HT)$	HALT Delay Time From Falling Edge of Clock		300	nsec	$C_L = 50pF$
INT	$t_s(IT)$	INT Setup Time to Rising Edge of Clock	80		nsec	
NMI	$t_w(NML)$	Pulse Width, NMI Low	80		nsec	
BUSRQ	$t_s(BQ)$	BUSRQ Setup Time to Rising Edge of Clock	80		nsec	
BUSAK	$t_{DL}(BA)$	BUSAK Delay From Rising Edge of Clock, BUSAK Low		120	nsec	$C_L = 50pF$
	$t_{DH}(BA)$	BUSAK Delay From Falling Edge of Clock, BUSAK High		110	nsec	
RESET	$t_s(RS)$	RESET Setup Time to Rising Edge of Clock	90		nsec	
	$t_F(C)$	Delay to Float (MREQ, IORQ, RD and WR)		100	nsec	
	t_{mr}	M1 Stable Prior to IORQ (Interrupt Ack.)	[11]		nsec	

[12] $t_c = t_w(\Phi H) + t_w(\Phi L) + t_r + t_f$

[1] $t_{acm} = t_w(\Phi H) + t_f - 75$

[2] $t_{aci} = t_c - 80$

[3] $t_{ca} = t_w(\Phi L) + t_r - 40$

[4] $t_{caf} = t_w(\Phi L) + t_r - 60$

[5] $t_{dcm} = t_c - 210$

[6] $t_{dci} = t_w(\Phi L) + t_r - 210$

[7] $t_{cdf} = t_w(\Phi L) + t_r - 80$

[8] $t_w(MRL) = t_c - 40$

[9] $t_{w(MRH)} = t_w(\Phi H) + t_f - 30$

[10] $t_{w(WRL)} = t_c - 40$

[11] $t_{mr} = 2t_c + t_w(\Phi H) + t_f - 80$

NOTES:

A. Data should be enabled onto the CPU data bus when RD is active. During interrupt acknowledge data should be enabled when M1 and IORQ are both active.

B. All control signals are internally synchronized, so they may be totally asynchronous with respect to the clock.

C. The RESET signal must be active for a minimum of 3 clock cycles.

D. Output Delay vs. Loaded Capacitance
TA = 70°C   Vcc = +5V ±5%

Add 10nsec delay for each 50pf increase in load up to a maximum of 200pf for the data bus & 100pf for address & control lines

E. Although static by design, testing guarantees $t_{w(\Phi H)}$ of 200 μsec maximum

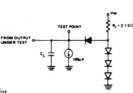

Load circuit for Output

A.C. Timing Diagram

Timing measurements are made at the following
voltages, unless otherwise specified:

	"1"	"0"
CLOCK	V_{cc} -.6V	.45V
OUTPUT	2.0 V	.8 V
INPUT	2.0 V	.8 V
FLOAT	Δ V	± 0.5 V

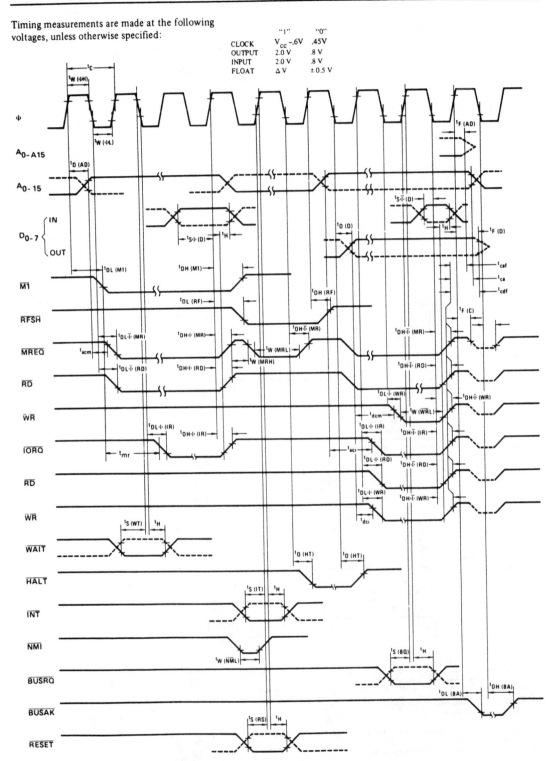

472

T_A = 0°C to 70°C, V_{cc} = +5V ± 5%, Unless Otherwise Noted.

Signal	Symbol	Parameter	Min	Max	Unit	Test Condition
Φ	t_c	Clock Period	.25	[12]	μsec	
	$t_w(\Phi H)$	Clock Pulse Width, Clock High	110	[E]	nsec	
	$t_w(\Phi L)$	Clock Pulse Width, Clock Low	110	2000	nsec	
	$t_{r,f}$	Clock Rise and Fall Time		30	nsec	
A_{0-15}	$t_D(AD)$	Address Output Delay		110	nsec	
	$t_F(AD)$	Delay to Float		90	nsec	
	t_{acm}	Address Stable Prior to $\overline{MREQ}$ (Memory Cycle)	[1]		nsec	C_L = 50pF
	t_{aci}	Address Stable Prior to $\overline{IORQ}$, $\overline{RD}$ or $\overline{WR}$ (I/O Cycle)	[2]		nsec	
	t_{ca}	Address Stable from $\overline{RD}$, $\overline{WR}$, $\overline{IORQ}$ or $\overline{MREQ}$	[3]		nsec	
	t_{caf}	Address Stable From $\overline{RD}$ or $\overline{WR}$ During Float	[4]		nsec	
D_{0-7}	$t_D(D)$	Data Output Delay		150	nsec	
	$t_F(D)$	Delay to Float During Write Cycle		90	nsec	
	$t_{S\Phi}(D)$	Data Setup Time to Rising Edge of Clock During M1 Cycle	35		nsec	C_L = 50pF
	$t_{S\Phi}(D)$	Data Setup Time to Falling Edge of Clock During M2 to M5	50		nsec	
	t_{dcm}	Data Stable Prior to $\overline{WR}$ (Memory Cycle)	[5]		nsec	
	t_{dci}	Data Stable Prior to $\overline{WR}$ (I/O Cycle)	[6]		nsec	
	t_{cdf}	Data Stable From $\overline{WR}$	[7]		nsec	
	t_H	Any Hold Time for Setup Time		0	nsec	
$\overline{MREQ}$	$t_{DL\Phi}(MR)$	$\overline{MREQ}$ Delay From Falling Edge of Clock, $\overline{MREQ}$ Low		85	nsec	
	$t_{DH\Phi}(MR)$	$\overline{MREQ}$ Delay From Rising Edge of Clock, $\overline{MREQ}$ High		85	nsec	
	$t_{DH\Phi}(MR)$	$\overline{MREQ}$ Delay From Falling Edge of Clock, $\overline{MREQ}$ High		85	nsec	C_L = 50pF
	$t_w(\overline{MRL})$	Pulse Width, $\overline{MREQ}$ Low	[8]		nsec	
	$t_w(\overline{MRH})$	Pulse Width, $\overline{MREQ}$ High	[9]		nsec	
$\overline{IORQ}$	$t_{DL\Phi}(IR)$	$\overline{IORQ}$ Delay From Rising Edge of Clock, $\overline{IORQ}$ Low		75	nsec	
	$t_{DL\Phi}(IR)$	$\overline{IORQ}$ Delay From Falling Edge of Clock, $\overline{IORQ}$ Low		85	nsec	
	$t_{DH\Phi}(IR)$	$\overline{IORQ}$ Delay From Rising Edge of Clock, $\overline{IORQ}$ High		85	nsec	C_L = 50pF
	$t_{DH\Phi}(IR)$	$\overline{IORQ}$ Delay From Falling Edge of Clock, $\overline{IORQ}$ High		85	nsec	
$\overline{RD}$	$t_{DL\Phi}(RD)$	$\overline{RD}$ Delay From Rising Edge of Clock, $\overline{RD}$ Low		85	nsec	
	$t_{DL\Phi}(RD)$	$\overline{RD}$ Delay From Falling Edge of Clock, $\overline{RD}$ Low		95	nsec	
	$t_{DH\Phi}(RD)$	$\overline{RD}$ Delay From Rising Edge of Clock, $\overline{RD}$ High		85	nsec	C_L = 50pF
	$t_{DH\Phi}(RD)$	$\overline{RD}$ Delay From Falling Edge of Clock, $\overline{RD}$ High		85	nsec	
$\overline{WR}$	$t_{DL\Phi}(WR)$	$\overline{WR}$ Delay From Rising Edge of Clock, $\overline{WR}$ Low		65	nsec	
	$t_{DL\Phi}(WR)$	$\overline{WR}$ Delay From Falling Edge of Clock, $\overline{WR}$ Low		80	nsec	
	$t_{DH\Phi}(WR)$	$\overline{WR}$ Delay From Falling Edge of Clock, $\overline{WR}$ High		80	nsec	C_L = 50pF
	$t_w(\overline{WRL})$	Pulse Width, $\overline{WR}$ Low	[10]		nsec	
$\overline{M1}$	$t_{DL}(M1)$	$\overline{M1}$ Delay From Rising Edge of Clock, $\overline{M1}$ Low		100	nsec	C_L = 50pF
	$t_{DH}(M1)$	$\overline{M1}$ Delay From Rising Edge of Clock, $\overline{M1}$ High		100	nsec	
$\overline{RFSH}$	$t_{DL}(RF)$	$\overline{RFSH}$ Delay From Rising Edge of Clock, $\overline{RFSH}$ Low		130	nsec	C_L = 50pF
	$t_{DH}(RF)$	$\overline{RFSH}$ Delay From Rising Edge of Clock, $\overline{RFSH}$ High		120	nsec	
$\overline{WAIT}$	$t_s(WT)$	$\overline{WAIT}$ Setup Time to Falling Edge of Clock	70		nsec	
$\overline{HALT}$	$t_D(HT)$	$\overline{HALT}$ Delay Time From Falling Edge of Clock		300	nsec	C_L = 50pF
$\overline{INT}$	$t_s(IT)$	$\overline{INT}$ Setup Time to Rising Edge of Clock	80		nsec	
$\overline{NMI}$	$t_w(\overline{NML})$	Pulse Width, $\overline{NMI}$ Low	80		nsec	
$\overline{BUSRQ}$	$t_s(BQ)$	$\overline{BUSRQ}$ Setup Time to Rising Edge of Clock	50		nsec	
$\overline{BUSAK}$	$t_{DL}(BA)$	$\overline{BUSAK}$ Delay From Rising Edge of Clock, $\overline{BUSAK}$ Low		100	nsec	
	$t_{DH}(BA)$	$\overline{BUSAK}$ Delay From Falling Edge of Clock, $\overline{BUSAK}$ High		100	nsec	C_L = 50pF
$\overline{RESET}$	$t_s(RS)$	$\overline{RESET}$ Setup Time to Rising Edge of Clock	60		nsec	
	$t_F(C)$	Delay to Float ($\overline{MREQ}$, $\overline{IORQ}$, $\overline{RD}$ and $\overline{WR}$)		80	nsec	
	t_{mr}	M1 Stable Prior to IORQ (Interrupt Ack.)	[11]		nsec	

[12] $t_c = t_w(\Phi H) + t_w(\Phi L) + t_r + t_f$

[1] $t_{acm} = t_w(\Phi H) + t_f - 65$

[2] $t_{aci} = t_c - 70$

[3] $t_{ca} = t_w(\Phi L) + t_r - 50$

[4] $t_{caf} = t_w(\Phi L) + t_r - 45$

[5] $t_{dcm} = t_c - 170$

[6] $t_{dci} = t_w(\Phi L) + t_r - 170$

[7] $t_{cdf} = t_w(\Phi L) + t_r - 70$

[8] $t_w(\overline{MRL}) = t_c - 30$

[9] $t_w(\overline{MRH}) = t_w(\Phi H) + t_f - 20$

[10] $t_w(\overline{WRL}) = t_c - 30$

[11] $t_{mr} = 2t_c + t_w(\Phi H) + t_f - 65$

NOTES:

A. Data should be enabled onto the CPU data bus when $\overline{RD}$ is active. During interrupt acknowledge data should be enabled when $\overline{M1}$ and $\overline{IORQ}$ are both active.

B. All control signals are internally synchronized, so they may be totally asynchronous with respect to the clock.

C. The $\overline{RESET}$ signal must be active for a minimum of 3 clock cycles.

D. Output Delay vs. Loaded Capacitance
    TA = 70°C   Vcc = +5V ±5%
    Add 10nsec delay for each 50pf increase in load up to maximum of 200pf for data bus and 100pf for address & control lines.

E. Although static by design, testing guarantees $t_{w(\Phi H)}$ of 200 μsec maximum

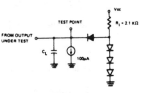

Load circuit for Output

Zilog
Z80–CPU
INSTRUCTION SET

ADC HL, ss	Add with Carry Reg. pair ss to HL
ADC A, s	Add with carry operand s to Acc.
ADD A, n	Add value n to Acc.
ADD A, r	Add Reg. r to Acc.
ADD A, (HL)	Add location (HL) to Acc.
ADD A, (IX+d)	Add location (IX+d) to Acc.
ADD A, (IY+d)	Add location (IY+d) to Acc.
ADD HL, ss	Add Reg. pair ss to HL
ADD IX, pp	Add Reg. pair pp to IX
ADD IY, rr	Add Reg. pair rr to IY
AND s	Logical 'AND' of operand s and Acc.
BIT b, (HL)	Test BIT b of location (HL)
BIT b, (IX+d)	Test BIT b of location (IX+d)
BIT b, (IY+d)	Test BIT b of location (IY+d)
BIT b, r	Test BIT b of Reg. r
CALL cc, nn	Call subroutine at location nn if condition cc if true
CALL nn	Unconditional call subroutine at location nn
CCF	Complement carry flag
CP s	Compare operand s with Acc.
CPD	Compare location (HL) and Acc. decrement HL and BC
CPDR	Compare location (HL) and Acc. decrement HL and BC, repeat until BC=0
CPI	Compare location (HL) and Acc. increment HL and decrement BC
CPIR	Compare location (HL) and Acc. increment HL, decrement BC repeat until BC=0
CPL	Complement Acc. (1's comp)
DAA	Decimal adjust Acc.
DEC m	Decrement operand m
DEC IX	Decrement IX
DEC IY	Decrement IY
DEC ss	Decrement Reg. pair ss
DI	Disable interrupts
DJNZ e	Decrement B and Jump relative if B≠0
EI	Enable interrupts
EX (SP), HL	Exchange the location (SP) and HL
EX (SP), IX	Exchange the location (SP) and IX
EX (SP), IY	Exchange the location (SP) and IY
EX AF, AF'	Exchange the contents of AF and AF'
EX DE, HL	Exchange the contents of DE and HL
EXX	Exchange the contents of BC, DE, HL with contents of BC', DE', HL' respectively
HALT	HALT (wait for interrupt or reset)
IM 0	Set interrupt mode 0
IM 1	Set interrupt mode 1
IM 2	Set interrupt mode 2
IN A, (n)	Load the Acc. with input from device n
IN r, (C)	Load the Reg. r with input from device (C)
INC (HL)	Increment location (HL)
INC IX	Increment IX
INC (IX+d)	Increment location (IX+d)
INC IY	Increment IY
INC (IY+d)	Increment location (IY+d)
INC r	Increment Reg. r
INC ss	Increment Reg. pair ss
IND	Load location (HL) with input from port (C), decrement HL and B
INDR	Load location (HL) with input from port (C), decrement HL and decrement B, repeat until B=0
INI	Load location (HL) with input from port (C); and increment HL and decrement B

INIR	Load location (HL) with input from port (C), increment HL and decrement B, repeat until B=0	LD (nn), A	Load location (nn) with Acc.
		LD (nn), dd	Load location (nn) with Reg. pair dd
		LD (nn), HL	Load location (nn) with HL
JP (HL)	Unconditional Jump to (HL)	LD (nn), IX	Load location (nn) with IX
JP (IX)	Unconditional Jump to (IX)	LD (nn), IY	Load location (nn) with IY
JP (IY)	Unconditonal Jump to (IY)	LD R, A	Load R with Acc.
JP cc, nn	Jump to location nn if condition cc is true	LD r, (HL)	Load Reg. r with location (HL)
		LD r, (IX+d)	Load Reg. r with location (IX+d)
JP nn	Unconditional jump to location nn	LD r, (IY+d)	Load Reg. r with location (IY+d)
		LD r, n	Load Reg. r with value n
JP C, e	Jump relative to PC+e if carry=1	LD r, r'	Load Reg. r with Reg. r'
JR e	Unconditional Jump relative to PC+e	LD SP, HL	Load SP with HL
		LD SP, IX	Load SP with IX
JP NC, e	Jump relative to PC+e if carry=0	LD SP, IY	Load SP with IY
JR NZ, e	Jump relative to PC+e if non zero (Z=0)	LDD	Load location (DE) with location (HL), decrement DE, HL and BC
JR Z, e	Jump relative to PC+e if zero (Z=1)	LDDR	Load location (DE) with location (HL), decrement DE, HL and BC; repeat until BC=0
LD A, (BC)	Load Acc. with location (BC)		
LD A, (DE)	Load Acc. with location (DE)	LDI	Load location (DE) with location (HL), increment DE, HL, decrement BC
LD A, I	Load Acc. with I		
LD A, (nn)	Load Acc. with location nn	LDIR	Load location (DE) with location (HL), increment DE, HL, decrement BC and repeat until BC=0
LD A, R	Load Acc. with Reg. R		
LD (BC), A	Load location (BC) with Acc.		
LD (DE), A	Load location (DE) with Acc.	NEG	Negate Acc. (2's complement)
LD (HL), n	Load location (HL) with value n	NOP	No operation
LD dd, nn	Load Reg. pair dd with value nn	OR s	Logical 'OR' or operand s and Acc.
LD HL, (nn)	Load HL with location (nn)	OTDR	Load output port (C) with location (HL) decrement HL and B, repeat until B=0
LD (HL), r	Load location (HL) with Reg. r		
LD I, A	Load I with Acc.		
LF IX, nn	Load IX with value nn	OTIR	Load output port (C) with location (HL), increment HL, decrement B, repeat until B=0
LD IX, (nn)	Load IX with location (nn)		
LD (IX+d), n	Load location (IX+d) with value n		
LD (IX+d), r	Load location (IX+d) with Reg. r	OUT (C), r	Load output port (C) with Reg. r
LD IY, nn	Load IY with value nn	OUT (n), A	Load output port (n) with Acc.
LD IY, (nn)	Load IY with location (nn)	OUTD	Load output port (C) with location (HL), decrement HL and B
LD (IY+d), n	Load location (IY+d) with value n	OUTI	Load output port (C) with location (HL), increment HL and decrement B
LD (IY+d), r	Load location (IY+d) with Reg. r		

POP IX	Load IX with top of stack
POP IY	Load IY with top of stack
POP qq	Load Reg. pair qq with top of stack
PUSH IX	Load IX onto stack
PUSH IY	Load IY onto stack
PUSH qq	Load Reg. pair qq onto stack
RES b, m	Reset Bit b of operand m
RET	Return from subroutine
RET cc	Return from subroutine if condition cc is true
RETI	Return from interrupt
RETN	Return from non maskable interrupt
RL m	Rotate left through carry operand m
RLA	Rotate left Acc. through carry
RLC (HL)	Rotate location (HL) left circular
RLC (IX+d)	Rotate location (IX+d) left circular
RLC (IY+d)	Rotate location (IY+d) left circular
RLC r	Rotate Reg. r left circular
RLCA	Rotate left circular Acc.
RLD	Rotate digit left and right between Acc. and location (HL)

RR m	Rotate right through carry operand m
RRA	Rotate right Acc. through carry
RRC m	Rotate operand m right circular
RRCA	Rotate right circular Acc.
RRD	Rotate digit right and left between Acc. and location (HL)
RST p	Restart to location p
SBC A, s	Subtract operand s from Acc. with carry
SBC HL, ss	Subtract Reg. pair ss from HL with carry
SCF	Set carry flag (C=1)
SET b, (HL)	Set Bit b of location (HL)
SET b, (IX+d)	Set Bit b of location (IX+d)
SET b, (IY+d)	Set Bit b of location (IY+d)
SET b, r	Set Bit b of Reg. r
SLA m	Shift operand m left arithmetic
SRA m	Shift operand m right arithmetic
SRL m	Shift operand m right logical
SUB s	Subtract operand s from Acc.
XOR s	Exclusive 'OR' operand s and Acc.

Appendix E

8080 SPECIFICATION SHEETS *

*Courtesy of Intel Corporation

8080A/8080A-1/8080A-2
8-BIT N-CHANNEL MICROPROCESSOR

- **TTL Drive Capability**

- **2 μs (− 1:1.3 μs, − 2:1.5 μs) Instruction Cycle**

- **Powerful Problem Solving Instruction Set**

- **6 General Purpose Registers and an Accumulator**

- **16-Bit Program Counter for Directly Addressing up to 64K Bytes of Memory**

- **16-Bit Stack Pointer and Stack Manipulation Instructions for Rapid Switching of the Program Environment**

- **Decimal, Binary, and Double Precision Arithmetic**

- **Ability to Provide Priority Vectored Interrupts**

- **512 Directly Addressed I/O Ports**

The Intel® 8080A is a complete 8-bit parallel central processing unit (CPU). It is fabricated on a single LSI chip using Intel's n-channel silicon gate MOS process. This offers the user a high performance solution to control and processing applications.

The 8080A contains 6 8-bit general purpose working registers and an accumulator. The 6 general purpose registers may be addressed individually or in pairs providing both single and double precision operators. Arithmetic and logical instructions set or reset 4 testable flags. A fifth flag provides decimal arithmetic operation.

The 8080A has an external stack feature wherein any portion of memory may be used as a last in/first out stack to store/retrieve the contents of the accumulator, flags, program counter, and all of the 6 general purpose registers. The 16-bit stack pointer controls the addressing of this external stack. This stack gives the 8080A the ability to easily handle multiple level priority interrupts by rapidly storing and restoring processor status. It also provides almost unlimited subroutine nesting.

This microprocessor has been designed to simplify systems design. Separate 16-line address and 8-line bidirectional data busses are used to facilitate easy interface to memory and I/O. Signals to control the interface to memory and I/O are provided directly by the 8080A. Ultimate control of the address and data busses resides with the HOLD signal. It provides the ability to suspend processor operation and force the address and data busses into a high impedance state. This permits OR-tying these busses with other controlling devices for (DMA) direct memory access or multi-processor operation.

NOTE:
The 8080A is functionally and electrically compatible with the Intel® 8080.

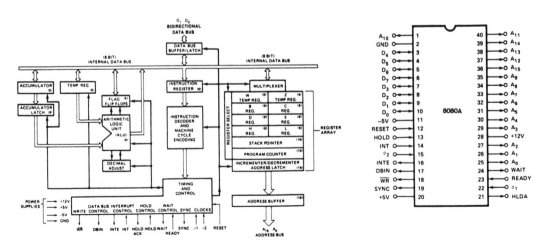

Figure 1. Block Diagram   Figure 2. Pin Configuration

intel

Table 1. Pin Description

Symbol	Type	Name and Function
A_{15}-A_0	O	**Address Bus:** The address bus provides the address to memory (up to 64K 8-bit words) or denotes the I/O device number for up to 256 input and 256 output devices. A_0 is the least significant address bit.
D_7-D_0	I/O	**Data Bus:** The data bus provides bi-directional communication betweeen the CPU, memory, and I/O devices for instructions and data transfers. Also, during the first clock cycle of each machine cycle, the 8080A outputs a status word on the data bus that describes the current machine cycle. D_0 is the least significant bit.
SYNC	O	**Synchronizing Signal:** The SYNC pin provides a signal to indicate the beginning of each machine cycle.
DBIN	O	**Data Bus In:** The DBIN signal indicates to external circuits that the data bus is in the input mode. This signal should be used to enable the gating of data onto the 8080A data bus from memory or I/O.
READY	I	**Ready:** The READY signal indicates to the 8080A that valid memory or input data is available on the 8080A data bus. This signal is used to synchronize the CPU with slower memory or I/O devices. If after sending an address out the 8080A does not receive a READY input, the 8080A will enter a WAIT state for as long as the READY line is low. READY can also be used to single step the CPU.
WAIT	O	**Wait:** The WAIT signal acknowledges that the CPU is in a WAIT state.
$\overline{WR}$	O	**Write:** The $\overline{WR}$ signal is used for memory WRITE or I/O output control. The data on the data bus is stable while the $\overline{WR}$ signal is active low ($\overline{WR}$ = 0).
HOLD	I	**Hold:** The HOLD signal requests the CPU to enter the HOLD state. The HOLD state allows an external device to gain control of the 8080A address and data bus as soon as the 8080A has completed its use of these busses for the current machine cycle. It is recognized under the following conditions: • the CPU is in the HALT state. • the CPU is in the T2 or TW state and the READY signal is active. As a result of entering the HOLD state the CPU ADDRESS BUS (A_{15}-A_0) and DATA BUS (D_7-D_0) will be in their high impedance state. The CPU acknowledges its state with the HOLD ACKNOWLEDGE (HLDA) pin.
HLDA	O	**Hold Acknowledge:** The HLDA signal appears in response to the HOLD signal and indicates that the data and address bus will go to the high impedance state. The HLDA signal begins at: • T3 for READ memory or input. • The Clock Period following T3 for WRITE memory or OUTPUT operation. In either case, the HLDA signal appears after the rising edge of ϕ_2.
INTE	O	**Interrupt Enable:** Indicates the content of the internal interrupt enable flip/flop. This flip/flop may be set or reset by the Enable and Disable Interrupt instructions and inhibits interrupts from being accepted by the CPU when it is reset. It is automatically reset (disabling further interrupts) at time T1 of the instruction fetch cycle (M1) when an interrupt is accepted and is also reset by the RESET signal.
INT	I	**Interrupt Request:** The CPU recognizes an interrupt request on this line at the end of the current instruction or while halted. If the CPU is in the HOLD state or if the Interrupt Enable flip/flop is reset it will not honor the request.
RESET[1]	I	**Reset:** While the RESET signal is activated, the content of the program counter is cleared. After RESET, the program will start at location 0 in memory. The INTE and HLDA flip/flops are also reset. Note that the flags, accumulator, stack pointer, and registers are not cleared.
V_{SS}		**Ground:** Reference.
V_{DD}		**Power:** +12 ±5% Volts.
V_{CC}		**Power:** +5 ±5% Volts.
V_{BB}		**Power:** −5 ±5% Volts.
ϕ_1, ϕ_2		**Clock Phases:** 2 externally supplied clock phases. (non TTL compatible)

Appendix F

8085A SPECIFICATION SHEETS*

*Courtesy of Intel Corporation

8085A/8085A-2
SINGLE CHIP 8-BIT N-CHANNEL MICROPROCESSORS

- **Single +5V Power Supply**
- **100% Software Compatible with 8080A**
- **1.3 μs Instruction Cycle (8085A); 0.8 μs (8085A-2)**
- **On-Chip Clock Generator (with External Crystal, LC or RC Network)**
- **On-Chip System Controller; Advanced Cycle Status Information Available for Large System Control**

- **Four Vectored Interrupt Inputs (One is Non-Maskable) Plus an 8080A-Compatible Interrupt**
- **Serial In/Serial Out Port**
- **Decimal, Binary and Double Precision Arithmetic**
- **Direct Addressing Capability to 64k Bytes of Memory**

The Intel® 8085A is a complete 8 bit parallel Central Processing Unit (CPU). Its instruction set is 100% software compatible with the 8080A microprocessor, and it is designed to improve the present 8080A's performance by higher system speed. Its high level of system integration allows a minimum system of three IC's [8085A (CPU), 8156 (RAM/IO) and 8355/8755A (ROM/PROM/IO)] while maintaining total system expandability. The 8085A-2 is a faster version of the 8085A.

The 8085A incorporates all of the features that the 8224 (clock generator) and 8228 (system controller) provided for the 8080A, thereby offering a high level of system integration.

The 8085A uses a multiplexed data bus. The address is split between the 8 bit address bus and the 8 bit data bus. The on-chip address latches of 8155/8156/8355/8755A memory products allow a direct interface with the 8085A.

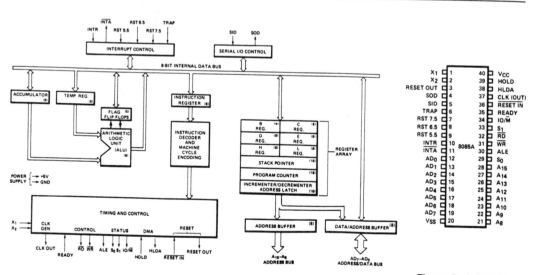

Figure 1. 8085A CPU Functional Block Diagram

Figure 2. 8085A Pin Configuration

8085A/8085A-2

ABSOLUTE MAXIMUM RATINGS*

Ambient Temperature Under Bias. . . . . 0°C to 70°C
Storage Temperature . . . . −65°C to +150°C
Voltage on Any Pin
  With Respect to Ground. . . . . −0.5V to +7V
Power Dissipation . . . . 1.5 Watt

NOTICE: Stresses above those listed under "Absolute Maximum Ratings" may cause permanent damage to the device. This is a stress rating only and functional operation of the device at these or any other conditions above those indicated in the operational sections of this specification is not implied. Exposure to absolute maximum rating conditions for extended periods may affect device reliability.

D.C. CHARACTERISTICS (T_A = 0°C to 70°C, V_{CC} = 0V ±5%, V_{SS} = 0V; unless otherwise specified)

Symbol	Parameter	Min.	Max.	Units	Test Conditions
V_{IL}	Input Low Voltage	−0.5	+0.8	V	
V_{IH}	Input High Voltage	2.0	V_{CC}+0.5	V	
V_{OL}	Output Low Voltage		0.45	V	I_{OL} = 2mA
V_{OH}	Output High Voltage	2.4		V	I_{OH} = −400μA
I_{CC}	Power Supply Current		170	mA	
I_{IL}	Input Leakage		±10	μA	0≤ V_{IN} ≤V_{CC}
I_{LO}	Output Leakage		±10	μA	0.45V ≤ V_{out} ≤ V_{CC}
V_{ILR}	Input Low Level, RESET	−0.5	+0.8	V	
V_{IHR}	Input High Level, RESET	2.4	V_{CC} +0.5	V	
V_{HY}	Hysteresis, RESET	0.25		V	

intel

A.C. CHARACTERISTICS (T_A = 0°C to 70°C, V_{CC} = 0V ±5%, V_{SS} = 0V)

Symbol	Parameter	8085A[2] Min.	8085A[2] Max.	8085A-2[2] Min.	8085A-2[2] Max.	Units
t_{CYC}	CLK Cycle Period	320	2000	200	2000	ns
t_1	CLK Low Time (Standard CLK Loading)	80		40		ns
t_2	CLK High Time (Standard CLK Loading)	120		70		ns
t_r, t_f	CLK Rise and Fall Time		30		30	ns
t_{XKR}	X_1 Rising to CLK Rising	30	120	30	100	ns
t_{XKF}	X_1 Rising to CLK Falling	30	150	30	110	ns
t_{AC}	A_{8-15} Valid to Leading Edge of Control[1]	270		115		ns
t_{ACL}	A_{0-7} Valid to Leading Edge of Control	240		115		ns
t_{AD}	A_{0-15} Valid to Valid Data In		575		350	ns
t_{AFR}	Address Float After Leading Edge of READ (INTA)		0		0	ns
t_{AL}	A_{8-15} Valid Before Trailing Edge of ALE[1]	115		50		ns
t_{ALL}	A_{0-7} Valid Before Trailing Edge of ALE	90		50		ns
t_{ARY}	READY Valid from Address Valid		220		100	ns
t_{CA}	Address (A_{8-15}) Valid After Control	120		60		ns
t_{CC}	Width of Control Low (RD, WR, INTA) Edge of ALE	400		230		ns
t_{CL}	Trailing Edge of Control to Leading Edge of ALE	50		25		ns
t_{DW}	Data Valid to Trailing Edge of WRITE	420		230		ns
t_{HABE}	HLDA to Bus Enable		210		150	ns
t_{HABF}	Bus Float After HLDA		210		150	ns
t_{HACK}	HLDA Valid to Trailing Edge of CLK	110		40		ns
t_{HDH}	HOLD Hold Time	0		0		ns
t_{HDS}	HOLD Setup Time to Trailing Edge of CLK	170		120		ns
t_{INH}	INTR Hold Time	0		0		ns
t_{INS}	INTR, RST, and TRAP Setup Time to Falling Edge of CLK	160		150		ns
t_{LA}	Address Hold Time After ALE	100		50		ns
t_{LC}	Trailing Edge of ALE to Leading Edge of Control	130		60		ns
t_{LCK}	ALE Low During CLK High	100		50		ns
t_{LDR}	ALE to Valid Data During Read		460		270	ns
t_{LDW}	ALE to Valid Data During Write		200		120	ns
t_{LL}	ALE Width	140		80		ns
t_{LRY}	ALE to READY Stable		110		30	ns

8085A/8085A-2

A.C. CHARACTERISTICS (Continued)

Symbol	Parameter	8085A[2]		8085A-2[2]		Units
		Min.	Max.	Min.	Max.	
t_{RAE}	Trailing Edge of $\overline{READ}$ to Re-Enabling of Address	150		90		ns
t_{RD}	$\overline{READ}$ (or $\overline{INTA}$) to Valid Data		300		150	ns
t_{RV}	Control Trailing Edge to Leading Edge of Next Control	400		220		ns
t_{RDH}	Data Hold Time After $\overline{READ}$ $\overline{INTA}$[7]	0		0		ns
t_{RYH}	READY Hold Time	0		0		ns
t_{RYS}	READY Setup Time to Leading Edge of CLK	110		100		ns
t_{WD}	Data Valid After Trailing Edge of $\overline{WRITE}$	100		60		ns
t_{WDL}	LEADING Edge of WRITE to Data Valid		40		20	ns

NOTES:

1. A_8-A_{15} address Specs apply to IO/$\overline{M}$, S_0, and S_1 except A_8-A_{15} are undefined during T_4-T_6 of OF cycle whereas IO/$\overline{M}$, S_0, and S_1 are stable.
2. Test conditions: t_{CYC} = 320 ns (8085A)/200 ns (8085A-2); C_L = 150 pF.
3. For all output timing where C_L = 150 pF use the following correction factors:
   25 pF $\leqslant$ C_L < 150 pF: -0.10 ns/pF
   150 pF < C_L $\leqslant$ 300 pF: $+0.30$ ns/pF
4. Output timings are measured with purely capacitive load.
5. All timings are measured at output votage V_L = 0.8V, V_H = 2.0V, and 1.5V with 20 ns rise and fall time on inputs.
6. To calculate timing specifications at other values of t_{CYC} use Table 7.
7. Data hold time is guaranteed under all loading conditions.

A.C. TESTING INPUT, OUTPUT WAVEFORM

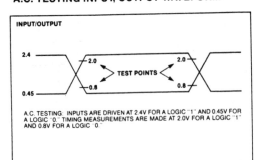

A.C. TESTING LOAD CIRCUIT

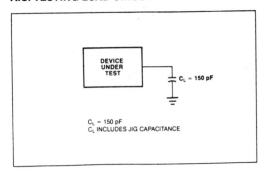

Appendix G

Number Conversion Tables

Conversion Table

OCTAL	HEX	OCTAL	HEX	OCTAL	HEX	OCTAL	HEX	OCTAL	HEX
000	00	063	33	146	66	231	99	314	CC
001	01	064	34	147	67	232	9A	315	CD
002	02	065	35	150	68	233	9B	316	CE
003	03	066	36	151	69	234	9C	317	CF
004	04	067	37	152	6A	235	9D	320	D0
005	05	070	38	153	6B	236	9E	321	D1
006	06	071	39	154	6C	237	9F	322	D2
007	07	072	3A	155	6D	240	A0	323	D3
010	08	073	3B	156	6E	241	A1	324	D4
011	09	074	3C	157	6F	242	A2	325	D5
012	0A	075	3D	160	70	243	A3	326	D6
013	0B	076	3E	161	71	244	A4	327	D7
014	0C	077	3F	162	72	245	A5	330	D8
015	0D	100	40	163	73	246	A6	331	D9
016	0E	101	41	164	74	247	A7	332	DA
017	0F	102	42	165	75	250	A8	333	DB
020	10	103	43	166	76	251	A9	334	DC
021	11	104	44	167	77	252	AA	335	DD
022	12	105	45	170	78	253	AB	336	DE
023	13	106	46	171	79	254	AC	337	DF
024	14	107	47	172	7A	255	AD	340	E0

Conversion Table (*continued*)

OCTAL	HEX	OCTAL	HEX	OCTAL	HEX	OCTAL	HEX	OCTAL	HEX
025	15	110	48	173	7B	256	AE	341	E1
026	16	111	49	174	7C	257	AF	342	E2
027	17	112	4A	175	7D	260	B0	343	E3
030	18	113	4B	176	7E	261	B1	344	E4
031	19	114	4C	177	7F	262	B2	345	E5
032	1A	115	4D	200	80	263	B3	346	E6
033	1B	116	4E	201	81	264	B4	347	E7
034	1C	117	4F	202	82	265	B5	350	E8
035	1D	120	50	203	83	266	B6	351	E9
036	1E	121	51	204	84	267	B7	352	EA
037	1F	122	52	205	85	270	B8	353	EB
040	20	123	53	206	86	271	B9	354	EC
041	21	124	54	207	87	272	BA	355	ED
042	22	125	55	210	88	273	BB	356	EE
043	23	126	56	211	89	274	BC	357	EF
044	24	127	57	212	8A	275	BD	360	F0
045	25	130	58	213	8B	276	BE	361	F1
046	26	131	59	214	8C	277	BF	362	F2
047	27	132	5A	215	8D	300	C0	363	F3
050	28	133	5B	216	8E	301	C1	364	F4
051	29	134	5C	217	8F	302	C2	365	F5
052	2A	135	5D	220	90	303	C3	366	F6
053	2B	136	5E	221	91	304	C4	367	F7
054	2C	137	5F	222	92	305	C5	370	F8
055	2D	140	60	223	93	306	C6	371	F9
056	2E	141	61	224	94	307	C7	372	FA
057	2F	142	62	225	95	310	C8	373	FB
060	30	143	63	226	96	311	C9	374	FC
061	31	144	64	227	97	312	CA	375	FD
062	32	145	65	230	98	313	CB	376	FE
								377	FF

GLOSSARY

accumulator—a register within the CPU. This register will be one of the operands in an arithmetic or logical operation.

address—a binary pattern used to select a location in memory. In this text, addresses are 16 bits wide.

addressing modes—techniques used by software or hardware in calculating an address.

ALU—arithmetic logic unit; the section of the CPU that performs calculations for arithmetic and logical operations.

assembler—a program that translates mnemonic code into machine-level code.

asynchronous—an event or operation not controlled by the master clock.

base address—the location of the first datum in a data table.

bit—a binary digit.

BCD—binary coded decimal; a number system in which each group of 4 bits (referred to as *decades*) represents a single decimal digit.

breakpoint—a place in a program where execution is temporarily stopped. Once a breakpoint is reached, analysis of the program can be performed.

buffer—a circuit that can be used to isolate one part of the computer from another. Buffers often provide extra current capabilities not found in the circuit driving the inputs. A buffer can also be used as a temporary storage register.

bus—a set of lines used to move information from one part of the computer to another. Typically, a bus is divided into three functional groups: data, address, and control.

bus contention—two or more circuits trying to place information on a common line at the same time.

byte—a group of 8 bits.

CPU—central processing unit; a section of a computer responsible for execution of programs. This section manipulates the data, generates control signals, and stores results. In modern computers these functions have been integrated into a single IC. The 8080, 8085, and Z80 are examples of CPUs.

clock cycle—the basic unit of processor activity.

compiler—a program that translates high-level code into machine code.

controller—a circuit that acts as an interface between the computer and a device such as a disk drive. The controller will pass information back and forth between the computer and the device and will generate specialized control signals needed to operate the device.

DAC—digital-to-analog converter.

device-select pulse—a control pulse created by logically combining a port address with an IN or OUT control signal.

DMA—direct memory access; a process in which circuits other than the CPU can read from or write to memory without processor intervention.

displacement—the amount by which a location differs from a reference point. When using data tables, the reference point is usually the base address.

duplex—two-way data transfers. *Half duplex* is two-way communication, with each end of the system taking turns transmitting. *Full duplex* is two-way communication that occurs simultaneously.

dynamic memory—a memory in which information is stored capacitively. This type of memory requires periodic refresh to replenish capacitor charges.

EEPROM—electrically erasable programmable read only memory.

EPROM—erasable by ultraviolet light.

firmware—a software routine that has been stored in a read only memory and thus is available at power up without the need for reloading the code.

flag—a flip-flop used to indicate the status of an operation. For example, the zero flag will indicate if an operation results in zero if it is set.

flowchart—a pictorial diagram of the logical sequence of a program.

handshaking—the exchange of control and status information between two circuits. Handshaking is used to coordinate the transfer of data between circuits.

hardware—the physical parts of a system.

high-level language—a computer language such as FORTRAN or COBOL. Such languages are Englishlike, requiring a compiler to translate them into machine code.

ICE—in circuit emulator.

index register—a special-purpose register used by a processor when performing indexed addressing. The value in the index register is usually the reference location to which a displacement will be added.

I/O—input/output; the process by which the computer communicates with the outside world.

instruction—a computer command.

instruction cycle—the time and activities associated with the performance of an instruction.

instruction fetch—a machine cycle used by the processor to obtain instructions from memory.

instruction register—the part of the CPU that stores the instruction while it is being decoded.

instruction set—the group of instructions that is recognized by a processor.

interrupt—an asynchronous request by a circuit asking for the processor's attention. If acknowledged, the processor will temporarily stop what it was doing and interact with the circuit that generated the interrupt.

interrupt service routine—a section of code written to handle the tasks associated with an interrupt request.

interrupt vector—a special code that identifies the circuit requesting an interrupt.

invisible subtraction—a subtraction in which the answer is not stored back in the accumulator. The results of the subtraction can, however, affect the flags, making it possible to make decisions based on the result.

isolated I/O—a method of I/O that differentiates between memory and I/O ports. In this text, the only register that can be used with isolated I/O is the accumulator.

linear decoding—a method of addressing a circuit using a single address line.

logical construct—a method of organizing how a task will be performed. When used in programming, constructs partition the code into sections in which each section has but one entry point and one exit point.

machine cycle—a set of clock states grouped together to perform a data transfer.

machine language—a computer language that is directly executable by a computer without the need for translation by a compiler or an assembler. Although the computer works on binary patterns, the program can usually be entered in octal or hexadecimal.

masking—a process in which an operation can be performed on a single bit.

memory cell—a circuit in memory that represents a single bit.

memory map—documentation that lists or shows the function of each location in memory.

memory-mapped I/O—a system of I/O in which each I/O location is treated as if it were memory.

microprocessor—an integrated circuit in which CPU, ALU, and control functions are combined.

mnemonic—an Englishlike representation of an instruction.

monitor program—a program, usually stored in ROM, that is responsible for basic computer operations.

nesting—the technique of placing a loop or subroutine within another loop or subroutine.

nibble—4 bits.

non-maskable interrupt—an interrupt that cannot be turned off.

operating system—a program similar to a monitor program, but more sophisticated. Not only does it handle basic computer functions, it is capable of interacting with peripherals such as disk drives and printers.

op code—a binary pattern that when loaded into the instruction register will cause the CPU to perform tasks associated with the instruction.

page—256 bytes of memory.

parallel—a bus system in which information is moved in multibit units simultaneously.

polling—a process in which the status of devices attached to a bus system is periodically sampled.

port—an interface circuit capable of receiving from or placing information on the bus.

priority—the level of importance of an event. Most often, interrupts are assigned priorities.

program counter—a 16-bit register that places addresses on the bus to retrieve information stored within a program.

programmable interface chip—an IC in which the specific tasks to be performed are not hardwired into the chip, but selectable through the use of command words.

PROM—programmable read only memory.

random access—each location within memory can be directly accessed without the need to sequence through prior locations. *Direct access* is probably more appropriate, as this access method is not really random.

read—to transfer information into the CPU.

relative addressing—an addressing mode that calculates a new address based on the position of an instruction within a program.

sequential access—a method of access in which all prior records or locations must be traversed before reaching the desired location or record.

signature analysis—a troubleshooting technique in which a stream of serial data is converted into a binary pattern that can then be compared to a pattern known to represent a functional circuit.

simplex—one-way communication.

single step—a process in which a program can be performed one instruction or one machine cycle at a time.

stack—an area of memory used to implement a data structure that follows the last in, first out method of access. In most cases, the stack is used by the processor to keep track of subroutine calls and returns.

stack pointer—a special-purpose register that tracks the location of the last entry in the stack.

static memory—memory in which the basic cell circuit consists of a flip-flop.

synchronous—an event or operation that takes place in step with a master clock.

throughput—the amount of information processed in a given time.

USART—universal synchronous asynchronous receiver transmitter; a special-purpose IC used in data communications.

volatile—memory in which data is lost when power is removed.

word—16 bits.

write—data transfer out of the CPU.

ANSWERS

CHAPTER ONE

1. A binary digit.
3. 8 bits.
5. Memory-mapped architecture.
7. The ALU performs arithmetic and logic functions.
9. The address buffer places addresses onto the address bus.
11. Sequential access is a method of access in which every record must be traversed prior to arriving at the required data.
13. A simple control program is often referred to as a *monitor*.
15. An instruction cycle is performed each time the step button is pressed.
17. The Z80 has the largest number of general-purpose registers.
19. When ALE is high, a valid address byte is present on the data/address pins. Consequently, this signal can be used to activate a latch that will hold the address during the rest of the operation.
21. One.

CHAPTER 2

1. A mnemonic is an Englishlike representation of a computer instruction. It is not directly executable by a computer. An op code is a binary pattern that can be executed directly by the computer. Assemblers translate mnemonics into op codes that can then be performed by the computer.
3. No.
5.

LXI SP − 061 octal	31 hex
ORI − 366 octal	F6 hex
CMP C − 271 octal	69 hex

7. Five.
9. The second byte of the MVI instruction is a data byte.
11. INX D.
13. Nested loops allow the programmer to perform different tasks within the body of each loop, where the number of times each task is performed can be controlled by different loop counters.
15. Invisible subtraction does not store the result back into the accumulator.
17. C1 hex.
19. 9F with the carry flag set.
21. DE is in the B register and CF is in the C register.

L1. Use an INR instruction; use the ADI with an immediate byte of 0.1 hex; use an SUI with an immediate byte of FF (minus 1 in two's complement).

L3. No. Counting up by 1 involves the use of an ADI which uses the A register. It could also be done through the use of an INR. It might seem that the INR suggestion could eliminate the use of the A register, but to compare the incremented value to 25 will require the use of the accumulator.

L5. Your program must include an OUT within the body of the loop. Another option would be to use register mode each time through the loop to inspect the loop counter.

CHAPTER 3

1. Organize the logic of a program; use a tool in the debugging of software.

3. A special code is a binary pattern with an assigned meaning that might not be apparent unless the meaning is documented. A code can be used to represent a condition that a computer must monitor or it can be used by a computer to activate devices that require more than simple on/off control pulses.

5. One.

7. One entry point; one exit point.

9. One.

11. One.

13. A dummy subroutine is a section of code that outputs a signature or value that tells an operator that the logic of the main-level program called the subroutine correctly. The dummy routine will be replaced as the programmer codes lower-level routines in programs developed using top-down design.

15. The program counter.

17. A binary search is a search technique that divides the area to be searched in halves. As each part is examined, the inappropriate part is discarded, with the remaining part again divided in half. This progression continues until the value desired is found.

19. The IN instruction will not set flags.

CHAPTER 4

1. The clock state.

3. Data transfers.

5. Three.

7. A cold reset occurs when power is first applied. A warm reset occurs when a reset pulse is delivered to a CPU that is already powered.

9. The Z80 will sample the data bus looking for an op code if the machine cycle underway is an op code fetch.

11. The Z80 will continuously perform NOPs so that dynamic refresh pulses can be generated.

13. At the falling edge of T2 and every falling edge of Tw.

15. During T1 of a machine cycle.

17. Overlapping cycles are used to complete one instruction while the next is being fetched from memory.

19. The instruction register.

21. 10111000.

L1. 1953.12 With a clock state lasting 1 μs, a delay of 500 ms requires a total of 500,000 states. Since a single-byte loop counter can handle a maximum of 256 iterations, each pass through the loop will need 1953 T states.

CHAPTER 5

1. I/0 request* and MEMRQ*.

3. A port address and either the IN* or OUT* control signals.

5. Eight for a port, 16 when decoding an address used in an address select pulse.

7. T3.

9. An ambiguity results when a single address can turn on many different devices or memory locations. It can occur when decoders are not absolute.

11. An address-select pulse is comprised of a decoded address and either a MEMRD* or MEMWR* control signal.

13. 00000011.

15. A software bottleneck arises when information not involved in I/O must be moved into or out of the accumulator prior to performing I/O operations.

17. 10011000.

19. Wire all control signals before connecting to the data bus. Verify that data-bus pins are tristate before the connection is complete.

21. Status-driven I/O relies on handshaking signals to control data transfers. A data transfer will be conditional based on the status signals.

CHAPTER 6

1. In applications where calculations would slow down processing by adding extra code, answers can be prestored.

   Trig functions.

   Wave generation—sine, triangular, sawtooth, etc.

   Control applications—where special codes control some sequence, the codes can be stored in the correct sequence in a table.

3. Indexed.

5. Base address and the index.

7. In hex – FFFE – FFFD – FFFB – FFF7 – FFEF – FFDF – FFBF – FF7F – FEFF – FDFF – FBFF – F7FF – EFFF – DFFF – BFFF – 7FFF.

In octal – 377 376 – 377 375 – 377 373 – 377 367 – 377 357 – 377 337 – 377 277 – 377 177 – 376 377 – 375 377 – 373 377 – 367 377 – 357 377 – 337 377 – 277 377 – 177 377.

Note: Because the 74154 has 16 outputs, each of the patterns given above would have to be stored in two consecutive memory locations with a test routine alternating between a test for the high-order byte and a low-order byte.

9. If a table were longer than 256 bytes, it would cross a page boundary. Using an INX instruction assures that the high-order address byte would change automatically when required.

11. The value of the test pattern could have been checked. The value of the loop counter stored in B could also have been tested.

13. There are two delays that need to be considered when an 8212 is used. The first is the time from data to output delay, which is a maximum of 30 ns. The second is the time from write enable to output delay, which is a maximum of 40 ns. A study of the output machine cycle shows that the write control signal is activated after the data is present on the bus. Therefore, we will use the 40 ns delay. The 7432 has a maximum worst case delay of 22 ns (tph1). Thus, the worst-case delay, once the circuit is activated by the device-select pulse, is 62 ns.

1/62 ns yields a frequency of 16,129,032 Hz. Since the processor driving the circuit cannot operate this fast, the data out of the OR gates will be present by the time the processor activates the IN buffer to sample the answers.

15. 32.

17. Yes. It is very unlikely that a bad strobe line will cause the chip to generate a 252.

19. See diagram:

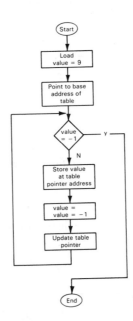

CHAPTER 7

1. The STA instruction stores the A register in a memory location specified by the second and third bytes of the instruction.
   It uses the direct form of addressing.
3. 0110 binary.
5. 896, 75, 36, and 27.
7. 100 base 10, when the CPU is 8 bits wide.
9. B, D, H, and the SP register pairs can be used with a DAD.
11. Two.
13. If the PUSHes and POPs are not balanced, the stack pointer will not be able to correctly locate return addresses.
15. The PCHL instruction transfers the contents of the H register pair into the program counter.
17. Place one memory pointer in the H register pair and a secondary memory pointer in the D register pair. Then use the XCHG instruction to toggle between the two pointers as each is required to act as the memory pointer.
19. Indexed.
21. Code compression is reducing the amount of code needed to perform a task without changing the program logic.
23. A. Access time differs depending on the function selected.
    B. Skip chains usually require more code than address tables.

CHAPTER 8

1. T1.
3. After the falling edge of T1.
5. By the manufacturer.
7. Electrical erasable programmable read only memory.
9. Direct access allows a record or datum to be retrieved without the need to sequence through every record in a file before reaching the required information.
11. Data are stored as charges or lack of charges across a capacitor.
13. A refresh cycle will replenish capacitor charges lost due to leakage currents and discharge currents.
15. 32.
17. BUSRQ* and BUSAK*.
19. RDY is used by the Z8410 to determine if a peripheral is ready for a read or write operation.

CHAPTER 9

1. 128.

3. Resolution is the smallest difference that can be produced at the output. It is equal to the value of the LSB. This can be calculated by taking the maximum output of the converter and dividing this value by the number of states the converter can handle.

5. Accuracy is a measure of how close the actual output is to the theoretical output. Resolution is explained in answer 3.

7. A1 is the MSB of the DAC. It corresponds to D7 on the data bus.

9. No.

11. A large amount of hardware is required.

13. 128.

15. CS*—chip select; WR*—write; RD*—read; EOC—end of conversion; CLK—clock.

17. Output interface.

19. Instant on and zero crossing.

21. To smooth out step changes in the staircase waveform.

CHAPTER 10

1. Fan out is a measure of the number of unit inputs that can be attached to a single output.

3. Z80—1.8 mA low, 250 μA high; 8080—1.9 mA low, 150 μa high; 8085—2 mA low, 400 μA high.
   If the current levels are exceeded, the voltage specifications are not guaranteed.

5. One capacitor for every four ICs.

7. So the outputs of the buffer drivers are tristated when the CPU tristates its bus lines.

9. Leakage currents used by devices when in the tristate condition.

11. 22 ns.

13. A. Memory—RAMS, ROMs.
    B. Arithmetic units.
    C. Multilevel logic paths.

15. A. Slow down the master clock.
    B. Buy chips with faster access times.
    C. Add wait states.

17. It is an active low tristate line.

19. MEMREQ* and RD*.

21. The 7475 provides a path to ground for key closures (a column at a time).

23. A bootstrap program contains enough logic to power up a computer and load the

rest of the monitor. The monitor should contain all the logic needed to operate the computer.

25. A. Breakpoint capability.
    B. Register mode.
    C. R/W storage capabilities to a backup memory device such as a cassette tape.

CHAPTER 11

1. Reset the system or interrupt the system.
3. EI.
5. By waiting to acknowledge the interrupt request until the end of the current instruction cycle.
7. The INTA signal can be used by a peripheral as a control signal that indicates when it should gate a restart instruction onto the data bus.
9. A RST instruction acts like a single-byte CALL. The RST has a predefined address and does not require a second and third byte for addressing.
11. If a false interrupt request is received, none of the peripherals should respond to the INTA signal. Thus, when the processor samples the data bus, there will be no valid information on the bus. The processor will interpret this as FF, which is the op code pattern for RST 7. This address is usually within the monitor. Thus, control will pass to the monitor.
13. OR logic.
15. *Jamming* is used to refer to a peripheral placing an instruction on the bus in response to an INTA signal. The op code will be transferred into the instruction register.
17. Save all the registers.
19. A priority chain is a hardware circuit where the physical location of a card determines the priority of the circuit. The circuit that first receives the INTA signal can respond or pass the INTA signal to the next card in the chain. If the card responds to the INTA signal, it will break the chain by preventing the INTA signal from reaching the next card.
21. Bracket the time-sensitive code with DI and then EI.
23. Place EI at the start of the low-order service routine.
25. A. Fully nested.
    B. Rotating priority.
    C. Special mask.
    D. Polled.
27. Fully nested.
29. TRAP.
31. IMO—mode 0.

CHAPTER 12

1. Loading effect of the probe; size of the probe tip.

3. You can obtain a false reading. A logic probe will indicate a positive at 2 or more volts when set to TTL thresholds. Vcc requires at least 4.75 V.

5. A. Read from memory.
   B. Write to memory.
   C. Read from I/O.
   D. Write to I/O.
   E. Perform internal operations.

7. Test the control inputs.

9. In an 8080 system, check the following inputs:
    power supplies and ground
    free-running clock
    reset input
    the ready input
    the HOLD input
    the INT line

  In an 8085 system, check the following inputs:
    input voltage and ground
    clock input
    READY
    HOLD
    INT
    TRAP
    reset IN

  In a Z80 system, check the following inputs:
    input power and ground
    INT*
    RESET*
    BUSRQ*
    Clock
    WAIT*
    NMI*

11. Insert a current-limiting resistor between the generator output and the injection point.

13. So the INT function can be used to transfer control to other test programs within the ROM.

15. A. RAM test.
   B. ROM test looking for bus contentions as well as bad data.
   C. Keyboard test.

17. 10.

19. Use a control signal associated with the operation to be tested to mark the time on the scope in which the data is valid.

INDEX

A

Accumulator, 4
Accumulator I/O, 13, 151
ADC:
  binary counting conversions, 309
  chip interface, 311
  direct conversions, 307
  dual slope conversions, 306
  pulse width conversions, 308
  successive approximation, 310
ADD, 52
Address bus:
  buffer, 6
  function, 7
Addressing modes:
  bit addressing, 261
  direct addressing, 260
  immediate addressing, 257
  immediate extended addressing, 257
  implied addressing, 260
  indexed addressing, 260
  indirect addressing, 253
  register addressing, 260
  register indirect addressing, 260
  relative addressing, 260
Address select pulse, 169
Address tables, 253–55
ADI, 52, 237
ANA, 38
Analog-to-digital conversions (*See* ADC)
ANI, 43
Arithmetic instructions, 52
Arithmetic logic unit, 4
Assemblers, 21
Asynchronous transmissions:
  description, 194
  frame, 194–95
  start bit, 195
  stop bits, 195
AY-3-1015:
  function, 195
  pin out, 195

B

Bit, 2
Block transfers, 250
Bootstrap, 347
Branch instructions, 28
Breakpoints:
  function, 11
  placement, 87
  usage, 87
BUSAK*, 280
BUSRQ*, 280, 406
Byte, 2

C

CALL, 75
Central processing unit, 2
Clock state:
  function, 100, 106
  8080 states (table), 107
  8085 states (table), 108
  Z80 states (table), 109
CMA, 41
CMP, 46
Code compression, 52, 254
Compare instructions, 46
Computer bus, 6
Condition codes, 29
Control bus, 7
Control loop:
  configuration, 315
  transducer, 315
Control pulses:
  generation, 172
  using select pulses as, 171
Counting instructions, 31
CPI, 47
Critical path, 331
Current probe, 429

D

DAA, 236
DAC:
  accuracy, 298
  applications, 305
  binary ladder, 298
  bipolar operation, 303
  converters (*See* 1408)
  fault analysis, 304
  resolution, 297
DAD, 242
Data bus:
  buffer, 6
  function, 6
Data communication equipment (*See* DCE)
Data tables:
  base address, 207
  index, 207
  usage, 207
Data terminal equipment (*See* DTE)
Data transfer group, 23
DBIN, 154, 157
DCE, 191
DCR, 32
DCX, 36
Debugging, 85
Decoupling capacitors, 322
Device select pulse:
  function, 152
  signal components, 152, 163
Digital-to-analog conversions (*See* DAC)
Direct access, 8
Direct memory access (*See* DMA)
Display ports, 346
DMA:
  operations, 280
  z8410 controller, 282
Documentation, 60
DTE, 190
DTE-DCE interface, 191
Dummy subroutines, 74

E

EI:
  activating interrupts, 373
  turning on INTE, 214
8080:
  instruction set, 465–68
  introduction, 2
  pin out, 149
  specifications, 477–79
  status bits, 155
8085:
  introduction, 14
  multiplexed data bus, 175
  pin out, 149
  specifications, 480–84
81C128:
  internal logic, 277
  pin out, 277
8212:
  address latch, 176
  data bus buffer, 323
  input port, 176
  internal logic, 174
  interrupting port, 442
  latch, 330
  pin out, 174
8224, 100
8228:
  bus controller, 323
8253:
  introduction, 131
  modes of operation, 135
  pin out, 132
  programming, 134
  reading count values, 138
  system interface, 133
  uses, 131
8255:
  internal logic, 178
  introduction, 177
  mode 0 operation, 177
  mode 1 operation, 179, 406
  mode 2 operation, 179

  pin out, 178
  programming, 179
  set/reset control, 181
    format, 183
  status driven I/O, 181
  status register, 409
8259A:
  internal logic, 389
  introduction, 388
  programming, 390
  system interface, 391
  typical interrupt sequence, 390

F

Fanout, 321
51C67:
  internal logic, 278
  pin out, 278
Flag control, 30
Flags:
  auxilliary flag, 5
  carry flag, 6
  half carry flag, 18
  overflow flag, 18
  parity flag, 5
  sign flag, 5
  understanding responses, 48
  zero flag, 5
Flowchart:
  introduction, 59–64
  symbols:
    connectors, 65
    decisions, 65
    process, 65
    terminal interrupt, 65
Forcing, 88
1408:
  pin out, 299
  system interface, 301
  typical circuitry, 300

H

HALT, 54
Hardware timing support, 130
Hexadecimal, 23
High-level languages, 22
HOLD, 281
HOLDA, 281

I

IN, 26
IN*, 151, 153
In-circuit emulators, 454
INR, 31
Instruction cycles:
  functions, 114
  in, 156
  out, 154
  tables, 114–18
INTE, 217, 376
Internal data bus, 6
Interrupt request, 372
Interrupts:
  half restarts, 402
  high priority lockout, 387
  INTA, 373, 376
  introduction, 11
  jump tables, 375
  low priority lockout, 386
  masking, 384
  multiline systems, 400
  priority chains, 382
  priority controllers, 383, 388
  restarts, 374
  service routines:
    functions, 373
    layout, 379
  single line system, 375
  TRAP, 401
  vectors, 381

Z80:
  mode 0, 403
  mode 1, 404
  mode 2, 404
Invisible subtraction, 46
INX, 36
I/O loop, 64
IO/M*, 148
IOR*, 148, 151
IOW*, 151
Isolated I/O, 13, 151

J

JPE, 44
JPO, 44, 46

K

Keypads, 340

L

LDA, 235
LDAX, 252
LDIR, 250
LHLD, 246
Loading, capacitive, 322
Logical constructs:
  coding, 70
  command, 67
  do-until, 69
  do-while, 68, 71
  if-then, 67
  if-then-else, 68, 71

Logical instructions, 38
Logic analyzers, 454
Logic probes, 427
Long word, 2
Loop counters, 33
LXI, 25

M

Machine cycles:
  bus request/acknowledge, 281
  8080, 110
  8085, 111
  input read, 111, 157
  instruction fetch, 113
  introduction, 102
  invisible, 121
  memory read, 110
    8085, 167
    Z80, 265
  memory write, 110
    8085, 167
    Z80, 266
  op code fetch, 110
  output write, 111, 155
  stepper circuitry, 434
  Z80, 112
Machine-level coding, 22
Masking:
  mask bytes, 44–45
  uses, 43
Master clock, 13, 100
Memory:
  holes, 7
  page, 27
  read only (ROM), 9
  system RAM, 9
Memory map:
  documentation, 7
  holes, 166
Memory mapped decoders, 169

Memory mapped I/O:
  A15, used for control, 166
  concept, 157
  pointers, 252
  ports, 13
Memory mapped system, 165
Memory operand, 24
Memory pointer, 26, 206
  multiple, 250
  updating, 218
MEMRQ*, 148
Microprocessing unit, 2
Mnemonics, 21
Modems, 199
Modular programming, 72
M1*, 114
Monitors:
  control programs, 9, 347
  minimum functions, 347
MVI, 26

N

Nesting:
  loops, 33
Nibble, 2
Nine's complement numbers, 240
NOP, 124
Number conversions:
  octal to hex (tables), 485–86

O

Operation code, 4, 21
ORA, 39
Oscilloscope, 428
OUT, 26
OUT*, 151, 153

P

Patches, 60
PCHL, 248
Polling, 378
POP, 78
Port address, 27
Port decoders:
   absolute, 158
   ambiguity, 158–59
   linear, 158
   overview, 157
   partial, 158
   ports (bidirectional), 164
   system function, 12
Power supply droop, 322
Power up reset, 106
Power up timing, 105
Program counter, 11
Project layout sheet, 61
Propagation delay, 331
PUSH, 77

R

RAM:
   decoder circuitry, 277
   dynamic, 289
     refresh of, 290
   introduction, 273
Random access memory (*See* RAM)
Read only memory (*See* ROM)
Read/write memory, 273
Ready, 114
Register(s):
   flag register layout, 5
   general purpose, 2
   global, 63
   index, 16
   instruction, 4

   interrupt vector, 16
   memory refresh, 16
Register mode, 11
Register pair operations, 25, 36
Reset, 106
Reset in, 104
RET, 75, 376
RETN, 405
RFSH*, 114
ROM:
   absolute address decoders, 271
   interfacing circuitry, 269
   types, 266
Rotate instructions, 47
RS-232C:
   overview, 191
   pin functions, 192
   uses, 199

S

Sample and hold, 314
Sequential access, 8
Serial interfacing, 193
74154:
   function table, 160
   pin out, 160
74LS245:
   internal logic, 328
   pin out, 328
74367:
   address bus buffer, 323
SHLD, 246
Signature analysis, 453
Single tasking, 11
Sixteen-bit arithmetic, 242
Skip chain logic, 255
Software timing, 121
Special codes, 61
SPHL, 249
STA, 235

Stack:
  architecture, 243
  system, 247
  uses, 75
Stack pointer:
  function, 77
  reading its contents, 245
Standardized bus systems, 334
Status strobe, 102
STAX, 250
STD bus:
  introduction, 335
  memory map, 339
  pin assignments, 336
Step button, 11
Structured programming, 69
SUB, 54
Subroutines, 73
SUI, 54
Summing amplifier, 295
Sync pulse, 154, 373

T

Ten's complement arithmetic, 239
Time delay subroutines, 462
Top-down design, 74
Trace, 87–88
Troubleshooting:
  AUTO TEST ROM, 436
  reading:
    address bus signals, 452
    control signals, 445
    data bus signals, 447
  signal injection, 433
  single stepping, 434
  techniques, 429
2147H:
  internal logic, 274
  pin out, 274

2716:
  pin out, 268
  timing analysis, 332
2732A, 268
Two's complement numbers, 459

U

UART, 195
  interface, 198

W

WAIT*, 114
Word, 2

X

XCHG, 253
XRA, 40

Z

Z80:
  introduction, 16
  pin out, 149
  specifications, 469–76
Z8410:
  introduction, 282
  modes of operation, 286
  pin out, 283
  programming, 286
  system interface, 284